AF361257

The Age of Discontent

THE AGE OF DISCONTENT

HOW WORKERS AND FARMERS REINVENTED AMERICAN DEMOCRACY

RALPH BRAUER

Georgetown University Press / Washington, DC

A bibliography of cited sources appears online at press.georgetown.edu.

The publisher is not responsible for third-party websites or their content. URL links were active at time of publication.

Library of Congress Cataloging-in-Publication Data

Names: Brauer, Ralph, author.
Title: The age of discontent : how workers and farmers reinvented American democracy / Ralph Brauer.
Description: Washington, DC : Georgetown University Press, [2025] | Includes bibliographical references and index.
Identifiers: LCCN 2024018126 (print) | LCCN 2024018127 (ebook) | ISBN 9781647124946 (hardcover) | ISBN 9781647125707 (paperback) | ISBN 9781647124953 (ebook)
Subjects: LCSH: Working class—United States—History—19th century. | Farmers—United States—History—19th century. | United States—History—1865–1921.
Classification: LCC E661 .B797 2024 (print) | LCC E661 (ebook) | DDC 305.5/62097309034—dc23/eng/20240515
LC record available at https://lccn.loc.gov/2024018126
LC ebook record available at https://lccn.loc.gov/2024018127

∞ This paper meets the requirements of ANSI/NISO Z39.48-1992 (Permanence of Paper).

26 25   9 8 7 6 5 4 3 2 First printing

EU GPSR Authorized Representative
LOGOS EUROPE, 9 rue Nicolas Poussin, 17000, LA ROCHELLE, France
Email: Contact@logoseurope.eu

Printed in the United States of America
Cover design by TG Design Studio
Interior design by Paul Hotvedt

To Lloyd and Anne Svendsbye and Bill and Judith Moyers,
who believed in the dream,

To Doctors Carole Warnes, Douglas Packer, Erskine Caperton,
Carrie Wojick, Robert Albright, and Andrew Nottleson and the nurses
and staff of the Mayo Clinic, for literally keeping the dream alive,

To my son, Max, and daughter-in-law, Caitlin,
who embraced the dream and made it theirs and
will pass it on to Anna, William, and Samuel, and

To my wife and coauthor, Donna, with whom I have
shared many dreams and hope to share many more.

If God would give me my choice of living in any age I would say,
"O God, let me live here and now, in this day of the world's history."
—*Mary Lease, speech to the National Council of Women, 1891*

CONTENTS

Preface: Fables of Identity

Been in the storm so long
Give me more time to pray
—*From the song "Been in the Storm So Long,"*
sung by the Fisk Jubilee Singers, ca. 1880

This book began as a follow-up to my previous work, *The Strange Death of Liberal America.* That book identified a counterrevolution aimed at rolling back New Deal and Progressive reforms to the supposed laissez-faire days of the late nineteenth century.[1] I thought the journey to understand those roots might take a few years; it took fifteen, years made more difficult by medical crises that had me writing drafts in hospital rooms. Instead of finding "the golden age of laissez-faire capitalism," I discovered the roots of Liberal America. Along the way I found a trove of new sources, built a massive database, and formed a new view of late nineteenth-century America that contradicts what many of us learned in school.

Several key experiences kept me focused, among them a conversation with a Mayo Clinic emergency room nurse, my reading W. E. B. Du Bois, and my correspondence with Bill Moyers. The nurse asked what I was writing about; when I told her, her rapt attention and the words "I never knew all this" convinced me I was on the right track. I read and reread the chapter "The Propaganda of History" in Du Bois's *Black Reconstruction.* What is the single most important piece of American historiographic writing spells out how the historical establishment buried and distorted critical parts of our past. Bill Moyers saw the potential of the manuscript even in its early stages. His encouragement and willingness to help extended beyond reading drafts. I still remember a day we met in Saint Paul, Minnesota, when I was at one of the lowest points in this project and he encouraged me in his inimitable fashion.

The nurse, Du Bois's writing, and Moyers provided what a writer needs when tackling a difficult project: affirmation, inspiration, and encouragement. Sometimes I wished that someone more famous had been gifted with the insights of this book, but as time passed I realized no one was looking through the same lens.

For much of the twentieth century we viewed the past through three historical narratives. Historical narratives are accounts that groups use to instill values and make sense of the world. They are what literary critic Northrop Frye terms, in another context, "fables of identity."[2] These narratives become lenses through which we view events, coloring our sense of who we are.

The first, the "Plantation Narrative," depicts a *Gone with the Wind* view of slavery and Reconstruction. The "Frontier Narrative" preaches individualism and manifest destiny. The "Industrial Narrative" sees industrialists and financiers as responsible for America's rise to economic greatness. Over time the Plantation Narrative undergirded the apartheid of segregation. The Frontier Narrative rode roughshod over Indigenous Americans and the West's natural resources. In a process resembling a Houdini illusion, the Industrial Narrative linked progress to laissez-faire capitalism.

Subsequent generations embellished these narratives. The Plantation Narrative sprouted Strom Thurmond's *Southern Manifesto*. The Frontier Narrative shaped Ayn Rand's *The Fountainhead*, with Gary Cooper in the movie version. The Industrial Narrative yielded Ronald Reagan's phrase, "Government is not the solution to our problem; government *is* the problem."[3] Like the three panels of Peter Paul Rubens's *The Raising of the Cross*, the elements of the American tryptic reinforced each other. Frontier individualism sustained the Wild West acquisitiveness of the Industrial Narrative. States' rights segregation reinforced industrial laissez-faire capitalism, and individualism augmented segregation.

As reflected in recent westerns like *Unforgiven* and *Open Range*, research has poked large holes in the Frontier Narrative. Collective action, not the lone gunfighter, tamed the West. Historians like Richard Maxwell Brown have recast the gunfights of the Frontier Narrative as a "Civil War of Incorporation" in "a small drama in which conservative forces consolidated authority in the West in the interest of property, order, and law."[4] Bolstering the Plantation Narrative, historian Ulrich Phillips wrote that Black and white were "fundamentally in accord."[5] But works like Larry Rivers's *Slaves and Runaways: Resistance in Nineteenth-Century Florida* show us the absurdity of that assertion. The claim by Phillips, that slavery was "the most efficient mechanism ever devised for use of stupid labor in agriculture on a large scale," today seems perverse.[6]

Instead of waning like the Frontier and Plantation Narratives, the Industrial Narrative remains strong. People find inventive methods of discrimination, but de jure segregation is illegal. Although some behave as if the frontier is in their backyard, Frederick Jackson Turner proclaimed it dead over a century ago. We may admire *Gone with the Wind*'s cinematography, but the plantation scenes are so discomforting that HBO removed the film from its available library. We may be fans of Clint Eastwood westerns, but few want gunslingers to administer summary justice.

While no text or history today supports the Plantation or Frontier Narratives, texts and histories continue to fortify the Industrial Narrative. David M. Kennedy and Lizabeth Cohen's *The Brief American Pageant* (2016) states: "The standard of living rose sharply, and well-fed American workers enjoyed more physical comforts than their counterparts in any other industrial nation." "[The] corporate world provided significant opportunities for a better life," says *Liberty, Equality, Power: A History of the American People* (2016). "The average laborer gained consistently and substantially during this period" according to *A Patriot's History of the United States* (2014). Writing about "the triumph of capitalism," H. W. Brands asserts that industrialists "effected a stunning transformation of American life" that lifted "the standard of living of ordinary people."[7] Even *Robber Barons* author Mathew Josephson concedes that industrialists were "agents of progress."[8]

The Industrial Narrative has received aid and comfort from interesting places. In *Railroads and Regulation*, Gabriel Kolko proposes, "The railroads, not the farmers and shippers, were the most important single advocates of federal regulation from 1877 to 1916."[9] Aided by Murray Rothbard, Kolko became the darling of libertarians. In 2002 *The New Libertarian Manifesto* proclaimed, "Kolko's *Triumph of Conservatism* detailed how 'capitalists' thwarted the relatively free marketplace of the late 19th century and conspired with the State to become 'robber barons' and monopolists."[10]

An unintentional contribution to the Industrial Narrative comes from appraisals of late nineteenth-century reforms. From Richard Hofstadter's *Age of Reform* to the debate over Lawrence Goodwyn's "movement" thesis, many historians have viewed them as ineffective. Thomas Ferguson's *Golden Rule* offers one of the more radical interpretations. In proposing that "blocs of major investors define the core of political parties," Ferguson asserts, "Not until the New Deal did any important segment of the mass population acquire much importance as political investors."[11]

The Industrial Narrative remains a key part of the counterrevolution. "Bring back the Gilded Age" trumpeted the Foundation for Economic Education in 2013.[12] Republican strategist Karl Rove pines for the McKinley administration. When Donald Trump describes the late nineteenth century as a time when "we had so much money we could do whatever we wanted," he echoes a view of those years as an era of progress and increasing prosperity.[13] During his administration, ideologues flush with a belief in "economic freedom" opposed COVID-19 restrictions and cut taxes and regulations.[14] These views have even breached the marble walls of the US Supreme Court Building, where justices have expressed distaste for government agencies using arguments implicitly evoking the Industrial Narrative. In *Seila Law LLC v. Consumer Financial Protection Bureau*, Justices Clarence Thomas and Neil Gorsuch called for the abolishment of "the numerous, unaccountable independent agencies that currently exercise vast executive power outside the bounds of our constitutional structure."[15]

Not from a Small Elite of Billionaires

My journey was not so much to understand how or why the counterrevolution bonded with the Industrial Narrative as it was to determine whether the narrative was even true. Was laissez-faire capitalism of the late nineteenth century as benign as it has been portrayed in the textbooks? And how much were late nineteenth-century laissez-faire policies responsible for America's rise to a world power?

What I found suggests that the Industrial Narrative rests on some shaky assumptions. For example, the narrative tells us wages rose from 1870 to 1900 and those increases were due to the largesse of industrialists. That interpretation has largely rested on an 1893 report that was criticized the moment it was issued. Statistician Charles Spahr charged the report was "out of harmony with scientific research abroad and common observation at home."[16] Spahr suggested looking at other data: "We have so much contributory evidence from the reports of the State and National Labor Bureaus that serious errors are easily avoided."[17] In the years since he made that suggestion, few have followed up on it. What I discovered in those sources was a far more complex view of wages and little confirmation that laissez-faire capitalists were responsible for the increase. Not coincidentally, this mistaken idea reinforced something Du Bois alludes to in *Black Reconstruction*, where he shows that the evidence lay in plain sight but was being ignored and overlooked.

Instead what has emerged in this book is an alternative to the Industrial Narrative, one that turns it upside down. The wrong people and the wrong initiatives have received too much credit for laying the foundations for America's rise. It wasn't Wall Street, but Main Street that rescued America from what some regarded as a Second Civil War. Those foundations do not consist of Bessemer converters or trains of coal. They consist of a systemic package that transformed America: broadening and improving education, providing supply-side aid for transportation and telecommunications, priming the demand side to increase discretionary spending, and ensuring a fair and competitive marketplace.

Education remains the most important. Thomas Piketty affirms, "U.S. economic leadership came from mass education, not from a small elite of billionaires."[18] What drove—and continues to drive—American productivity was and is not machines, but the world's most educated workforce. What intrigues foreign observers of this country is our commitment to coeducation and universal higher education.

In my journey I also uncovered a darker side to the Industrial Narrative. In the late nineteenth century, corporations cloaked in a custom-tailored suit the nullification theory that had produced a civil war. They held that government had no right to dictate to business; in recasting the states' rights ideas John Calhoun championed, business owners believed they could decide which laws to obey.

The 1883 US Supreme Court's *Civil Rights Cases* decision illustrates the entanglement of states' rights and corporate rights. In several cases involving the denial of accommodations to people of color, Justice Joseph Bradley ruled the 1875 Civil Rights Act's prohibition of such actions was invalid because it allowed the government to "lay down rules for the conduct of individuals in society towards each other."[19] What was unsaid was simple: if courts could force railroads to serve African Americans, they could intervene in any business dealing.

Bradley's words looked back to *Dred Scott v. Sandford* (1857) and forward to *Plessy v. Ferguson* (1896). Chief Justice Roger B. Taney wrote in *Dred Scott*, "No word can be found in the Constitution which gives Congress a greater power over slave *property*, or which entitles property of *that kind* to less protection than property of any other description."[20] In *Plessy v. Ferguson*, which involved a railroad evicting a passenger who was seven-eighths white because he refused to sit in the "colored" car, the majority performed an interesting verbal sleight of hand: where Bradley held the federal government could not impose antidiscrimination laws on a business, the ruling from *Plessy* says *states* could enforce segregation. Echoing Bradley, *Plessy* ruled, "If the two races are to meet upon terms of social equality, it must be the result of natural affinities, a mutual appreciation of each other's merits, and a voluntary consent of individuals."[21] Note the final words, which must have been music to corporate ears.

Justice John Harlan saw through the decisions in *Plessy* and the *Civil Rights Cases*. Both revolved around railroads denying Blacks the freedom to ride a train that they willingly granted to the most uncouth, rancid-greased buffalo hunter. Harlan, who grew up on a plantation, believed Bradley had turned the Thirteenth and Fourteenth Amendments into "splendid baubles, thrown out to delude those who deserved fair and generous treatment at the hands of the nation."[22] Harlan went on to assert anyone who "devotes his property to a use in which the public has an interest . . . must submit to be controlled by the public for the common good." In *Plessy* he insisted that citizens "ought never to cease objecting, to the proposition that citizens of the white and black race can be adjudged criminals because they sit, or claim the right to sit, in the same public coach on a public highway."[23]

Running through the majority decisions in *Dred Scott*, *Plessy*, and the *Civil Rights Cases* was the belief that property rights were so sacred they upheld enslaving or discriminating against other human beings. It is little wonder that late nineteenth-century American corporations flunked one of our most momentous tests. They could have employed millions of newly freed slaves to work in factories and mines. Instead, they spent millions to recruit workers from Europe and Asia while discriminating against those freed by Emancipation.

Like those misguided Supreme Court decisions, the Industrial Narrative conveniently sidesteps the fact that prejudice flooded the late nineteenth century like a river that knew no boundaries. We should not be surprised that the views of plutocrats and courts contributed to these swirling waters. Company towns, city neighborhoods, and frontier communities were segregated by race and nationality. Even though most plutocrats were not Jews, anti-Semitism reared its head cloaked in dog whistles such as Shylock and the moneylender. These ingredients spiced the wicked stew of eugenics as the final solution to racial and ethnic clashes. Ivy League universities were no more immune than the most unreconstructed redneck.

I Stand Aghast

In *Black Reconstruction*, Du Bois writes, "I stand aghast at what American historians have done to this field."[24] He was responding to the errors, omissions, and egregious distortions that characterized American historiography of slavery and Reconstruction when he wrote that in 1934. While I am not so much aghast at how deeply the Industrial Narrative has penetrated the history that American children learn in school or ongoing government policies or even that motivate the counterrevolution, I admit to being perplexed. The late nineteenth century I discovered is a far different world than the one many of us know, but what makes the insights I discovered so perplexing is how the counterevidence has been there all along. With few exceptions, it is because we haven't recognized what was already there.

Some of those "I never heard this before" examples reveal a side to this country that some would prefer remain in the attic where it has been shut up for so long. They are disturbing because they were unnecessary. The knowledge that people were starved and murdered to serve greed is not something any nation wants to confront. It is difficult to face and, as with slavery, it will take time to comprehend its implications and heal the wounds it created. What should not be in doubt is that it is high time we begin the process.

Slave owners, perpetrators of lynchings and massacres, and leaders of the armed rebellion that produced the highest casualty rate of any American war are being held to account for their sins. Yet no one has been called to reckon for needlessly starving people, or gunning down workers at places like Lattimer, Mussel Slough, and Morewood, or for refusing to make workplaces safe. Plantation owners beat their slaves; corporate masters beat their workers. The Ku Klux Klan terrorized innocent African Americans; detectives, mine police, and hired goons terrorized workers and their families. Slaves and tenant farmers had to get permission to leave their plantations; so also did residents of company towns, where they paid exorbitant prices at company stores. The blacklist restricted the freedom of workers much like the Jim Crow laws of segregation restricted the freedoms of former slaves. Plantation owners built ostentatious estates on the backs of the enslaved as did the plutocrats whose millions came from workers oppressed by what the author of one state report termed "a central evil."[25] It should be just as impossible to look at a mansion on a Newport beach as it is look at one in a Southern bayou without thinking of the lives sacrificed to make it possible. Until this country has its reckoning with the costs of industrialization as it has and is with slavery, until this country cleanses itself of the sins committed in the service of greed, it will never be whole.

I should interject that I do not believe making money is wrong. But *how* you do it *does* matter. This book is no muckraking job. It is quite the opposite. It tells the story of how the people I call the Discontented responded to one of history's most complex transformations. Despite its sordid side, the late nineteenth century brought forth one of the world's greatest expressions of popular democracy. That it took place in America is something we should celebrate. What Lincoln called "the better angels of our nature" surfaced in a way that transformed us. As Geoffry Ward once told an interviewer, "In extraordinary times there turn out to be no ordinary lives."[26]

What kept me grounded throughout this journey (with more than its share of rabbit holes) were the methods and principles dating to my undergraduate and graduate years. They served as compass points. My training was a bit unusual in that my mentors emphasized using primary sources, not textbooks, a habit that has guided me since. That habit produced this book's emphasis on primary sources, many cited for the first time. Given the territory covered, citing every secondary source or wandering into bibliographic discussions would have drowned out the message. As it is, the bibliography of sources cited is so long it must be posted online. Those looking for a bibliography more heavy on secondary sources should consult Richard White's masterful bibliographic essay in *The Republic for Which It Stands*.[27] Although I cite only the secondary sources that helped me understand the evidence, this is no reflection on the sources omitted and definitely is not an indication that I do not know about them.

The emphasis on primary sources also resulted in tracing secondary quotations back to their originals. I found, more often than I expected, that some sources were inaccurately quoted. For example, "Raise less corn and more hell" has often been attributed to Mary Lease. Astute historians deem it apocryphal. But it appears no one has correctly identified that it was in fact first uttered by Farmers' Alliance official Ralph Beaumont, who was also a prominent leader with the Knights of Labor.[28] The emphasis on primary sources also prompted me to seek out new examples in lieu of using ones that have been cited multiple times elsewhere.

Many sources are government reports that, for whatever reason, have been overlooked. While they have their quirks, including that they sometimes engage in boosterism, they contain evidence found nowhere else: investigations into women workers, child labor, tenements, railroads, and the cost of living. At a national meeting of state labor statisticians, one speaker remarked those reports are "the only medium by which the most numerous class of citizens and taxpayers can speak for themselves."[29]

Historians like Lawrence Goodwyn pioneered using newspapers because they are often the only place one finds perspectives on events. The book cites over a hundred different newspapers covering most of the country, some of them cited multiple times. They were not without biases, in an era when the words "Republican" and "Democrat" reflected editorial sympathies and editors were not above concocting fake news. It should be no surprise that *Wizard of Oz* author L. Frank Baum mastered his craft by serving as a newspaper reporter and editor.

Archival references shape the manuscript, but are not the major resource. The COVID-19 pandemic and a disability that makes flying impossible were partly responsible for this, but the main reason was that I wanted to show the Discontenteds' public face because we need to know what the country knew and felt about their efforts. I also had no desire to retrace the steps of scholars like Craig Phelan, who delved into the papers of people such as Terence Powderly and John Mitchell.

Regrettably, this book also does not focus on local actions. That local actions preceded many national efforts is a matter of record. States and cities passed laws regulating railroads, mandating factory, food, and sanitary inspections, and establishing measures like arbitration. The simultaneous formation of state health departments and bureaus of labor statistics testifies to the depth of the Discontenteds' reforms. My hope is future researchers will more fully explore these efforts and recognize the leaders who made them possible.

Another piece of my background that played a role was postgraduate training in system dynamics. Rarely used by historians, this discipline stressing dynamic interrelationships and feedbacks led me to the theory that volatile conditions produced a need for control by business owners, farmers, and workers. This is not a replay of Robert Wiebe's *The Search for Order*. As a verb, "control" is an activist concept: how to solve problems. As a noun, "order" is an analytical concept: how to organize reality. Control is also the word *they* used. For example, it appears one hundred times in the transcript of the 1899 Chicago Civic Federation conference on trusts.

Because systemic approaches are multidisciplinary, this book draws on everything from film theory to regression analyses. The period covered begins after the Civil War and ends in the early 1890s with the passage of five critical pieces of legislation: the Sherman Act, the Interstate Commerce Act, the Hatch Act, the Second Morrill Act, and the Safety Appliance Act. Those years laid the groundwork for the Progressive Era and the New Deal. Despite historians' love for the Progressives, they also killed much Discontented activism, such as when doctors suppressed nurse midwives and academically trained experts replaced "amateurs" like Jane Addams and Eleanor Roosevelt.

One term you will not see is "Gilded Age," a name for me that grates like squeaky chalk on a blackboard. It emphasizes the gilding and gilders instead of the people they oppressed. The term also isn't even accurate, because most people who lived then would have settled for regular employment. Instead of a Gilded Age, for them it was an Age of Discontent.

The book that has emerged is divided into three parts. Part 1 provides background for the discontent. Chapter 1 introduces the people. Chapter 2 explains the megatrends that shaped their lives: the progress and poverty paradox, the Great Retreat from rural America, the rise of the consumer culture, the machine process, and Rag Time and Movie Space. Chapter 3 explores social and workplace conditions like starvation, wages, and industrial accidents. Chapter 4 brings the trends and conditions to a personal level with the stories of homesteader Anna Pavelka and miner's wife and organizer Mary Septak. Part 2 (chapters 5 through 10) details the deeds of the Discontented and is divided into two parts by decade. Those parts appear in groups of three: one for workers, one for farmers, and a third explaining their combined efforts. Part 3 analyzes the Discontenteds' legacy. Chapter 11 examines the impact of their systemic initiatives. Chapter 12 reveals how aid for the demand side increased discretionary spending. The conclusion shows the culmination of the Discontenteds' efforts in the 1902 Anthracite Strike and the *Northern Securities* decision.

Because our dominant historical and nonfiction form is the personal narrative, either as biography or memoir, other works are now the almost-exclusive territory of scholars, who continue working like medieval monks in these dark ages. This book stands on their shoulders. My experience as a scholar, community organizer, and wilderness guide has taught me that exploration should not be a solitary enterprise.

One advantage I have enjoyed as someone who has held positions both inside and outside the academy is the friendship and insights of those from a variety of perspectives. As every historian knows, your training stays with you forever. I was fortunate to learn from two giants of late nineteenth-century history: Joe Wall and David Noble. Joe was my undergraduate advisor and David served as my dissertation advisor. My graduate advisor, Mary Turpie, ingrained in me the importance of an interdisciplinary perspective. Her stories of teaching in a one-room Nebraska schoolhouse remain a priceless addition to this book.

The energy needed to sustain over a decade of research cannot be sustained by the author alone. No one did more to support the manuscript through a difficult process than my editor, Hilary Claggett, with whom I also worked on *The Strange Death of Liberal America*. She is responsible for shaping a longer and disjointed manuscript into a finished product. Authors know that producing a book is a team effort. Copyeditor Ann Baker's incredible work took the mess I gave her and shaped and polished it into a finished product. Rachel McCarthy ably oversaw final production of the book. Marketing coordinator Francys Reed and publicist Stephanie Rojas made me feel like I was a big name author at some major publishing house. Reviewers at Georgetown University Press were also helpful in suggesting needed changes.

My wife, Donna, endured years of reading multiple drafts, supplied valuable stat analysis, and furnished insights into medical data and terminology. My son, Max, and daughter-in-law, Caitlin, were rocks through this process, even though spending years on a book must have seemed strange. Max, a Maryland assistant attorney general with degrees in law and public policy, was especially helpful with the economics portions, pointing me toward sources I did not know and correcting misguided ideas.

The late Augustana and Luther Seminary president and historian Lloyd Svendsbye and his wife, Anne, grasped the importance of this book before I did and gave me much-needed swift kicks when I was ready to abandon it. I confess to getting a tear when I remember reading sections to Anne on her deathbed. Lloyd's experiences as the son of a North Dakota homesteader helped me understand that life.

Historian and system dynamics modeler Jeff Potash aided me through the daunting task of modeling economic and social changes. My colleague Jeremy Young, with whom I have worked on the *Progressive Historians* blog, provided the support and insights of a historian of the Progressives and nineteenth-century oratory. Jane Addams biographer Victoria Brown read sections of the manuscript and offered valuable ideas about writing and approach. I contacted Rebecca Edwards about her work on Mary Lease, which led to her offering ideas and criticisms. Eric Foner graciously offered his time and advice on several subjects. George Drake of Grinnell College read several chapters. Thomas Woods gave me the benefit of his knowledge about the Grange movement and Caroline Hall. Economist Louis Johnston reviewed and recomputed some of my calculations and values. Historian Ellen Langill read parts of the manuscript and contributed her insights about business leaders. Paul Shackel shared unpublished data from his work and subsequent book about the Lattimer Massacre. Marc Wortman read portions of the manuscript and offered suggestions. Friends Tom and Judy Jackson, Rod Brown, John and Martha Bordwell, Dennis Spencer, and Tom Lannom never once wondered why I spent so much time on one book.

My views of the challenges faced by business were shaped by system dynamics modelers and consultants Barry Richmond and Peter Senge. Public sector colleagues such as Minnesota Department of Natural Resources commissioner Sarah Strommen and Ted Marchese of the American Association of Higher

Education gave me insights into the consequences of government programs. Bill Norris, founder of Control Data and the Norris Institute, offered a lifetime of insights on afternoons when we were the only ones still working. My years as executive director of the Transforming Schools Consortium influenced my views of the importance of public education. I am grateful for the insights and friendship of Jack Nelson, Jim Oraskovich, Bill Crocoll, Al Meyers, John Rinaldi, Jim Boos, Ken Bird, Ron Gillespie, Jeanne Harmon, and Jim Minerich. Lees Stuntz of the Creative Learning Exchange introduced me to system dynamics and has tolerated my misunderstandings.

The archivists at the Library of Congress did their usual superb job. That this resource is subject to budget cuts to pay for tax cuts for the rich shows how distorted our country has become. Archivists from the University of Minnesota, the Minnesota Historical Society, the Chesapeake and Ohio Railroad, Grinnell College, and the New York City Public Library aided my research. The National Weather Service researched records that provided details for described events.

The Bush Foundation provided a fellowship that allowed me to enhance my knowledge of system dynamics. Without that fellowship this book would have been a far different one.

Doctors Carole Warnes, Douglas Packer, Erskine Caperton, Carrie Wojick, Robert Albright, and Andrew Nottleson may have made the most important contribution by keeping me alive and functioning. I also want to thank the Mayo Clinic nurses who have cared for me.

I finish this project with the mixed feelings that come with every difficult journey. I regret leaving and will miss the many voices of the Age of Discontent, who showed me what Herbert Croly once called "the promise of American democracy." I also know there are still dozens of questions to be asked and sources waiting to be rediscovered. Jeff Potash says the best books make you ask better questions. I hope this one meets that standard.

THE DISCONTENTED

Up with your standard! For ever and ever,
Shall labor's grand emblem reign over the land!
—*From "Labor's War Cry," music by George Mainey,*
lyrics by Edmund Mortimer, 1887

At rest. Words chiseled into the gravestones of Sarah Jane Geary and her husband, Henry. Nearby lies daughter Maud, who was four when she died in 1882. Daughter Florence probably commissioned the stones in the early twentieth century, since they are identical and Henry did not pass away until 1901. The cross-shaped alignment of the trees shading the graves asks more questions than maybe what those who planted them intended.

While the Gearys lived, bitter coalfield wars added three bodies to this cemetery in Girardville, Pennsylvania. The 1875 murders of Thomas Gwyther, Thomas Sanger, and William Uren shocked the community. Justice of the Peace Gwyther was shot while walking from his office to serve a warrant. Sanger, a mine shift boss, and Uren, a Cornish immigrant who roomed in Sanger's house, were killed a month later. Nearby sits the Hibernia House tavern once run by John "Black Jack" Kehoe, who was an alleged leader of the Molly Maguires, a group accused of those murders and others. Ten alleged Mollies went to the gallows on July 21, 1877, which became known as the Day of the Rope, one of the largest mass executions in US history. Another ten, including Kehoe, were executed later. Kehoe's framed pardon, dated 1979, hangs in the tavern.

A visitor might overlook the graves, for nothing suggests they hold dark, suppressed memories that question how we perceive and use history. The *North American Review* described Sarah's 1885 death:

Mrs. Sarah Jane Geary, an English woman, residing in this city, committed suicide a few days since. Her husband is a miner and owing to the frequent suspension of business in the mines during this past winter, his meager earnings were insufficient to support the family. That fact preyed on Mrs. Geary's mind, and she resolved to end her life, that her children might receive her share of the food, otherwise, they would go hungry.[1]

In the context of generalizations about "well-fed American workers" and laborers gaining "consistently and substantially," Sarah's death is especially unsettling. Her story clashes with the traditional image of progress in the years after the Civil War. Take the railroads. From 1871 to 1898 the milling of rails tripled, passenger car construction increased tenfold, and the production of freight cars grew by a factor of fifty.[2] The manufacturing index increased from 25 to 100, patents doubled, and exports tripled.[3] In 1898 American Bankers Association president Joseph C. Hendrix boasted to a hall of financiers, "We now hold the three winning cards in the game for commercial greatness, to wit: iron, steel, and coal."[4]

No one could miss the signs of progress. Inventors created blue jeans, Coca-Cola, flush toilets, vacuum cleaners, dishwashers, traffic lights, and the zipper. In 1870 railroads operated 52,922 miles of track, but most people traveled as they had for centuries—on horseback, by boat, and on foot. By 1900 the train was the preferred method of long-distance travel for those who did not own one of eight thousand registered automobiles.[5] Three years later the Wright brothers filed US Patent 821,393 for a flying machine. After Charles Guiteau fired two rounds into James Garfield on July 2, 1881, the president endured hellish ministrations as physicians probed for the bullets with unsterilized instruments. In 1901 Thomas Edison offered his X-ray machine to help locate a bullet lodged near William McKinley's stomach. It took nine days after the Battle of the Little Bighorn for headlines to announce "Massacre of Our Troops."[6] In 1903 Guglielmo Marconi broadcast Pres. Theodore Roosevelt's message to King Edward VII across the Atlantic.

Late nineteenth-century future shock puts to shame Alvin Toffler's 1970 book. The Toffler of his time was Cincinnati minister Josiah Strong, whose 1885 bestseller *Our Country* made him a celebrity. Strong described the pace of change: "For [an American born in 1800] the first thirty-three years of his life he had to rely on the tinder-box for fire. He was thirty-eight when steam communication between Europe and America was established. He had arrived at middle life (forty-four) when the first telegram was sent. Thirty-six years later the world had 604,000 miles of telegraph lines."[7] A century before consultants began hyping the Information Age, Mary Lease employed similar language: "We are living in an age of thought. The mighty dynamite of thought is upheaving the social and political structure and stirring the hearts of men from centre to circumference."[8] Ideas were in the air, fluttering like moths around a flame kindled by despair and desire.

The nation burst its buttons celebrating the 1893 World's Columbian Exposition in Chicago. Tourists marveled at the sights from atop a 264-foot rotating wheel designed by bridge builder George Washington Ferris in response to calls for something to rival the newly completed Eiffel Tower in Paris. The exposition inspired reporter L. Frank Baum to write a story named after a filing cabinet labeled O–Z and moved the son of construction worker Elias Disney to invent Disneyland.

Sitting atop the Ferris wheel or standing in the shadow of the immense Corliss engine, someone might momentarily forget how this progress created a substantial gap between the real and the possible. One who recognized that gap was Connecticut Bureau of Labor Statistics commissioner Samuel Hotchkiss, when he wrote: "[The workers] do not complain of these larger incomes, but they do believe most profoundly that they are not receiving their fair share of the benefits conferred upon society by these inventions and labor-saving machines. In this belief lies the principal source of their unrest."[9] Hotchkiss alludes to two crucial qualities of the gap: what mattered was people's perceptions of their lives and what technological progress promised, and the size of the gap indicated how far the playing field was tilted.

Nothing better embodied the shifting playing field than when *what was* clashed dramatically with *what could be.* The perception that the fruits of productivity were not distributed fairly produced much resentment, especially since many tycoons avoided Civil War military service by paying substitutes to serve in their place. Workers also resented what Thorstein Veblen termed the "machine process," with its monotonous specialized tasks performed in soulless factories and mines. As a cabinetmaker testified, "Yet improvements in machinery and division of labor[,] though it relieved the workingman of hard labor, converted the trained worker to a mere attendant upon a machine."[10]

Farmers also believed their toil also did not receive its just reward. They worked hard to produce a crop in hazardous and uncertain conditions on which they mortgaged their families' futures. Meanwhile, railroad owners, bankers, elevator and seed store operators, plus assorted middlemen walked away with a majority of the profits. One farmer complained: "Middle men and railroads take . . . shoes to Iowa and sell them at $3 per pair. Farmers pay for them with corn at twenty-five cents per bushel or twelve bushels for the shoes. The shoes are constructed or manufactured for two and sold to the consumer for twelve bushels of corn. Who goes off with the odd ten bushels has much to do with the failure of farmers."[11]

The resentments of those like the farmer and cabinetmaker were compounded by the tycoons' ostentatious lifestyles during the era that coined the term "conspicuous consumption." Stories about millionaires lighting cigars with $100 bills or hosting parties where guests bobbed for apples containing diamonds were spread rapidly by newspapers into every hamlet. The authors of state reports recognized this explosive friction between the real and the possible. Indiana Bureau of Statistics chief William Peelle observed:

> Our much boasted of progress and advance in our social life is not in just proportion to the increase of wealth, knowledge, and appliances. In our age, progress on the one and poverty on the other hand seem to be the concomitants of our civilization. Labor does not receive a fair share of these advantages which bring out the inequalities of our modern life and the so-called refinement of the wealthy classes does not apply to the working masses.[12]

The author of the *North American Review* essay, Knights of Labor leader Terence Powderly, highlighted the Geary family's story in his essay because it was such a dramatic example of the chasm between the real and the possible. He no doubt had read the article about Sarah's death in a local paper. He may have also heard details about what happened or even known friends of the family. He certainly was familiar with the conditions that caused her to take such a dramatic action.

Some might point to Henry Geary as the cause of his family's dire condition, but the fact that his daughter erected identical tombstones for him and Sarah after his death suggests that neither she nor the community blamed him. We also know that he was a skilled worker in a critical industry cited by banker Hendrix as a mark of America's progress. He was killed while repairing the pulleys controlling the cars bringing men and supplies from underground, a job requiring expertise and trust. So it is unlikely he was unemployed because of incompetence or the disapproval of supervisors or fellow workers.

The Geary family's story suggests the Gilded Age may be more tarnished than we thought. Henry did not earn enough to provide for his family because his employment was intermittent. Powderly's essay pointed out, "In the two years ending December 1, 1884, those employed in and around the coal mines worked but little over half-time."[13] This was common in Pennsylvania's anthracite fields, where owners periodically closed mines for a variety of reasons, sometimes without warning or any indication of when production would resume. Of approximately 500 Pennsylvania anthracite mines monitored over six years yielding a total of 1,668 data points, there were only 236 instances when mines were open for more than 250 days, or 14.1 percent. In contrast, there were 690 instances when mines were open fewer than 200 days, or 41.3 percent.[14]

In a wage table, Henry's official salary might look good, but what he actually *earned* each month or annually was another matter. When they were laid off, workers like him had to fend for themselves in an era with no unemployment or workers' compensation insurance, food stamps, or medical assistance. Being at the whims of owners for their daily bread must have weighed heavily on the Geary family. It certainly weighed on one Luzerne County miner, who vented his frustration by saying, "We often talk about the condition of the slaves in the South before they had their freedom. I am compelled to say our condition is far worse today when there are hundreds of our fellow men who cannot get what they ought to eat and are willing to work at the same time."[15]

Henry's death in a mining accident reveals another dimension of late nineteenth-century America. Mining remains one of the deadliest occupations, but over a century ago dying on the job was even more frequent. Several articles on Henry's death mention three other mine deaths that day. In the year Sarah died, Pennsylvania mine inspectors reported 130 fatal and 378 nonfatal accidents, during an average of 208½ days worked.[16] The state Bureau of Industrial Statistics commented, "Accidents continue to be frequent and whether their causes are due to the want of law or of non-conformity to the provisions of existing law, the fact that they occur so often shows the many hidden perils to which the men who mine the coal are liable."[17] The possibility that even on the days that Henry was working he might not come home, must also have weighed on Sarah Geary.

In these unsafe workplaces, workers were kept in line by discipline resembling what Simon Legree administered on a plantation. Pennsylvania's Lattimer Massacre occurred during a strike that began after superintendent Gomer Jones, "the worst slave driver who ever set foot in the coal region," beat a miner with an ax handle.[18] A factory foreman testified to a congressional committee, "I was told that if a man did not do what I told him to do to take a club and knock his damned head off."[19]

Terence Powderly recounted Sarah's story in his essay to shock his audience, just as it shocks us today. By dramatizing industrial conditions, he sought to cast a light into the dark corners of the late nineteenth century. The essay was a classic American jeremiad warning of the consequences of industrialization. After presenting data showing that 22 percent of the workforce was unemployed in 1885, Powderly reflected, "It is safe to assume that the 2,000,000 unemployed persons are discontented with their lot; and not only are they discontented, but those who labor at the same occupations that they previously followed have every reason to be dissatisfied also."[20]

Powderly wasn't the only one worried about discontent. Indiana Bureau of Statistics Commissioner William Peelle issued this assessment:

When we behold hundreds of millions of dollars concentrated in the hands of a single person under sanction of law by processes if not illegal, at least morally very objectionable, and on the other hand look upon the thousands of honest workingmen, who by constant toil and labor and self-denial year after year, are strugling [sic] hard for the support of their families, we can not wonder that the contrast between this superfluity of the few and the impoverished condition of the many should evoke discontent among the masses and even threatening language here and there.[21]

That such discontent existed was well known. A study by the federal Bureau of Labor Statistics found 22,304 strikes had taken place from 1881 to 1886. Employers ordered an additional 1,753 lockouts that involved a total of 175,270 employees.[22] In truth, the late nineteenth century was a highly combustible atmosphere that frequently exploded. "Violence flickered incessantly on every man's horizon," wrote historian Robert Bruce.[23] The three bodies buried near the Geary family attest to this. Lynchings averaged 150 per year between 1881 and 1900, or one every 2.4 days.[24] Another 1,400 people perished in riots.[25] According to Randolph Roth's *American Homicide*, by 1900 we had become the world's most murderous society.[26]

The true extent of the discontent can be seen in various state reports. Ohio Bureau of Labor Statistics commissioner H. J. Walls wrote:

The wages system is but a slight improvement on the system of villeinage or serfdom . . . for while the serf or villein was always assured of a supply of food, clothing, and a home such as they were, the wages laborer has no such assurance his food, clothing, and home is only assured so long as he has remunerative employment and that employment is dependent on the whim or will of another or on circumstances over which the laborer at least has no control.[27]

His New York colleague, Charles Peck, employed flowery language not normally seen in state reports to contrast what he witnessed on a visit to a tenement sweatshop and the domains of the plutocrats: "From the window of this wretched room in which squalor, want, and suffering revealed with joined hands, could be seen the towering walls of magnificent business blocks and other evidences of fabulous wealth. The hum of the factory wheel, the roar of business traffic, and the throbbing of great industries could be heard and from Trinity's graceful spire the chime of bells pealed forth in sacred notes peace on earth, good will to men."[28]

In this context, the Geary family becomes a proverbial canary in the mine shaft. Powderly was well aware of this, issuing a warning in his essay:

That the army of the discontented is gathering fresh recruits day by day is true, and if this army should become so large that, driven to desperation, it should one day arise in its wrath and grapple with its real or fancied enemy, the responsibility for that act must fall upon the heads of those who could have averted the blow, but who turned a deaf ear to the supplication of suffering humanity, and gave the screw of oppression an extra turn because they had the power.[29]

Powderly does not mention he was part of that army. He knew of the reality gap and what Sarah faced because he faced it himself. He described hitting bottom: "I have sampled in all its awful reality the desolation and misery of tramp life that at times, during blinding storms of sleet and snow, seemed to shut out all sight and sound and hope of God."[30] Like so many leaders of that time—people like John Mitchell and Mary Lease—he emerged from his personal wilderness transformed. A decade after his desperate journey, he found himself as the head of the Knights.

Over the last three decades of the late nineteenth century, thousands like Powderly arose in a series of eruptions as discontent built up under economic and social pressures generated by the tension between the promise of progress and the realities of their own lives. They met in churches and saloons, whispered new ideas a mile underground, and shouted fighting words under the unforgiving sun of the prairies. They were murdered, beaten, blackballed, cheated, and humiliated, but they refused to surrender. Though flawed, they strove to rebuild their country in a world never imagined by the Founders. How could the constitutional compromises of gentlemen in powdered wigs apply to Western Union, the Associated Press, locomotives traveling a mile a minute, steel mills that could swallow an ocean liner, and dynamos that stopped nearby watches?

These eruptions occurred in two main theaters: the rural regions of the Midwest and South and the factories and mines of the industrial North. They were shaped by community characteristics, ethnic, racial, and gender conflicts, and the personalities of local leaders. Southern farmers had different villains than northern ones. The grievances of miners were not those of steelworkers. Women, people of color, and immigrants brought their agendas.

Actors mingled between these theaters to a degree still largely unrecognized by historians. Detroit labor leader Richard Trevellick was a temperance orator and official in New Orleans and Nebraska, spoke on women's suffrage in Colorado, debated labor's representation in the Democratic Party in Ohio, and lectured on the financial crisis in Idaho. Henry Demarest Lloyd covered mining strikes, investigated Standard Oil, befriended Jane Addams, Florence Kelley, John Dewey, and other Chicago change agents, and campaigned as a Populist congressional candidate before serving as cocounsel with Clarence Darrow during the 1902 Anthracite Strike.

Many leaders like Powderly rose from humble beginnings. There was Leonora Barry, a silver-tongued, blacklisted factory worker who exposed the deplorable conditions of working women and then worked to change them. There was Seaman Knapp, a failed pig and sheep farmer who inspired the Hatch Act, providing federal funding for agricultural experiment stations. There was Caroline Hall, a former rural schoolteacher who became the soul of the Grange movement.

Like flocks of migrating birds, resolutions flitted between organizations. Some were carried word for word for more than a decade. The 1892 People's Party platform echoed the 1878 Greenback Party platform, in part because the hyperkinetic Ignatius Donnelly had a hand in writing both. The Farmers' Alliances borrowed the Grange motto and some of the Knights' aims.

The diffuse nature of this revolt was its greatest strength and its chief weakness. If it had set an agenda or centralized its leadership, its impact would probably not have been as significant and it would have been an easier target for the opposition. Instead, opponents struggled to contain one spontaneous uprising after another. On the other hand, leaders were often frustrated by the lack of unity. Groups like the Knights and the Farmers' Alliances fought internally and with each other over conflicting agendas. Those upset by our current political divisiveness might ponder an 1891 Arkansas Farmers' Alliance meeting, which escalated into a shooting war that left five dead. Replies of workers in state reports show the diversity that made the Discontented so difficult to organize. Some favored unions while others wanted to bargain individually. Of those favoring unions, some were against strikes while others were ready to walk at the slightest grievance.

I refer to the Discontented with a capital "D" to differentiate between those who organized and those who did not. Their achievements often resulted from fortuitous circumstances and temporary alliances as windows of opportunity opened, then slammed shut. This gives the discontent an ebb and flow, as people joined together and then broke apart. Attempts at unity paralleled the state of the economy and testify to the depth of peoples' despair and their determination to overcome its causes.

The civil rights movement of the 1950s and 1960s offers an instructive parallel. Partisan efforts, like the Freedom Democratic Party, parallel the Greenback and People's Parties. Activist groups like the Student Nonviolent Coordinating Committee (SNCC) and Congress of Racial Equality (CORE) have counterparts in the Knights of Labor and the Farmers' Alliances. Religious organizations such as the Southern Christian Leadership Conference (SCLC) have their equivalent in the social gospel.

If a commitment to racial justice united the civil rights movement, a commitment to a level playing field bonded the Discontented. They believed America had become dangerously tilted. Ohio Republican senator John Sherman, who did not consider himself one of the Discontented, stated, "The popular mind is agitated with problems that may disturb social order, and among them all none is more threatening than the inequality of condition, of wealth, and opportunity." Arkansas Democratic senator James Jones used similar words: "It is not the aggregation of wealth, property, or money that makes a people prosperous, but its even, fair, and equitable distribution."[31] Pres. James A. Garfield gave the most succinct expression of the principle when he said, "Our modern feudalism can be subordinated to the public good only by the great body of the people acting through government by wise and just laws."[32]

Despite the concerns expressed in my previous book, *The Strange Death of Liberal America*, the belief that government's role is to maintain a level playing field remains one of our core values. We all can recall examples, such as Title IX and Pell grants. James Madison's *Federalist #10* contains our most compelling statement of that value. Madison believed "the various and unequal distribution of property" is "the most common and durable source of factions," contending *"the regulation of these various and interfering interests forms the principal task of modern legislation."*[33] Despite numerous attempts to disparage "regulation," the intent of the principal author of the Bill of Rights remains clear. The words of the Declaration, "To secure these rights, *governments are instituted*," testify to the importance placed on that role. The signers knew from experience that rights are only an abstraction if no one enforces them.

In an 1860 Connecticut speech, the author of the Gettysburg Address agreed: "While we do not propose any war upon capital, we do wish to allow the humblest man an equal chance to get rich with everybody else." To anyone puzzled about those words, historian Gabor Borritt makes a compelling case that Abraham Lincoln embraced "an intense and continually developing commitment" that everyone should receive "a full, good, and ever-increasing reward for their labors so that they might have the opportunity to rise in life."[34]

To these views, we can add recent research findings about the importance of a level playing field. The World Bank issued one of the more succinct statements about it: "Institutions and policies that promote a level playing field—where all members of society have similar chances to become socially active, politically influential, and economically productive—contribute to sustainable growth and development."[35]

Although the level playing field principle runs through the varied ideals and experiences of the Discontented, they had widely different interpretations of it, some hypocritical and others even dangerous. In general, they viewed the playing field as exclusive rather than inclusive. Racial, gender, and ethnic prejudices colored their intentions, no matter how laudable they may seem to us today. Former Confederate postmaster general John Reagan, known as the father of the Interstate Commerce Act, supported permitting separate but equal accommodations. Populist Mary Lease was an anti-Semite whose prejudice hardened over time. AFL founder Samuel Gompers was anti-intellectual and discouraged granting leadership positions to women and people of color. Powderly's Knights drove away the organizer who championed female workers and never fulfilled its promise of equal pay. The Knights also lobbied for Chinese exclusion.

The Discontented may not have been a movement, but they reinvented American democracy. By the end of the 1902 Anthracite Strike, most Americans accepted that government had a role to play in maintaining a level playing field. It was the equivalent of a third American revolution. In the Second, the Civil War and ensuing constitutional amendments did away with the notion that African Americans were not citizens and that states could nullify laws. The third did away with the idea that labor had no rights and corporations could decide which laws to obey.

In the process, the Discontented turned the tattered and stained pages of the Industrial Narrative upside down. The narrative's script is found in works like Charles Calhoun's 2007 *The Gilded Age*, which claims, "From Appomattox to the years before World War I, the business executive, the engineer, and the wizards of marketing would assume their roles as the most powerful shapers of American civilization."[36] Like other apologists for the Industrial Narrative, Calhoun has it wrong. Leaders of labor and farm organizations were the engineers of a new America. Government programs, not laissez-faire capitalism, were the bricks and mortar.

When they worked together, the Discontented produced an impressive list of achievements: expanded education, collective bargaining, unemployment offices, women's economic rights, factory inspection, child labor laws, and federal and state bureaus of labor statistics. They also laid the groundwork for three constitutional amendments. Although an income tax financed the Civil War, the Sixteenth Amendment came two decades after a pro-business Supreme Court struck down the first peacetime income tax in 1895. In 1913, the preceding decades of agitation for the direct election of senators yielded the Seventeenth Amendment. After women won the vote in several states, it took until 1920 for the Nineteenth Amendment to extend it to the entire country.

The Discontenteds' most outstanding achievement was a flurry of legislation in the late 1880s and early 1890s: the Sherman Antitrust Act, the Interstate Commerce Act, the Hatch Act funding agricultural experiment stations, the Second Morrill Act expanding higher education, and the Safety Appliance Act mandating railroad airbrakes and other safety measures. The Sherman and Interstate Commerce Acts have been much discussed, but not as much has been said about the others and how they all fit together.

This combined legislation represents a still-relevant systemic package that transformed America: broadening education, providing supply-side aid for transportation and telecommunications, priming the demand side to increase discretionary spending, and ensuring a fair and competitive marketplace. Wheat production is an example of how the elements reinforced each other. The Hatch Act allowed farmers to hold homesteaded land and increased yields, the Interstate Commerce Act facilitated crop distribution, the Sherman Act prevented monopolistic practices, and the Safety Appliance Act assured crops reached their destination. Add to this the creation of the federal US Bureau of Labor Statistics to monitor the process.

This strategy produced a country better positioned to deal with a new century. We forget that history's value lies in helping us know where we are and where we came from. In this sense, history is our compass. Reflecting on the 1897 Lattimer Massacre, the *Kansas Agitator* wrote, "One of the most stupendous crimes of this generation should be enough to rouse from lethargy every

American who has a particle of respect for the sacredness of life or the rights of men."[37] That is the power of history: to rouse "from lethargy" those who seek to learn from it.

The Geary graves mark one of those compass points. From them radiate all the crosscurrents of the late nineteenth century: capricious wages, workplace accidents, frayed safety nets, and record-setting negative social and public health indicators. The graves also attest that the Geary family did not crumble after Maud and Sarah died, nor did the country during the times some termed a Second Civil War. Their story—and America's—is not one of tragedy, but triumph. Facing some of the most daunting challenges, farmers and workers reinvented our country.

Although we live in a world where the equivalent of the Alexandria Library is only a click away, knowledge is precarious. The late nineteenth century reminds us that when serious history is ignored or distorted, serious thought suffers. The subsequent vacuum erodes democratic institutions and spawns toxic behavior. Today, when we desperately need to feel good about ourselves, there may be no more relevant period than the late nineteenth century. It offers an inspiring lesson of what citizens can accomplish through government. The Homestead steel mill, once celebrated as a major achievement of industrialization, is now a shopping mall, but the reinvention of America continues paying dividends.

PART ONE

THE WORLD OF THE DISCONTENTED

Chapter One

The Grittiest Generation

Oh, the moonlight's fair tonight along the Wabash,
From the fields there comes the breath of new-mown hay,
Through the sycamores, the candle lights are gleaming,
On the banks of the Wabash, far away.
—*From "On the Banks of the Wabash, Far Away,"*
music and lyrics by Paul Dresser, 1897

Panic. It began under leaden skies that oracles believed foreshadowed portentous events. Drizzle failed to prevent crowds from spilling into the streets, where rumors reverberated like thunderbolts. Messengers shoved through the churning throngs they feared would swallow them. From clusters of umbrellas rose an unsettling Babel needing little translation. Witnesses confirm the crisis began at half-past ten on September 19, 1873, a day they christened Black Friday.[1] The crowd milling outside the New York Stock Exchange heard an uproar not even stone walls could contain. On the floor, traders screaming with rasping voices wildly thrust their fists in the air like drowning men caught in an undertow.

"Good God, there will be no one left to be suspended," shouted a man darting to and fro like a runaway horse, as the rifle-like crack of the gavel announced another firm had suspended business.[2] At a nearby bank, slope-shouldered men indifferent to the rain stood in a lengthening line, hands in their pockets to foil thieves, who were among the few making money. "Others were so intent upon working themselves forward," commented an observer, "that a man desirous of being martyred in the cause of the panic might have accomplished this purpose without any extraordinary effort."[3] A youth netted $1,500 holding places in the line.[4] Others, like Civil War photographer Mathew Brady, were not so lucky. He could not pay to store his negatives.

Newspapers reassured readers the storm would pass like a summer squall. A reporter blamed "railways, inflated currency, or an idiotic public."[5] Using one of the era's favorite metaphors, Cigar-Makers' Union president William J. Cannon reflected, "The panic, with all its attending evils, came upon us like a whirlwind, carrying destruction and desolation in its path, making fearful havoc and ghastly inroads into the prosperous and happy homes of the working people, effectually closing every avenue of prosperity and every channel of industry."[6] The Panic of 1873 made an indelible mark on their character.

One of them was a woman named Sarah Murray, who began an improbable journey in Atlanta, where she boarded a train to meet her husband and son, who were working as herders in North Platte, Nebraska. The men's likely employers, Omaha millionaires Morrill Keith and Guy Barton, paid hands $30–$50 a month plus room and board to tend stock.

When Murray stepped on the train, she probably carried a single carpetbag and not much else. She probably slept fitfully on her seat as the wooden car lurched through the night. When the train reached St. Joseph, Missouri, she discovered her money was gone. She began walking the 150 miles to Omaha. The rhythmic scuffling of her shoes accompanied her for the next twelve days. Although she was fortunate for "the many kind favors from charitable people along her route," the *Omaha Bee* admitted she "suffered considerable" on the journey.[7] Fortunately, only a day of heavy rain marred the mild weather, allowing her to average more than ten miles a day. She arrived just ahead of a snowstorm with a wind chill of 15 degrees.[8] A good Samaritan brought her to the Union Pacific station, where kindly "ticket agent Kimball" offered her free passage to North Platte.[9]

A mere one inch in the *Bee* covered Sarah Murray's story, but it defined her generation: they found themselves without prospects, but they started walking. No one was very comfortable for very long, but instead of giving up or giving in, they fought back. They are our Grittiest Generation.

The fates of other Sarah Murrays offer revealing snapshots. One in Stroudsburg, Pennsylvania, paid $14.19 in taxes on 225 acres. One in Springfield, Ohio, bought 25 acres for $1,590. One homesteaded near Dodge City, Kansas, on half a quarter section. In San Francisco, some Murray sisters held an elegant party "where games and singing were indulged in till midnight when all present adjourned to the conservatory, where an elegant table arranged by the Misses Murray was in readiness, and a bountiful repast was indulged in." Others faced more trying circumstances. One Murray lost a three-year-old daughter; another landed in an asylum; police arrested a third for public drunkenness.[10]

Sarah Murray wasn't the only one taking a long walk. A blackballed Italian laborer who revolted against intolerable working conditions in South Carolina had only a dollar to use to get back to New York. "After forty-two days I arrived in the city utterly exhausted," he told an interviewer.[11] Princeton professor Walter Wycoff spent eighteen months rambling 2,500 miles from Connecticut to California, to "get a better knowledge of the people and the country," issuing periodic reports on the state of the nation like a nineteenth-century Charles Kuralt.[12]

If Sarah Murray represented the heart of the Grittiest Generation, Thomas Kimball represented its soul. This man, who became assistant to the first vice president of the Union Pacific Railroad, was the son and grandson of men who had fought in the Revolution and the War of 1812. A 1917 biography gushes with praise for his "strong human sympathy," "unusual moral sensitiveness," and "extreme conscientiousness." Those who worked under him "were the best paid and best satisfied force of any railway system in the west."[13] Combine Murray's grit with Kimball's values and you have a movement.

Every One Was Talking

To understand the Grittiest Generation you need to ponder the contrast between their lighting and ours. In 1873, when dusk descended, the only illumination for most came from candles and oil lamps. A light bulb insinuates itself into the darkest corner; a candle casts an uncertain glow. A candle fragilely holds the darkness at bay; a light bulb confidently banishes it. A candle-lit world left evenings unmediated by wall-clinging televisions. People contemplated their lives without radio, television, Facebook, or Twitter. The era's spectacular growth in civic engagement gestated during evenings when people sat and pondered the possible. Darkness was a blank canvas daring them to fill the void.

Maybe this explains the era's popular songs. Theodore Dreiser's brother Paul Dresser sentimentalized a world lost in "On the Banks of the Wabash, Far Away." Eva Tanguay's "I Don't Care" expressed the defiant energy of people like Sarah Murray. The exuberant "Rings on My Fingers" is an homage to opportunity. The most telling song was also the most popular: "After the Ball" told a maudlin story of things not being what they seem. A man glimpses his sweetheart kissing another and breaks off their engagement, but years later finds out the man was her brother.

No, they were not *that* naïve. They *were* living in a time when venerable principles and behavior codes faced new realities for which they were ill-adapted and unprepared. The tension between the ideal and the real worked on them, even when circumstances said it shouldn't. As a result, they found themselves constantly recalibrating their values.

They carried haunting names like Eadweard Muybridge and Voltairine de Cleyre. Few public figures lacked colorful monikers like those of Chicago ward healer John "the Bath" Coughlin or Kansas lightning bolt "Sockless Jerry" Simpson. Newspapers sported titles like the Frankfort (Kentucky) *Roundabout*, the Laramie (Wyoming) *Boomerang*, the Sedalia (Missouri) *Weekly Bazoo*, and the Lexington (Missouri) *Weekly Caucasian*.[14] Wealthy men wore silk stockings ("socks") and liberated women revived bloomers to ride bicycles. Neither sex wore shorts and jeans were for workers. The zeal to photograph victims of train wrecks, gunfights, and lynchings seems certifiable, as was the custom of posing dead infants with living family members. Their humor could be perverse: "Put a little strychnine or arsenic in the meat or other supplies furnished the tramp," wrote the *Chicago Tribune*. Their stoicism is incomprehensible. A Cincinnati cigar maker confessed, "We get meat once a week. The rest of the week, we have dry bread and coffee."[15] Their combativeness was extreme. Tammany Hall boss Charles Croker wrote, "Chess is war; business is war; the rivalry of students and of athletes is war. Everything is war in which men strive for mastery and power as against other men, and this is one of the essential conditions of progress."[16]

Their record levels of civic engagement remain difficult to grasp. What Gerald Gamm and Robert Putnam term "associational density" rocketed, as Americans created a "dramatic proliferation of voluntary groups" that were "concentrated in smaller cities and towns."[17] Jane Addams described its impact in Chicago: "All through our neighborhood, as in every neighborhood of workingmen, little societies spring up, sometimes without any formal organization."[18]

A prime example was the Chautauqua, which began in 1874 near a New York lake and grew into a national circuit of "assemblies" that mixed lectures by public figures with entertainment. William Jennings Bryan's wife, Mary, noted for her husband: "Chautauqua is something deeper than concerts or inspirational lectures." It was about "listening to and speaking to the mind of his country."[19] The importance of this "something deeper" is shown by the Chautauqua Literary and Science Circle's membership increase, from 100,000 in 1888 to 2.5 million in 1900.[20] *Everybody's Magazine* noted Chautauqua "grew up in the forests and on the prairies, not in the cities . . . where the native American runs free and true to type, not where he has been infected by the worldly and effete European notion of going out and having a gauzy and gaseous Good Time utterly unbuttressed by Uplift."[21]

The explosion of civic engagement that hatched Chautauqua included "single taxers," Christian and Marxian socialists, prison and mental health reformers, and what Gerald Carson termed the "Corn Flake Crusade."[22] A fad called "Fletcherism" attracted William James, with its belief that chewing each bite one hundred times could cure a variety of ailments. One who had the right cure for whatever ailed the country was Dr. John Harvey Kellogg, the cornflakes inventor who turned a struggling "sanitarium" in Battle Creek, Michigan, into a facility whose clients included Theodore Roosevelt and John D. Rockefeller. "Guests" faced regimens such as eating 14 pounds of grapes a day to cure high blood pressure.

Civic engagement played a role in producing voter turnouts that reached 67.2 percent (1892), 65.7 percent (1876), and 65.2 percent (1880).[23] Disillusionment with the major parties generated new ones. Longest-lived were the Socialist Labor Party, which fielded its first presidential candidate in 1892 and was on the ballot into the 1950s, and the Prohibition Party, which fielded candidates from 1876 to 1920.

What drove and sustained this civic engagement—as it sustained Sarah Murray—was grit. A nineteenth-century author provided a better definition than the "perseverance" emphasized by current research: "Grit is in the grain of character. It may generally be described as heroism materialized—spirit and will thrust into heart, brain, and backbone, so as to form part of the physical substance of the man."[24] In the Age of Discontent, perseverance without purpose was like a locomotive without coal. W. E. B. Du Bois tells of one enterprising African American: "I happened to pick up a bouquet of flowers that had been thrown out on an ash-pile. I untied the seemingly dead flowers and found a rose-geranium which seemed to have a little life in it by its smell, and I carried it home and planted it. . . . I have been growing flowers ever since."[25] Without glossing over the realities of segregation, Du Bois makes sure we understand what sustained African Americans—hope and a refusal to be broken.

The Country Was in Real Danger

Sarah Murray needed all the grit she could muster to traverse an area that was home to notorious ex–Civil War guerillas. In 1866 a front-page story read: "Unionists Murdered in Platte City, Missouri, by Rebels."[26] Six months after Black Friday, former guerilla Jesse James married in Kearney, just southeast of St. Joe. The year of Sarah Murray's walk, the James gang robbed a Missouri train in January and a Kansas one in November. Sarah Murray's husband probably fought for the Confederacy, which made her at home in a region where some still refused to acknowledge the Union.

The Civil War hung over the country like collective post-traumatic stress disorder, prowling every town. The veteran in his service cap swayed down the street while mumbling about fires in the Battle of the Wilderness; the Shiloh survivor staggered on one leg with a vacant look in his eyes. In a debate over veterans' pensions, a congressman described what we term PTSD:

> [The war] wounded a hundred times as many; wounds unseen perhaps and felt for years, insidious, subtle, hiding away in nerve, muscle, brain, heart, tissue, and bone; seeds of decay planted in the constitution weakened by the stress and strain of the service, germs of infirmity sown in the system in the swamps of the Carolinas, the sands of Florida, the mud of Virginia, or in the heat and flame of the deadly encounter when nerve and brain and heart were subjected to strains from which they never entirely recovered.[27]

We know the Civil War from photographs and memoirs, some long out of print. What we do not know are the sounds and smells that years later would awaken veterans as they lay in their beds. The Civil War casualty rate of 34 percent far surpasses America's World War II rate of 6 percent.[28] Although disease killed many, those deaths could be as cruel as perishing on the battlefield. Especially controversial were mass assaults like Pickett's Charge at Gettysburg. Soldiers who pinned letters to their uniforms while waiting for orders to charge had to wonder if they were no better than cannon fodder. After losing a third of his men at Malvern Hill, Confederate general David Hill lamented, "It was not war—it was murder."[29]

For most soldiers the war formed their first experience with industrial technology and management. New weapons produced battles that resembled modern versions of Agincourt, the horrific medieval battle where English archers slaughtered armored French knights. The Civil War also marked many soldiers' first experiences with the leadership of nonprofessional officers, who regularly took license with their power. One historian remarked that Civil War soldiers "had always followed freely their own wishes, restrained only by the civil law of a free people."[30] Some draftees felt "they were being used chiefly for the benefit of cotton speculators, officers, and outsiders."[31]

It is little wonder desertion rates were 11 percent among Union soldiers and 10 percent among Confederates—higher than for any other conflict.[32] Ella Lonn listed the causes: poor rations and lack of proper clothing. One officer described what they faced: "For twenty days I have been constantly marching, and part of this time in drenching rain, and have only drawn three days' rations in that time. A great many of my men are nearly naked."[33]

Those who survived battles like Cold Harbor near Mechanicsville, Virginia, resented those who avoided the draft by hiring someone to serve in their place. Knowing that those who bought substitutes were reaping profits while others were trying to keep from being roasted alive in the Battle of the Wilderness "left resentments that lasted long after the war."[34] Eight years after Appomattox, George Templeton Strong observed, "Great wealth . . . is now, as a general rule, presumptive evidence against the character of its owner."[35] He did not need to add it also marked the tilted playing field.

There is little question veterans brought home itchy trigger fingers and short fuses. The late nineteenth century still stands as the most violent thirty years in our nation's history. Too many killings also had a purpose, whose most troubling symbol is a gnarled tree branch, thrust like a skeletal finger, with a dangling rope. People of color were driven off their lands by whites bearing nooses. Ken Gonzalez-Day uncovered 350 lynching cases in California alone, with Latinos a majority of the victims of whites coveting their land.[36]

The absurdity of lynching rationalizations are found in a medical journal's discussion of "the sexual criminal." Between articles on "Pernicious Delay in Surgical Cases" and "Hypertrophy of the Prostate," a doctor wrote: "The fear of death—sudden, violent, terrible—is about the only thing that will hold the sexual criminal in check and teach him that he must restrain his savage lust. . . . The mad dog is not granted the formality of a legal trial before we blow out his brains. He is destroyed at once."[37] Newspapers carried stories with sentences like "Clinton Anderson, colored, was hanged at Little Rock, Ark., on the 30th, for outraging a white woman."[38] The article doesn't specify the "outrage," but it shows how the press spread the lynching-as-retribution idea. An 1897 front-page illustrated story of a lynching, headlined "Trio of Reds Swing Off," confessed, "Few, if any, will admit that the fate of the men was undeserved."[39] The retribution-through-violence theme sometimes acquired a political tinge. "The home of George Herron at Borne's station on the Big Four railroad, east of this city, was entered on Monday night by ten masked men, Herron was taken from his bed, bound to a telephone pole, and whipped," read a story about a man who dared to open a saloon.[40] An 1896 article in the *Railroad Trainmen's Journal* shows the undercurrent of violence coursing through the age: "Thousands of professors and educated mechanics are tramps in every country, while millions of idle men are drilling to prepare for a war that all men feel impending."[41]

The penultimate intimidation symbol was the Gatling gun. This 1862 invention fired two hundred rounds a minute, enough to mow down people like a reaper leveling a wheat field. Only lightly used during the Civil War, in 8½ minutes Gatlings won the Spanish American War, firing thirty-six hundred rounds into entrenched positions on San Juan Hill.[42] Anyone could methodically turn the crank of this killing machine and snuff out more lives than an entire company of Civil War sharpshooters. Julia Keller notes the gun's gleaming brass barrel became a potent symbol "of the iron rule of the dominant classes."[43]

Sarah Murray was not merely walking through one of America's most contentious regions; a year after the panic she walked into a thicket called the Long Depression. The term remains controversial, even though those who lived through the Age of Discontent were not reticent about using it.[44] One was William McKinley, who mentioned it in his Second Inaugural Address: "There was deep solicitude because of the long depression in our manufacturing, mining, agricultural, and mercantile industries and the consequent distress of our laboring population."[45]

Although the years from 1873 to 1903 do not meet the criteria for a depression, evidence suggests something extraordinary occurred. The National Bureau of Economic Research (NBER), the authority on recessions, identifies 202 months (54 percent of the time) from 1873 to 1904 as recessions.[46] There were only 282 months for the entire twentieth century. Between 1873 and 1885, 71 percent of the months were recessions, versus 47 percent during the Great Depression. The consumer price index fell 13 points from 1870 to 1900, leading some to refer to those years as the Great Deflation.[47] For farmers and workers, deflation meant crops and wages were worth less than they had been the year before, even though debt amounts remained the same.

This economic climate shaped people like Sarah Murray, sowing fear and confusion. The financial undertow of the Panic of 1873 probably exceeded Great Depression figures. An 1877 Ohio report noted, "The wages of machinists, machine blacksmiths, machine molders, and other employés in foundries, etc., have been reduced on an average of from 25 to 40 per cent since 1872."[48] Business output and durable goods production fell by 25 percent and wheat prices by 50 percent during the mid-1880s downturn. Overall unemployment in the Panic of 1893 hit 18.4 percent and in Connecticut, manufacturing wages fell by 25 percent.[49] If the Great Recession unnerved you, imagine facing three depressions in twenty years with no Federal Reserve, no Securities and Exchange Commission, and a questionable safety net.

Two Directions

A late nineteenth-century glass ceiling also loomed over Sarah Murray's walk. Women found themselves bound by prejudice as tightly as the corsets that imprisoned them. Popular opinion viewed women as keepers of morality with expectations they behave accordingly. This led to bizarre positions, such as when National Labor Union leader William Sylvis proclaimed he favored "limited female suffrage" in which women "should have a vote on all questions involving a moral issue."[50] Of course, suffrage *was* a defining moral issue, when the Fourteenth Amendment dictated that no state shall "deprive any person of life, liberty, or property, without due process of law." Deprived of their rights, women picked themselves up and, instead of walking, embraced the fad of cycling. You could not ride a bicycle in restrictive clothing nor could your freedom of movement be restricted. Others strode toward freedom one step at a time.

Although Sarah Murray's story does not mention it, no doubt some wondered "what kind of woman" chose to walk alone through Jesse James's backyard. The need to look over their shoulders colored women's participation in organizations like the Farmers' Alliance. An Alliance history noted, "There is nothing with which she comes in contact that is not purified, refined, ennobled."[51] One woman noted how this shaped the agenda: "While we may not enter the arena of politics, or mingle in the busy commercial mart with the sterner sex, in our sphere at home, by the fireside, and in the social circle, we can make our influence felt for the good of our noble Order."

In the Age of Discontent, cultural forces made women's choices difficult. The US president's LGBTQ sister, Rose Cleveland, wrote: "An intense emotion of the age . . . takes two directions . . . which running parallel are permanently divergent and can never meet. The one claims that in the home alone can be attained a true education and development of women; the other claims that the home furnishes everything except the opportunity for higher education and development."[52] Her words were part of a lively debate in the pages of *The Chautauquan*—and in America. Noting the number of female workers increased 50 percent between 1870 and 1880, Mary Lowe Dickinson explained, "There remains hardly an art or an industry that does not now include them"; Ida Tarbell reported on "Women in Journalism"; Julia Ward Howe wrote about "Women in the Professions."[53] They were part of a surging undercurrent of women determined to meet the world on their terms. In 1848 New York became the first state to permit married women to hold property in their names. By the 1870s similar laws existed in many states, allowing women to collect their earnings and share custody of their children.[54]

An example of this taking control is Elizabeth Colt, who managed the firearms company after her husband died in 1862, along with maintaining her involvement with the suffrage movement and other causes.[55] While Samuel Colt had reduced costs through machine production, her marketing genius is reflected by her slogan, "The gun that won the West." William Hosley recognized her contributions: "Colt invented . . . a system of myths, symbols, stagecraft, and distribution that has been mimicked by generations of industrial mass marketers and has rarely been improved upon."[56] Victoria Woodhull saluted her character by saying, "The most honorable chapter in her biography is the interest she takes in the welfare and advancement of her work, people, and dependents."[57]

Industrialization increased working opportunities for women. An 1889 study listed some of the occupations: box, cigar, flower, feather, and candy makers, chair seaters, gold polishers, silk weavers, and upholsterers. It noted "the encouragement employment brings to marriage," since a working woman "has certainly a better chance of securing a home suited to her station in life."[58] The average woman worker was twenty-two years old, began employment at fifteen, and was single, but earned only 53 percent of men's wages.[59] The 1889 report admits, "These figures tell a sad story, and one is forced to ask how women can live on such earnings." Although the study decried "dangerously low" women's wages, its male author wrote, "Woman has come in as a . . . new economic factor, and as such must take her place at the bottom of the ladder."[60] Several states also published studies on women workers and business owners. An 1890 Massachusetts report found 1,760 women as partners in manufacturing industries and another 13,332 as stockholders.[61]

By 1901, *Statistics of Women at Work* was citing "economic necessity" as the "impelling motive" increasing female workers from 1,836,000 in 1870 to 5,319,000 in 1900. A passage that would have had Elizabeth Colt rolling her eyes admitted: "A considerable number of women . . . are actuated by motives that do not differ materially from those which appeal to men in similar circumstances, such as some form of ambition, a love of activity, or a desire for social usefulness."[62] The report classified 275,000 women in "professional service," with 200,000 teachers, 4,488 doctors, 6,132 government officials, and 1,164 "literary and scientific persons." Of the 233,000 women in "trade and transportation," 10,471 were "merchants and dealers," 60,129 "saleswomen," and 35,911 "bookkeepers and accountants."[63] A woman whose name should be more widely known—Helen

Sumner—enhanced the data with a 1910 study.[64] While Sumner's data reveals an increase in many occupations, it still shows a thick glass ceiling (see table 1.1).

Rural women faced other issues. The Nebraska Board of Agriculture observed: "The woman ... is obliged to rise in the ice-cold morning and kindle the fire; she ... must scrub the rough floors and keep the interior of the house clean ... milk the cows and look after the cattle sheds ... care after the children and provide them with clothes; it is she who in seed time and harvest must do a full grown servant's work in addition to her daily chores."[65]

Some believed this work bred insanity. A Wisconsin Grange lecturer estimated that in 1878, farm wives accounted for half the women housed in state asylums. Kansas Populist Annie Diggs cited a similar figure.[66] One 1899 *Iowa Bulletin* illustrated how the stereotype of the mad farm wife inspired a backlash:

> The governor's wife queried: I would like to ask Superintendent Hoyt if statistics show that a larger proportion of farmers and farmers' wives become insane than any other class of people?
>
> Superintendent Hoyt: I think not. Farmers' wives probably form the bulk of our lady patients, but that is because this is an agricultural state.[67]

An Ohioan agreed: "It always makes me indignant when I hear the statement that a larger proportion of our farmers' wives are insane than any other class because it is not true."[68] One study found that from 1885 to 1928, women's admissions at the North Dakota Hospital for the Insane were lower than their proportion among the overall state population.[69]

This does not alter the reality that the lives of rural women could be lonely and even brutal.[70] Willa Cather makes the attempted rape of a farm girl who was boarding in town a central scene in *My Ántonia*. Annie Diggs described what she called women's "eternal climb" of the economic treadmill: "For more than a quarter of a century, these churning, washing, ironing, baking, darning, sewing, cooking, scrubbing, drudging women, whose toilsome, dreary lives were unrelieved by the slight incident or by-play of town life, felt that their treadmills slipped cogs. Climb as they would, they slipped—down two steps while they climbed one."[71]

To counter prejudice, women bonded in organizations that worked to better their lives. The largest and most influential was the Women's Christian Temperance Union (WCTU). Even as the number of saloons increased from one hundred thousand in the early 1870s to three hundred thousand by 1890, the

Table 1.1 Women's Employment, Selected Occupations

Occupation	1870 number	1870 percent	1880 number	1880 percent	1890 number	1890 percent	1900 number	1900 percent
Hucksters and peddlers	1,463	4.3	2,420	4.5	2,182	3.8	2,792	3.5
Stenographers; clerks; bookkeepers	9,982	3.3	28,698	5.7	168,808	16.9	238,782	75.7; 12.9; 28.6
Telephone and telegraph operators	350	4.3	1,224	5.3	8,403	16.2	21,980	29.3
Printing and publishing	2,800	9.1	6,777	11.6	19,026	13.9	28,765	17.6
Bank and company officials	68	0.5	0	0	217	0.5	1,271	1.7
Undertakers	20	1.0	54	1.1	83	0.8	323	2.0
Bankers and brokers	20	0.2	133	0.7	510	1.4	293	0.4
Nonwholesale merchants and dealers	5,651	4.3	14,741	3.1	25,480	3.7	33,825	4.3
Livery stable keepers	11	0.1	33	0.2	47	0.2	190	0.6
Other managers	591	1.3	1,524	2.7	1,473	4.9	3,345	5.3
Dressmakers	—	—	—	—	47,164	97.0	40,835	89.5
Men's clothing	58,466	54.8	80,994	50.4	96,077	44.2	89,874	47.0
Custom milliners	—	—	—	—	16,457	96.4	32,487	97.6
Boarding house keepers	7,050	55.2	12,513	54.6	37,583	73.5	59,455	83.4
Servants and waitresses	786,635	88.4	876,377	75.9	1,231,344	84.5	116,5561	74.7
Laundresses	55,218	91.5	107,136	87.8	215,121	87.2	328,935	85.3
Hotel keepers	855	5.3	2,126	6.6	4,276	13.0	6,533	15.8
Restaurant keepers	714	1.4	2,196	2.8	4,837	3.3	4,845	14.3
Nurses and midwives	11,356	93.4	14,097	90.4	41,265	87.0	108,691	89.9
Total	2,799		52,344		191,378		301,353	

Note: Dashes indicate no attempt was made to categorize the occupation or data; zero indicates none were found.

Source: Sumner, *Report on the Conditions of Women:* table 12, "Domestic & Personal Service," 254; table 17, "Transportation," 259; and table 11, "Clothing Industries," 253.

WCTU had women saying, "Lips that have ever touched liquor will never touch mine," while others sang hymns outside saloons.[72] WCTU member Mary Bryan wrote that her husband "was deeply grieved over the sorrow and misery directly traceable to intemperance."[73] Two other members were First Ladies Frances Cleveland and Lucy Hayes, the latter of whom earned the nickname "Lemonade Lucy," for advising her husband to ban liquor from the White House.

Wendell Phillips, who went from abolitionist to prohibitionist, linked temperance to economics: "Law can shut up those bars and dramshops which facilitate and feed intemperance, which double our taxes, make our streets unsafe ... treble the peril to property and life."[74] Phillips's charge, that drinkers were "tools in the hands of designing men," hinted at the anti-immigrant dimensions of the temperance movement. Its zealotry closed many immigrant pubs.

The surge of women into an organization that gave them leadership roles increased WCTU membership from 22,800 in 1880 to 158,477 in 1901, a growth only matched by what took place in the Farmers' Alliances.[75] Led by Frances Willard, an LGBTQ woman with a talent for analyzing, organizing, and collaborating, the WCTU also focused on activities other than temperance.[76] Willard's 1894 presidential address spoke of the "wage workers war" as a "wonderful uprising against the power of the dollar."[77] The WCTU worked with the Knights of Labor in supporting prison reform and lobbying to protect working women and eliminate child labor. Willard's statement of principles begins, "We believe in a living wage; in an eight-hour day."[78] She also made controversial alliances with "morality czar" Anthony Comstock (who prosecuted presidential candidate Victoria Woodhull) and failed to make alliances with others (giving only lukewarm support to the anti-lynching movement).

Willard maintained, "Women are varied in their methods; they are born to be branchers out."[79] As a "brancher out," Willard herself offered an example of how collaboration offered an alternative to the social Darwinism embraced by many tycoons.[80] Under the umbrella of the National Council of Women she brought together "orthodox and heterodox, Republican, Democrat, and Prohibitionist, native and foreign ... [and] agreed that while loyal each to her own belief, we had met to counsel for the further advancement of Woman's sacred cause."[81] She defined this in scathing terms: "When we are not toys, when we are not dolls, when we stand before them royal, crowned with heart of love and brain of fire, then shall come the new day." Willard was speaking from experience. She lost her position at Northwestern University after being harassed by male students.

The Color Line

Like women, people of color faced old prejudices in new packages. Industrial racism differed from antebellum racism in its intellectual "fit" between the emerging "scientific" classification mania and the hierarchy and specialization demanded by the factory system. Standardization demanded everything have its place. Complex organizations demanded everyone know their place.

It was one thing to standardize nuts and bolts of the work of a factory, but another to classify the people. The obsession with classification included pseudosciences such as phrenology, which used a device resembling a fiendish hair dryer to examine skulls for clues about personality and intelligence. Jane Addams was among those who fell prey to this fad, receiving an evaluation stating, "Vital power not great, but still an element of toughness in her that will endure a great deal."[82]

More troubling were respected academics who measured skulls and anatomical features to shackle Black, Indigenous, and people of color (BIPOC) Americans as surely as the leg-irons of slave traders. Anthropologist Daniel Brinton announced, "The Parisians of today have a cranial capacity of 1448 cubic centimeters; the Negroes 1344 c.c.; the American Indians 1376."[83] The potent poison flowing from the pens of Theodore Roosevelt and others insisted industrialization signaled the triumph of the Angle-Saxon race. In his best-selling *Our Country*, Josiah Strong asked, "Does it not look as if God were preparing in our Anglo-Saxon civilization the die with which to stamp the peoples of the earth?"[84]

In the common perception, racial and ethnic traits were immutable; ethnic Slavs could no more change their qualities than tigers could lose their stripes. Ohio senator and presidential candidate George Pendleton repudiated the right of African Americans to vote: "They have different blood and bones and organization. They have different tastes and habits and capacities.... It is an adherent and radical difference of race, of blood, of nature, of intellect, of capacity, which no training can efface, no associations, or habits, or discipline can extinguish."[85]

These ideas provided cover for all manner of perversities. They justified violent, extralegal takings of Hispanic land grants and Indigenous American homelands. They bolstered the connection between laissez-faire capitalism and race that figured in the *Civil Rights Cases*. Most of all they granted respectability to the unspeakable. African Americans celebrated the Thirteenth, Fourteenth, and Fifteenth Amendments as they listened to speeches about justice, only to watch both political parties throw the rulings under the bus. Mary Lease may have had her faults but she understood: during a tumultuous tour of the South with 1892 Populist presidential candidate James Weaver, during which they were pelted with rotten eggs, vegetables, and threats of violence, she recognized the suppression of African American voters: "There has not been an honest election in the South for years. After the negro had been enfranchised the democracy started out with the proposition that it was right to count out his vote, and they have followed that up with the idea that it is right to count out any political opponent. Democracy holds power in the South by fraudulent voting."[86] The dreaded night riders have come to symbolize these setbacks, but the pervasive unemployment and hunger were more feared nightmares.

When W. E .B. Du Bois wrote about "the problem of the color-line," he recognized "an upheaval of humanity like the Reformation and the French Revolution" that added over 4 million newly freed enslaved workers to the economy.[87] Although people of color worked in steel mills and coal mines, managers and union officials did not encourage diversity. A coal region country doctor spoke for many when he said, "A highly educated negro was absolutely useless for all practical purposes."[88]

A few companies employed significant numbers of African Americans. Two fascinating examples are the extinct Iowa towns of Buxton and Muchakinock. In 1879, the McNeill brothers, H. W. and W. A., known as "Big Mac" and "Little Mac," recruited formerly enslaved people to work their Muchakinock mine in response to a strike. When the Chicago and Northwestern Railroad bought out the McNeills in 1881, officials enlisted John Buxton to manage the new acquisition. By 1885 almost two-thirds of Muchakinock's 1,200 residents were African American. When the mine petered out, Buxton's son Ben designed the new company town of Buxton to replace it, incorporating the latest ideas about municipal development. Buxton's population exceeded Muchakinock's, reaching 2,700 African Americans and 1,991 whites in 1905. Three decades later, plagued by a decline in the demand for coal, Buxton was a ghost town. At its height it boasted African American doctors, lawyers, and other professionals and an African American YMCA with a gymnasium and indoor swimming pool.[89]

To this country's discredit, there were too few Buxtons. Like many, African Americans did find some opportunities in the West where an estimated 25 percent of Texas cattle drive cowboys were African American.[90] Corporate employment of more African Americans might have changed the course of industrial racism. It is hard to maintain prejudice against someone who increases production or saves lives. The real tragedy is that companies deprived themselves of *ideas*. Despite corporate America's failure, rarely has anyone mentioned it in discussions of reparations for African Americans.

An 1893 publication written by Frederick Douglass, Ida B. Wells, Irvine Garland Penn, and Ferdinand Barnett (who later married Wells) offers a prime example of the African American response to industrial racism. *The Reason Why the Colored American Is Not in the World's Columbian Exposition* indicted the nation while celebrating African American achievement. In its most hard-hitting chapter, Wells describes the terrorism of "Lynch Law" that could condemn African Americans to a brutal death on a whim. The included tables revealed 27 people who were murdered for "race prejudice," 13 for "quarreling with white men," and 10 for "making threats." Wells classified 32 deaths as "no reason given."[91]

In his chapter Douglass protests the exposition's midway, which featured the "barbaric rites" of "African savages brought here to act the monkey."[92] In dramatizing civilization's "advance" over "primitive peoples," the midway featured an "Algerian and Tunisian Village" with snake charmers and a harem, a "Dahomey Village" with "Amazon warriors," a "Wild East" show with "Bedouin warriors" in imitation of Buffalo Bill's nearby Wild West Show, and an attraction named "The Streets of Cairo" featuring a dancer named Little Egypt (who was in fact a Syrian named Farida Mazar Spyropoulos).[93]

The midway exemplified an era when science supplied theories that sold freak show tickets. In P. T. Barnum's "Grand Scientific and Musical Theater," an African American dwarf held a sign asking: "Is it man? Is it monkey?"[94] The "coon song" fad made minstrel show bigotry seem tame. The lyrics of a song like "The Coon's Trademark: A Watermelon, Razor, Chicken and a Coon," are a national embarrassment:

> A coon he loves to sing and dance,
> Until he is out of breath;
> All you've got to do is jolly him 'long,
> And he'll work himself to death.[95]

Contrasted with the midway was the exposition's White City, named for the luminous stucco exterior of buildings symbolizing the Anglo-Saxon superiority celebrated by Theodore Roosevelt in his *The Winning of the West*. For him, America "will be lost unless we grasp, however roughly, the past race-history of the nations who took part therein."[96] In the exposition's most famous chapter, "The Significance of the Frontier in American History," one of Woodrow Wilson's prized pupils, Frederick Jackson Turner, wrapped manifest destiny in social Darwinism: "At last, the slender paths of aboriginal intercourse have been broadened and interwoven into the complex mazes of modern commercial lines; the wilderness has been interpenetrated by lines of civilization, growing ever more numerous."[97]

The Reason Why's four authors challenged these perceptions by showing how African Americans used their new freedom. The main argument came from Penn, a Virginia journalist, who at nineteen became editor of *The Lynchburg Laborer* and then turned a few heads with his 1891 book, *The Afro-American Press*. Penn's work includes tables showing that in 1892 African Americans owned $253 million in property, a majority of it in the South. In the Midwest, African American assets totaled $2.5 million in Iowa and Nebraska and $3.9 million in Kansas, suggesting how many African Americans established businesses or homesteads.[98]

Penn noted in 1890 there were 215 lawyers, 417 physicians, and 23,866 African Americans teaching 1,460,447 pupils throughout the country. Douglass rejoiced: "It is proof the Negro is not standing still. He is not dead, but alive and active."[99] Although Penn does not cite literacy results, others documented the grit of African Americans in learning to read and write. An Indiana state report noted that before Emancipation, only 3.4 percent of African Americans in the South were literate, versus 20.9 percent in the North. By 1870 the literacy rate in former Confederate states had risen to 26 percent, in part because of the efforts of the Freedmen's Bureau and institutions like African American churches.[100]

Herrings in a Barrel

Immigrants also felt industrialization's prejudices. Sarah Murray and her husband may have been two of them. The staggering number of those who entered this country after the Civil War remains difficult to comprehend. Following the Long Depression's rhythms, over 8.5 million people entered between 1870 and 1890, with the peak coming in 1882, when bank suspensions and business failures were the lowest of any three years before 1900. That year immigrants equaled 1.5 percent of the total population, a figure that today would total 4.9 million.[101] In just one example, the number of Slavs in Luzerne County, Pennsylvania, swelled from 449 in 1880 to 19,330 in 1890.[102]

Those who entered this country between 1881 and 1890 were mostly male (61 percent) and between fifteen and forty years of age (65 percent).[103] Reports classed almost half of them (49.8 percent) as having no occupation, a total that probably reflects immigration officials befuddled by language rather than a lack of skill. Slightly less than a quarter (24 percent) were laborers, another classification that contained a variety of nuances. Just under 11 percent were skilled workers, 7.7 percent were farmers, and 3.9 percent were domestic workers. Professionals accounted for less than 1 percent.[104]

A massive advertising campaign attracted them with low fares and fanciful pictures of the wonders awaiting them. Steamship companies deluged Europe with posters promising steerage rates to America that averaged $22.50. To supplement the advertising, companies hired recruiting agents who promised free land and jobs paying up to $3.50 a day.[105] Railroads were among the most active marketers, enticing immigrants to settle on their government-granted lands. The Union Pacific spent $855,414.92 on advertising in Nebraska alone; the Burlington spent $969,500.25 on its national efforts.[106] A recruiter boasted he "swiped a whole trainload from the two Kansas roads."[107] A town's recruiting pitch captures the boosterism:

> Beatrice is not dead or dying,
> Real estate is simply flying,
> He who buys to-day is wise,
> For Beatrice dirt is on the rise.[108]

Those who journeyed to this country endured what Oscar Handlin termed the "harsh and brutal filter" of the ocean voyage.[109] Most immigrants journeyed in steerage quarters like the following:

> Imagine a wooden cell some 36 feet or so in length, 12 feet wide at one end, but narrowing to about 5 feet at the further extremity; instead of a ceiling, a hatchway opening on to the main deck; two dirty ladders, placed almost perpendicularly, forming a staircase. On two sides, running the length of the den, a wooden partition had been constructed of bare boards, reaching to within 10 inches of the top. At intervals in this boarding were eight doors, numbered, showing that behind these were our sleeping berths. The boards had once upon a time—evidently a very remote time—been painted. The floor was strewn with sawdust.[110]

The cramped quarters reeking of human waste and unwashed bodies forced passengers to escape on deck when they could. Robert Louis Stevenson wrote of his experiences in *The Amateur Immigrant* (1885). Likening passengers to "herrings in a barrel," he recalled a terrified man shouting, "The ship's going down!"[111] While shipwrecks were rare, the deplorable conditions meant some did not survive. They received a brief ceremony, then were dumped rudely over the side.

Exhausted passengers arrived at New York's Castle Garden, where they underwent the process that became infamous at Ellis Island, which replaced Castle Garden in 1890. Abandoning the living hell of steerage, passengers experienced the brief liberation of open air and solid ground before learning that American officials could be as petty as those of their home countries. Doctors screened for physical, mental, and political diseases. While the newly arrived shuffled through various stations, wolves circled, looking for victims. For exorbitant fees they helped with currency exchanges and railroad tickets. After leaving Castle Garden, some experienced what immigrant Mary Antin described as a "spinning" vision: "Bells, whistles, hammers, locomotives shrieking madly, men's voices, peddlers' cries, horses' hoofs, dogs' barkings—all united in doing their best to drown every other sound but their own, and made such a deafening uproar in the attempt that nothing could keep it out."[112]

The screening was only the immigrants' first taste of prejudice. A *Century* article on the Pennsylvania coalfields, complete with cartoonish caricatures of "an Irish American," "a Hun" and "A Factor in the Problem (Italian)," informed readers, "The first purchase made by a Slovak or a Polack is a revolver, by Italian or Sicilian a stiletto."[113] These words reflected the belief that every immigrant harbored a variety of vices. The temperance movement linked immigrants with drunkenness since they consumed wine or beer with meals and socialized in bars. Temperance crusaders criminalized "immigrant cultural mores regardless of how important alcohol was to German and Irish cultures," observes Fred Stopsky.[114]

The depth of anti-immigrant feelings is clear in the many protests voiced by workers and farmers. Typical was an Iowa wagon maker who vented his feelings: "This importation of foreign labor is using up American labor and the sooner the emigration of foreign labor is stopped, the better it will be for the American laborers and there will be a demand for labor on good wages paid for good men."[115] More surprising is the unvarnished nativism voiced by those charged with gathering the facts for volumes officially issued by state governments. The stream of anti-Chinese diatribes that runs through several years of California reports provides a sense of why cities like San Francisco discriminated against the Chinese. "I know that the Chinese differ from us in habits, tastes and moral principles, and I know that they are a race which cannot assimilate with us, and I know their presence among us to be an evil and detrimental to the welfare of our people and institutions, and we should always give preference in employment to our own people," said the 1884 report.[116]

Those on the other side of the continent vented their prejudices against different groups. An 1885 Pennsylvania report ranted about Italians in saying, "The illiteracy, turpitude, and degraded habits of this class of immigrants, innate and lasting as they are, stamp them as a most undesirable set whose affiliation with our own people must in time work great injury."[117] The state that was the door for millions of immigrants issued this warning in 1886, "If the tide of immigration is not checked the unskilled American laborer must get down to the level of the foreigner or else he must leave and go in search of a better country."

That officials entrusted to provide information to legislators and the public should openly vent about immigration peels back the curtain covering the views behind a predictable backlash. In 1882 the country passed its first anti-immigration law—the infamous Chinese Exclusion Act—stating "the coming of Chinese laborers to this country endangers the good order of certain localities."[118] In 1897 the Pennsylvania legislature approved what became known as the "Hunkie Law," placing a tax on the wages of so-called alien workers.

When the 1890 Census showed an increasingly diverse America, historian Richard Gray says it "was enough to generate a moral panic."[119] That census was especially controversial because it used punch cards like those that eventually fed mainframe computers. The system's inventor, Herman Hollerith, founded International Business Machines. Much the way machines replaced manual labor, his machines tabulated over a million entries, doing the work of twenty hand tabulators—and with more accuracy.

Rhetoric stressing the need to preserve Anglo-Saxon purity was common. In 1892 the *Boston Traveler* predicted that if restrictions were not placed on immigration, the government "will be in the hands of and controlled by the alien-born citizens."[120] Some Harvard alumni formed the Immigration Restriction League. A founder, Prescott Hall, received star billing at a 1901 Industrial Commission hearing, where he argued that Northern European immigrants were less likely to commit crimes. These attitudes reinforced a resurgence of nativism that played a role in introducing the Pledge of Allegiance in 1892 and the flag salute in 1898.

We will never know how much these attitudes contributed to the desire of immigrants to return to their homelands. While we lack definitive late nineteenth-century data, early twentieth-century figures show nearly a third returned after less than five years, carrying with them an average of $160—several thousand dollars in today's money.[121] Historian Dean Strang observes that, for

Italians, "America could not match the imaginings that led many to leave Italy."[122] Kerby Miller, who studied Irish immigrants, notes letters and memoirs reflected "a generalized unease—indeed, often a deep dissatisfaction" with life in their new country.[123]

Through Difficulties Without and Within

Nimrod Smith was well-acquainted with "no reason given." His photograph in an 1890 government report shows a man with long hair, a mustache, a watch chain, and a penetrating stare above a caption translating his Cherokee name, Cha-la-di-heh, as Charles the Killer. The Eastern Cherokee were among 14,339 Indigenous people in the East enumerated by the 1890 Census. The descendants of those who refused to be forcefully removed to Oklahoma on the Trail of Tears lived relatively unmolested in a remote Smoky Mountain shadowland that the *Omaha Bee* described as "a perfectly organized republic" that was "practically independent of both state and national governments."[124]

Indigenous people like Smith faced increasing pressure from one of the most misguided pieces of legislation ever approved by Congress. Passed in 1887, the Dawes or Indian Allotment Act divided communal lands into individual holdings. Payments went to anyone claiming tribal membership. From 1890 to 1900 the number alleging Cherokee heritage in Smith's North Carolina home state nearly tripled. Seeking aid to fend off Oklahoma pretenders, Chickasaw governor R. M. Harris complained, "We regret to be forced to give up the institutions laid and founded by our parents."[125]

The act was part of a larger effort to wipe out traditional Indigenous life, forcing people to choose between survival and culture. The standardization demanded by industrialization fell on those with no desire to be standardized, especially children forcibly sent to boarding schools that were determined to beat their culture out of them.

The chasm between Nimrod Smith and Sarah Murray is wide but they share with their generation a need to break free of what boxed them in. They may have had different perspectives, but they shared resiliency and grit. Two examples stand in for members of the Grittiest Generation. One was Joseph Grewe, "the Human Badger," a Nebraska immigrant who was better at digging wells than planting wheat. They said he never stopped until he hit water, using hand tools to burrow as much as 65 feet a day.[126] Without his help many homesteaders would have failed. The second was the formerly enslaved Andrew Jackson Beard, who found a solution every time he saw a problem. In the late 1870s he patented a plow, whose rights he sold for $4,000. By 1890 his inventions, including a rotary steam engine, had brought him $30,000. His fame came from patent number 594,059 for a railroad safety coupler.[127] After Congress mandated better couplers, Beard sold the rights for $50,000.

The examples of Grewe and Beard reinforce the importance of knowing the lives behind the numbers. Today, who could endure a bone-jarring wagon ride to a land without a tree in sight to arrive at a grass-covered cave and call it home, as did Willa Cather's Ántonia Shimerda? In a keening winter wind, would we go mad in a twelve-foot room, its smoky air lit by a lamp whose flame flickered uncertainly because refilling it required fighting thigh-high drifts and money you did not have? Seated in work cubicles, can we imagine steel mills where molten metal surged through the cavernous spaces?

Walter Wycoff recalled: "Each [has] his own salvation to work out through difficulties without and within that are little understood from the outside."[128] Sarah Murray's generation embraced this task of salvation. Instead of putting the jagged pieces back together (although some favored doing so), they took the pieces that mattered and rebuilt them into something inspirational.

CHAPTER TWO

TRANSITION STAGES ARE ALWAYS HARSH

The railroads and banks combined, the lawyers paid to find,
Out a way to rob me of my home.
—From "Dear Prairie Home,"
music and lyrics by Mrs. J. T. Kellie, ca. 1890

Four people embody the trends that shaped the Age of Discontent. Henry George rose from beggar to best-selling author by highlighting the paradox of poverty and progress in a vision of *what should be*. Carroll Wright's zeal for numbers cast light on *what was* by illuminating the Great Migration from rural to urban America and the rise of a consumer culture. The quest of the *why of it all* by Thorstein Veblen brought attention to industrialization's consequences. Edwin S. Porter was a gifted tinkerer who caught the eye of Thomas Edison by showing he understood as well as anyone the new meanings of *where and when*.

Desperate Enough

Like a biblical prophet, Henry George crawled out from industrialization's dark side with a revelation. With his wife near starvation, he did the only thing he could: "I stopped a man—a stranger—and told him I wanted $5. He asked what I wanted it for. I told him that my wife was confined and that I had nothing to give her to eat. He gave me the money. If he had not, I think I was desperate enough to kill him."[1] Fortunately, his natural writing ability and typesetting skills caught the eye of a discerning editor. In 1871 he had modest success with a book about the railroads' growing power.

One day while riding, he learned nearby land might sell for a thousand dollars an acre. "Like a flash it came upon me that there was the reason of advancing poverty with advancing wealth."[2] That insight made him America's third most famous person after Mark Twain and Thomas Edison. *Progress and Poverty* became a bestseller because it neatly captured three concerns: progress, poverty, and equity. The 1879 book warned the "prodigious increase in wealth-producing power" had increased the gap between rich and poor.[3] Though production was "most highly developed," it contrasted with "the deepest poverty." If it continued unchecked, "progress must turn to decadence, and modern civilization decline to barbarism."

One of the best at documenting poverty was photojournalist Jacob Riis. Arriving on the *Iowa* from Glasgow, Scotland, the Danish immigrant spent his last $40 to buy a revolver. Given the places he chose to haunt, it was an astute purchase. Like Henry George, Riis hit bottom, sleeping anywhere he could find. His low point came when he watched a stray dog he had adopted being clubbed to death by a policeman.[4] After becoming a police reporter, he brought back from alleys that were as narrow and sunless as a mine shaft numerous compelling images with a Rembrandt-like transcendence. As he later explained, "I hate darkness and dirt anywhere, and naturally want to let in the light."[5]

After hearing about flash photography, Riis bought a camera. With a flash rigged from a frying pan, he photographed Bottle Alley, the lair of the notorious Why-o Gang, and Bandits Roost, where men with chiseled faces and stony eyes dared the intruding lens to come further. Like Civil War photographer Mathew Brady, Riis knew the power of images. A health board report's description was uninspiring: "Until my negatives, dripping from the dark-room, came to reinforce [it]. From them, there was no appeal."[6] His image of youngsters curled on a doorstep like abandoned kittens captured late nineteenth-century destitution. A young New York police commissioner named Theodore Roosevelt coined the term "muckraking" to describe Riis's work.

It is difficult to comprehend the miseries of places like those Riis photographed. Tomb-like apartments sometimes had so little air that people struggled to breathe. On the streets, refuse as high as eighteen inches blocked ground-level windows. A New York Report described it: "The stench, the filth, the utter wretchedness, and seeming hopelessness of the inmates and the thought of the future of the little children brought up under such circumstances is simply heartsickening."[7] A committee investigating tenements concluded, "The rents here are nearly, if not more than double, the prices paid in many of the European cities."[8] Europe had nothing like the "narrow rooms and dark and narrow halls as exist in the double-decker on the 25-foot lot in New York to-day." The seven-hundred-page report described ceilings and walls near collapse and "garbage and filth of every description."

If Riis was the era's most famous chronicler of poverty, its preeminent booster of progress was improbably a former pastor dismissed for sexually molesting boys. After leaving his post in disgrace, Horatio Alger remade himself as the author of bestsellers like *Ben the Luggage Boy* (1870) and *Phil the Fiddler* (1872). In them Alger distilled a formula we still consume: "Serve your employer well, learn business as rapidly as possible, don't fall into bad habits and you will get on."[9]

Ample examples reinforced Alger's sermons. After Thomas Edison rescued three-year-old Jimmie MacKenzie from a runaway train, the boy's grateful father trained him as a telegrapher. Thirteen-year-old Andrew Carnegie's ability to translate Morse code by ear dazzled Pennsylvania Railroad president Thomas Scott, who made him his protégé. Although historians like Howard Zinn have pointed out such stories were rare, their power has not diminished.[10]

The increase in millionaires captured the public imagination; cities cited their numbers as evidence of their prosperity. In 1845, *New York Sun* publisher Moses Beach reported the metropolis had nineteen millionaires.[11] By 1892 there were over a thousand.[12] An 1891 Ohio report highlighted a machinery owner who made $700,000 with $350,000 in expenses, a farm equipment manufacturer who netted $1.5 million from $525,000 in expenses, and a whiskey distiller who earned $1.5 million with only $127,000 in expenses.[13]

The handiwork of Alger-like heroes was visible in American homes. Melville Bissell built his first sweeper in 1876. Gas stove ads promised to the average household the kitchen of a millionaire. Of all the new home gadgets, none may have been more critical than the sewing machine. Emerging from a protracted series of patent wars during the 1850s, it entered mass production after the Civil War. An 1885 Massachusetts report celebrated this achievement, noting, "In the application of natural forces in labor saving machinery, the introduction of the sewing machine was in many respects the most important epoch of this period."[14] Indiana reported the increase in ownership of sewing machines rose from 39,746 in 1881 to 149,533 in 1884.[15] Richard Sears was more than happy to ship by mail the new appliances and anything else. In 1888 he began advertising watches and jewelry. As envelopes piled up he realized he had stumbled across a brilliant idea that gave birth to his catalog's slogan as the "Book of Bargains."

Nothing embodied the muscle of progress more than the railroad industry, which expanded at a furious pace after the war.[16] Railroads were everyone's favorite hero and despised villain. Farmers ranted about the railroads' sins while small towns hoped they would lay track to their locales. In 1872 and 1873 they laid almost 13,000 miles of track, the largest two-year figure ever.[17] A judge described the rails "as necessary to life and health and comfort of the people of this country as are the arteries of the human body."[18] Locomotives brought fish from Boston to Kansas City and cattle from Abilene to Chicago. A farmer observed, "Every man in the country now has a market at his door."[19] Besides introducing the latest fashions to once-isolated homesteads, the tracks brought voices with strange accents and new ideas.

In the years after the Civil War, the belief grew that progress bent to the wealthy. Thomas Nast, the cartoonist who created our now-accepted image of Santa Claus, caricatured a rotund tycoon with a pile of money bags. Mr. Dooley, humorist Finley Peter Dunne's Chicago Irish bartender–political pundit, specialized in quips like: "A Ti-tan iv Fi-nance is a man that's got more money thin he can carry without bein' disorderly."[20]

When protests about the tilt of the playing field prompted the Census Bureau to hire George Holmes to study inequality, he revealed that the richest 9 percent held 71 percent of the nation's wealth, with 20 percent in the hands of the top .03 percent. Worried that inequity could "vex the coming ages of the Republic," Holmes proposed "progressive taxes on incomes, gifts, and inheritances."[21] Wisconsin University professor William Scott used Holmes's data to identify monopolies "as the chief source of inequalities."[22] In another study, Charles Spahr found "seven-eighths of American families hold but one-eighth of the national wealth."[23]

Nothing symbolized the cavernous gap between rich and poor more than the 1895 wedding of Consuelo Vanderbilt and the Duke of Marlborough. What *Leslie's Weekly* termed "the most imposing Anglo-American marriage since the Declaration of Independence" had reporters swarming to dig up the latest nugget about what some termed an "alliance" sealed by the bride's $10 million dowry and $100,000 trousseau featuring a corset with gold clasps and inset diamonds.[24] Cartoonist Richard Outcault's Yellow Kid offered a satirical view of the wedding as performed by the children of Shantytown. The minister stood under a dollar sign, a wedding guest arrived in a child's wagon pulled by a goat, and "the press" sat on a board to observe the event. Outcault summed up the extravagances of an age when Leland Stanford paid "upward of $600,000" for Queen Isabella's diamonds, and the aptly named John "Bet-a-Million" Gates wagered on which of two raindrops sliding down a window would first reach the bottom.[25] He lost. So did others.

In defense, the tycoons merged the Puritan concept of election with the idea of evolution. "While the law [of survival] may be sometimes hard for the individual, it is best for the race, because it ensures the survival of the fittest in every department," wrote Andrew Carnegie in his famous 1889 essay "Wealth." Few remember the more devastating next sentence, which blessed the marriage between racism and laissez-faire capitalism: "We accept and welcome … great inequality of environment, the concentration of business, industrial and commercial, in the hands of a few" because it is "essential for the future progress of the race."[26]

Carnegie wasn't the only millionaire enthralled with what came to be called social Darwinism. In 1902 John D. Rockefeller Jr. preached, "The American Beauty rose can be produced in the splendor and fragrance which bring cheer to its beholder only by sacrificing the early buds which grow up around it. This is … merely the working out of a law of nature and a law of God."[27] He didn't spell out what those sacrifices involved.

Yale professor William Graham Sumner, who believed wealth indicated superior talent and character, supplied ammunition for the tycoons.[28] He wrote: "The weak who constantly arouse the pity of humanitarians and philanthropists are the shiftless, the imprudent, the negligent, the impractical, and the inefficient, or they are the idle, the intemperate, the extravagant, and the vicious."[29] The words are from "The Forgotten Man" (1883), whose subject he characterized as the hardworking wage earner ignored by reformers.

Standard Oil's chief counsel, S. C. T. Dodd, turned Henry George's ideas upside down in 1902 when he rhetorically asked, "Why is there still so much poverty?" His answer would have earned an "A" from Sumner: "If people are content to work for barely sufficient wages to supply them with barbarous needs, they will find the work and wages suited to their wants."[30] Some went further. A professor visiting Pennsylvania mining towns evoked the dark undercurrent of eugenics: "Men have applied artificial selection to plants and animals and the results are gratifying. Man can only claim true distinction from other animals when he has the courage to apply it to himself."[31] Boston minister Brooke Herford preached that "good, wholesome starvation" was needed to make the poor more prudent.[32]

Transition Stages Are Always Harsh

A decade after George published *Progress and Poverty*, Carroll Wright illuminated two crucial transitions: from staples society to consumer culture and from a rural to an urban nation. Wright summed up their lesson: "Transition stages are always harsh on the generation that experiences them."[33] As much as any other individual, Wright was responsible for systematically applying statistics to public policy, especially as his work at the Massachusetts Bureau of Labor Statistics became a model for others.

The use of numbers to gauge fairness altered America as dramatically as the instant replay changed sports; like those replays, it remains controversial. Much credit for this goes to organizations like the Knights of Labor, whose constitution states: "To arrive at the true condition of the producing masses, in their educational, moral, and financial condition, [we demand] the establishment of bureaus of labor statistics."[34] The formation of these bureaus may be the era's most overlooked achievement.

A day before a January 1885 blizzard closed the Smithsonian Institution, Wright became commissioner of the newly formed National Bureau of Labor Statistics. In a faded picture, Wright's bushy eyebrows hover over a snowy walrus mustache. A contemporary wrote, "You would trust the man with that kind of face without knowing him, and you should not be mistaken."[35] That trust became important, as Wright professionalized information analysis. A statistician recalled, "We had to tentaculate our way step by step, often in doubt, at times feeling that we might be wrong, and must return and take a new departure, sometimes bewildered by diversity of counsel."[36]

Wright was not without faults. In one article he contended that women's freedom tended to "increase the divorce rate."[37] He referred to French Canadians as the "Chinese of the Eastern States." His evocation of manifest destiny no doubt pleased Theodore Roosevelt: "The pioneer element of the Anglo-Saxon race could not content itself until it had reached the utmost western boundary of its American inheritance."[38] His support of the Aldrich Report (discussed in the next chapter) was criticized for cherry-picking data. In a muckraking pamphlet, H. L. Bliss termed Wright "The Official Statistical Liar" who orchestrated a critic's dismissal.[39]

Words like leisure, hobby, and recreation were not in the vocabulary of pre–Civil War America, when shoes cost a farm laborer one-fourth of his monthly wage.[40] During Wright's childhood, a Nebraska farmer's letter offered an aphorism befitting the times: "The useful comes before the ornamental you know."[41] Antebellum society was built around staples—the basic goods needed to survive[42]—as illustrated by the description of a successful farmstead: "A complete farm ought to have woodland, pasture land, meadow or grass land, arable land, an orchard, a garden spot, and space for roads. . . . A husbandman also wants capital to stock his farm with cattle and other animals, and to furnish it with carts, wagons, plows, and other tools."[43]

In many communities, barter was critical. "The country storekeeper cannot expect to be paid for his goods in cash," wrote one foreign visitor, "and is obliged to barter if he wishes to have business."[44] Store owners knew "when to press for debts and when to be more lenient."[45] The detailed ledgers that were used to track what people traded to pay their debts demanded an exacting calculus that was cultural as well as economic. From these relationships, people built communities where country stores cushioned families against hard times. "The role of credit as a form of relief," observes Michael Katz, "never has received the attention it deserves from students of poverty."[46]

The Hollywood version of the general store was not far from reality. One ledger listed axes, curry combs, hoes, horse collars, suspenders, bed ticking, gunpowder, washboards, thimbles, lamps, castor oil, and iron tonic.[47] Another tallied sewing supplies, clothing, tableware, chamber pots, scythes, rifles, bridles, plows, paint, and nails.[48] While country stores carried many goods, city stores more often specialized. Sam Bass Warner's Philadelphia study lists shops owned by weavers, shoemakers, grocers, butchers, tobacco dealers, and cabinetmakers. "The small size of the shops in which most of these trades were practiced," he says, "made the mixed wards of homes, workplaces, foreign-born, and native Americans possible."[49]

The icon of the staples society was the Yankee tinkerer. "Every man can use an ax, a saw, and a hammer. Scarcely one cannot do any job of rough carpentry and mind a plow or a wagon," commented an English immigrant. A wine merchant had been a railway director, sold watches, and peddled shoes. A farmer once ran a calico factory. "Such men, whose flexibility equaled their energy," observed Stanley Lebergott, "flourished in a social order that permitted them to freely shift from task to task, whenever the opportunity of gain appeared."[50]

When Wright assumed his post, the Jeffersonian vision of a nation of small farmers was already fading.[51] Elbowing it aside was a consumer culture that valued what you bought, not what you made. Edward Bellamy's 1888 novel *Looking Backward* imagined something like Amazon.com, "a gigantic mill, into the hopper of which goods are being constantly poured by the train-load and ship-load, to issue at the other end in packages of pounds and ounces, yards and inches, pints and gallons, corresponding to . . . infinitely complex personal needs."[52] Given the uneven character of economic development, the consumer culture arrived in local communities at different times and in varying intensities.[53] Davy Crockett roamed "the wild frontier," while Francis Cabot Lowell's Massachusetts mills began mass-producing textiles. By 1912 the staples society had passed, causing Louis Brandeis to reflect: "Half a century ago, nearly every American boy could look forward to becoming independent. . . . Today most

American boys have reason to believe that throughout life they will work in some capacity as employees of others."[54]

Two paintings capture the transformation. Asher Durand's 1849 *Kindred Spirits* depicts poet William Cullen Bryant on a cliff overlooking a stream, with waterfalls and mountains in the background. The gritty browns of Thomas Eakins's *Between Rounds*, painted fifty years later, portray a pallid fighter slumped in his corner. Dim light falls on a policeman and a dark-suited timekeeper. Shadowy shapes capture the anonymity of urban life.

Documentation also comes from rural photographs. The earliest images depict families proudly standing in front of homes with a few farm animals and implements. Later, prize possessions creep into the frame. In one a Nebraska family poses in the front yard around a large organ with ornately carved decorations, which it is doubtful they hauled on their journey west. The organ pushes into the background the staples society's success symbol: a well-fed team of mules hitched to a wagon. By the turn of the century, photographs move indoors to show off carpets, curtains, and new furniture.[55]

The consumer culture gave us professional sports (which eclipsed town teams), the phonograph (which quieted parlor pianos), and motion pictures (which challenged local live theater). To entice Americans into singing the same tunes, sheet music adopted eye-catching graphics and scores with lyrics that people could easily play and sing. Even the congenitally tone-deaf could warble "After the Ball," whose chorus had that ingratiating quality of staying in your head.

Advertising was the consumer culture's lifeblood. Although newspaper ads arose in the previous century, not until 1880 did Wanamaker's Department Store debut the first full-page ad.[56] Not coincidentally, the first full-service advertising agency, N. W. Ayer & Son, opened inside Wanamaker's Philadelphia in 1869. Fifteen years later the *New York Times* compared "a pot of printer's ink" to "the greatest gold mine ever discovered."[57] Once J. C. Ayer turned Ayer's Cherry Pectoral into a household word through clever ads, others followed. "The evolution of the science of American advertising can be traced by a review of Ayer announcements," proclaimed *Advertising Success* in 1900.[58] In 1894 Ayer spent $900,000 a year on ads, less than the $1 million spent to advertise "Scott's Emulsion" but more than the $500,000 for "Pink Pills for Pale People."[59] Jackson Lears perceptively recognizes that advertising sought to manage desire within what he terms a "broader rhetoric of control."[60]

Storekeepers learned that selling consumer goods required divining purchases fed by advertisers. It did not help when local papers reported, "Several of our citizens have been to Keokuk the past week, and from all appearances found new suits cheap."[61] The demand for "inventory" meant knowing what was "in fashion." *Hardware* advised: "Taboo all obsolete and out-of-date goods, no matter what the allurements in price or blandishments of the traveling salesman."[62]

Arriving in the city, Theodore Dreiser's Carrie Meeber mused, "There was nothing there she could not have used—nothing which she did not long to own."[63] She was one of many for whom department stores became shrines where advertising was the hymn and emulating the rich the sermon. The equivalent of stained-glass windows presented images of the good life expounded by magazines that coined a new term: housewife. Trappings such as Marshall Fields's Tiffany glass dome preached "a new ideal of domestic womanhood" that Lori Merish terms "sentimental materialism" and Gillian Brown labels "domestic individualism."[64] "A woman who does not read advertisements would not be a woman," announced advertising consultant Nathaniel Fowler.[65]

Every sermon has its thou-shalt-nots. In 1878 a store manager testified: "There are a great many people who cannot withstand the temptation to pick off little articles when they see a good opportunity."[66] From this truism, medical experts of the time constructed what Elaine Abelson terms "a social and psychological reality: kleptomania."[67] This "reality" stemmed from the belief that women could not control themselves when tempted by the items in Macy's store windows.

Kleptomania was only one worry about the consumer culture's theme of instant gratification. Goods like the sewing machine and processed baked goods threatened to turn the importance of hard work inside out. An advertising card for Lily corn starch began: "Poor Mrs. Brown, the more she tries, the worse become her cakes and pies," and in turn, the worse becomes her marriage, until she buys the right ingredients.[68]

The consumer culture also muddled old relationships. Margaret Walsh and Barbara Handy-Marchello affirm that the staples society farm rarely was a "going concern" without women's efforts.[69] A newspaper remembered husband and wife "worked together behind the counter and on the farm, each understanding the labor of the other and joining as a true yoke fellow in drawing the mutual load."[70]

Towns Have Been Depopulated

The second transformation Carroll Wright documented involved the Great Migration of millions who moved from rural to urban America during the largest spontaneous mass migration in American history. "Over a considerable portion of our fair land, the Death Angel has spread his black wings; towns, cities, and parishes have been depopulated," Minnesotan Samuel Adams told an 1878 Grange annual meeting.[71] Thirty years later rural residents had become a minority.

Farmers faced Hamlin Garland's "lion's paw" and the hardships of the Age of Discontent. Caught in what Steven Hahn calls the "vortex of the cotton economy," southerners did not need anyone to tell them they were in a depression when their major crop lost three-fourths of its value in a little over a quarter of a century.[72] Under this pressure, the average farm in the South declined from 214 acres in 1870 to 138 acres in 1900.[73] In South Carolina, crop values were static from 1870 to 1890.[74]

When rural Americans needed help coping with panics and oscillating prices, they faced "Cash Only" signs, reflecting the perils of merchants squeezed by faraway imperatives. Meanwhile, national firms began opening outlets, with the Singer Sewing Machine Company eventually owning five hundred stores.[75] In 1879 Frank Woolworth opened a store in Utica, New York, using a formula of low prices and allowing customers to inspect the merchandise. By 1910, when he commissioned the world's tallest building, his chain stores were fixtures across the country.

In response, farmers kept moving in quest of the promised land. Historian James Malin found that only a quarter of Kansas farmers stayed in one place, a figure comparable to what Merle Curti found in Trempeleau County, Wisconsin.[76] Where farmers went was as important as how many times they moved. A study of Iowa migration discovered that between 1880 and 1890, the proportion of the population living in cities with 2,500 inhabitants or more rose from 15.2 to 21.2 percent. Between 1875 and 1895 the state's largest city, Des Moines, grew from 14,443 to 56,559, and Dubuque, the second-largest city, almost doubled in population during the same period, from 21,234 to 40,574.[77]

If rural populations were declining while homestead applications were increasing, then many homesteaders had failed. The National Park Service estimates the median homestead success rate was only 40 percent.[78] Sometimes a neighbor would venture out to look in on a family. The smokeless chimney told them what they would find. They kept details to themselves like soldiers do after a harrowing battle. The systemic implications of homestead failure reverberated throughout America.

The Predatory Community's Scheme of Life

The habit of asking why came at an early age on Veblen family farmsteads, whose most extraordinary crop was eight brothers and sisters, of whom seven completed high school and three graduated from college, including the first daughter of Norwegian immigrants to earn a college degree. Intense family conversations sharpened their minds.[79] Although Emily was probably the smartest, brother Ed remembered that Thorstein "knew everything."[80] His knowledge earned him a doctorate at Yale, where his dissertation advisor was William Graham Sumner.

In one photograph Veblen resembles a stereotypical bomb-thrower, with dark hair draping carelessly over one eye and a face punctuated by a thick mustache and unruly beard. The image fits the opinion of fellow professor Jacob Warshaw, who remembered Veblen had a reputation as a "dangerous iconoclast."[81] In contrast, Edwin Child's portrait depicts Veblen as a Victorian rake with a Van Dyke beard holding a cigarette. Child may have remembered Harvard president Lawrence Lowell's remark, that if he hired Veblen, "some professors might be a little nervous about their wives." Veblen reportedly replied, "They need not worry; I have seen their wives."[82] Albert Einstein offered an alternate opinion, proclaiming Veblen and Bertrand Russell the only writers to whom he owed "innumerable happy hours."[83] In *The Encyclopedia of Political Economy*, C. M. A. Clark calls Veblen "the last man in America who knew everything."[84]

In 1899 Veblen set off a theoretical bomb with *The Theory of the Leisure Class*, where he coined the term conspicuous consumption. Veblen's leisure class were those whose income was enough they didn't need to labor, but instead devoured "the best, in food, drink, narcotics, shelter, services, ornaments, apparel, weapons and accoutrements, amusements, amulets, and idols or divinities."[85] While conspicuous consumption has become watered down to a keep-up-with-the-Joneses mindset, Veblen's original concept displayed the bite of a generation that deeply resented in-your-face ostentation. The Vanderbilt wedding did not impress the *Kansas Agitator*: "This money which now goes to fatten British nobility would better have been left among the farmers of the United States from whom it has been drawn by excessive railroad charges."[86] A former Speaker of the House even advocated a tax on what he termed "the insignia of wealth" in the hope that "a deserved stigma will be fastened on one form of miserable social affectation."[87]

One word lost in the homogenization of *The Theory of the Leisure Class*, "predatory," explodes a hundred times in four hundred pages, especially when Veblen compares it to slavery: "The pervading norm in the predatory community's scheme of life is the relation of superior and inferior, noble and base, dominant and subservient persons and classes, master and slave."[88]

Five years later Veblen dropped another theoretical bomb when *The Theory of Business Enterprise* announced, "The present is the age of the machine process."[89] For confirmation, people could gawk at the three-story dynamos of the 1893 Chicago Exposition. Workmen had dinner pails jerked from their hands by the current as they walked by them. Watches "[ran] crazy; sometimes fast and again slow but always in an erratic manner."[90] Those watches symbolized Veblen's most radical idea: instead of people molding institutions, industrial institutions molded people.

Veblen recognized the machine process required standardization and control. A prime example was the railroad industry. Managing a national network meant standardizing time in a nation that had allowed local communities to decide when the clock tower would chime. On November 18, 1883, people awoke to find railroads had changed time, dictating the zones we have today. The *Indianapolis Centennial* joked, "The sun will be required to rise and set by railroad time."[91] Three years later, "detailed and prolonged discussion among the managers of many roads," led to a commonly used gauge for railroad track.[92]

Thorstein Veblen believed the standardization and control demanded by the machine process influenced broad areas of society. The eccentric, who hosed off his dishes, was one of the first to connect standardization with pressure to conform. Such pressure is, of course, human nature, but in the Age of Discontent it acquired new dimensions.

A century that began with handmade custom shoes and clothes ended with machine-made standard sizes. Veblen explained the change by saying, "Modern industry has little use for, and can make little use of, what does not conform to the standard."[93] Further commenting on the demise of local color, he described the new pressure with a mouthful of a sentence: "The idiosyncrasies of the individual consumers are required to conform to the uniform gradations imposed upon consumable goods by the comprehensive mechanical processes of industry."

Industrialization also demanded standardized workers. Managers sought to create the nineteenth-century equivalent of a fast-food restaurant, where they could hire anyone off the street—and pay them accordingly. Charles Schwab, who became U.S. Steel's president, boasted he could take a farmer and make him a skilled worker in six weeks. This meant using automation to reduce manufacturing to small, easily taught tasks. A state report described it thus: "He forms one of a company of specialists each being a link in an industrial chain and each like himself confined to a particular field of effort."[94] As craftsmanship became taskmanship a new phrase emerged for an insufferable boss: "slave driver."[95]

In 1873 offices resounded with keystroke volleys, when the Remington Arms

Company marketed the typewriter six years after Christopher Latham Sholes invented it. Veblen saw it coming: people were becoming numbers and many resented it. Harry Houdini's popularity expressed the ambivalence about progress. Even though they suspected him of cheating, his fans cheered his triumphs over the fiendish devices of technology in a staged version of John Henry's mythical battle against a steam drill.

Veblen recognized the problem was how to manage those who mistrusted industrialization. Corporations found it in the Civil War. "When we look at organization charts even today, we are looking at something descended from the organization charts developed by the military in the nineteenth century," according to Morgan Witzel.[96] Because operating a coast-to-coast system required a degree of control far different than running a single local store, railroads were among the first to apply the Civil War's command structure.

Researching post–Civil War careers of second- and third-tier officers, Mark Enrique Van Rhyn reports, "In later life they were often the middle managers, providing the professional competence that was the nation's foundation."[97] Railroads hired them because many had graduated from the only place that trained civil engineers, West Point. In *Looking Backward* Edward Bellamy imagined a military structure for his utopia. Mark Twain's Sir Boss applied Civil War organization to the Knights of the Round Table. The real-life Sir Boss was former Midvale Steel Company foreman Frederic W. Taylor, who used a stopwatch to improve productivity through what he termed "scientific management." John Phillip Sousa applied Taylor's stopwatch to music, using a metronome so his Marine Band performed like dynamos.

In this transitional period, what arose might be termed feudal capitalism. Medieval historian Marc Bloch's classic definition is instructive: feudalism combined "the right to the revenues from the land with the right to exercise authority."[98] A Pennsylvania report described the process: "Capital too often regards the laborer with little, if any, more consideration than a beast of burden, while the laborer, too often with justice, esteems the employer, if not an absolute oppressor, as utterly wanting in human feeling toward him."[99] When visiting Carnegie's Homestead steel mill, Charles Spahr commented, "All that I saw of the management of the company carried out this idea, feudalism."[100]

The era's supreme capitalist, J. P. Morgan, merged autocracy with bureaucracy by choosing good managers and employing them in numbers that Carroll Wright would applaud. Morgan, who claimed pirate Sir Henry Morgan as a relative, sailed his black yacht, the *Corsair*, along the Hudson River as if searching for prizes. Handed a position in his father's banking empire, young Pierpont bought five thousand obsolete rifles at $11.50 each, had them rebored, and resold them to the army for $22 apiece.

The rifle deal haunted Morgan, but he was no speculator. Instead, he was a proponent of what Alfred Chandler called "the visible hand" of the managerial revolution. Obsessed with control, Morgan told a congressional committee, "Unless you have got actual control, you can not control anything."[101] In a process termed "Morganization," he hired professional managers, replaced machinery, and organized for efficiency. He also recognized bad data were as worthless as stock certificates from a Rocky Mountain silver mine. He equipped his office with telegraph and phone lines, which he played like a master puppeteer. Fittingly, Morgan acquired Carnegie's steel company from a man who complained "the ablest presidents are hampered by boards of directors and shareholders, who can know but little of the business."[102]

The most famous deal brokered by the man Ron Chernow terms "a Victorian gentleman" involved not a business but the US government, which he rescued in 1895.[103] Morgan knew of plans to redeem $10 million worth of gold certificates from a Treasury with only $9 million in bullion. He warned President Cleveland that without immediate action, the country could be bankrupt. Morgan prevailed on European banking allies to cover the shortage. The agreement drawn up by his attorney and Cleveland's friend Francis Lynde Stetson, obligated the government to repay the bailout at a rate of 3.25 percent.[104] A poem reflected on the transaction:

"What a great old country it is!" I cried;
And a man with his chest in the air replied:
"It's Morgan's."[105]

No one valued control more than John D. Rockefeller. At sixteen, he obsessively recorded income and expenses in a little red book known as Ledger A. He fretted over buying gloves for $2.50, but he was no Scrooge, giving $5.58 to charity the same year.[106] All his life Rockefeller kept a mental Ledger A, astonishing employees with his knowledge of finances. This need for control ruled his Standard Oil Company, which muckrakers termed an octopus.[107] The metaphor fits his vision of a firm whose "tentacles" reached from wellhead to distribution site. Rockefeller put it bluntly: "What a blessing it was that the idea of cooperation . . . came in and prevailed."[108] Company attorney S. C. T. Dodd crafted the ingenious solution by twisting the legal instrument of a trust into an alliance of thirty-nine companies. "Under their agreement . . . a few men united to do things no incorporated company could do. It was a situation as puzzling as it was new," wrote Ida Tarbell.[109] Veblen saw it as a natural part of the machine process, where "the captain's strategy is commonly directed to gaining control of some large portion of the industrial system."[110]

Others adopted similar business models. Railroad baron Leland Stanford told Congress that "control is the essence of ownership."[111] As trusts multiplied, one muckraker claimed they controlled "nearly every staple article in the market," including "anthracite coal, turpentine, opium, jute, augers, axes, planes, files, hammers, door knobs, mortise locks, chisels, meat, building materials, linseed oil, furniture, tobacco, nails, petroleum, cottonseed oil, lard, tallow, eggs, codfish, herring, crackers, glucose, barbed wire, copper wire, pepper, molasses, salt, shovels, and pig iron."[112] Cashing in on the fascination, rotund comedian Billy Watson formed the Beef Trust, made up of chorus girls who each weighed at least two hundred pounds. Despite the act's popularity, few thought trusts were a joke.

In 1901 a US Census table showed trust consolidation concentration ratios of 100 percent in rubber, 46.8 percent in petroleum, 49.9 percent in tobacco, 57 percent in transportation products, and 45 percent in primary metal products.[113] Between 1895 and 1904 over eighteen hundred manufacturing firms disappeared into consolidations. According to Naomi Lamoreaux, "this meant that nearly half the consolidations absorbed over 40% of their industries and over a fourth were in excess of 70%."[114]

A dramatic example is barbed wire. Patented in 1874 by Illinois farmer Joseph Glidden, barbed wire accomplished what mountain men and Indigenous Americans thought impossible by fencing the prairie and its most precious commodity, water. Under the American Wire and Steel Company monopoly, barbed wire prices increased from an average of $1.85 per hundred pounds in 1898 to $3.17 in 1899. Some thought America had become a barbed wire nation. Judge T. A. Minshall's 1892 Ohio Supreme Court ruling against Standard Oil decried "a society in which a few men are the employers and the great body are merely employees or servants, is not the most desirable in a republic."[115]

John D. Rockefeller wasn't the only one enamored with control. In numerous cities arose what might be termed political trusts, which fittingly came to be called political machines. They transported immigrants to the polls, "interpreted" ballots, and distributed favors, including jobs, legal aid, health care, food, and cash.[116] Jane Addams described the ideal ward politician: "He must be a man kind to the poor—not only in a general way, but with particular and unfailing attention to their every want and misfortune."[117] A Lithuanian immigrant put it in more practical terms: "I voted as I was told, and then they got me back into the yards to work."[118]

Patronage, the oil that greased the machines, increased from in half of the thirty cities surveyed by M. Craig Brown and Charles N. Halaby in 1870 to operating in over 70 percent between 1890 and 1910.[119] The informal title for the heads of political machines—boss—reveals much about machine politics. Richard Croker proudly boasted that governing Tammany Hall was "precisely the same as that which governs the workings of a railway, or a bank, or a factory."[120] After the Panic of 1893, the official history of Tammany observed: "Tammany was busy striving to alleviate the distress of the unemployed poor in the City of New York, by raising large sums of money in all the Assembly districts, furnishing fuel and food to thousands thrown out of work."[121]

Changing city budgets provide an idea of those sums. In 1897 New York allocated $487,000 for public works and $1.1 million for street cleaning.[122] Given that street cleaning was a notorious patronage job, extrapolating New York's $1.1 million to other cities adds up to a considerable sum. Graft also fed the conspicuous consumption of big-city bosses. Croker owned a $5,000 bulldog, a Fifth Avenue mansion, and champion racehorses like his friend August Belmont.

City bosses and factory-building industrialists weren't the only ones to see the virtues of combination. "It has been a peculiarity of American politics since the Civil War that the two political parties have been controlled, in the main, either by men of a conservative type who are naturally opposed to taking up any new or radical issues, or by professional politicians," wrote Farmers' Alliance historian Solon Buck.[123] In six key votes on monetary policy during the years before the Panic of 1893, over 40 percent of the Democrats crossed the aisle.[124]

People called these Democrats Bourbons, referring to French royalty, not whiskey—although some liked the whiskey parallel. The American Tariff League explained, "Between the exit of Buchanan and the entrance of Cleveland . . . a large percentage of [Democratic Party] campaign funds came from railroad companies and among railroad men they found many of their best counselors."[125] Tycoons like August Belmont served as convention delegates, and Congress boasted its share of millionaires. The *Harvard Advocate* wryly noted, "[The millionaire] has seized control of this legislative citadel. . . . He holds chairmanships of seventeen of the sixty-seven committees, and is well represented on all the others." The article pointed out they "can prevent the passage of any law or treaty."

The king of the Bourbons was Grover Cleveland, the only president so far to serve two nonconsecutive terms. If Nast's portly tycoons symbolized the era, central casting could not have found a better political symbol than Cleveland. He served as a pallbearer for Belmont and worked for J. P. Morgan's father-in-law. Supporters included railroad baron James J. Hill, financier William Whitney, Chesapeake and Ohio Canal president Arthur Gorman, and Morgan.

Cleveland rose to fame following a script borrowed by Theodore Roosevelt and his cousin Franklin, becoming a New York reform governor. A man of impeccable but rigid character, he held a Sumner-like view of charity, as illustrated by vetoing an 1887 bill providing seed to drought-stricken farmers. Echoing Sumner, he lectured: "Federal aid, in such cases, encourages the expectations of paternal care on the part of the government and weakens the sturdiness of our national character."[126] Historian Allan Nevins admits, "[Cleveland] was not interested in the Buffalo Hospital or in raising money for the victims of the Chicago fire."[127] The 1896 Democratic *Campaign Text-Book* stated Cleveland "profoundly disbelieved in the ability of government, through paternal legislation or otherwise, to increase the happiness of the nations."[128] These views have fueled speculation that Cleveland was the Wicked Witch of the East in *The Wizard of Oz*, while William McKinley was the Wicked Witch of the West.[129]

That Most Orderly and Methodical of Things

Thorstein Veblen was an astute observer of American culture, but he missed two trends. The syncopated beat of ragtime music and the growth of moving pictures expressed new ideas about space and time that Albert Einstein could have explained to him. No one better understood the application of these ideas than movie director Edwin S. Porter. After a stint in the US Navy, Porter went to work for Thomas Edison, who was showing moving pictures using Vitascope, a projection system purchase by the Menlo Park wizard to compete with the cinema being pioneered by France's Lumiere brothers. Porter served as a projectionist for the first Vitascope screening in New York on April 23, 1896. British director Birt Acres's *Rough Sea at Dover* became a hit when he placed his camera on a stone pier where breaking waves threatened the lens. Some recoiled as if the waves were real. *Rough Sea at Dover* wasn't the only sensation. The *Los Angeles Herald* observed that no scene caught "the popular fancy" more than "where May Irwin is kissed by John H. Hush."[130]

Despite attempts to make people work according to a stopwatch, life does not march to a metronome. Perhaps that is why syncopated beats born in Africa reached a broad audience as ragtime pianists performed near the 1893 Columbian Exposition. Ragtime seized what a writer termed "that most orderly and methodical of things—time," then gave it a shaking.[131] Although what a critic termed "the tower of depravity" had roused moralists like Anthony Comstock, ragtime escaped most attempts to cage it.[132] Mining baron William Clark's ragtime ball at the 1900 Democratic Convention signaled that moralists had lost the battle.

Ragtime redefined time; movies redefined space. Porter combined the camera work of *Rough Sea at Dover* with the human interest of *The Kiss*, creating mini-dramas like *The Life of an American Fireman* (1903). People flocked to see *The Great Train Robbery* (1903), whose imaginative ending depicted a mustached outlaw pointing his pistol directly into the camera. The *Washington Times* noted, "Women put their fingers in their ears to shut out the noise of the firing."[133] Despite these early reactions, people soon could not get enough of what Noel Burch termed the "conquest of space."[134]

It was a time when people like Henry Adams wondered where their world had gone. His father was Civil War ambassador to the United Kingdom. His brother Charles Francis headed the Union Pacific Railroad. His best friend, John Hay, was Lincoln's private secretary and McKinley's secretary of state. Yet Adams struggled to understand industrialization, where "the old universe was thrown into the ash-heap and a new one created." A child born in 1900 would enter a world that would not be a "unity but a multiverse."[135] Charles Francis had another view. Observing the Erie Railroad War, he wrote, "They had . . . turned back the wheels of progress and reduced the America of the nineteenth century to the level of the France of the sixteenth."[136]

The new elbowed aside the old, as inventors like George Westinghouse and Goodyear founder Frank Seiberling hastened the extinction of skilled independent workers. Those able to adapt redefined occupations; others stepped off the elevator into free fall. A pamphlet captured the new normal: "To-day [farmers and mechanics] are, for the most part, in the employ of great corporations depending entirely upon wages paid. They have no shops, no places of business, and nearly two-thirds of them are . . . the tenants of the rich."[137]

Progress stretched institutions to the breaking point; poverty put them on trial. Rural Americans watched neighbors move away, while urban America saw an influx of people as telephone wires latticed the sky and sunsets bled crimson from pollution. As the machine process standardized lives, the challenge was how to deal with a country threatening to become a runaway train.

Dark Corners

Oh, it's hard to hear the hungry children crying
When I have two hands that want to do their share.
Oh, you rich men in the city, won't you have a little pity
And just listen to a miner's prayer?
—*From the folk song "The Miner's Prayer," recorded by Vernon Dalhart, 1928*

On New Year's Eve 1883 Mary Hennessey died "alone and friendless" near what is now the United Nations Building. Mary was an Irish immigrant who devoted her life to caring for what the *New York Times* termed her "perfectly helpless" older brother.[1] The *Times* says they survived on what she could earn scrubbing and washing, probably at any place that would hire her, be it a saloon or small shop whose owner was barely better off than she. An 1880 Census report lists her age as fifty-two and her occupation as "washer woman," and notes she could neither read nor write.[2]

A New York report written shortly after she died provides a window into her life:

The most deplorable aspect of woman's labor is to be found among those unfortunates who having no specific calling are reduced to seek casual labor by chance at scrubbing or washing. The more respectable of them have one or two regular customers from whom perhaps they are sure of a job for one or two days a week with their meals. This transient work is liable to be interrupted by any of the trifling events so common in every household, such as sickness or change of residence. Bad weather too may be the cause of a regular scrub woman losing her job, but these are lucky compared to the casual whose mean work is miserably paid. Visits have been made to these women's resorts of which it can only be said that the condition of debasement is beyond description, if not belief.[3]

Given her age and background, it is not hard to imagine Mary's appearance. Poor nutrition meant she very likely was thin, with prominently protruding bones and sunken cheeks and eyes. Her hair was prematurely gray from both her diet and the hardships she endured. She walked bent over from too many years of scouring floors. She spoke with the hesitation that comes from a lifetime of being told what to do. Her lonely death meant she was not gregarious and had no close relatives.

A "perfectly helpless" brother would not have evaded the immigration police, so his condition must have occurred after they arrived. One possibility is laboring in the Brooklyn Bridge caissons, the underwater chambers used to build the bridge's massive stone foundations. Several hundred men worked in a space half the size of a football field that was protected by what was essentially a large log cabin held down by slabs of Vermont stone. Built by experts in fabricating watertight hulls, it had a fifteen-foot thick roof and walls tapering from eight feet to eight inches.[4]

A reporter described the caisson's interior as "a continued expanse of water, slime, and stones, with winches, planking, iron shafts, and other paraphernalia of bridge engineering scattered about in confusion."[5] A few lithographs of the time show a funereal space that probably required considerable willpower to enter. Left unsaid is the odor of sweat, muck, and human waste—plus water pressure reaching 18 to 36 pounds per square inch.[6] Periodically the crew would drive a metal probe into the muck, listening for the distinctive ring of bedrock, but they heard nothing and found only sheep bones and pottery shards.

The deeper they dug, the greater the pressure. They didn't know it, but the caisson was a human pressure cooker. Some emerged with excruciating cramps—the "bends" divers get if they surface too fast. The term comes from the Grecian Bend, an 1860s fashion trend that employed a daunting array of undergarments to force "an S-like curvature of the upper figure, caused by thrusting out the chest, bending forward the head, contracting the stomach, and elevating the hips."[7] The Grecian Bend tortured women; the bends could bring paralysis or death.[8]

The perils of bridge construction claimed its two chief engineers. John Roebling died of gangrene after a ferry crushed his leg while surveying bridge locations. His son, Washington, took over, only to fall victim to the bends after spending seven hours suppressing a caisson fire. Although paralyzed, he observed construction from a telescope mounted in a nearby apartment window. After teaching herself engineering, Washington's wife, Emily, became the project's savior.

The year the workers finished the bridge, Mary Hennessey's brother fell in the street, where the cobblestones finished off his battered brain. This suggests "perfectly helpless" exaggerated her brother's condition since, unlike Washington Roebling, he could walk. Injecting himself into the story, the *Times* reporter wrote, "With her main purpose for living gone," Mary became ill and unable to work. With no safety net, she fell as hard as her brother. On New Year's Eve the neighbors called a doctor. He came too late.[9]

Authorities probably buried Mary and her brother in one of the mass graves on Hart Island, which still serves as the city's potter's field. The siblings faced another potential indignity: the late nineteenth century faced an epidemic of grave-robbing. A scandal occurred when future president Benjamin Harrison discovered his ostensibly buried father's body at the Medical College of Ohio.[10]

A decade and a half after the Hennesseys died, philosopher and psychologist William James wove a famous essay that helps put into context what happened to the Hennesseys. Written around an idyllic visit to Chautauqua, New York, "What Makes Life Significant" contains James's impressions of this "middle-class paradise" that gave him "a foretaste of what human society might be, were it all in the light, with no suffering and no dark corners."[11]

The essay revolves around a classic rhetorical trick. After celebrating Chautauqua's idyllic pleasures, James turns to the dark corner. "Let me take my chances again in the big outside worldly wilderness with all its sins and sufferings," he says. There he "noticed the great fields of heroism lying all around me. . . . Here it was before me in the daily lives of the laboring classes." He added, "Not in clanging fights and desperate marches only is heroism to be looked for, but on every railway bridge and fire-proof building that is going up to-day." Couple that courage with an ideal, wrote James, and the extraordinary happens. He could have been describing the Army of the Discontented, telling us we cannot understand them without knowing the dark corners where those like the Hennesseys lived.

You Are Safer in the Army

Despite his injuries, Mary Hennessey's brother was lucky to work for the Roeblings, who, despite the challenges, "created a safer workplace."[12] At one point they shut down the caissons because of the bends. Evidence tells us just how unusual were their attempts to ensure workplace safety.

Start with coal mining. It remains a hazardous occupation, but according to the 1903 Anthracite Strike Commission, the average fatality rate for laborers digging hard coal between 1870 and 1900 was 3.38 per thousand, or 338 per

100,000.[13] This compares to a 2010 rate of 248 per 100,000.[14] Reading Coal Company records show one of every seven workers was injured in the years 1891 to 1901.[15] A 1900 report on 1,107 injured anthracite miners provides details about those accidents: almost half suffered fractures and there were 201 burns, 220 bruises, 20 severed fingers, and 19 crushed hands. Widows of killed miners received $75 from the Lackawanna Coal Company; Hazleton Coal paid $50 and Lehigh $30. The families of boys under sixteen who were killed received half those amounts.[16] A reporter commented, "Truly, this is a land where life is held cheap."[17]

Accident rates in other countries show the degree to which these deaths were preventable. A review of coal mining accidents between 1887 and 1896 found Pennsylvania anthracite mine death rates were double those in French mines and 87 percent higher than in British and Belgian mines.[18] The Anthracite Strike Commission confirmed this fact, finding deaths for Pennsylvania miners almost double that of their European counterparts.[19]

Next to mines, railroads had the nation's highest accident rates.[20] In 1890 the Interstate Commerce Commission pointed out that American railroad passenger deaths were double those in England.[21] Such numbers caused an American consul to comment, "Europeans shudder over the statistics of employees slaughtered annually on the railroads of the United States and say that such a wholesale sacrifice of life and limb is barbarism."[22] The *Railroad Trainmen's Journal* was blunt: "Human life is cheap: property is dear."[23] One of the most tragic moments of sheer terror occurred the night of December 29, 1876, when an estimated 80 people died, and another 60 suffered injuries when a faulty bridge near Ashtabula, Ohio, collapsed during a snowstorm. Many perished in flames started by the stoves used to heat the train. A photo of the aftermath shows a thicket of metal twisted and contorted as if by some fiendish sculptor.

While notable for its severity, Ashtabula was one case in an epidemic of train wrecks. In catering to an obsession with pictures of mangled railroad cars, photographers sought ever-more spectacular images of smashed locomotives. *Railroad Gazette* editor H. O. Prout's data revealed railroad accidents annually averaged 483 killed and 1,790 injured from 1880 to 1890, with the highest total coming in the final year.[24] It is no wonder there was a growing outcry. The *Railroad Trainmen's Journal* raged about corporate refusals to spend on worker safety: "It was cheaper to kill a few thousand men annually and pay small damages in settlement than to spend millions of dollars on something for which there was no prospect of immediate return."[25]

The author of the article was right to be concerned. Testimony before the US

Senate revealed brakemen sustained a 23 percent casualty rate, which compares to 34 percent war casualties during the Civil War. Given that approximately one-third of those casualties were caused by disease, this yields a battlefield in-jury rate of 23 percent, meaning every brakeman faced a similar probability of violent death or injury as a Civil War soldier. A senator commented, "You are safer in the Army."[26] Maybe that is why a *Railroad Gazette* article referred to "The Car Coupler Holocaust."[27]

Roll calls of the dead from railroad commission reports, union publications, and trade journals show other ways death came unexpectedly to brakemen. Two days of fatal accidents in September 1882 put faces on the casualties:

September 6. A. P. Ammerman, Brakeman on the Pennsylvania, jumped from the cars while in motion and was instantly killed at New Brunswick, N.J.

September 6. Jas. McGovern, Brakeman on the Chicago, Milwaukee & St. Paul, was fatally crushed while coupling cars at Beloit, Wis.

Cole Montee, the oldest brakeman on the Delaware, Lackawanna & West-ern, was thrown into the firebox by a collision at Delaware, N.J., Sept. 7, and burned to a crisp.

John Link, Brakeman on the Indiana, Bloomington & Western, caught his foot in a rail while coupling cars at Sandusky, O., September 7, and was killed.[28]

These jobs came with built-in hazards. To set the brakes, workers turned a wheel on the roof of each car by hand. If it was tough to turn, they employed a "persuader" inserted between the spokes for leverage. Since each car's brakes worked independently, stopping a train meant running from car to car. A brake-man described doing this in a sleet storm: "In attempting to get at those brakes a great many of the brakemen lose their lives, slip off the cars, and, again, even if they do reach the brakes, it is more often the case than it is not that they find that the brakes are frozen up, and they can not twist them."[29] The matter-of-fact tone betrays the battlefield-like fatalism of railroad workers, since if the brakes are frozen, the train can't stop.

You can get some idea of what brakemen faced by laying boards on the ground in two parallel rows. A gap of three feet between sets of boards simulates the distance between cars. Spray the boards with water and try running from one to another without slipping off. Then imagine doing that on a moving train. High winds made it more likely brakemen would fall into the chasms between cars, fail to see oncoming tunnels, or be pitched into the darkness by a sudden turn, like a dog flicking off a flea. Falling from trains killed 493 railroad employees in 1889 (25 percent of all fatalities), 456 in 1890 (31 percent), and 467 in 1891 (30 percent), or an average of more than one a day every day for three years. The highest casualty rates came from coupling cars, injuring 6,757 in 1889 (34 percent of all injuries), 6,073 in 1890 (46 percent), and 7,155 in 1891 (46 percent).[30]

A reporter attending an 1884 coupler test observed most were "made of very cheap and poor material and are turned out in the most expeditious manner."[31] To ease into place the pin joining the cars, workers straddled the rails with one foot in and one foot out. A brakeman explained: "The brake-beam could catch him and throw him down. That is one of the dangers. The other is when he has to make a coupling between draw-bars. . . . The draw-bars are between the dead woods [bumpers]. Therefore, to get to the draw-bar, you have to place your hand either over the top of this dead-wood or underneath or right in there quick and set your link in and pull your hand out."[32]

Thanks to people like H. O. Prout, we have data about railroad accidents, but determining accident rates for factory work is difficult. Not until widespread inspection laws in the 1890s does extensive data about what workers faced appear. Stories like Hamlin Garland's 1894 tour through the Homestead steel mill illustrate the hazards. As he dodged 175-pound wrenches while coping with 110-degree heat, Garland did not need to make explicit comparisons with Satan's kingdom. Black-and-white illustrations fill where imaginations needed a nudge. When an immense crane upended a cauldron of molten metal, unleashing a hail of multicolored sparks with a searing blast of heat, Garland jumped out the nearest door into the rain. "They call this the death trap!" shouted his guide, smiling at Garland's reaction.[33]

A steelworker described life in the Homestead mill: "That big wrench swinging round in the air is the source of much danger, and many a time have I seen the man on top of the rolls jump over it and heard it crash against the housing behind him."[34] He goes on to report over a thousand accidents and at least a dozen deaths for that year. In what the *Pittsburgh Dispatch* termed "one of those unexpected catastrophes that frequently happen in iron works," four men died and another five were seriously burned when a ladle carrying molten metal exploded.[35] One desperately tried to outrun the glowing river, but he tripped and fell, entombing him in steel. When coworkers finally freed his body, the steel retained an imprint of his features. Pennsylvania inspector Robert Watchorn acknowledged, "The manufacturing of iron is one of the most prolific sources of casualties, and its every phase, from the unloading of the ore, to the dumping of the slag, should be subjected to the most painstaking care and precaution."[36]

Not until 1913 did the US Bureau of Labor Statistics report on steel mill accidents. It showed slightly fewer than two workers per thousand died on the job, while nearly three per thousand suffered permanent injury.[37] Garland's description implies that conditions were probably far worse nineteen years earlier. That it took almost two decades to issue a report testifies to the effectiveness of Andrew Carnegie and others in suppressing accident data. There also were no Ashtabulas to generate outrage at the mills. Like snipers, they picked off workers one by one.

Garland's descriptions of working in a steel mill have much in common with reports in which injuries could be bizarre and unpredictable. One recorded elevator accidents: "Emma Sochek, 15 years old, working in J. K. Farley's candy factory, at 161 South Jefferson Street, was carrying boxes of candy to the freight elevator. The elevator was moved while she was gathering boxes, and the child, approaching with boxes piled so high that she could not see over them, stepped into the open shaft and fell four stories. She died the next day."[38] Due to corporate resistance, it wasn't until 1921 that the American Society of Mechanical Engineers published the first elevator safety code.

This Was Not in India

Shocking accident rates offer some perspective on life in the new industrial workplaces. The death of Mary Hennessey offers a window into life at home. Almost two hundred articles on starvation published between 1870 and 1900 in the *Times* confirm that Hennessey's death was not an aberration. A sampling is sobering: five thousand "represented as starving to death in Virginia," (1882), "Starvation in Iowa" (1873), "Starving Texans" (1887), "In Danger of Starvation" (Dakota Territory, 1889), "People Who Are Starving" (Kansas, 1889), "Starving in Oklahoma" (1890), "Families Subsist Mainly on Dandelions" (1894), and "Starving in Hocking Valley" (1895).[39]

If today starvation occurs invisibly, during the Age of Discontent it could not be avoided. In a memorable article, Stephen Crane wrote "The country died," as he watched a blizzard slash across the windows of a hotel room where the *inside* temperature hovered near zero. He had witnessed drought scorch the plains until the "vast tract was now a fit place for the nomads of Sahara." His descriptions recall stark photographs from the 1930s Dust Bowl. "Visitors to the country have looked from [railroad] car windows to see the famine-stricken bodies of the farmers lying in the fields," he wrote, "and have trod lightly in the streets of Omaha to keep from crushing the bodies of babes."[40]

Reports like Crane's became cries for help by those desperately needing relief. The *Buffalo Enquirer* reported 5,000 Poles in "imminent danger of starvation."[41] The *Chicago Post* reported an appeal by the state Conference of Charities: "Want and starvation, are at the doors of thousands of the homes of our people."[42] The *San Francisco Call* described men in San Luis Obispo County felling oak trees to eat the leaves.[43] Lamenting how "many people literally starved to death as in the past few months," an Indiana minister asked, "Have you noticed in the newspapers how many men and women . . . have been found dead, the post mortem examination stating the cause of death was hunger?"[44]

Locating valid statistics to put these accounts in context is complicated by the difficulty of making any diagnosis from a distance of more than a century. Since their immune systems are compromised, malnourished people may die from a variety of causes. In its recent, widely cited "Guidelines for Investigating Suspected Starvation Deaths," Hunger Watch advises, "The diagnosis of a 'malnutrition death' cannot just be an individual diagnosis, we have to document the circumstances prevailing in the family and community along with the individual to reach such a conclusion."[45] Archaic medical terminology adds to the problem. In their study of deaths in two Massachusetts cities, Douglas Anderton and Susan Leonard explain, "The radical transitions in disease environments, medical understanding, and cause-of-death recording over the latter half of the nineteenth century present a significant challenge to cause-specific mortality analyses during an important period in U.S. mortality experience, precisely because contexts of mortality changed so radically over this period of demographic history."[46]

One reason historians have not discussed starvation lies in an inability to decipher unfamiliar medical terminology. A late nineteenth-century medical dictionary uses the terms atrophy, inanition, and debility as synonyms for nutrition deaths, although the meaning of those terms today is different. Other sources confirm this.[47] The main statistics for deaths from these causes come from the 1880, 1890, and 1900 Censuses, most authored by Dr. John Billings, the founder of the National Medical Library, who has been called the "father of medical and vital statistics in the United States."[48] There also are a limited number of other reports. We need to be careful in equating deaths from atrophy, inanition, and debility with actual starvation deaths, because poor nutrition was a factor in all three in late nineteenth-century deaths. As you ponder them, remember they represent a fraction of those who faced what today is termed "food insecurity."

This ever-present fear hung like a shroud over the Age of Discontent. It was why factory organizer Leonora Barry reported women made the oft-repeated request, "God's sake, do not give me away, as I would lose my work and it is all I have to depend on."[49] Barry isn't the only one who reported this fear. It appears again and again in state reports, like one where a mill worker admitted, "I have got two little boys at home one of them three years and a half and the other one year and a half old and how am I to find something for them to eat."[50]

The numbers are sobering. First, contrary to what the Industrial Narrative claims, death rates from atrophy, inanition, and debility increased dramatically during the 1880s. In 1880 the death rate per 100,000 from all three was 38.04, versus 51.50 in 1890 and 37.71 in 1900.[51] (Chapter 12 explores a theory for the 1890s decline.) These compute to an average of 42.41 over three decades. In 2020 the worst death rate from malnutrition was 43.92 in the Democratic Republic of the Congo.[52] The numbers show that in each of the three Census years, an average of 26,665 people died of atrophy, inanition, and debility, equating to almost 800,000 Mary Hennesseys from 1870 to 1900.

Existing state and local data are more problematic, partly because we lack precise annual population figures to compute accurate estimates of deaths per 100,000. Standing out among those states is Illinois, which recorded deaths from debility, atrophy, and inanition during the 1880s. From 1881 to 1886 its numbers range from highs of 25.75 per 100,000 in 1881 and 27.85 in 1883 to 19.0 in 1884. Because Illinois tabulated discrete data for the Chicago–Cook County area, we can see that in that state, nutrition-related deaths were largely an urban affliction, accounting for an average of 90 percent of all cases, with an 1883 Cook County death rate from debility, atrophy and inanition of 82.28 per 100,000.[53]

Data from New York and Philadelphia seem to confirm the high urban death tolls from atrophy, debility, and inanition. Philadelphia recorded a rate of 53.25 per 100,000 in 1884. The 1890 annual report of the Health Department of the City of New York recorded a staggering death rate of 84.47 per 100,000 from "Debility, Marasmus, Inanition." Half of these deaths were children under one, but only 1 percent of them were listed as "colored."[54] That year, malnutrition-related deaths in that city even exceeded those of the dreaded scourge of diphtheria.

Hard Duty

The *Times* edition with Mary Hennessey's story also contained the year-end report of the New York City Bureau of Vital Statistics. Among its tables is the number of deaths of children under age two, which public health experts view as a possible indication of malnutrition.[55] In 1882 they accounted for more than one-third of the *total deaths* for all ages.[56] In comparison, in 2014 children under five accounted for only 1 percent of total US deaths.[57]

In *Fatal Years: Infant Mortality in Late Nineteenth-Century America*, Samuel Preston and Michael Haines analyze data about the most vulnerable Americans. Their discoveries illustrate the tilt of the playing field. "The infant mortality rate was 167 per 1,000 live births for families in which the father's annual income was less than $450, and only 59 per 1,000 for families with father's annual earnings in excess of $1250."[58] Child mortality was 43 percent higher for those with working mothers and 26 percent higher in families with unemployed fathers. In cities with more than 25,000 residents, the child mortality index was 46 percent greater for laborers' families than those of professionals. Numbers for adults were equally grim. The age-adjusted death rate for African Americans of both sexes was 27.8 per 1,000, versus 17.6 for whites.[59]

Other evidence reinforces this picture. Nobel laureate Robert Fogel provides a measure of the nation's "physical and mental health" by examining height. Using data from 1710 to 1970, he found the average height during the late nineteenth century was the lowest ever recorded in this country. He notes: "The conflict between vigorous economic growth and very limited improvements or reversals in the nutritional status and health of a majority of the population suggests that the modernization of the late nineteenth century was a mixed blessing for those who went through it."[60] Economic historians Dora Costa and Richard Steckel reinforce Fogel's findings. Using the United Nations Human Development Index (HDI), they determined that 1890 was the low point for the United States' HDI. Countering the Industrial Narrative, Costa and Steckel conclude, "Conventional estimates of the growth rates of per capita GNP overestimate well-being by 30–75 percent during the increases in mortality from the 1870s to the 1890s."[61]

This evidence suggests that for Americans like Mary Hennessey, malnutrition was not uncommon, making starvation more likely. A second key statistic in the 1882 New York City report—deaths from contagious diseases—bolsters the impression that the lives of many Mary Hennesseys were suspended by the frayed threads of unhealthy sanitary and social conditions. In New York City, 18,763—or slightly less than half the deaths—came from scarlet fever, diphtheria, and measles. What the report does not tell us is that 54.5 percent of the deaths that year took place in tenements, suggesting a link between those who perished and their living conditions.[62] A New York report commented, "The only comparison that I could make, or that I could compare the New York tenement houses to, would be the black hole of Calcutta."[63]

Other evidence provides a perspective on Hennessey's death. "Ten Thousand Starving in Nebraska" read one story, referring to a blot on our history.[64] In 1874 the most massive horde of flying insects ever recorded—an estimated 12.5 trillion Rocky Mountain locusts—flew from Minnesota to the Rio Grande, eating "everything but the mortgage."[65] The courageous efforts of Gen. E. O. C. Ord prevented a catastrophe. William Tecumseh Sherman wrote words that should be on Ord's tombstone: "He has always been called on when hard duty was expected, and never flinched."[66] An 1839 West Point graduate who served in the campaign against the Seminoles, Ord was "one of the chief causes of Lee's surrender," according to Sherman.

In Nebraska, Ord faced a crisis like no other he had encountered. A November 6, 1874, report from Maj. Nathan Dudley described the situation:

> Great suffering exists in all five of these extreme frontier counties to a fearful extent. . . . If the winter should be as severe as that of Seventy and Seventy-one, and as deep snows fall, beyond a doubt hundreds will starve unless a supply of provisions sufficient to last them through the winter is thrown into the valley and they are provisioned for an emergency of this character, for it would be out of the question for any aid society, or the Government even, to reach anything like a majority of them in deep snows.[67]

Press reports support Dudley's assessment. An Ohio front-page story describes a family sitting down to a supper of a watermelon and two pieces of bread and a Civil War widow baking her last loaf. The reporter summarized the situation: "Nearly the whole population in many places is barefooted, and half the people are nearly naked . . . and wherever I traveled not over ten or twenty days' supplies of rations were to be found."[68] Three days later, in his annual report to Congress, General Sherman said nothing about Nebraska.

On November 11, Ord sought permission from his superiors to distribute extra army rations to the starving farmers, writing, "Unless relieved soon, many poor frontier people will certainly starve to death, while the Army store-houses within 100 miles are filled with provisions."[69] Two weeks after a newspaper reported homesteaders had only ten to twenty days of food remaining, Ord's superior, Gen. Philip Sheridan, replied, "It is a little unwise to compromise the Government by the action of its military officers in regard to any general distribution of supplies to the people residing in the section devastated."

People then moved to convince Congress to pass an emergency bill to provide the ration units, but it did not act until December 17. Meanwhile, private and state action attempted to fill the gap. When the Kansas Legislature refused to help, the governor commented, "I tremble to anticipate the judgment of mankind upon a commonwealth which, having encouraged appeals to the charity of the people of the whole country, steadfastly refuses to relieve a single want at the expense of its own treasury."[70] Nebraska's legislature was more charitable, passing a small relief bill. In the end, "hundreds succumbed," according to Jeffrey Lockwood.[71]

That Sheridan turned away starving farmers isn't surprising, since waging war against families was a favorite tactic. In the 1864 Shenandoah Valley Campaign Sheridan aggressively followed Ulysses S. Grant's order to destroy the land "so that crows flying over it for the balance of this season will have to carry their provender with them."[72] Sheridan-style warfare was also used with Indigenous Americans. Hinmatóowyalahtq'it (Chief Joseph), Tatanka Iyotake (Sitting Bull), and Goyaałé (Geronimo) surrendered because their bands were short of food.

Sheridan wasn't the only one to use starvation as a weapon. Corporations borrowed what had worked in the Shenandoah Valley to suppress worker strikes. One example occurred during the building of the transcontinental railroad. When Chinese workers struck for higher wages, Charles Crocker severed supply lines to starve them into submission.[73] In 1875 Franklin Gowen closed company stores to striking Pennsylvania miners. Such stories infuriated Henry Demarest Lloyd: "To get lower and lower wages, and more and more work out of your men, it is indispensable that they should not be allowed to unite, that they should be starved, that, when starved, they should be cut off from outside relief."[74]

They Must Work or They Must Starve

There is another critical dimension of Mary Hennessey's death: her sex. In an address dedicating the Women's Building at the 1893 Columbian Exposition, Mrs. Potter Palmer described women's dilemma in saying, "They must work, or they must starve."[75] An 1888 California report detailed the equation facing women like Hennessey: "At this rate, a self-supporting woman has all she can do to make both ends meet. It is a never-ending struggle with her to procure the necessaries of life without the means to lay anything by for a rainy day."[76]

This script appeared with many variations: "To save his children from starvation … Henry Borck, an old engineer, had committed suicide in order that his children might receive the $8,000 insurance on his life."[77] The *Kansas Agitator* lived up to its name with this kind of writing: "During the last four months, twenty men and women committed suicide rather than live by beggary or crime. This was not in India, Africa, or any other heathen land, but in New York, in the midst of the blessings of free American institutions, Christian civilization, 'triumphant Democracy,' etc., etc."[78]

Over 300,000 late nineteenth-century references to suicide in the Library of Congress newspaper database suggest the magnitude of the problem. Stories about suicide and starvation occurred so frequently, people complained. "Read the daily press with its budget of crime, starvation, misery, suicide, and sensational headlines announcing to the greedy public the carrion on which the minds of the nineteenth-century civilization feeds," said an 1895 reader's letter.

Emile Durkheim's 1897 classic *Le Suicide* identified a significant cause of suicide as the disconnect between people and society.[79] An obscure 1893 paper by D. R. Dewey on suicide in Massachusetts, Rhode Island, Vermont, and Connecticut makes a similar point. After presenting data showing suicide rates were America's highest ever, Dewey offers a disturbing conclusion: "It seems probable from the data presented that suicides have increased from thirty to forty per cent since 1860."[80] These numbers reveal a troubling systemic problem: death, disease, malnutrition, and social conditions formed a web that entrapped innumerable people like Mary Hennessey.

Nothing better symbolizes this web than child labor. In 1894 Florence Kelley and Alzina Stevens found children composed 10 percent of those employed in 2,452 establishments.[81] Reports agree that for some families, children needed to work. Consider this 1875 sketch of a laborer with a wife and five children: "[They] live in a tenement of 5 rooms, in a poor locality, with filthy surroundings. There is no drain, and the foul water from the sink runs from the sides of the building into the yard and remains there … causing a strong smell throughout the house." The father earned only $375 a year; his two sons earned $308. Even with the boys' incomes, the little meat the family purchased was "scarcely fit for food." Author Carroll Wright drew two conclusions: many families relied on children for "from one-quarter to one-third" of their income, and if the children did not work, families starved. He comments: "[The system] uses men and women when they are strong and leaves them to shift for themselves when they are sick, infirm, or without employment. This it does by paying no more for labor than the bare cost of existence of the body."[82] People knew the consequences of paying no more than "the bare cost of existence of the body" because, as one analyst stated, those consequences were a "common observation."[83]

A Hurtful Extent

The systemic relationship between child labor and starvation brings us to a critical element in Mary Hennessey's death: wages. People starve because they can't afford the food needed to keep them alive. Mary Hennessey was one of many scraping by on an assortment of odd jobs. Henry George would have understood, because before he became a best-selling author, his main paycheck came from his work as a part-time meter reader for the city of San Francisco.

Table 3.1 shows some of the major wage studies that are usually cited in histories of the late nineteenth century.

To understand the table, we must return to where so many of the numbers first began a life that would make them one of the country's most influential and controversial datasets. Virtually all the wage estimates descend from a committee headed by Rhode Island senator Nelson Aldrich, a prominent tariff supporter and an influential figure, especially after his daughter married John D. Rockefeller's son in 1901. Lincoln Steffens's 1905 article, "Rhode Island for Sale," skewered Aldrich as "the political representative of . . . that System which is coming more and more to take the place of the passing paper government of the United States."[84]

In 1893 Aldrich decided to determine "the relative purchasing power of [the] earnings of the great mass of people in the country."[85] His raw data came from Carroll Wright and Joseph Weeks, who had authored a wage study for the 1880 Census.[86] University of Pennsylvania professor Roland Falkner conducted the analysis. The Aldrich Report found that by 1891, wages had increased from an 1860 base index of 100 to 168.2. It boasted: "No other investigation has been made with so wide a scope, such variety of detail, and covering so extensive a period."[87] The boast was not unfounded. In 1984 H. M. Douty affirmed that "despite its many limitations, the Bureau's work for the Aldrich Committee is the major source of information on the structure and course of wages in this country from 1860 to 1890."[88] As late as 2002, the book *History of the American Economy* by Gary M. Walton and Hugh Rockoff was still relying on Aldrich data.[89]

The Aldrich conclusion about rising wages from 1860 to 1890 has become the dominant view. In his 1960 book Clarence Long concludes that between 1860 and 1890 wages had risen "roughly 50 percent."[90] Among the most prominent proponents of acknowledging a wage increase using Aldrich data is the distinguished economist Robert Margo. In *The Labor Force in the Late Nineteenth Century*, Margo concludes, "There is abundant evidence that real wages were higher at the end of the century than the beginning."[91] He adds, "The average worker was better off in 1900 than a century earlier." Margo's use of Aldrich data is not to be taken lightly. His innovative ideas on antebellum wage data using sources like reports from frontier forts mean his conclusions come from someone who has navigated the minefield of nineteenth-century wage numbers.

Questions about the Aldrich results began even before the report's ink was dry. Given little time to review the text, the committee minority issued a statement that should give us pause: "No accurate or reliable approximate conclusion as to the movement in prices can be reached."[92] An 1894 paper presented by US Department of Agriculture economist Frederick Waite to the American Statistical Association issued a scathing critique of the Aldrich Report: "It is moreover, accurate neither for our chief occupation nor for any occupation."[93] After endorsing the findings the association appointed a committee, including Joseph Nimmo, ex-chief of the Bureau of Statistics, and Armin Shuman, special agent in charge of results for the Eleventh Census, to convey Waite's conclusions to Congress, which rebuffed them.

Another vocal critic was statistician Charles Spahr, who charged that the report was "out of harmony with scientific research abroad and common observation at home."[94] He accused Falkner of errors that would earn first-year statistics students a failing grade, like averaging the wages of clerks and workers. Contrary to the conclusion that wages had increased, Spahr revealed the average wage *fell* from $2.04 per day in 1873 to $1.69 per day in 1891. He charged that the statisticians "were to a hurtful extent in sympathy with the political aim of the investigation."[95] Since then, others added criticisms. In 1908 economist Wesley Mitchell pointed out, "Professor Falkner treated each wage series as having the same importance, whether it represented the relative wages of one man or a hundred men."[96] Although he used Aldrich numbers, Stanley Lebergott termed the report a "haphazard collection of wage data that need analysis, allowance for bias, and careful weighting before they can be utilized."[97] In 2002 Mary Furner affirmed Spahr's criticisms. She noted the data were exclusively Northern, disproportionally drawn from higher-paid skilled trades, and often atypical.[98]

Even if we accept the numbers, the Aldrich Report has problems, the chief one being the use of 1860 as a base year. This can immediately be seen in the table. The 1870 index was 167.1, meaning the gain in wages during the war was 67 percent. The gain from 1870 to 1890 was a minuscule .50 percent using the

Table 3.1 Selected Late Nineteenth-Century Wage Estimates

Year	Aldrich	Aldrich Weighted	Long 1960 Manufacturing	Long 1960 Building Trade	Lebergott 1964 Census Real Annual	Abbot 1905 Unskilled per Day	Officer 2009 Hourly	Misc. State Reports
1870	162.2	167.1	151	187	375	1.89	0.113	N/A
1871	163.6	166.4	153	174	386	1.87	0.116	N/A
1872	166.0	167.1	154	172	416	1.88	0.117	N/A
1873	167.1	166.1	156	169	407	1.81	0.120	N/A
1874	161.5	162.5	151	164	403	1.70	0.118	N/A
1875	158.4	158.0	145	159	403	1.58	0.116	N/A
1876	152.5	151.4	141	144	393	1.48	0.114	N/A
1877	144.9	143.8	134	135	388	1.35	0.110	N/A
1878	142.5	140.9	128	128	397	1.34	0.108	N/A
1879	139.9	139.4	125	128	391	1.29	0.107	$314.10 (OH-Mine)
1880	141.5	143.0	130	126	395	1.31	0.111	$385 (CT); $417 (IN); $335.50 (PA-Carp.)
1881	146.5	150.7	131	139	415	1.35	0.110	N/A
1882	149.9	152.9	134	150	431	1.42	0.113	$396.66 (IN)
1883	152.7	159.2	138	150	459	1.44	0.114	$417.18 (OH-Mine); $430 (IL); $358 (MA)
1884	152.7	155.1	140	151	478	1.43	0.116	$333.18 (IN); $204.29 (IA-Farm)
1885	150.7	155.9	136	151	492	1.45	0.116	$369.60 (MI)
1886	150.9	155.8	136	156	499	1.41	0.119	$405.81 (IN)
1887	153.7	156.6	141	153	509	1.45	0.126	$372.50 (IA Mine)
1888	155.4	157.9	142	154	505	1.45	0.128	$441.33 (CT); $478.33 (NJ)

1889	156.7	162.9	146	156	510	1.47	0.133	$363.42 (OH); $435.16 (CT); $413.32 (IA-Mine); $409.46 (MI)
1890	158.9	168.2	148	159	519	1.48	0.133	$492.91 (OH); $384 (IL-Mine); $467.02 (MI)
Percent increase	−2.0	0.5	−1.0	−15	38	−21.0	17.0	

Note: The first two columns show indexed wages as computed by an 1893 Senate committee led by Nelson Aldrich. The Aldrich index uses 1860 as the base year. Statisticians chose that year because it "represents a period in our industrial development midway between the older methods of production that prevailed before the war and those which have come into use since that period. It is also a period of comparatively normal prices." Thus 100 represents the average wage in 1860. The Aldrich weighted average column reflects the relative importance of various industries. The next two columns are reworkings of the Aldrich data by Clarence Long in 1960, one for manufacturing and the other for building trades. Using data from Aldrich and Joseph Weeks, Stanley Lebergott produced the next column in his 1964 book, *Manpower & Economic Growth*, using the values corresponding to actual wages, factored for inflation. The word "Census" refers to the bicentennial edition of the US Census Bureau's *Statistical Abstracts*, which used Lebergott's numbers. Edith Abbott produced a table of wages for unskilled labor based on Aldrich's data. Lawrence Officer's wage computations appeared in 2009; those state reports are cited for the first time here. They are labeled by state and occupation if they do not include all occupations. For example, OH-Mine indicates only mining wages in Ohio.

Sources: US Senate Committee on Finance, *Wholesale Prices, Wages and Transportation* (Washington, DC: GPO, 1893), 13; Clarence Long, *Wages and Earnings in the United States: 1860–1890* (Princeton, NJ: Princeton University Press, 1960); H. M. Douty, *Nineteenth Century Wage Trends, BLS Staff Paper No. 2* (Washington, DC: GPO, 1970), 13; Stanley Lebergott, *Manpower in Economic Growth* (New York: McGraw-Hill, 1964), 528; Edith Abbott, "The Wages of Unskilled Labor in the United States: 1850–1900," *Journal of Political Economy* 13, no. 3 (June 1905): 363; Lawrence Officer, *Two Centuries of Compensation for Production Workers in Manufacturing* (New York: Palgrave Macmillan, 2009), 166–67.

State statistics (some values computed by dividing total wage dollars by total number of workers; where possible, child workers were excluded): 1879: OHBLS, *Third Annual Report*, 85; 1880: CTBLS, *Second Annual Report*, 43; INBLS, *Second Annual Report*, 29; PBIS, *Volume 17*, D31; 1882: INBLS, *Fourth Annual Report* (title page mislabeled as Third), xii; 1883: OHBLS, *Seventh Annual Report*, 15; ILBLS, *Third Biennial Report*, 128; 1884: INBLS, *Sixth Annual Report*, ix; IABLS, *First Biennial Report*, 189; 1885: MIBLS, *Third Annual Report*, 148; 1886: INBLS, *First Biennial Report*, 311; 1887: IABLS, *Second Biennial Report*, 179; 1888: CTBLS, *Fourth Annual Report*, 37; NJBLS, *Eleventh Annual Report*, 245; 1889: OHBLS, *Fourteenth Annual Report*, 42; CTBLS, *Sixth Annual Report*, 39; IABLS, *Third Biennial Report*, 133; MIBLS, *Seventh Annual*, xvi (report gives two amounts, one computed by the bureau and the other based on blanks returned); 1890: OHBLS, *Fourteenth Annual Report*, 111; ILBLS, *Biennial Report, Volume 6, Part 1890*, xlvii; MIBLS, *Eighth Annual Report*, xv.

weighted data. Columns with Long's data are similar, showing increases of 51 percent and 87 percent during the war, but little gain thereafter. The only two sources showing increases are Lebergott's and Officer's, each of whom reworked Aldrich data. In the end the information shows no definitive answer to whether wages did indeed rise. That distinguished researchers can hold widely divergent views should alert us to the fact that we face something more than mere methodology differences.

The Cruel Logic of Figures

To enter the world of late nineteenth-century wages is to fall into a deep rabbit hole. Data resemble the results of a mad tea party, especially when caught up in boosterism. An 1892 Colorado report crowed, "Colorado leads the world as a wagepaying [sic] community, with few exceptions."[99] Iowa might challenge this by saying, "A careful study of the following pages and a comparison of them with similar data gathered in other states will disclose the gratifying fact that the wage workers of Iowa are fully as prosperous as elsewhere."[100] In various reports, numbers appear as shape-shifting as a Cheshire cat.

At the time most wage numbers came from questionnaires submitted to employers (the term was "blanks"). Little comes from employees or trained enumerators. Gathering data was an impossible task. If the constant griping of state statisticians is any indication, inadequate funding, some purposeful, made administering such surveys difficult. It was not unusual for one or two people to collect statistics for an entire state. The blanks lived up to their name because that is often all the statisticians received. An 1877 Ohio report noted employers returned only 405 out of 1021 surveys.[101] Employers were not about to allow the government to pry into their affairs. "There were hundreds of cases during the past year which manufacturers and others not only treated with silent [sic] the schedules sent them, but actually abused and insulted the agents of the State while they were engaged in the work of statistical information."[102] The haphazard nature of the responses colors the data. The coal mining wages in Joseph Weeks's highly regarded study omit mines in Pennsylvania, the nation's leading coal producer. The task of acquiring data became so onerous that in 1886 a national meeting of state bureaus of labor statistics recommended employers be guilty of a misdemeanor for not answering questionnaires.

Even when employers submitted replies, enumerators had to sort out their truthfulness. An 1889 report on railroad labor observed, "[When] employers are called upon to return the number of persons employed . . . the vagueness of the information resulting from such an inquiry becomes apparent."[103] An Ohio report author bluntly related the problem: "I made inquiry regarding the wages of employees and in those establishments where labor was well paid, the proprietors promptly responded to all inquiries, while employers of poorly paid labor gave me much trouble in securing this information and in some cases prevented it."[104] California's surveys demonstrate the absurdity of employers' answers. In answering a question about working conditions, an inordinate number replied, "Good." One owner went overboard when he crowed, "Splendid!"[105] Nothing indicates that anyone verified the responses. In Ohio the workplaces' reports of being in operation for fifty-two weeks seems fanciful. The state admitted, "The system of collecting information by mail is an absolute failure."[106]

Some employers' replies would be comical if the implications were not so serious. Testifying before a committee investigating the Homestead lockout, Carnegie Steel's Henry Frick offered, "Some men [were] counted as boys."[107] He meant that totals for jobs usually performed by youngsters also included older workers. Frick's answer is not so funny when you ask whether wage figures for various occupations included children, who usually received a fraction of adult wages.

Curiously, no wage study refers to an 1885 report filed by Joel McCamant, chief of Pennsylvania's Bureau of Industrial Statistics. Born in 1823, this former cabinetmaker, lawyer, banker, and delegate to the state's 1872 constitutional convention, questioned a crucial dimension of late nineteenth-century wage data. Because reported *wages* often failed to account for the days worked, they did not match actual *earnings*. He termed the discrepancy between wages and earnings "theoretical" versus "actual." The information tables in figure 3.1 are illustrative.[108]

Those quick with math will note "actual wages" are as low as 53 percent of "theoretical wages." Unless we know the circumstances, the numbers are suspect. As McCamant put it, the reporting system was "calculated to deceive the wage-workers themselves," even as it deceives us today.[109]

McCamant points to the elephant in the room: *actual* days worked. He comments, "A wageworker must sustain himself and his dependents for a period of fifty-two weeks on wages received for labor performed during forty-two weeks."[110] In the shape-shifting reality of late nineteenth-century wages, the salaries appearing in a table might refer to an annual full-time wage rate, but few worked full-time in an era when jobs were subject to employers' whims.

Unlike workers today, people of Mary Hennessey's generation had no idea whether they would work each day or for how long. Histories fail to mention the toll this precarious employment situation took on workers and their families. Having lived that life, Terence Powderly knew exactly why he selected Sarah

TABLE 1.—*Exhibit of highest average wages paid in the anthracite coal mines of Pennsylvania, based on full working time.*

Theoretical wages.	Day.	Week.	Year.
Employés.			
Miners on contract, .	$2 70	$16 20	$842 40
Miners on wages, . .	2 00	12 00	624 00
Laborers, inside, . .	1 78	10 68	555 36
Laborers, outside, .	1 40	8 40	436 80
Boys, . .	65	3 90	202 80
Drivers and runners,	1 43	8 58	446 16
Firemen, ...	1 58	9 48	492 96
Engineers, ...	1 88	11 28	586 56
Blacksmiths, ...	1 91	11 46	595 92
Slate-pickers, boss, .	1 55	9 30	483 60
Slate-pickers, boys, .	50	3 00	156 00

TABLE 2.—*Exhibit of actual wages paid in the anthracite coal mines of Pennsylvania, based on actual time employed.*

Actual wages.	Day.	Week.	Year.
Employés.			
Miners on contract,	$2 70	$8 84	$459 68
Miners on wages, .	2 00	7 00	364 00
Laborers, inside, .	1 78	6 14	319 28
Laborers, outside, .	1 40	4 91	255 82
Boys, . . .	65	2 07	107 64
Drivers and runners,	1 43	5 32	276 64
Firemen, ...	1 58	5 73	297 96
Engineers, ...	1 88	8 84	459 68
Blacksmiths, . . .	1 91	7 16	372 82
Slate-pickers, boss,	1 55	5 60	291 20
Slate-pickers, boys,	50	1 70	88 40

Figure 3.1 Pennsylvania Mining Wages

Jane Geary to dramatize the situation. In congressional testimony, one of Mc-Camant's colleagues declared, "As a rule, no miner knows what wages he is getting until pay-day comes, as wages in the anthracite regions are not regulated in any certain, simple, honest, straightforward manner, as elsewhere, but upon some varying principle said to depend on the price of coal at the mines or at tide-water [where the coal was shipped], either of which prices is made by the railroad to suit itself."[111]

McCamant wasn't the only one to recognize the issue of employment time. Investigating employers' self-reported claims of days worked, Ohio commissioner A. D. Fassett found, "These 600 employees therefore instead of working 7,200 months as the returns indicate, worked but 5,160 months or an average of but eight and one-half months each."[112] Few states had the resources to follow up as thoroughly as Fassett had done. A worker explained: "As to our earnings we are left entirely at the mercy of the boss. When times are dull our wages are cut down and if we grumble we are told that there are plenty waiting to take our place. In busy times, we are worse off yet, for then we are told that we are making too much time and money."[113]

Reports show significant numbers of workers were idle for substantial amounts of time. From 1878 to 1889 Pennsylvania anthracite miners worked only 58 percent of the year, which is why Sarah Jane Geary's family was near starvation. Of the 224,570 employee records examined in an 1889 Bureau of Labor Statistics study of railroad labor, 58.1 percent showed employees worked less than 150 days.[114] An extensive examination of days worked came from an 1887 Massachusetts Bureau of Labor Statistics report. It discovered part-time jobs drifted along the rivers that powered mill towns such as Fall River and Lawrence, where a third of those employed were idle for a third of the year.[115] Investigating miners' wages, Illinois found that "working time is only 51.2 per cent of the actual number of days during which the miner must subsist, that is, 30 days in each month, or 365 days in the year; in brief that the earnings of one day must, on an average, maintain the miner and his family two days."[116]

We can see just how much workers endured when we seek additional clues in places Charles Spahr suggested we look. "We have so much contributory evidence from the reports of the State and National Labor Bureaus that serious errors are easily avoided," he observed.[117] What is remarkable is that there has been little examination of these reports since Spahr made his suggestion. As figure 3.1 shows, nearly all state reports record earnings at odds with the other data. Additional state data show 75 percent of workers received less than the annual wage reported by Lebergott/Census.[118] To cite just one example, in 1891, Ohio reported a state average earning for "wage earners" of $470.05 versus the Lebergott census average wage of $519.00. Six of twenty-one occupations earned less than $400 a year.[119] Several reports contain an alarming number of near-starvation wages. How did West Virginia piece workers live on salaries of $162 per year?[120] It would take another book and more years to analyze these reports in more detail, but these examples suggest the information to be gained and raise the question of why no one has conducted those studies.

Other studies show a similar pattern. In 1890, of the 219,132 people employed in wool manufacturing, the average earnings was $349.84 or 75 percent of the Lebergott annual wage. The 1880 average earnings for 172,544 cotton textile workers was 62 percent of the Lebergott wage, and in 1890 it was 63.5 percent.[121] The Bureau of Labor Statistics found that the 1889 average annual wage for 90,104 railroad laborers was $124, with almost 65 percent of railroad workers earning under $300, versus the Lebergott wage of over $500. The Brotherhood of Locomotive Firemen commented, "These men receive less than an average of $243 a year for their work, a fraction over 77 cents a day for 313 days of work. Such is the cruel logic of figures."[122]

The 1903 Anthracite Strike Commission further documented the shape-shifting nature of wages. It found the size of ore cars ranged from Delaware and Hudson Railway's 66 cubic feet to Reading Railroad's 127 cubic feet, making Reading's wages half the Delaware and Hudson's.[123] So-called dockage bosses deducted the cost of any waste from workers' wages, creating "a systematic means of robbery."[124] It was "heads, I win; tails, you lose," lamented United Mine Workers president John Mitchell.[125]

Historian Perry Blatz has used the word "capricious" to describe a system where miners blasting ore were paid by the yard and those who extracted it paid by the carload.[126] State reports acknowledge miners' earnings depended on the whims of supervisors and owners. A Pennsylvania report noted: "Not only is the coal more easily cut in some mines than in others but even in the same mine the quality and position of the coal may be unlike in different places."[127]

Miners weren't the only ones whose earnings were subject to whim. What you found in your pay envelope could depend on a cozy relationship with those making work assignments. In George Pullman's sleeping car factory, Myrtle Webb sewed hems on carpets for 10¢ per carpet, a task that took her a little over an hour. Annie Lynn sewed a hundred pillowcases in seven hours, for which she received 35¢.[128] The women toiled under the dictatorship of supervisor Mary Schub. If she liked you, you might land a position like Myrtle Webb's. If she didn't, you sewed pillowcases with Annie Lynn.

Accounting ruses used by employers also show the difficulty of determining earnings. Some employers did not pay wages on time. Others paid in vouchers to be used at the company store. Weeks estimated that 12 percent of all workplaces included company store vouchers (scrip) as wages.[129] In New Jersey the use of paper "shinnies" (shin-plasters) to pay workers in lieu of cash became so rampant in one community they even made their way into the church collection plate.[130]

Companies used other tactics to maximize profits and lower workers' earnings. Miners were required to buy supplies at the company store, where a keg of blasting powder that cost the company $1.10 sold for $2.75. In 1877 an Ohio miner reported these costs: "We have to buy all the tools we use as follows: Shovel 1.00, Sledge 1.75, Drilling machine 12.00, Needle 1.00, Scraper .40, Steeling machine drill .75, Pick 1.12, Wedge .60, Rake 1.00, Tamping box 1.25, Steeling pick .50. All these tools we have to keep in repair which is not done by the company."[131] The most bizarre example of forcing workers to pay for supplies comes from Leonora Barry. She relates how a textile factory required each employee to purchase a sewing machine and the thread to run it from a supervisor who was an agent for the sewing machine and thread companies. If a worker became ill, fell too far behind in paying off a debt, or was fired, she forfeited everything and the factory sold the machine to the next victim.[132]

Employers' creativity in devising schemes to avoid paying workers knew no sense of morality or empathy. One tactic was to fine workers for petty infractions. A New York woman revealed some of them: "Five minutes late 25c and half hour's time, for washing your hands 25c, eating a piece of bread at your loom, also for imperfect work, sitting on a stool, taking a drink of water, and many trifling things too numerous to mention. The amounts of same being optional with foreman or superintendent and frequently offset the whole pay of employee."[133]

The final indignity for workers were the agreements governing employment. Western Union required workers to sign what became known as the Iron Clad Oath: "I will abandon any and all membership connection or affiliation with any organization or society whether secret or open in anywise attempts to regulate the conditions of my services or the payment therefor."[134] An Iowa mining firm stipulated, "Said first party hereby reserves the right and privilege, however, of closing the mines at any time or of reducing the number of miners employed by the discharge of all or such of them, including said second party, as the superintendent or person in charge of the mine for the time may think proper."[135]

Such language and the fickle nature of wages help us to better understand the discontent. Earnings figures reveal how many lived on a razor's edge. The Bureau of Labor Statistics record shows 16 percent of 25,440 families reported an average deficit of $65.58; author Carroll Wright comments, "They most likely had less of furniture, clothing, fuel, and food on hand than at the close of the preceding year."[136] A balance sheet used by Josiah Strong showed expenses for an Illinois family were $754.42, though earnings for the father were typically only $555.68, forcing everyone else in the family to work, leading him to comment, "This is modern and republican feudalism."[137]

There is a final important piece of the wage puzzle. Assume that reported wage increases are accurate. The Industrial Narrative gives employers credit for those gains, but that assumption ignores records having few examples of companies voluntarily raising salaries. In reality, the dynamic of those years revolves around employers cutting wages and resisting, sometimes violently, attempts to raise wages. Strikes like the 1894 one against Pullman and the 1897 Lattimer Massacre revolved around employers lowering wages or refusing to grant increases.

In the days before the National Labor Relations Board existed, employers routinely refused to submit wage disputes to arbitration. States like New Jersey attempted to provide arbitration, but without corporate cooperation they were ineffective. One report summed up the problem: "The first obstacle in the way of the successful introduction of arbitration is the hostile attitude or contemptuous indifference of many employers to the wants and needs of their employees."[138]

Rather than credit employers for raising wages or improving working conditions, several state reports viewed unions as responsible. New York observed, "As a rule non-union men work longer hours and receive less pay than union men." New Jersey was blunt in saying, "Every day experience proves also that it is equally foolish to assert, as has been the custom with many economic writers, that to industrial progress is alone due the credit for the rise of wages and the shorter work day which would have come without trades union intervention."[139]

These findings bring Mary Hennessey's story full circle. Poor nutrition, unsafe workplaces, and capricious wages tightened a noose around those who, through no fault of their own, found themselves in extremely difficult circumstances. We also know most wage data comes from workers in major industries, not people like Hennessey, who toiled wherever they could for whatever meager earnings they could command. These people left no records.

Mary Hennessey's death must be multiplied by the thousands who lie with her on Hart Island and in other such places. Everyone should stand on the island's wind-swept flats and look from this bleak place at skyscrapers across the water and ponder the disconnect. For those who do not know New York, it is shocking to know that Mary Hennessey spent her life near the still-fashionable Murray Hill. J. P. Morgan moved to the neighborhood in 1886, but his attorney, Lewis Ledyard, had a mansion at 137 East 35th Street. He may have seen her on the street, but the distance between them was more than feet and inches. It was wide enough to spawn a popular revolution.

CHAPTER FOUR

A Threat of Endlessness

Oh, the hinges are of leather and the windows have no glass,
The board roof lets the howling blizzards in.
—*From the song "Little Old Sod Shanty," ca. 1880*

She was known as Big Mary, "the most forcible and picturesque character of the mining region ... a queen who rules with a high hand."[1] This boardinghouse owner and activist in Pennsylvania's anthracite fields relished how the feared mine police avoided eye contact because her eyes said "I will not be broken." A sketch shows a dark-haired woman with a light-colored kerchief, proclaiming the melting pot's limits. Although *The Century* called her an "Amazon" whose words were "well punctuated by profanity," it also depicted tender moments. "As [her husband] passes her from time to time," observed the writer, "he says some pleasant word or pats her cheek."[2]

You cannot understand the Age of Discontent without looking into the eyes of people like Mary Septak. They reflect communities, workplaces, and the forces governing their actions. A Slav immigrant, Septak lived where the tilt of the playing field was especially pronounced, something recognized by area newspapers: "No part of the world ever presented so favorable an opportunity as the coal regions for the rich to oppress the poor working man. In many instances, the opportunity was not neglected."[3] Only the strong survived the harsh realities of company towns, where coal dust transformed trees into skeletons and converted streams into inky, foul-smelling tributaries similar to the River Styx. Curses accompanied the ritual scrubbing of blackness from clothes and walls, but prayers could not prevent it from coating a miner's lungs.

Stephen Crane described his journey into a mining community. "A journey that held a threat of endlessness" opened with the ominous image of mine breakers dominating the land like enormous preying monsters, "eating the sunshine, the grass, the green leaves."[4] These distinctive-looking buildings resembling massive ski jumps housed one of industrialization's most notorious workplaces, where boys worked shifts of eight to ten hours, sorting black nuggets in air so thick with coal dust that by the end of the day they acquired a distinctive "breaker boy mask" that made them resemble impish raccoons. They needed nimble fingers to pick out the slag (waste) and sort the rock into grades with names like "grate, egg, chestnut, pea," and "buckwheat" referring to the size of the nuggets. Sorting coal with bare fingers was especially difficult in the winter when the breakers had no heat.[5] Paid by the bucket, these soot-faced youngsters swore foul-tongued oaths as they harassed Crane for cigarettes.

If you have never entered a coal mine, the experience can trigger an atavistic fear of darkness. In those depths, nothing is so disconcerting as the feeling that you are in the grip of powerful natural forces. Reflecting on the miners' lot, an Illinois report affirmed their common reality: "So long as mines are worked[,] so long will they continue to furnish their annual crop of accidents."[6] One miner asked Crane's guide to measure the coal they excavated. "Yeh wanta hurry up," said the miner. "I don't wanta get killed."[7] A fellow worker joked, "You'll be carried out o' there feet first before long." Recalling a blast that echoed through the tunnels, Crane wrote, "It is war; these miners are grimly in the van," then listed their odds: "If a man may escape the gas, the floods, the 'squeezes' of falling rock, the cars shooting through the tunnels, the precarious elevators, the hundred perils, there usually comes to him an attack of 'miners' asthma' that slowly racks and shakes him into the grave."

Today we know "miners' asthma" as a disease defined by an occupation: coal workers' pneumoconiosis (CWP), commonly known as black lung disease. It is a terrible fate; lungs fill with dust and fluid, choking off air in an equivalent of drowning with no one to throw a rescue line. "The wonder is not that men die of clogged lungs, but that they manage to exist so long in an atmosphere which contains fifty per cent of solid matter," wrote a doctor using the fluid coughed up by a miner as his ink.[8] It wasn't until 1969 that a black lung bill became law.[9]

The worst moments for miners and their families came when the wail of the breaker whistle signaled disaster. Then came anxious hours, even days, as comrades attempted to rescue those trapped in darkness. Trapped miners scratched messages into the rock walls. After one mine disaster, rescuers found their last words on the paper normally used for dynamite cartridges: "My Darling Mother and Sister: I am going to Heaven. I want you all to meet me in Heaven. . . . Bury me in black clothes. . . . Ellen I want you to live right and come to Heaven. There are a few of us alive yet. Oh, God, for one more breath."[10] No one better summed up these varied dimensions of life for a coal miner than Andrew Roy, a former miner who served as an Ohio mine inspector:

> The inhalation of an atmosphere contaminated by the noxious and poisonous gases of the mine blanches the human face and impoverishes the human blood like vegetable products similarly deprived of solar light and a life sustaining atmosphere. Moreover, the danger to life and limb to which there is no parallel on earth and which the miner often can not see to guard against, added to the awful hardness and gloom of the coal mine, affect the minds and emotions of our subterranean workmen.[11]

Conditions like these made miners some of industrialization's most militant workers. It was as if the volatility of their working conditions produced a corresponding explosiveness in their strikes and other confrontations with those who controlled their lives. One miner reflected, "We often talk about the condition of the slaves in the South before they had their freedom. I am compelled to say our condition is far worse to-day, when there are hundreds of our fellow-men who cannot get what they ought to eat, and are willing to work at the same time."[12]

Those looking for work found themselves in a position like Ishmael's in *Moby Dick*, inquiring about a ship's reputation. A legal catch-22 colored the decision: if you agreed to work in unsafe conditions you presumably knew the risks. An 1883 US Supreme Court decision stated a worker "cannot, in reason, complain if he suffers from a risk which he has voluntarily assumed."[13]

In addition to the risks below ground, the lives of the miners and their families above ground could be surreal. When *The Century's* portrait appeared, only one of Mary Septak's ten children was alive. Statistics show slightly over half of immigrant infants survived, versus 70 percent for those of native-born parents. Another study found an infant mortality rate of 56.1 percent among immigrant Slav children, with 13.9 percent dying between the ages of two and five.[14] Mary Septak's lost children reflect what civil rights leader Fannie Lou Hamer said: there wasn't much else they could take from her.

The physical geography of a company town like Mary Septak's Lattimer mirrored the miners' cultural geography. Each ethnic group had its neighborhood, or "patch," like "Scotch Road," "Welsh Hill," and "Little Italy." It says much about Mary Septak that her boardinghouse was located in a non-Slavic neighborhood. "The attempt of aspiring members of the Sclav [*sic*] races to move into the better sections of town is speedily resented," wrote Peter Roberts.[15] In these towns, mine police collected gossip from informers, monitored mail, and specialized in intimidation. In some towns, miners had to procure a pass to walk beyond town boundaries.

Depending on what people could afford or scrounge, houses ranged from small frame structures to rude shacks. In a phrase that describes the tilt of the playing field, Roberts recorded the stinginess "of coal companies when they erect homes for the people, and the taste of the men themselves when they put up their own dwellings!"[16] An 1898 report painted a bleak picture of a company town: "The privy wells are full up to the top of the ground, and the contents of the wells flow out into surface ditches, new houses excepted."[17] Families might share a house, pool their food, and share childcare. Single miners bunked in boardinghouses that crammed as many as fourteen into a room, where they might share a bed with a worker from a different shift.

Mary Septak's boardinghouse contained seven beds and eight trunks in space, which she, her husband, and her fourteen-year-old daughter shared with twelve to fifteen men. She tried to make it pleasant by hanging religious pictures over each bed. Septak's efforts show that long before today's two-income households, women often determined whether a family had economic stability. While Septak's fees are not known, even a dollar a month per boarder would have added substantially to the family income.

In addition to boarders, women in mining towns took in washing, mended clothes, and scrounged for coal. Because the mine police guarded waste piles, women slipped out at night to pick nuggets. One family living near a mineshaft dug their fuel supply. Francis Nichols encountered a frightened mother who cringed in fear that she had been caught gathering coal. The mother explained, "All the people round here is striking, so, of course, the company wants them to starve, and if they can't get coal to cook their food with, they will starve faster."[18]

If you entered a late nineteenth-century mining company town you passed "naked gray [tree] limbs uplifted as if crying for help," on a road that either cast up clouds of black dust or encased your shoes in asphalt-like mud.[19] "Everything is black," wrote a reporter who saw the region in 1876.[20] Like Lady Macbeth washing blood from her hands, women scrubbed away blackness that, in Merle Travis's words, will "seep in your soul."[21] In 1904 Roberts wrote, "The waters of nearly 400 collieries impregnated with sulfur, flowing into the creeks and rivers have killed the fish."[22] Company towns had no sewage systems and what we might put in the trash was thrown into a stream of fetid water that ran behind the shacks. Keeping children from this mess tasked women when they weren't hauling water or scrounging for fuel.

Those whom Francis Nichols termed "children of the coal shadow" had "no child life. The little tots are sullen, the older children fight; they rarely play."[23] As soon as they were able, children were pressed into work to help feed the family. Girls aided their mothers by taking in washing or gathering fuel. When old enough they watched the younger children while their mothers were busy. Boys were destined for the mines as soon as they could put in a shift at the breaker. As many as one-third of the breaker boys employed in Pennsylvania were under age twelve.[24] The 1902 Anthracite Strike commission found their wages ranged from $69 to $129 per year, or 51¢ to 72¢ a day. An unfortunate soul received 1¢ a month.[25]

Those wages reveal the miners' precarious situation, for if a family felt compelled to send children to the breaker for 72¢ a day, they surely needed it to survive. If the boys were strong enough they might work underground as miners' assistants. "The girls . . . are on the one hand subject to serious temptations because of their lack of means, and on the other tend to enter inconsiderably into marriage to relieve the economic tension of the home," noted Roberts.[26]

When miners were sick or injured, the company doctor treated them, with the monthly cost of 50¢ to 75¢ deducted from wages. Mining families shopped at the company store, where they paid 18¢ for canned goods and 21¢ per pound of coffee, items that at the time cost most other Americans 13¢ and 18¢, respectively.[27] United Mine Workers president John Mitchell charged that companies earned money "not only by mining coal but by mining miners."[28] If families bought elsewhere, they risked dismissal.[29] An 1885 report calculated the impact: "The prices paid by the wage-worker . . . on store orders, are equivalent to a reduction of from ten to fifteen per cent of his wages."[30] In towns where outsiders ran the company stores, mine owners received 10 percent of the profits.[31]

Evidence points to a community that valued those who refused to be broken. Jay Hambidge recalled a miner whose bandage covered a recently amputated hand that had been shattered by an explosion. When asked if he feared another accident, the defiant reply was flavored with an ample dose of gumption: "No," he growled. "Me no afraid."[32]

The miners' housing mirrored their stubborn individualism:

Each little house with the boxes, cubby-holes, and fences about it, has been built by the man who lives in it. . . . One portion will have eaves, while its companion will scorn the luxury. . . . Some of the small openings used for windows are high, while others are low. One door will open in, and another out. . . . Some of the roofs have shingles, others weather-boards, while others are formed of great pieces of rusty sheet-iron.[33]

Mary Jones reflected on the lives of the miners, who had nicknamed her Mother Jones: "No more loyal, courageous men could be found than those southern miners, scornfully referred to by 'citizens' alliances' as 'foreigners.'"[34]

Originally and Distinctively American

Mary Septak's counterpart on the midwestern prairies was Anna Sadilek Pavelka, an immigrant homesteader who was the model for the title character of Willa Cather's *My Ántonia* and Cather's close friend. What greeted the Sadilek family when they arrived at the homestead her father had purchased sight unseen while still in Europe was a cave dug into the side of a hill with a crude board bed and an old stove. Cather described where Anna and her sister slept: "In the rear wall was another little cave; a round hole, not much bigger than an oil barrel, scooped out in the black earth."[35]

What brought settlers like the Sadileks was the Homestead Act of 1862 and its siren song of free land, the first time a nation promised citizens an opportunity to achieve financial independence. The act guaranteed that anyone with gumption could own 160 acres if they registered their claim and lived on it for five years. Having "proved up," the land was theirs.

The quintessential image of western settlement remains carved into our collective memory, in technicolor. With white canvas tops billowing above boat-like hulls, a wagon train of prairie schooners sails through the waving tall grasses into the realm of myth. The godfathers of those movie scenes were nineteenth-century painters like Albert Bierstadt, whose expansive canvasses depicted endless landscapes using a palette of glowing colors.[36] In reality most homesteaders trickled into the West family by family, usually in a farm wagon or on horseback. As with Sarah Murray, the men often went first, marking their claims then erecting crude structures the coyotes bypassed in that nose-down, ears-back trot they adopt when eager to move on.

Today the descendants of many homesteaders still keep their original deeds hanging in a place of honor. In a country where property-holding was still a requirement for voting and holding office, the act provided a chance for people to improve their lot.[37] In an 1884 Land Commission report, Thomas Donaldson unabashedly waved the flag when he pointed out the act was "originally and distinctively American."[38] He failed to mention that the act contained a large flaw: it never fulfilled the hopes of the newly freed enslaved for "40 acres and a mule." Gen. William Tecumseh Sherman's famous Field Order #15 had provided several hundred thousand acres and army mules for the emancipated people living in the lands he had liberated, but after Abraham Lincoln's death Andrew Johnson rescinded the order. The 1866 Southern Homestead Act held the promise of providing land for the enslaved who had been freed, but in the rollback of Reconstruction it was repealed.

Not surprisingly, African Americans had mixed experiences with the Homestead Act and its successors.[39] In his history of the "buffalo soldiers"—African Americans who served on the frontier—Clinton Cox tells of former troops who were barred from settling lands they helped protect.[40] A buffalo soldier who witnessed the attempted lynching of a fellow cavalryman near Fort Robinson, Nebraska, typifies the gumption of frontier African Americans. The soldier reported that he and his fellow troops issued an ultimatum that if such activities persisted "while we have shot and shell . . . we will repeat the horrors of Santa Domingo," a reference to the 1801 revolt of Toussaint Louverture.[41]

Texas forbade African Americans from homesteading, but Kansas was more hospitable, as the former state of John Brown became home to African American settlements in Morton City, Hodgman, and Nicodemus. In Oklahoma, African Americans owned more than a million acres.[42] Census data provide the big picture: in the north-central region of the plains, the African American population doubled from 1870 to 1880 but then declined by more than 25 percent for the remainder of the century. By 1900 there were only 30,000 African Americans in the West, out of a total population of 4.3 million, or a mere .60 percent.[43]

Susan Sessions Rugh perceptively identifies the post–Civil War generation's view of the land as an important indicator of a change in values: younger people saw the land as a commodity to buy and sell like a bushel of corn.[44] The most audacious scheme came from the banking firm of Chubb Brothers and Barrows, which purchased land to move the national capital to Nebraska. Speculation helped to double land values between 1870 and 1900. Jeffrey Williamson's data indicate that the largest increase took place from 1875 to 1885, which is not surprising, given that the early 1880s were the best for farmers in the late nineteenth century.[45] Despite traps laid by speculators, people kept coming, because America was not a place but an idea. In Nebraska, homesteaders settled 45 percent of the land.[46]

In contrast to the tales spun by one of America's earliest mass advertising campaigns, settlers like the Sadileks faced Four Horsemen that rode on steeds named Drought, Disease, Devastation, and Despair. An Iowa minister writing east pulled no punches: "Get clothes firm, durable, something that will go through the hazel brush without tearing. Don't be afraid of a good, hard hand, or a tanned face."[47] After laying out these realities, the minister ended, "I never expect to see one of you west of the Mississippi as long as I live."

Willa Cather, Hamlin Garland, Ole Rølvaag, and others filled in those harsh realities with exacting details that lent weight to homesteaders' testimony. Although plots and characters were fictitious, the novelists captured the experiences of farmers struggling to keep their heads above swirling waters. In *O Pioneers!*, Cather describes a land seeming "to overwhelm the little beginnings of human society that struggled in its somber wastes."[48] Garland's *Main-Travelled Roads* relates the grim story of a family forced to move by grasshopper plagues and unscrupulous speculators. The father was "hid in a mist, and there was no path out."[49]

The situation became even more grim for new settlers like the Sadileks if they arrived too late in the year to plant a crop and needed enough money to buy food for the winter. One estimate of the capital required to successfully homestead shows the odds:

Registering, etc. $50.00
Horses and implements. $500.00
Furniture, small stock, etc. $200.00
House (sod), staples, and seed. $150.00
Breaking forty acres sod. $100.00
Total $1000.00[50]

Most farmers required funds for *two years'* subsistence—the time it took to establish a regular crop. A lucky few reaped good harvests with their first crops.

Because lumber was scarce or nonexistent, Nebraska settlers lived in dugouts like Anna's family or the sod houses that symbolized prairie homesteading. The dugouts were caves carved into a hill with a door and window in the front. While primitive, they were cool in summer and easy to heat in the winter, along with being able to weather storms that battered those living aboveground. A Nebraska doctor recalled locating a family during the winter by finding a smoke-stack poking out of the snow.[51]

Records of sod houses date from the Civil War. There was an art to building with "Nebraska marble." Some struggled, but others were masters, like the family that constructed a two-story showplace. Start with the walls: How thick should they be? How did you lay the sod and frame windows and doors? One settler explained to his mother: "I cut my sod 2½ ft. long and plowed about 4½ in. deep and 10 in. wide and it is pretty heavy work to handle them."[52] They used sod pieces like bricks, alternating them so there were no seams from top to bottom. A 16-by-20-foot sod house contained up to three thousand of these "bricks."[53] To start, they placed two rows on the ground, alternating the breaks. Next came a layer laid perpendicularly. Some put the root side up so the layers grew into each other to strengthen the walls.

For the roof, settlers scrounged materials. One farmer stole them from a neighbor.[54] The fortunate laid tree limbs and covered them with sod, brush, and anything else handy. Ideally a sod house had a sloped roof to shed rain and snow and provide a loft for sleeping or storage. One famous sod house photograph shows a cow standing on a grass roof; another shows the four Chrisman sisters in front of a sod dwelling smaller than a millionaire's closet.[55] Even if they could support the weight of a cow, poorly constructed roofs leaked. One homesteader joked that they had running water—it dripped through the roof.[56] Settlers had to be careful not to make the roof too thick, since weighted by snow it could turn a shelter into a tomb.

Sod houses had another problem: they attracted rodents and other critters, including centipedes and tarantula-like wolf spiders that could leave painful but not fatal bites.[57] To thwart rattlesnakes, settlers hung cloth from the ceiling so snakes did not fall on beds or tables. Prairie homesteaders lacked our squeamishness about mice. In the city, those attitudes began to change after William Hooker patented the mousetrap in 1894. Thanks to Mr. Hooker, the absence of mice became the sign of a well-managed home. The stereotypical shriek of a woman seeing a mouse was as much a comment on the state of the home as it was the residents' fear. Women who maintained a proper home were supposed to be startled by mice.

Keeping out mice was nothing compared to dealing with grasshopper plagues of biblical dimensions, plagues that may have been triggered by the settling of the prairie. Settlers watching the churning darkness gnawing away the sun probably felt the throat-gripping realization that the sky was alive. They grabbed children and shut doors and windows, stuffing gaps with rags. "I could hear the hoppers dropping from the grain to the ground, they make a noise like a heavy shower of rain," said a farmer.[58] Grange founder Oliver Kelley described one invasion: "If a window or door chanced to be open in their track, they entered and did not hesitate to feed upon anything they came in contact with—clothing, tobacco, shoes, even thick cowhide boots."[59]

Grasshoppers (actually they were locusts) weren't the only disasters that could drop from the sky. Summer storms generated tornadoes or hurled lightning bolts that ignited every prairie dweller's greatest fear: a massive fire that consumed everything in its path. In one ghastly accident, a child running from the flames caught her foot in a gopher hole. Her mother struggled to pull her free as the child's clothes and then her own caught fire. Ripping off the burning garments she carried her child to safety only to have her die an excruciating death nine hours later. The mother lived eleven more days.[60]

The winter sky could be equally cruel. Nebraska's most famous snowstorm is the Schoolchildren's Blizzard of 1888, named because it struck in the afternoon before pupils went home at the end of the school day. In the town of Valentine the temperature plummeted from 30 degrees at 6:00 a.m. to 6 below by 2:00 in the afternoon. What made the storm lethal were winds that turned the prairie into a whiteout. As many as 500 perished from that storm, some only yards from their homes. The heroism of teachers who guided students to safety made newspaper front pages across the country.[61] One article described how searchers kept in touch "by long ropes held by all of them."[62]

The blizzard was a particularly potent reminder of how a homesteader's life could turn deadly in an instant. A sudden illness or injury presented families with the awful dilemma of when to call a doctor. A study of one Nebraska township noted that living a long distance from a physician had two disadvantages: "First, the inability to get medical attendance promptly, and second, the cost of it when obtained."[63] If a patient needed surgery, it was performed on the nearest table with primitive anesthesia and a high risk of infection. Questionable elixirs whose chief ingredient was often alcohol or opium treated various maladies. A Nebraska doctor listed twelve remedies in his medicine cabinet, several of which today are considered dangerous. The doctor's wife reported their kitchen table could "tell some tales of pioneer surgery."[64]

The lives of homesteaders could be as cruel and uncertain as those of anthracite miners. In *O Pioneers!*, Amedee Chevalier dies suddenly of a ruptured appendix while supervising the harvest of a bumper crop. Anna Pavelka's father, depressed by his family's situation and perhaps, like Sarah Jane Geary, believing they would have one less mouth to feed, took his own life, a lesson Cather implies had economic causes. His death strips the thin gilding off the so-called Gilded Age, showing us how precarious lives could be in an era with an inadequate safety net.

The numbers tell the larger story. Between 1870 and 1900 settlers registered 175,529,625 homestead acres, of which 79,330,000—or only 45 percent—proved up. The lucky found the promised land. Rains came, grasshoppers stayed away, and they never glimpsed a fire or tornado or faced a blizzard. Yet even good yields faced crop prices oscillating to an inexplicable rhythm.

A Pernicious Error

Whether they lived in company towns, tenements, or sod houses, if people like Mary Septak and Anna Pavelka fell while walking the late nineteenth-century tightrope, there was little to catch them. What people called relief was a tattered net of haphazard policies that varied from state to state, along with an even more disorganized collection of private efforts. The terms for them were "outdoor relief" and "indoor relief." Outdoor relief meant aid delivered directly in the form of money or food. Indoor relief meant an odious institution imported from England: the poor house. Jails were another housing option. Eric Monkkonen found that "during very bad depression years or harsh winters, the number of overnight lodgings provided by a police department exceeded all annual arrests."[65]

The difference in opinions between New York secretary of state J. V. N. Yates and Pennsylvania activist Matthew Carey characterize the attitudes toward aid held by most in the early decades of the century. In 1823 Yates conducted one of the first investigations of American poverty. His report divides paupers into two classes: permanent and impermanent. The first group includes "ideots [*sic*] and lunatics," the blind, and "the extremely aged and infirm, the lame, or in such ill health as to be wholly unfit for labor."[66] The impermanent were those "who could earn their living if proper labor were assigned them." His tally of permanent paupers ranged from Massachusetts, with 1 per 68, to Pennsylvania, with 1 per 265. Yates concludes that "intemperance" was the primary cause of pauperism and poorhouses were the remedy. He points out that in Salem, Massachusetts, "a *profit* has been made on the keeping of the poor."

Mathew Carey's 1830 pamphlet addresses the fallacy "that benevolent and assistance societies foster idleness and improvidence."[67] In criticizing this "pernicious error," Carey extolled the Good Samaritan parable: "We are all offenders, in a greater or less degree, and have no right to hope for mercy, if we extend it not to others." Carey took readers into Philadelphia's dark side:

A room . . . contained no furniture, but a miserable bed, covered with a pair of ragged blankets. . . . The day was intensely cold. The occupant, a woman, far too slenderly clad, had two children, one about five years old, the other about fifteen months. . . . *The younger child had had its hands and feet severely frost-bitten, and the inside of the fingers so much cracked with the frost, that a small blade of straw might lie in the fissures!*

In contrast to Yates, Cary rests his case on equity: "This state of things calls for a remedy whereby burdens, the benefits of which are enjoyed by all, should be more equally distributed."

As the country struggled to claw its way out of the Panic of 1873, calls for aid multiplied just as governments strapped for revenues were cutting back. Sounding like Henry George, in 1876 the Michigan Board of Corrections and Charities commented, "Poverty and destitution keep more than even pace in the census with advancing civilization, and its percentage on the population grows larger and larger."[68] The board reported, "The inmates of the poor-houses increased from 1871 to 1875 at an annual rate more than four times greater than the increase of the population." Wisconsin tallied 3,429 paupers in 1879 compared with 1,185 the previous year. In 1877 New York charities spent over $2 million for 43,095 paupers, orphans, and people with mental illnesses. Another 114,893 received outdoor relief.[69]

In the aftermath of the panic New York undertook a new study on pauperism. Charles Hoyt found that of 12,614 paupers in poorhouses, a quarter of them were under twenty years old (3,078) and 16 percent were under ten. Over half were single, 2,599 were widows, and 1,223 were widowers. The most startling statistic: the average poorhouse resident spent almost half a decade in a poorhouse.[70] Hoyt's conclusion introduced a new element into the poverty debate in saying that "the greater number of paupers have reached that condition by idleness, improvidence, drunkenness, or some form of vicious indulgence. It is equally clear that these vices and weaknesses are . . . the result of tendencies which are to a greater or less degree hereditary."[71]

Goaded by such views, states with budget pressures reduced aid. A Wisconsin report justified the cuts: "[Aid] may often injure the recipient as well as others, by encouraging indolence, intemperance and other vicious courses of life."[72] Other states began requiring relatives to care for impoverished family members. In 1883 Nebraska stipulated, "Whenever any persons become paupers from intemperance or any other bad conduct, they shall not be entitled to support from any relative except parent or child."[73] It did not specify "other bad conduct."

Another solution was to deport the poor. Illinois decreed: "Should any town fail to pay for the support of its paupers, the county agent may be authorized by the county board to return such paupers to the town to which he or she may belong, or the county may sue for and recover the amount due for taking care of such paupers."[74] In 1891 New York reported deporting 15,071 paupers since 1873, to "states or countries where they had legal residence."[75] One county went further: "All tramps, and traveling paupers . . . shall present a certificate signed by a physician . . . stating that they are sick, and in need of assistance. . . . If they apply for relief without presenting such certificate they will be arrested as vagrants and dealt with according to law."

Budget cuts and bad management left poorhouses in deplorable condition. A Wisconsin report described one: "The siding has shrunk and is falling off. The foundations have settled so that the doors do not fit." A physician urged the end to "the inhuman and criminal custom of placing deceased persons in a room between the hospital laundry and vegetable cellar, and beneath rooms occupied by poor, unfortunate servant girls, recently confined with infants."[76] New York's Department of Social Welfare found that "some of the beds were not well filled with straw, and all of them were overrun by water bugs and other vermin."[77] The *New York Times* described a meal with butter smelling like a dead animal, red and blue tea, decomposed fish, and hash made from "everything left lying around."[78]

While state reports from the 1890s show that systematic inspections brought some improvement to poorhouse conditions overall, their descriptions are stomach-turning. Words like "cheaply built," "a dangerous fire trap," "tumble down," "not easily kept clean," and "a mere apology for a building" grace an 1890 Wisconsin report. These conditions occurred even as the state condemned outdoor relief as "a waste of public money" that "educates people into being paupers."[79] New York reported six people sharing the same bathwater, a sink drain connected to an outhouse, and "bread was unfit for a human stomach."[80] Inspectors facing such conditions were in a bind because closing a badly-run facility sent its residents into the streets.

Despite these reports of poorhouses, critics regarded outdoor relief as a boondoggle. Typical was Mrs. Charles Russell Lowell of New York, who reputedly said, "That certain persons need certain things is no reason for supplying them with those things."[81] Josephine Shaw Lowell was no ordinary welfare opponent. Her family had a distinguished tradition of defending equality, including a famous brother, Robert Gould Shaw, who commanded the first African American regiment. After the war Josephine became the chief fundraiser for the Freedman's Relief Association and then earned an appointment to the New York State Charities Aid Association.

Lowell shows that opposition to outdoor relief involved some of the most enlightened people of the time. She believed "the task of dealing with the poor and degraded has [to] become a science."[82] For her the solution was to put conditions on receiving outdoor relief, such that "persons not in danger of starvation will not consent to receive it."[83] Lowell did not explain how to determine who was "not in danger of starvation." She also revealed the unpleasant side of the welfare controversy with a familiar word: "The only way is for the community to refuse to support any except those whom it can control."[84]

Control became a justification for questionable actions. Spurred by Lowell and others, New York cut outdoor relief, with fewer people receiving it in 1890 than had in 1850, even though the total population had mushroomed.[85] New York was not alone. In the years around the Panic of 1893, ten of the nation's largest cities abolished outdoor relief.[86] A 1900 report sums up the administrators' reasons: "Nearly all the experiences in this country indicate that outdoor relief is a source of corruption to politics, of expense to the community, and of degradation and increased pauperization to the poor."[87] The unseemly side of this was deeply political: Republicans saw relief as the tool of big-city Democratic bosses and corporations believed aid encouraged idleness by supporting those who should work.

The cutbacks brought draconian measures to weed out the undeserving, such as the woodpile test, where candidates for assistance faced a catch-22 of splitting firewood (which meant they could work) or being labeled a shirker if they could not. Another practice was one of the great euphemisms of welfare policy: "friendly visitors," who insinuated themselves into homes to determine if families merited aid. The man behind the idea, S. Humphreys Gurteen, wrote in 1882, "There must be no sentiment in the matter. It must be treated as a business scheme, if success is to attend its operations."[88] Two excerpts from a "friendly visitors" handbook reveal they were little better than a unit of secret police:

1. Never state the object of a visit as being to see whether any *relief* is wanted.
2. Be on your guard against encouraging idleness, improvidence, or grosser misconduct, directly or indirectly.[89]

The knock of the friendly visitor must have rekindled bitter memories, since for immigrants, "friendly visits" in their homelands from the government often brought misery.

The most notorious scheme was that of Charles Loring Brace. His daughter described her father's insight: "It is in accord with a great natural principle that the Children's Aid Society is aiming at the removal of the children from the city streets to farmers' homes in the West."[90] Note the term "natural principle." Brace organized the infamous "orphan trains" that carried children to live with farm families in order to "benefit" from a rural upbringing. His daughter described when bewildered children stepped off the train into a new community:

> On the arrival of one of the parties, immense interest was displayed by the whole town.... The next day a meeting of the people, irrespective of religious sympathies, was held in the town-hall.... People who were childless came forward to adopt children. Others, who had not intended to take any into their families, were induced to apply for them; and many who really wanted the children's labor pressed forward to obtain it.

Stephen O'Connor reports that some children labored under brutal taskmasters; others landed with well-meaning parents who had difficulty understanding children who spoke with strange accents.

Like their parents, children were cast adrift without a compass to navigate the turbulent waters and fog of uncertainty enveloping everything. Packing inner-city children on a train to be rehabilitated is not the same as kidnapping Indigenous children and shipping them to boarding schools, but it does reflect a similar mindset. In a culture facing the "machine process," it was easy to believe you could produce standardized people.

What makes the late nineteenth century so dynamic is that people refused to be standardized. In taking stock of life on the prairies, Willa Cather describes a place that produced stubborn survivors where others did not think humans could live. "All the human effort that had gone into it was coming back in long, sweeping lines of fertility," she writes.[91] In the people of places like the Nebraska prairie or the anthracite coalfields, the American story becomes one of a people whose achievement is not the creation of great inventions or the building of steel mills but those who converted the ordinary into the extraordinary. What they accomplished is not the marvel of the exceptional but instead the persistence of the transcendent.

PART TWO

THE DEEDS OF THE DISCONTENTED

THE 1870s

CHAPTER FIVE

To Advance Agriculture

Come gather from the prairie wide, The hillside and the plain . . .
Come and make the world respect, The tillers of the ground.
—*From "The Hand that Holds the Bread"*
by Caroline Arabella Hall

Oliver Kelley was a seed swirling in capricious currents, propelled to great heights then fluttering uncertainly in free fall. He sold real estate, water pumps, Excelsior Metal Polish, fruit trees, and vegetable seeds, and never got rich from any of them. He contributed to a variety of publications, once saying, "My scribbling is my recreation—gratuitous."[1] A contemporary described him as "a greenhorn—given to small dickerings without a particle of discretion, and it would never do to take him into your confidence."

Kelley's niece, Caroline Hall, was also a visionary, but she kept her feet on the ground and paid attention to detail. She lived with his wife and family in a relationship so comfortable that he could name his last great scheme after her and not attract a hint of scandal. Her experiences as a rural schoolteacher sharpened her natural organizing skills when the profession faced major challenges and enhanced her understanding of rural needs, as she worked in communities whispering about what she bought and said.

Together they hatched a movement as American as rock and roll. Officially titled the Order of Patrons of Husbandry, it has been known for generations as the Grange, the name given to local units.[2] Kelley and Hall proposed it when rural Americans faced a new and incomprehensible world. For some the villains were the railroads and banks, which they saw as responsible for Scrooge-like loans, outrageous shipping rates, and rapacious seed and crop prices.

Kelley knew that world well. Before the Civil War he bought land on the Mississippi River near the town of Itasca, which speculators hoped might become

Minnesota's capital. Like many schemes, it failed. Left with a farm and little else, he had sense enough to know he was a greenhorn and vision enough to seek help from fledgling agricultural journals and a loose network of those practicing "scientific farming." His farm became the showpiece described by a reporter: "A large, well-filled barn, sleek, fat cattle, horses, hogs, chickens, etc. All convenient outhouses including a granary stored with every variety of choice cereals, the most approved plows, cultivators, drills, reapers, a horsepower wood saw (capable of turning out fifteen cords of wood per day) complete an array of conveniences that would put to the blush most Eastern farms."[3]

Biographer Thomas Woods describes Kelley as an "agrarian capitalist . . . tempered by a republican concern for fairness, equality and class solidarity."[4] Those qualities guided his formation of the Benton County (Minnesota) Agricultural Society and authorship of a column for the *Sauk Rapids Frontiersman*. In one article he envisioned a future of independent farms and "here and there a spire rising above the top of each tasty grove, beneath whose shadow, protected by a gaunt arm, shall stand a school house."[5] To help farmers obtain better varieties, he started an "agricultural depot."

Drought and the grasshoppers that chewed through science the way they chewed through everything else eventually busted him like so many others. Fortunately, he had connections. In 1864 Minnesota senator Alexander Ramsey procured a position for Kelley in the new US Department of Agriculture. After the war, Connecticut senator James Dixon took an interest in his proposal to assess the South's agricultural and mineral resources.

By pulling strings, including one from beleaguered President Andrew Johnson, Kelley was on his way to Dixie. A friend suggested he pack a pistol for protection. Instead, Kelley found a bond that had survived the carnage: Freemasonry, a secret order whose membership once included George Washington and Andrew Jackson. When Kelley received warm receptions from southern Masons, he made one of America's great connections, envisioning "a Secret Society of Agriculturists, as an element to restore kindly feelings among the people."[6]

He wrote Caroline Hall about his idea. She had served on the front lines of a key change in American education. In the words of *The National Teacher*, "One of the most vital social changes wrought by our great civil war was the rush of the schoolmistress to the front, and her capture of the common school."[7] After the war, publications like the *Teacher* advised against leaving children "exclusively in the hands of women."[8] If this continued, it warned, it would be "a very perilous thing for American society." Hall was on the front lines of women's battles to hold important gains.

She encouraged Kelley to pursue his idea. He also found support among fellow government employees for an organization whose name Kelley said came from the novel *Ivanhoe*.[9] Kelley later admitted the heavy involvement of federal employees fed the misperception that the Grange was a government organization. An August 1867 letter to Hall shows Kelley continued to refine his idea:

I suggest the project of organizing an Order to embrace in its membership only those persons directly interested in cultivating the soil. I should make it a secret order, with several degrees, and signs and passwords. The lectures in each degree should be practical, appertaining to agricultural work, at the same time convey a moral lesson. While the order would aim to advance agriculture to a higher rank, by encouraging education, it would at the same time naturally embrace the benefits to its members guaranteed by Masonry.[10]

As they drafted plans for the Grange, Kelley and Hall complemented each other. His mind wandered while hers was laser sharp. He stressed Masonic ritual and hierarchy; she emphasized learning and socializing. Hall balanced Kelley's entrepreneurial instincts with her activism. Charles Postel has argued that Kelley "actually assisted Hall."[11]

At the center of their discussions was an idea that changed the nation: including women members. Kelley recorded Hall's contribution in capital letters: "THIS FEATURE ORIGINATED WITH HER."[12] He admitted, "Had it not been for the influence of woman, the Order would probably never have been known."[13] The best place to find the vision behind Hall's idea is the Grange songbook she edited. In the song "Welcome Sister" she proclaims, "In the harvest and the vintage, you shall have a rightful share."[14] Eliza Gifford, a Granger who headed New York's Woman Suffrage Association, recalled pervasive opposition to Hall's ideas, but "insistence conquered."[15]

Historian Donald Marti believes the Grange was "the rural arm of the women's rights movement."[16] Still, it had a glass ceiling. Marti notes: "Women held mostly secondary Grange offices."[17] Although fenced in, women held their ground. A man who authored household hints in a Grange publication prompted a put-down from women, who resented his push into what they regarded as a women's domain. One letterwriter observed that he was "generally not the stuff of which our staunch men are made."[18]

There was another area where Hall influenced Kelley. In the 1860s Kelley had written, "Politics and farming ought not to be mixed together,"[19] but Hall moved him from that position.[20] Kelley's Grange rules stated politics should not be discussed during meetings; Hall argued that as soon as a meeting ended, members should be free to engage in political activity.

Arrangements Should Be Made

As civic engagement swept the country, the hunger for connections emerged from the cracks between the paving blocks of city streets, in the vacant lots of small towns, and along the fencerows of farm fields. Oliver Kelley was far from the only one to harbor ideas about establishing "an order" with signs and passwords in the years W. S. Harwood termed "the Golden Age of Fraternity," when groups like the Improved Order of Red Men popped up all over the country.[21] Enthusiastic fans convinced *Ben-Hur* author Lew Wallace to approve the Supreme Tribe of Ben Hur, whose rituals included reenacting the famous chariot race.

As people sought connection with others, midwestern fields echoed with the cacophony of excited voices accompanied by the low-pitched rumble of wagons punctuated by the occasional shriek of an ungreased wheel and the snap of whips.[22] These meetings were not small affairs, nor was it easy for farmers to attend them. One account that noted those attending a meeting at 7:00 in the evening "had considerable distances to go home, over bad roads in a dark night."[23] The pull of the Grange was strong enough that an 1873 Minnesota meeting attracted a mile-long procession and 5,000 people to Northfield.[24]

These open-air cathedrals symbolically had no walls; their pews were blankets or wagon boxes; their worshippers were people with calloused hands and windbeaten faces. Sermons condemned railroad barons, grain speculators, and greedy middlemen. Bible verses mixed with newspaper headlines. Hymns rang out with the trials of the here and now.

The audiences did not sit quietly, but instead played the role of a rustic Greek chorus punctuating the oratory with retorts. Abraham Lincoln became skilled at the rural give-and-take as he honed his skills in rural courthouses, taverns, and stores. Accounts of his face-offs with Stephen Douglas often portray them as if they were a genteel debate. Far from it. Like most nineteenth-century rallies, they were raucous affairs. A speaker who could not handle hecklers faced a short career.

Opponents feared Minnesotan Ignatius Donnelly as a fast-talking rhetorical gunslinger who could get off a quick retort before his opponent cleared the holster. Once, when someone lobbed a cabbage onto the speaker's platform, he examined it like Hamlet holding Yorick's skull before firing his response,

"Gentlemen, some Democrat has flung his head up here. I only asked him for his ears, and, lo! he has given me his whole head!" Then he unloaded: "Look at the fine, intelligent cast of that countenance! The man that head belongs to believes, I have no doubt, that slavery is ordained of God, and that the best way to prosecute the war is to stop fighting."[25]

Audiences were connoisseurs of vocal subtleties and body language that helped them determine if the speakers had tucked inside their waistcoat pockets a moral compass. Daniel Boorstin believes oratory became "the main form of American public ritual."[26] For immigrants who had lived under the heel of the Hapsburgs, political oratory, especially that from prairie lightning bolts like William Jennings Bryan, must have seemed a revelation. They were at ground zero of one of history's great upwellings, one dedicated to holding a nation accountable to its ideals.

These gatherings were the sinews of the rural Discontented. Through them leaders like Donnelly connected with the thousands living in towns and on isolated farmsteads, exchanging ideas and strategies. Propose a third political party only to receive a chorus of boos and the speaker knew where his audience stood. Policies were vetted along with a process to make them happen. Prairie meadows and cottonwood groves became incubators for reinvention.

Our Home Interests Demand

In one of history's more fascinating parallels, Kelley chartered the first Grange the year the Working Men's Benevolent Association sprouted in anthracite country and an Indigenous alliance formed around opposition to the Fort Laramie Treaty. Common to them all was a growing apprehension about industrialization. In rural America the Grange drew nourishment from verbal thunderclaps that rumbled over new homesteads. As the sense of community changed, granges offered sanctuary, hymns, rituals, and houses of worship. Grange buildings still dot landscapes, where they keep company with thick-trunked oaks. Built on April 26, 1873, the Bennett Valley Grange Hall in Santa Rosa, California, is the oldest still active.[27]

In the 1870s America produced a bumper crop of wandering farmers, a fact which contradicts a still-prevalent myth that our ancestors were deeply rooted. They showed no reluctance about packing their wagons to seek a better place, even if it meant enduring drenching downpours and parching heat. "Pulling up stakes" meant taking your boundary markers to a new place. Driving these restless farmers was their hope for a promised land that emanated a sensual odor, its pheromones enticing them with something stronger than gold fever. They yearned for moist earth that clung to their hands like fertile nuggets.

The Grange's rituals, secret signs, and arcane titles helped sate the farmers' hunger for community. As is often the case for someone who lived a disordered life, Kelley's handbook contains detailed instructions. The ceremony for the First Degree includes "Court Robes—White with proper colored trimmings; Yellow for Ceres, green for Pomona, and pink for Flora. Ladies may, if desired, wear sunbonnets pushed back from the face."[28] In the language of the Grange, borrowed from Greek and Roman myths, Ceres was grain, Pomona fruit, and Flora flowers. Somehow Hall, Kelley, and the other founders avoided falling apart over the picky arguments that can sometimes bring down organizing, such as the color assigned to Ceres or the penalty meted out to anyone who dared to wear blue for Flora. While the preciseness of ritual detail may seem obsessive, it is in keeping with the rites of other fraternal organizations and reflected a larger need for control.

Besides the inclusion of women, the Grange's most unique feature was the lecturer, a one-person Chautauqua. One account details their methods:

> These grange meetings are conducted on what might be called the inquiry plan. Such questions as the following are the leading ones: What is your membership? How are your meetings attended? What degree of interest is manifested in the objects of the order? What are they? What have you saved or gained by co-operation? etc. This brings out the condition of each grange, and gives a fair indication of the health of the order in the county.[29]

Note the term "inquiry plan," which teachers might recognize as the Socratic method. This was the glue that held the Grange together. Although Kelley officially became the Grange's first secretary, he also was its first lecturer.

One lecturer reported giving ninety lectures in a year, or about two a week.[30] The most challenging country they traveled lay along the back roads of rural minds, which they guided through a tangle of crop problems, market realities, and civic instruction, all illustrated by the latest headlines. A Vermont proposal gives an idea of their importance: "Arrangements should be made for lecturers to visit the different granges and speak upon such topics as our home interests' demand, the farm work, seeds, tools, modes of cultivation, etc. Our sanitary interests need attention, and our wives and daughters' instruction in regard to diet, dress, fashion, education, etc."[31] The schedule of some lecturers may have necessitated the use of canned presentations, but the inquiry plan meant they did not merely stand in front of an audience and talk, but instead provoked discussion.

Supplementing the lecturers was a feature called the query box, which allowed members to anonymously submit questions and concerns. A committee reviewed them and lecturers facilitated discussions of the answers at the next meeting. Since there were no rules about the questions, they could provoke debates over wheat varieties or how to finance the purchase of seeds. "This plan draws out a great deal of latent talent," commented one Grange publication.[32]

The lecturers and local granges were controlled by a national council largely consisting of the Washington officials who had encouraged Kelley. Known still as "the Founders," most of them were more experienced and held higher posts than Kelley. Unfortunately, they resembled the stereotypical bureaucrat more concerned with enforcing regulations than enacting visions. Of the senior officials, the one who was the biggest problem for Kelley and Hall was William Saunders, who was famous for designing the Gettysburg battlefield cemetery. A botanist credited with bringing the navel orange to California, Saunders's design has been praised, but it was an industrial solution to the country's first industrial war.[33] How could the thousands of dead be interred with dignity befitting their "last full measure of devotion"? Saunders's solution was to bury the Confederates separately in mass graves, while arranging the Union dead with the same standardization as the machine process. Every grave would be identical, right down to the typeface used on every headstone.

Saunders's vision of the Grange followed similar principles. His clashes with Kelley and Hall revolved around radically different ideas of equality. Saunders believed local granges should be the same and, like the inscriptions on the Gettysburg headstones, stick to the basics of providing planting and crop information. As disciples of a level playing field, Hall (especially) and Kelley believed the Grange existed to aid farmers in overcoming obstacles that had led them to believe the game was rigged. This meant providing current information, meeting their needs at reasonable prices, bringing families together for socializing and entertainment, and giving farmers a voice in determining their future. As leaders more familiar with rural America than Saunders, they knew the needs of Ohio were not those of Nebraska or Georgia. Nurturing this diversity without excessive standardization remains a quintessential American dilemma.

It should also be noted the Grange idea of a level playing field extended only so far. The Grange was largely a white organization. Like many fraternal societies, especially in the North, it did not specifically forbid African Americans from joining, but it did not encourage them. One historian explains, "If Negroes did join the order, and this must have been the case in Louisiana and elsewhere, this was the exception rather than the rule."[34] Neither Kelley nor Hall referred to race in materials they distributed, nor do Grange meeting minutes mention issues like lynching.

Success Is Certain

In February of 1868 the man who once risked his future on Itasca risked it again on the Grange, resigning his government post when the Founders authorized him "to establish the Order in any portion of any State or Territory."[35] Kelley admitted, "Probably one less fitted for such work could not be found."[36] One Founder bolstered his confidence by writing, "You are still driving on and will make your order go. I call it your order, as you not only conceived the idea but are making it go 'unaided and alone.'"[37] Kelley had a different take, borrowing a familiar word: "There is nothing visionary about it. One is not apt to build air castles and fairy scenes with [poverty] for a background. Hard friction is necessary to sharpen diamond grit. Every man, to be eminently successful in what he undertakes, and competent to enjoy prosperity, must be able to stand hard usage."[38] After recruiting his first grange in Fredonia, New York, Kelley found himself on a train to Madison, Wisconsin, with only three dollars to his name. He put his hopes in italics: *Success is certain. Our aim is to elevate and dignify the labor of cultivating the soil, and the education of the masses.*"[39] In reality, finances were precarious enough that Kelley's wife sold her inherited real estate to fund his work.

The newborn Grange faced daunting challenges in linking farmers from northeastern pastures and midwestern prairie grasslands to western fruit groves and southern cotton fields in the era before the telephone became widespread. In some parts of the country farmers who possessed a cussed independence lived so far apart they rarely saw each other, especially during the winter. Further complicating building a national group was the bad blood of the Civil War and regional prejudices. Perhaps naively, Grange officials held hopes they could bridge that substantial gap. They were part of a larger national debate between reclamation and retribution.

With her background as a rural teacher, Hall probably understood the challenges better than Kelley, which may explain why she journeyed from Boston to take an active role in aiding him. They blanketed newspapers with announcements. When a paper lampooned them, Kelley crowed, "Urge them to keep up the attack, for it will help advertise us all over the country."[40] By 1870 they had organized thirty-eight granges, most in Kelley's state of Minnesota, which had the first state grange. From the beginning, Hall and Kelley stressed education, germinating America's first systematic adult education effort as they sent articles from farm journals and other sources.

We can see these changes in one representative town, Willa Cather's Red Cloud, Nebraska. A July 18, 1874, note in the *Red Cloud Chief* commented, "The Grange has commenced its work under favorable auspices."[41] Towns like Red Cloud saw a grange as the mark of an established community, along with a post office, school, and church. In *A Son of the Middle Border* Hamlin Garland wrote of the Grange, "Nothing more picturesque, more delightful, more helpful, has ever arisen out of American life."[42] In the January 11, 1877, edition of the *Chief*, "society" columnist Betsey wrote about decorating her Christmas tree and looking forward to attending the "grange festival."[43] The Grange had become a part of the town's fabric.

National meeting minutes reveal the larger story. From the beginning, tension existed between the Founders and local granges, especially around what community organizers term WIIFM (What's in it for me). Kelley astutely perceived "the educational and social features offer inducements to some to join, but the majority desire pecuniary benefits—advantages in the purchase of machinery, and sales of produce."[44] A postmortem of the Grange written in a Connecticut grange history explains: "A common cause for abatement in Grange interest lies in the failure to realize pronounced monetary advantages."[45]

As the Grange evolved, Kelley, Hall, and local granges began seeking other benefits. In 1874 the national meeting passed the following resolution:

> The Executive Committee of the National Grange be instructed to give especial attention to furnishing Patrons with tools and implements for the cultivation of our farms, and all family and farm supplies, at as low a price as a legitimate business profit will permit, and also to make arrangements by which a mutual exchange of products between different sections of the country may be made; and they are hereby authorized to employ, if in their judgment it may be necessary, competent agents to aid them in the work.[46]

Local grangers who envisioned "a mutual exchange of products between different sections of the country" created a variety of initiatives that taxed the abilities of Hall, Kelley, and the national office to keep up. Grange stores providing "tools and supplies" were successful at first. Iowans bought fifteen hundred sewing machines and saved $50,000 in one year on plows and cultivators.[47] One wrote,

"We have already received our groceries from a wholesale house in Burlington at 80 percent less than we had to pay to local merchants here."[48] The array of local Grange activities was staggering. In Louisiana, grangers set up a state agency to serve stores. In Kentucky and Texas they conducted a livestock business. They devised the Direct Trade Union to ship crops to Europe, then sold stock in it. Grangers aided in founding Mississippi State College and befriended Texas A&M College.[49] Kelley had grander plans. Hoping to tie the Grange directly to producers, he met with New York wholesalers. The Grange had become more than just a social club.

Red Cloud reflected these changes. The December 16, 1874, *Chief* announced:

Grange Store in Red Cloud.
The store kept by John G. Potter having been appointed by the
   County Council.
Don't forget the place next door to the Post Office.

Note the appointment of the store manager by the county council, a sign that local officials were involved with the Grange. At first the Grange store advertised frequently, highlighting "Grange prices" for goods that included "a fresh stock of prints" [fabric, not art]. Threatened by this new competitor, one local merchant advertised farm implements "at Grange prices."[50] A grocer offered something the Grange could not match: fresh oysters that had traveled to central Nebraska.

Buoyed by efforts like the Red Cloud store, the number of granges grew from 8,667 in 1873 to 24,290 in 1876. Perhaps the only one not surprised was Kelley, who had predicted a million members. In less than a decade since he and Hall had proposed the idea, the Grange had become one of the largest independent organizations in the country. A report on publications given to the 1874 meeting reveals the logistical nightmare caused by this expansion. That year the Grange printed 170,000 constitutions, 135,000 manuals, and 884,000 tracts.[51] This mass mailing preceded Richard Sears's catalog by fourteen years.

By the mid-1870s the Grange had swelled to almost 800,000 members. At high tide it found itself drowning in success. Deluged with new members, it lacked a process to manage them. Imagine running a city of the same size with no staff and no telephones. Most of the workload fell on Kelley and Hall. For this Kelley earned $2,500 in 1874 and $2,000 in 1875. Hall received a token $25, but she shrewdly sold the rights to her songbook for $1,000.[52]

Meanwhile, economic difficulties precipitated a running argument between granges and national headquarters, with demands that fewer dollars stay in

Washington. A sister paper of the *Chief*, the *Nebraska Advertiser*, ran a front-page story about an Illinois grange that threatened to secede: "It is burdensome and expensive to the members of the order, without adequate compensation for money expenses; that it is now engendering a spirit of class legislation, mutual distrust between the agricultural and commercial intercourse of the land, thereby demoralizing and debasing the standard of relations the community bears to each other."[53]

These problems played out in a drama that ultimately drove Kelley and Hall from the organization. Meeting records report the tug-of-war between the national office and those who wanted the Grange to take a more active role in dealing with farm problems. In 1874 Samuel Adams, Worthy Master for the national Grange, put the question to the national meeting: "The questions of transportation, taxation, finance, corruption in public places, were such as come home to the conscience and pockets of our members, and they wish to know whether they will be denied the privilege of canvassing them on the ground of politics. This body should clearly set forth an authoritative interpretation for the guidance of members."[54] It is difficult to believe Adams had not discussed this with his friends Kelley and Hall.

The national office responded by issuing a gag order stating no member could "precipitate action upon any subject whatever that has not received the approval of the National Grange."[55] To reinforce this edict, they issued a Declaration of Purposes: "No Grange, if true to its obligations, can discuss political or religious questions, nor call political conventions, nor nominate candidates, nor even discuss their merits in its meetings."[56] Bureaucrats who served several administrations made no secret of their distaste for the main sport of the nation's capital.

Washington was not the sole cause of the Grange's problems, however. Oliver Kelley could be stubborn and erratic, frustrating officials by moving his office and dabbling in Florida real estate. Annual meeting attendance also reveals a dramatic change in membership during the late 1870s. The Grange began as a diverse organization with 85 national delegates from thirty-five states attending the 1873 and 1874 meetings. Ten percent represented border states, 36.5 percent the East, 25.9 percent the Midwest, 20 percent the South, and 5.9 percent the West. By 1878 easterners controlled 43 percent of the 30 delegates, only 5 of whom had attended a previous convention. This made the Grange top-heavy with people from states with a lot of factories, few homesteaders, and farmers whose operations differed from those in the Midwest.

Those who believed the Grange should deal with kings as well as cabbages kept pressing. In 1875 delegates offered a resolution urging members to withhold crops to drive up prices.[57] It failed. Another resolution, to "pass an act making greenbacks true legal-tender," also failed. In its place the convention affirmed, "The currency question is rapidly becoming a political question, and therefore should not be entertained by this Grange." This resolution passed 18–13, with easterners providing the majority. In 1879 New York's W. G. Wayne opened the meeting with an impassioned address, stating, "Great and powerful monied corporations control our State and National governments."[58] The delegates ignored his pleas.

The geographic split that rent the Grange came to characterize similar later efforts by the Discontented, as representatives from industrial states like New York clashed with midwesterners and southerners. The debate over political involvement also provided fuel for the creation of two third parties, which promised to satisfy those yearnings: the Greenbackers and the Populists.

By the late 1870s, as the Greenback Party gathered recruits, the Grange had squandered its chance to become a national political force. In 1871 W. W. Corbett, the influential editor of *Prairie Farmer*, had written Kelley to propose "We, as an order, have a work to perform in the war that is to be waged in this country, at no distant day, by the people, against the monstrous monopolies that are overshadowing us."[59] Corbett hoped the Grange could serve as the center of a farmers' organization that would back political candidates. Kelley enthusiastically urged Corbett to "get out a good, lively editorial" and then "liberally employ printer's ink" throughout the summer. Months passed. Little happened. In November 1872 a disillusioned Corbett declined to attend the annual meeting.

As the 1870s progressed, the two people who were the heart and soul of the Grange grew increasingly frustrated, as the national office continually jerked their short leash. Kelley complained, "I was never asked into [the national office] unless to be reprimanded for not obeying instructions that were usually as sensible as if given by boys of sixteen."[60] One packet sent by Hall and Kelley picked up Corbett's suggestion, with a call for farmers to array "the agricultural force in this country in some organization which shall be able to make its power felt as it deserves to be."[61] Hall reinforced these sentiments in her songbook. No doubt the national office cringed at Grangers singing, "Take a firm stand" to "rectify the mistakes of our land." Hall also cleverly repackaged the Civil War tune "Rally 'Round the Flag" as "Rally 'Round the Grange," with its line "We will gather for the right cause with honest heart and shouting the farmer's cry of Freedom."[62] Washington's frustration with the political tone of such lyrics became clear when it purged later editions of Hall's radical tunes.

The growing split over politics prompted Kelley to found a secret order within the Grange, the Degree of the Golden Sheaf, for "wholly political purposes."[63] The name is interesting, given that Golden Sheaf was a popular brand of wheat flour. What we know suggests the idea had little traction. In 1877 the National Grange adopted a resolution denouncing as conspirators anyone "found engaged in organizing a secret society within our order."[64]

Oliver Kelley and Caroline Hall remained with the Grange until 1878, but in the last few years they grew further away from the national office. On November 21 Kelley sent a short resignation letter: "On account of the demands upon my time by my private business, I hereby respectfully tender my resignation as Secretary of the National Grange."[65] Caroline Hall must have felt more frustrated. She had written songs, articles, and circulars that irked the national officials. She even initiated a member survey that might have linked granges, but the national office took no interest.

Hall watched as her dreams for women appeared to stall. She also must have become weary of continued personal assaults, such as the pointed omission of her name from an 1874 resolution naming the "founders" of the order.[66] Although women served as delegates to national meetings, minutes of the national gatherings in the 1870s indicate no woman offered any resolution or contributed to any debate. The rapid shrinking of the Grange after Hall left raises questions about the role of women in this decline. Annie Diggs described the situation: "The Granger sisters through the intervening years, climbing laboriously, patiently, felt their treadmill cogs a slipping three steps down to one step up."[67] After leaving the Grange, Kelley searched for another Itasca in Florida, starting the town of Carrabelle, named after Hall. Hall retired to a Wisconsin farm, eventually moving to Minnesota, where she died in 1918. Grange membership fell from 411,244 in 1877 to 124,880 in 1880.[68]

In retrospect, it seems the Grange could not decide if it was a rural organization or a farm organization, whether it should endorse candidates or just advise about planting corn. Red Cloud was a prime example. Articles in the *Chief* hint that the town's elite perhaps even ran the local Grange. In some communities, doctors and lawyers joined to attract clients, prompting a Granger to remark, "They are as interested in agriculture as the hawk is interested in the sparrow."[69] Predictably, Grange business and political activities ruffled feathers. Local merchants competed with "Grange prices" while being squeezed by the tentacles of the consumer culture. Bankers and grain buyers, the villains of rural rhetoric, also were people they met at church and other community functions. Susan Sessions Rugh found that in Hancock County, Illinois, the Grange disbanded due to conflicts with local merchants.[70]

The Grange never resolved its identity problem, as events in Red Cloud show. The *Chief* reprinted a long front-page article from the *Grand Island Independent* (in central Nebraska) on December 16, 1874, questioning the national office edict about politics. The wording suggests it might have come from material that Kelley and Hall periodically sent to local papers. "Members are at perfect liberty to take any action they choose as citizens. Whether it be to indulge in a dance or hold a regular political discussion, make stump speeches, give a theatrical performance, or form themselves into a camp meeting. Belonging to the order does not deprive any one of his perogatives [*sic*] as an American citizen." The paragraph that follows sounds like Hall: "When . . . the master declares the grange 'closed,' the members . . . are at once at liberty to hold a woman's rights convention if they choose. If by joining the Order of Patrons, one bartered away his civil rights as a citizen, its membership would be limited indeed."

The mention of women's rights on the Nebraska frontier provides a hint of the Grange's impact on suffrage. The article also broached the idea of a farmers' third party: "On election day the people are called upon to 'choose between two evils.' That there should be a reform in this respect is certain, and if the people do not strive to redress existing wrongs by taking steps to secure the reform, then there will be little pity for them while monopolies continue to grind them down."[71]

Nebraskans were not the only ones speaking about rural political power. Not long after the Panic of 1873, the Fourth of July gave birth to the publication *Farmers' Declaration of Independence*. It concluded, "We . . . will use all lawful and peaceable means to free ourselves from the tyranny of monopoly, and . . . will never cease our efforts for reform until every department of our Government gives token that the reign of licentious extravagance is over."[72] The *Kansas Chief* reported grangers had no problems recommending legislation: "We demand the passage of a law, by which justice shall be dealt alike to the rich and the poor, making taxation uniform."[73]

A major political action by farmers was the passage of what became known as the Granger Laws. Although not endorsed by the national organization, in the 1870s farmers in Illinois, Iowa, Wisconsin, and other states moved to regulate railroad rates and prohibit corporate collusion. Illinois rewrote the state constitution to require laws "to prevent unjust discrimination and extortion in the rates of freight and passenger tariffs."[74] The US Supreme Court decided the cases relating to these laws in *Munn v. Illinois* (1877). With a nationwide railroad strike raging in the background, the court issued a ruling that Solon Buck terms "The most significant achievement of the anti-monopoly movement of the seventies."[75] Contrary to the idea that government should leave business alone, Chief Justice Morrison Waite employed a playing field argument to uphold the Granger Laws: "When private property is devoted to a public use, it is subject to public regulation."[76]

Two interrelated questions hover over the Grange. Did it help to level the playing field and why did membership decline so quickly and drastically? We know the peak year for the business failure index did not occur until 1877, telling us the Panic of 1873 took years to roll through the system. Corn prices per bushel fell from 52¢ in 1870 to 31¢ in 1878, cotton went from 24¢ in 1870 to 11¢ in 1878; and potatoes from $1.18 per hundredweight in 1870 to 72¢ in 1879. Wheat prices reached a low in 1878.[77] Not surprisingly, the average value per farm declined from $2,799 in 1870 to $2,544 in 1880.[78] Farmers were not economists, but their primitive ledger books told them they were in trouble.

The numbers also tell us that Grange membership fell precipitously just when farmers hit bottom. It recovered slightly in the 1880s, reaching 205,740 registered members in 1893, only to fall steeply again after the Panic of 1893. The correlation between bad years and declines in membership tell us the Grange was not satisfying farmers' needs when they needed help the most. On the Dakota plains, the Svendsbye family could gaze out on their snow-covered fields and wonder whether the next spring might be their last.

As for helping to level the playing field, the most significant accomplishment usually noted by historians are the Granger Laws and their affirmation by the Supreme Court in the *Munn* decision. The Grange was founded as an organization to bring knowledge to farmers, so one would expect to see increases in crop yields or at least a decline in their variability. Before the blossoming of state agricultural experiment stations, the Grange was a key source of information about varieties and planting techniques. The average number of bushels per acre for wheat and corn in the early 1870s increased only slightly in the second half of the decade, even though weather statistics show better rainfalls in the plains during the latter years.[79] Whether due to a lag in disseminating this knowledge or other causes, the next decade was more favorable.

The Grange offered hard lessons about channeling the anger and frustrations of the Discontented. Multiply the difficulties between Kelley, Hall, and the national office by its thousands of members and you have an idea of the challenges of herding regionally diverse people in one direction, especially in areas lacking communications. Despite overreaching, the Grange was always about possibilities. As a systematic attempt to link rural Americans, it demonstrated the boundaries of those possibilities and their potential to seed meaningful change.

Much credit for these successes should go to those who shouldered most of the burden: the lecturers. They looked back to the traveling schoolmaster and looked forward to online education. "The lecturer is a teacher," observed one grange. "His grange is his school, the members are his pupils, the outside world contains the material for its enlargement."[80] The role required people who could learn quickly, easily bond with strangers, and project credibility without sounding like know-it-alls. Their real value lay in teaching people how to think. A grange explained:

> The grange is worth to-day almost as much to the agriculturists of the country as the common school. It is, in fact, the only primary school we have which is devoted to agricultural instruction; it is there that our sons and daughters are first taught the importance of agricultural instruction; it is there that they are taught to love and take pride in their calling; it is there that they are made to see possibilities in agricultural industry which past generations never dreamed of—and it is from thence that an influence is to go out which in a few years will fill up our agricultural colleges with young men, and young ladies, too; with a class of students that will not turn their backs on the farm, or seek other respectability or utility.[81]

Historian Thomas Woods believes the Grange was a radical group "eager to participate in the promise of a new industrial republic."[82] It brought together rural communities, teaching citizens to understand the issues facing them and explaining how to make their voices heard. A Grange lecturer reflected, "The educational work of the Grange . . . reaches out into the future, and will have an influence in solving the problem of self-government, or government by the people, which, sooner or later, must be the government of the entire world."[83] These lessons would come in handy for a new political party and a new organization germinating in rural America that built on what Oliver Kelley and Caroline Hall had created.

CHAPTER SIX

TO WIN FAIR TREATMENT FOR THE LIVING

No pen can write the awful fright
And horror that prevailed,
Among those dying victims,
In the mines of Avondale.
—*From the folk song "The Avondale Mine Disaster," ca. 1870*

On April 9, 1868, immigrant Pennsylvania anthracite miner John Siney filed the charter for the Workingmen's Benevolent Association (WBA). The child of an Irish family done in by the potato famine, Siney began working in a Manchester, England, cotton mill when he was seven. As a teenager he learned bricklaying and became a union member. Like many leaders of his generation, Siney had a conversion experience that changed his life—his wife died suddenly and he lost his job. With no prospects, he journeyed with his mother and daughter to the Pennsylvania anthracite fields in 1863.[1] His easygoing personality and organizing experience made him a natural spokesman. One contemporary described him this way: "His modesty, his honesty, his frankness were marked traits of his character."[2] Siney summarized his vision for organizing: "Single handed we can do nothing, but united there is no power of wrong we can not openly defy."[3]

Siney was one of many leaders who emerged during the decades after the Civil War, propelled by record levels of civic engagement and the consequences of the machine process. Some rose briefly and unexpectedly, then fell back into obscurity. Others were on stage for years, bringing together disparate groups and ideas. Behind them were hundreds who worked tirelessly for granges and unions. Channeling their energy and anger was a challenge.

Drawing from traditions as old as the medieval guilds, workers began organizing before the war in groups like the Boston Journeymen Bootmakers'

Society, whose members pledged "not to work for any master or person who should employ any workman not being a member."[4] The Bootmakers precipitated the 1842 Massachusetts Supreme Court decision *Commonwealth V. Hunt,* whose words haunt American labor: "Such a purpose . . . would give them a power which might be exerted for useful and honorable purposes, or for dangerous and pernicious ones."[5] During the Civil War numerous painters, plasterers, joiners, bricklayers, tailors, and others formed unions, eventually increasing membership to 300,000 by 1873.[6]

Seeing this growth, iron molder William Sylvis proposed a convention for "concerted and harmonious action upon all matters appertaining to the inauguration of labor reforms."[7] The son of an itinerant wagon mechanic, Sylvis favored wearing a pockmarked shawl resembling a battle flag that had seen many actions. When he visited the mills, molten iron left holes in the shawl as he listened to workers, hoping for the moment when he had made a connection and a slight smile of recognition cemented it as surely as a handshake. Sylvis told them, "We are now all one family of slaves together, and the labor reform movement is a second emancipation proclamation."[8]

Sylvis had formed a national iron molders union in 1859. In the decade that followed much changed. The increasing use of machines created thousands of John Henrys battling the equivalent of steam drills in dozens of industries. The shoe business is an example. Printing press salesman Gordon McKay and inventor Lyman Blake began perfecting a shoemaking machine the year Sylvis founded his union. Because it could produce identical footwear, the two won a Union Army contract for 275,000 pairs of shoes. Just as the standard track gauge eliminated producing different railroad cars for every size track, the standard-size shoe ended the crafting of shoes for individuals. Although his machines could produce 300 pairs of shoes a day while a cobbler could only make five, after the war McKay couldn't sell his shoe-makers, so he rented them out.[9] An 1885 report describes what happened next: "In 1845 the labor of each operative [worker] employed in Massachusetts produced slightly more than 455 pairs of boots and shoes. In 1875 the labor of each operative produced 1205 pairs."[10] It was a familiar story. In hatting, machines enabled one employee to do the work of nine; in cotton, three; in glass, six.[11] Carroll Wright saw the implications, writing, "These stories show positively the influence of inventions in bringing about industrial depression."[12]

In August 1866 over a hundred bricklayers, coopers, blacksmiths, ship joiners, bookbinders, painters, turners, harness makers, can makers, stone cutters, glassblowers, miners, masons, coach makers, and ship carpenters from Tennessee,

New York, Connecticut, Michigan, Illinois, Missouri, Massachusetts, Indiana, Georgia, Delaware, Virginia, Maryland, and Pennsylvania descended on Baltimore.[13] Note the paucity of representatives from the Deep South. On their way to the Front Street Theater, they passed under a huge banner proclaiming, "Welcome Sons of Toil—From North and South, East and West." To relax, they joined thousands watching the Maryland and Enterprise clubs play "Base Ball" as Professor Holland's Blues Band provided music. As Sylvis hoped, delegates created the country's first national labor organization: the National Labor Union (NLU). David Montgomery recognizes it as "the first enduring, nationwide institution created by the working class."[14]

The resolutions they approved included providing "mechanics' institutes, Lyceums, reading rooms, and the erection of buildings for that purpose." A second pledged "our individual and undivided support to the sewing women and daughters of toil in this land."[15] Others preserved public lands for settlers and abolished prison labor. The delegates' efforts bore fruit when, in June 1868, their resolution for an eight-hour day convinced Congress to pass an eight-hour law for government employees over President Andrew Johnson's veto. Lack of enforcement and employer resistance crippled the law.

Baltimore introduced the Discontented to others with whom they might find common ground. Sylvis took his shawl on the road over the next few years to enlist them. During meetings in Chicago (1867) and New York (1868), the NLU broadened its agenda to reflect increasing concerns about industrialization. Adopting a metaphor, he wrote: "A slavery exists in our land worse than ever existed under the old slave system."[16] The center of that power "has been transferred to Wall Street."

In 1868, at the height of its power with 600,000 members, the NLU's New York meeting reached out to African Americans and what the *New York Herald* unapologetically termed delegates from "the weaker half of creation."[17] As the story reported, seated at the center of the floor were the twin pillars of the suffrage movement, Elizabeth Cady Stanton and Susan B. Anthony, along with Mary McDonald of the Women's Protective Labor Union (WPLU), who told delegates she could "drive a team or a tandem abreast of any man." They influenced debates over two key issues.

In the 1860s many questioned the effectiveness of strikes. An 1866 NLU committee condemned them as "productive of great injury to the laboring classes; that many have been injudicious and ill-advised; and the result of impulse rather than principle."[18] At the New York meeting Anthony's assertion that strikes were a "weapon" to be "prominently put forward" prompted a martial metaphor from

Richard Trevellick, who proclaimed strikes are "the great shield of the working-man that should never be surrendered."[19] Swept up by these voices, delegates voted to retain strikes as a weapon.

The women also figured in deliberations over monetary reform. During a lively debate, Anthony rose from her seat waving a copy of the platform. The *New York Herald* relates that, "She did not wish it to go forth to the world that a workingman's Congress was unable to assemble and deliberate in New York City without being bought up by Wall Street," as had the Republican convention. She proposed the following resolution:

> With the actual application of the fundamental principle of our republican dem-ocratic government—the consent of the governed—to the whole people and a sound monetary system there would be no antagonism between the interests of the workingman and workingwoman of this country, nor between any of the branches of productive industry, the direct operation of each, when not pre-vented by an unjust suffrage and monetary laws, being to benefit all the others by the production and distribution of the comforts and necessities of life; and that the adoption by the national government of the political and financial policies set forth in the platform of this Congress will put an end to the oppression of work-ingwomen and are the only means of securing to them, as well as to workingmen, the just reward of their labor.[20]

Amid the twists and turns signaled by commas, Anthony cleverly weaved the cause of workers, putting workingmen first and then reversing the order. Her resolution passed without opposition.

The women also succeeded in passing a resolution honoring organizer Kate Mullaney, whom Sylvis termed one of the "smartest and most energetic women in America."[21] With Sylvis's encouragement, at nineteen Mullaney organized female laundry workers into the Laundry Collar Union. It became the country's first female union and one of the first to offer benefits to its members. Mullaney also was the first woman appointed to a union higher office when she became the NLU assistant secretary. By 1870 the machine process and its paper collars had made the Laundry Collar Union obsolete.

A year after that meeting, the NLU took a giant step backward when it re-jected Anthony as a delegate because she did not represent a union. Although women continued participating, they never fulfilled the promise predicted by the *New York Herald* in 1868: "What will be the result when in place of a few hundred females being represented, half a million send their delegates to speak on their behalf?"[22] The union also failed to fulfill its promises to African Americans. Despite recruitment efforts by Sylvis, at the meeting there were only 8 African American delegates of the total 225.[23] One was Isaac Myers. A Baltimore native, at sixteen he began working in local shipyards in 1851. When he formed a caulkers union in 1868, an astute Sylvis invited him to attend the 1868 congress. A credential fight over an African-American delegate prompted Myers to bolt the NLU and form the Colored National Labor Union. Sylvis might have been able to retain some of the NLU's African Americans, but he died in July 1869, leaving union leadership to the man who was at his bedside during his last days, Detroit ship carpenter Richard Trevellick. Although Trevellick attempted to hold the NLU together, by the early 1870s it was in intensive care.

Organization Was in the Air

Among those attending the 1870 NLU convention was John Siney, who served on a committee that created the National Labor Reform Party. Had you flown over the coalfields that year you might understand why Pennsylvania was an early battleground for the Discontented. Dotting the green, hump-backed Allegheny hills crouched the sloping hulks of coal breakers, surrounded by dark mounds of coal waste on which nothing grows. In their shadows lay the shanties of company towns. A local paper spelled out the tensions: "Nowhere in this country have capital and labor at so early a date been arrayed against each other as in the coal regions."[24]

G. O. Virtue wrote "Organization was in the air" to describe Siney's 1868 chartering of the WBA in Pennsylvania's Schuylkill County.[25] It was not the first miners' union, but others were short-lived. Under Siney the WBA membership reached 35,000 by 1871, making it one of the country's largest unions.[26] Organization may have been in the air, but Siney knew miners needed education, benefits, and political power. He founded a newspaper to provide education and raise political consciousness. A familiar figure at the Pennsylvania Legislature, in 1869 he achieved a significant victory with the passage of one of the first laws recognizing the right to unionize.

Not only was it one of the first unions to provide benefits, but the WBA was also instrumental in convincing the 1870 legislature to approve construction of a miners' hospital in Schuylkill County. To form alternatives to the notorious company stores, it developed co-ops, providing items at reasonable prices. Siney even explored buying a mine and running it as a cooperative. A WBA member reflected:

I shall remember it as long as I live; for a long time in the Hazleton region they had a very bad system; they paid us all in store goods; of course, some who were a little honorable paid $5 or $10 a month in cash; in some places they charged extraordinary prices for powder—more than we could purchase it for ready cash; it was no use for a man to speak above board to any of these gentlemen, because he knew it was immediate death or discharge, and then he might look in some other quarters for employment.[27]

The WBA's Achilles heel was its organization by county, each with an executive board. For every 1,000 members they also elected a member to the general council. This guaranteed the union became more unwieldy as it grew. A member identified another issue: "If a county or district does not wish to be governed by the law that is passed, they are at liberty to reject it."[28]

A major WBA priority was improving working conditions. The fear of being caught in a mine death trap became a nightmare on September 6, 1869, when the Avondale mine caught fire. Like the fuse on a stick of dynamite, a blaze ignited the coal dust, sending flames a hundred feet above the breaker. In the tunnels below the conflagration sucked away oxygen, suffocating 108 miners. The youngest was Willie Hatton, age ten, who died with his father; the oldest was fifty. After three days rescuers reached the bodies, lying in gruesome tableaux behind makeshift barriers. A father clutched his son in a last embrace. A man's hands were frozen in prayer. On September 9, John Siney spoke to those witnessing the rescuers bring up bodies so disfigured they were impossible to identify.[29] He issued a call to arms. "You can do nothing to win these dead men and boys back to life," he said, "but you can help to win fair treatment for the living who risk life and health in their daily toil."[30]

With the words "fair treatment" he linked Avondale to the Discontenteds' struggle for a level playing field. Terence Powderly was among many who resonated with this meaning, writing "I realized that there was something more to win through labor than dollars and cents for self. [It] was a call to the living to neglect no duty to fellow man."[31] After Avondale the WBA lobbied the legislature to pass a comprehensive mine safety law to replace an earlier one whose inadequacies the disaster illuminated. Their efforts rode a massive wave of sympathy. A notice in the *Charleston Daily News* was typical: "The Rev. Dr. W. W. Hicks will deliver a discourse in the Church in aid of the families of his countrymen who have been left destitute by the Avondale disaster."[32] Miners and their supporters used Avondale to rouse a national crusade that brought attention to working conditions and those who created them. The *Memphis*

Daily Appeal picked up the battle flag: "These honest, poor people deserve all the protection their fellow-citizens can give, and the Legislature of Pennsylvania will be recklessly criminal if, at its first meeting, it does not compel a safety as well as working shaft to every mine in the State." [33]

Pennsylvania governor John Geary's 1870 annual message made it clear Avondale was a matter of justice because "the mines in many cases are constructed and managed in the most selfish and parsimonious manner; consequently, some of them, like that of Avondale, are nothing but underground man traps."[34] In response, the legislature passed a law "providing for the health and safety of persons employed in coal mines."[35] Perhaps in response to the ten-year-old who died at Avondale, the law prohibited the employment of boys younger than twelve underground. Most of all the new law challenged laissez-faire capitalism, asserting that government was justified in intervening in corporate affairs. Without it, more than three thousand families might have lost their chief breadwinner.[36] Two studies found fatalities declined after the passage of the law.[37]

Frank Gowen Has the Say Now

By the time Franklin Gowen entered the coal business the promise of these actions had already faded. Some today believe the abandoned breakers haunting the region harbor the restless spirit of a man whose life and death continue to raise questions. Gowen rose to prominence as county attorney of Schuylkill County, then became counsel for the Reading Railroad in 1864 and its president from 1870 to 1886. Although a biographer admits he was ill-fitted to run the Reading, he had the gifts of an expert Monopoly player, using his profits to buy other mines. Flushed with success, he built an estate with 20 acres of lawn and gardens he named Cresheim, the name of the town of his ancestors.[38]

The ghostly glow of the gaslights illuminating the hearing room of the 1871 Pennsylvania Senate Judiciary Committee reveals how Gowen developed the Reading into one of America's most powerful companies. The hearings were scheduled to discuss railroad rates, but Gowen astutely turned the occasion into inspired political theater, putting Siney and the WBA on trial for making it "impossible to carry out the coal industry in this Commonwealth."[39] When the union realized it had walked into a rigged game, Siney requested the WBA also be allowed counsel. The sparring that took place peeled back the growing animosities in anthracite country.

An 1869 strike had produced a contract stipulating that miners be paid under a sliding scale that corresponded with the price of coal. For a short time there was peace, because management and labor could each influence the price. If it went too low, mine owners shut down, pinching supply, while workers could strike, also creating a shortage. Left out was Gowen's Reading Railroad. If owners or miners cut supply, shipments and Reading profits declined.

Faced with this squeeze, Gowen, like John D. Rockefeller, was obsessed with the need for control. He detested the union, complaining, "In the wildest flight of the imagination of the most pretentious charlatan there never was conceived such a cure for the ills with which we were afflicted as was suggested by these new doctors."[40] So Gowen created one of America's first price-fixing cartels.[41] Testimony at the 1871 hearings revealed he threatened to increase shipping prices if someone refused to join the cartel. One owner testified, "Frank Gowen has the say now."[42] Other owners defended the arrangement: "There has got to be some power from some quarter to arrest this constant striking and this constant demand upon the coal operators."

Although the hearings were intended to investigate the cartel, Gowen masterfully turned them upside down and put the WBA on trial. In his opening statement he arrogantly proclaimed the time had come for those who "labor with their hands" to yield to those "who labor with their minds."[43] Calling coal operators to the stand, Gowen's team elicited stories about the headaches caused by the union. "It got so bad that if it looked like rain, as it did one morning, my drivers would not go out," whined one owner.[44]

The owners had legitimate concerns because the WBA's unwieldy superstructure allowed local unions to engage in wildcat actions. If a miner objected to something, he only had to convince others to walk out. Consequently, in 1870 the Schuylkill County WBA was on strike but members in adjoining counties continued to work. Predictably, coal prices rose, which under the contract triggered an increase in wages. The imbalance between Schuylkill County and its neighbors created bad feelings among miners and owners.

Facing hostile questioning during the hearing, the WBA defended the right to negotiate contracts and workplace rules. The union noted that, although wildcat strikes continued, they were considerably reduced under the union, while wages increased. "Before this association was organized I have seen men making coffins out of store boxes to bury their children; I have seen men discharged for asking for $20 when $50 were due them," testified a WBA member.[45]

Despite the fireworks, the committee's report handed the union an important victory, affirming "the right of labor to combine is no longer an open question."[46] It added: "If any individual workman be at liberty to refuse work except on his own terms, any number of workmen must be equally at liberty collectively to refuse to work except on terms to which, after consulting together amongst themselves, they may have collectively agreed." In reality, the committee had no power to enforce this conclusion.

Armed Banditti

John Siney responded to Gowen's cartel by creating a new union, the American Miners' Association (AMA), whose national membership he hoped might provide more leverage. The AMA stated its objectives in a constitution that pledged to "promote the interests of the miners morally, socially and financially."[47] This document's systemic approach is remarkable. It urged miners to become citizens—that is, register to vote—to increase their political power. It included an education provision, "to spread general intelligence among them"; voting, "that we may secure by the use of the ballot"; and social and economic justice, "to promote the interests of the miners morally, socially and financially; for the protection of their health and lives." It also guaranteed "a weekly allowance for members when out of employment when resisting any unjust demands." Article 2 was crucial: "To assist all similar associations which have the same object in view, to wit: Mutual protection of members and the protection of labor against capital."

The AMA grew so quickly in its first year, Carroll Wright dubbed it "the best open labor organization that was introduced among the miners of the United States."[48] Covering the second national convention, the *Nashville Union* observed, "Delegates are present from Pennsylvania to Wyoming Territory."[49] The article mentioned a resolution about the use of "armed banditti" by mine operators, and recommended miners "immediately provide themselves with a full supply of the best breech-loaders the country affords."

Those armed banditti were central to Gowen's strategy to break the union by turning Schuylkill County into what Anthony F. C. Wallace terms a "state within a state."[50] Transforming the mine police into a coal country SS, enabled by the legislature's Act 228, allowed mine and steel mill owners to provide their own law enforcement. Gowen sprinkled the mine police with toughs who had no problem wielding their fists or other weapons to intimidate workers. One historian points out there was never "any attempt on the part of any responsible authority to determine the character or fitness of the persons for whom commissions were sought."[51] Under Gowen's direction they spied on citizens and visited those who needed "a lesson." Their word could cost a miner his job; their displeasure could cost him a broken leg. "Respect from fear" is a common thread in stories about the mine police from descendants of the miners.[52]

Gowen then went further, hiring the Pinkerton Detective Agency to serve as his gestapo. He had previously employed the Pinkerton Agency to spy on workers, but in 1873 that relationship expanded, much to the relief of Allan Pinkerton, whose firm was in financial difficulty. Appointing Pinkerton agent Robert Linden as captain of the mine police cemented the relationship.

Allan Pinkerton earned fame protecting Abraham Lincoln when he traveled to his inauguration. During the war he oversaw Union intelligence-gathering. After Appomattox, Pinkerton offered his services to industrialists. Books like *The Spy of the Rebellion* and *The Expressman and the Detective* publicized his use of modern methods, like fingerprinting. The real recipe for success by the agency, whose logo was a paranoid eye and the motto "we never sleep," mixed William Graham Sumner's philosophy of wealth and red-baiting: "The deadly spirit of Communism steals in and further embitters the workingman against that from which his very livelihood is secured, and gradually makes him an enemy of all law, order, and society."[53] When this tactic failed to attract customers, Pinkertons fomented unrest and then touted their expertise as spies for those "desirous of ascertaining the feeling of their employees."[54]

Contrary to their wish to be seen as dime novel heroes, Pinkertons represented a major threat. One story estimated Pinkertons even outnumbered US Army soldiers.[55] Samuel Gompers warned, "The maintenance of an armed force which has neither the dignity nor the federal authority of a standing army . . . is contrary to all American principles and ideas."[56] By 1893 the Pinkertons became so toxic, Congress passed a law stating "No employee of the Pinkerton Detective Agency, or similar agency, shall be employed in any Government service."[57]

Franklin Gowen's use of the Pinkertons and his heavy dictatorial hand betrayed a deep personal insecurity that extended to spying on Pennsylvania legislators. If Gowen could not find tasks for them to perform, Allan Pinkerton would find them. In May 1873 he urged his manager to "go to Franklin Gowan [*sic*] occasionally . . . suggest some things to Mr. Gowan [*sic*] about one thing and another which would be possible, and I have no doubt he will give us work."[58]

The Pinkertons and the mine police came in handy when Gowen and the cartel announced a 55 percent wage cut to cover losses caused by reduced demand after the Panic of 1873 and their own overspeculation. Throughout 1874 miners struggled to maintain their equilibrium. A common entry in reports by Pinkerton spy James McParlan refers to miners looking for work. One had an especially ominous tone: "McKeon said that if the operative [McParlan] made it till the New Year he would see some rough times, as both the Bosses and men claim that the Reading RR Company were responsible for the suspension [of work] in order to reduce the Bosses and break up the Union and if there was a suspension it would cause a rough time."[59]

In January 1875 the miners did the only thing they could: they went on strike. Gowen held all the cards in what became known as the Long Strike, having stockpiled coal to wait out the miners. When union members began harassing scabs, Gowen had Siney and twenty-five union officials arrested for "conspiracy" on May 12, crippling the leadership. Gowen then starved the miners into submission. On June 25 the *Chicago Tribune* announced the "unconditional surrender" of the union in an article that blamed the miners for starving their own families.[60] "The right to strike [does not] justify men in starving and abusing their families after it has been clearly demonstrated that their demands are exorbitant and will not be granted." Gowen was single-handedly asserting dictatorial control of the coalfields. Statistician Joseph Weeks described the atmosphere: "Strikes were the normal condition of the region and their outcome being for the most part the constant defeat of the workingmen, a feeling of utter hopelessness and blind recklessness became the ruling spirit of many of the workmen."[61]

To consolidate control Gowen needed to suppress the growing political power of the Irish. John Siney had immigrated to an area where ethnic antagonisms preceded the Civil War. In the 1850s Schuylkill County was a stronghold of the secretive, nativist Know-Nothing Party. In 1854 the Stroudsburg, Pennsylvania, newspaper, the *Jeffersonian*, reported, "There are said to be Know Nothing lodges in all the towns and villages in Dauphin, Cumberland, Perry, Lebanon, Adams, Franklin, Northumberland, Union, Lancaster, and Schuylkill counties numbering thousands of members."[62] Gowen grew up hearing the rants of ex–Know Nothing, anti-Irish *Pottsville Miners Journal* editor Benjamin Bannan.[63] Opinionated and controversial (as witnessed by several libel convictions), Bannan saw his paper as the sword of the Republican Party, which rewarded him with a seat on the state committee.[64] As early as 1854 Bannan was excoriating the Irish: "Coming into this country from the ignorance and poverty of the old world, they enter into any avocation which will yield a livelihood, and thoughtlessly plunge into vice and drunkenness."[65]

Bannan and Schuylkill County Republicans especially resented Irish actions during the Civil War. Irish miners hated the military draft as much as Irish New Yorkers did, especially when mine owners supplied draft boards with the names of workers who spoke out. Draft resistance became violent when the Irish blocked a train carrying draftees, causing mine owners to call in federal troops and leaving Schuylkill County as the only northern community with a standing army to keep order. A local paper remembered: "[Draft law opponents] were in numbers chained to ropes which were tied to the saddles of dragoons, and thus from distant points marched into Pottsville, sent to Fort Delaware and Fortress Monroe and left to languish in prison."[66] Grace Palladino believes the draft allowed industrialists to "impose managerial prerogative by force of law."[67]

After the war, Irish support for the Democratic Party continued antagonizing the local Republican establishment, who were "opposed to giving the Irish Catholic any alternative except to leave the region or become a hewer of wood and drawer of water for others."[68] Siney further fanned the fire by building the WBA into a political force whose reputation reached a Maine newspaper: "Schuylkill has been so thoroughly Democratic for years that the Republicans have given up all hope of ever subduing it; but this year the Democrats have nominated three men for the legislature so obnoxious to the Working Men's Benevolent Association that this powerful society largely composed of Democrats propose to nominate candidates of their own, which will most likely give the election to the Republicans."[69] In Schuylkill County, the area's US House of Representatives seat became a political football, as Irish immigrant James Reilly and German-American Charles Brumm traded election wins.[70] The *Shenandoah Herald* connected the 1874 selection of Reilly to WBA labor reforms: "The young Irish American element of the Democratic party, who, for the past few years, has been coquetting with the Labor Reform movement . . . triumphantly carried for him all the primaries in the county in which the Irish element of the party preponderates."[71] That antagonism became even more pronounced when rumors surfaced in 1875 that Republican governor John Hartranft had cut a deal with union leader John Kehoe to deliver the Irish vote.[72]

In Gowen's mind—and in those of others—the ultimate source of the troubles was the Ancient Order Hibernians (AOH), an Irish American organization that remains strong in the United States. Founded in 1836, as large numbers of Irish immigrants began entering the country, it has been a lifebuoy for them in troubled waters. In coal country, AOH members served as school directors, tax collectors, and township supervisors.

In the 1871 hearing Gowen referred to "an association which votes in secret, at night, that men's lives shall be taken, and that they shall be shot before their wives, murdered in cold blood, for daring to work against the order."[73] Knocked off guard by the attack, Siney fired back, saying, "I challenge Mr. Gowen, as a lawyer and a resident in our county, or any other man, to name one outrage which has been committed that can be traced to this association which I represent."[74]

From these charges emerged a coalfield Frankenstein created from paranoia, gunpowder, prejudice, and congealed blood, and brought to life by the region's high-voltage friction. Allan Pinkerton gave that creature a name. On October 9, 1873, he wrote the Reading president that operatives reported the "rumored existence at Glen Carbon of an organization known as the 'Molly Maguires.'"[75] This was less than a year after newspaper reports blamed the Mollies for the shootings of the three men buried near the Geary family in Girardville.[76]

The Mollies' ghostly footprints track through nativist tracts and century-old newspapers. An 1846 article in the Somerset, Pennsylvania, *Herald* includes a quote from an Irish circular, stating, "Brand us not with Molly Maguireism."[77] In 1857 the *Glasgow Weekly Times* of Glasgow, Missouri, reported Philadelphia Democrats were "much excited" by the discovery of "a secret organization that exists among them, whose object is to control . . . the Democratic party."[78] In the next decades, "Molly Maguire" became a widely employed epithet. Southern newspapers used it to defend resistance to Reconstruction. In 1871 the *Nashville Union* wrote, "If it is right and necessary for the Federal Government to crush out Ku-Kluxes, it would seem to be equally so in the same power to put down Buckshots and Mollie Maguires."[79] In the North the Mollies also proved useful. "There is known to exist among a certain portion of the miners in this region a secret society called the 'Molly Maguires,' one of whose laws, it is said, fully recognizes the atrocious crime of assassination," read a story with the subhead "Organized Assassins in Maryland."[80] An article subtitled "Evidence of Dangerous Secret Societies Among the Coal Miners" put the Mollies at the center of an Illinois trial.[81] Behind the articles were ancient prejudices and tactics that tar as dangerous those who are different, and then link them to shadowy outside organizations.

Histories sometimes conclude that we can never really know what happened with the Mollies, but thanks to recent efforts we know a great deal. The coalfield violence is a matter of historical record and the miscarriage of justice in their subsequent trials is well documented. Secret societies in Ireland with names like Whiteboys and Ribbonmen existed. American nativist groups used this connection to print inflammatory material, like the 1856 "Oath of the Irish Ribbonmen" to be "always faithful to the Society; to keep and conceal all the secrets, and its words of order; to be always ready to execute the commands of my superior officers, and, as far as it shall lie in my power, to extirpate all heretics, and All The Protestants, and to walk in their blood to the knee!"[82]

The conspiracy theories and the Pinkertons' dime-novel reality created a cloud over the coalfields. Veiled in that cloud is James McParlan, the detective who, two months after Pinkerton dropped his hint about the Molly Maguires, was on his way to Pennsylvania. A photograph shows a man with mole-like glasses and a brushy mustache who bears a slight resemblance to Teddy Roosevelt, perhaps because his body language projects a similar pugnacious image. An Irish immigrant, McParlan had a gift for self-promotion that clouded his past and inflated his importance, inducing Allan Pinkerton to hire him after his bar burned in the Chicago fire. Referring to himself as "the operative," his reports read like a third-grader playing detective, including a melodramatic story of winning over alleged conspirators by singing Irish songs. His most common entries are "Nothing to report" or accounts of frequent bar visits.

McParlan portrayed Schuylkill County as a place where too many men with chips on their shoulders and guns in their belts were ready to pull the trigger. On August 28, 1874, he reports three men were shot in a gun battle. On September 1 a constable shot a boy. Ten days later a drunk threatened a barkeeper with his pistol. On September 13, after a man threw rocks through the window of an alleged Molly, he was beaten so severely he was not expected to live.[83] McParlan's entries suggest he was more than willing to provoke such actions.

His reports culminated in several remarkable trials in which mine owner Gowen prosecuted his own miners by applying the totalitarian strategy of hanging the innocent to create more fear than hanging the guilty could create. With McParlan as the star witness, Gowen used his considerable oratorical skills to portray the Mollies as evil incarnate.[84] Psychologists might view Gowen's grammar of hate as a repudiation of his Irish past:

[The Molly Maguires get] authority . . . from a society . . . sitting in secret in Ireland and Scotland and England, and there concocting the secret passwords and signs and toasts, and sending them, once every three months to the members of the society here. . . . [You] will convict this society . . . so that no member will hereafter lift his hand to strike the blow that has so often carried terror to the community, which now looks to us as its last refuge.[85]

Gowen stacked the jury with German immigrants, some of whom could barely speak English. The presiding judge was the losing candidate for governor, a defeat he blamed on the AOH and the WBA. The prosecution cleverly indicted everyone connected to the allegedly planned murders, making it difficult to call rebuttal witnesses. On the stand McParlan proved unflappable in part because defense efforts seemed half-hearted. This stands in stark contrast to Clarence Darrow, who put McParlan's former stenographer and brother on the stand to question his character in the 1907 murder trial of union organizer William "Big Bill" Haywood.

The convictions of twenty miners broke any resistance remaining after the strike ended. On June 21, 1877, known as the Day of the Rope, ten walked to the gallows, one after the other. Ten more followed later. One of the condemned, Alexander Campbell, put his handprint on his cell wall to proclaim his innocence, where it remains, asking the questions he intended. The Reading Railroad offered to ship the bodies home for free.

In seeking to understand the Mollies we need to recall something John Siney stressed repeatedly. When Franklin Gowen lobbed his bomb about secret societies into the 1871 hearings, Siney and others pointed out that the WBA had curbed violence. Research backs up his point. Of twenty-four killings that took place from 1862 to 1876, Kevin Kenny classifies six from 1862 to 1868 as caused by the Civil War or robbery. Only three killings occurred from 1868 to 1874, when the WBA was strong. In 1874 and 1875 there were nine, with six coming in the wake of the Long Strike. A semiliterate letter written to the *Shenandoah Herald* explained, "The union is Broke up and we Have nothing to defend ourselves with but our Revolvers and if we dount [sic] use them we shal [sic] have to work for 50 cents a Day."[86] In an interesting coincidence, the lowest output per mine worker occurred during the trials.

Two local priests who sought control of the narrative penned a letter charging "a great conflagration cannot be ascribed to a match; combustible material also must have been there."[87] Citing "rapacity, extortion, and refusal to pay the laborer his just wages" they pointed out that "any attempt on the part of the men to ameliorate their condition was at all hazards immediately crushed. Those who took a prominent part in such movements among the men fell under the operators' displeasure, and were 'marked,' 'black listed.'"

A Question of Bread or Blood

The year marking the Day of the Rope was not a kind one, with state bank suspensions nearly totaling those for the entire decade. The business failure rate of 158 the following year remains the highest ever recorded, exceeding 153 in 1932.[88] The railroads were a favorite villain, especially since the air remained thick with the stench of Jay Cooke's collapse that precipitated the Panic of 1873 and the "king of frauds"—the Credit Mobilier scandal.[89]

No one saw a winter strike by icemen in Rondout, New York, as a warning sign about what was coming. Over 200 deputies guarded the town's icehouses while 500 men paraded with spades, shovels, and clubs "making incendiary threats" after ice magnates announced that "under no circumstances will the scale of wages be advanced."[90] The strike illustrated how corporations now exercised control over formerly local operations. For generations, harvesting ice blocks was such a critical industry that nature writer John Burroughs claimed, "Ice or no ice sometimes means bread or no bread."[91] By 1900 "Ice King" Charles Morse controlled every cake of ice sold in New York City.[92]

Like a terrible memory, 1877 featured some of the era's bloodiest battles. At their root were what Robert Bruce refers to as "combustibles." South Carolina's *Anderson Intelligencer* explained: "We do not hear so much of the measures of statesmanship necessary to control the overgrown corporations and monopolies of the country, and to emancipate trade and industry from the special and unwise legislation, which are at the bottom of our late troubles."[93] As the feeling grew that the playing field was indeed tilted and getting more so, people looked to remedy the imbalance.

Thrown into this smoldering situation was a particularly potent accelerant in the form of the many left destitute by the Panic of 1873. By 1877 they had created a life centered on the rails as they followed the rhythms of nature and the economy. For that reason they tended to hang around railroad yards, where they trolled for food, shelter, and good leads on jobs. Their eyes gave them away because they looked down like someone hoping to find whatever they lost between holes in the minimal safety net. In the years after the panic, time wore away their waning memories of stability, leaving only a desperate need to stay alive.

Fittingly, a railroad yard is where resentments boiled over. A 10 percent pay cut announced by the Baltimore & Ohio (B&O) lit the fuse. According to testimony, workers made between $1.45 and $2.45 per day.[94] Even working three hundred days, those wages amounted to $435–$735 per year. The one-third cut in less than a year put some workers near starvation, given information gathered in Carroll Wright's 1875 Massachusetts study, which found the average worker annually spent $422.16 on food. Facing these realities, railroad workers seized the Martinsburg, West Virginia, roundhouse on July 14, refusing to move any trains and reviving memories of John Brown's capture of the nearby Harpers Ferry armory.

A young labor organizer with a fondness for rye whiskey and the skills of an organizer had planted the seed for Martinsburg. Nearly forgotten today, Robert Ammon deserves better, for without him 1877 would have been far different. A burly six-footer with a commanding presence and a voice that rose above the din of a crowded meeting, Ammon packed a lifetime of experiences into his twenty-five years: a calf wound in the Plains War, a visit to China, a trek in the Arizona mountains searching for a lost diamond mine, and attendance at the University of Pittsburgh. Pennsylvania's *Biographical Encyclopedia* describes him as "possessing honesty and high social qualities [that] make him a general favorite with a large circle of friends."[95] A Pennsylvania legislative committee added: "Ammon had the nerve; was naturally shrewd and sharp, and knew how to control men."[96]

The Trainmen's Union he founded arose from a rowdy gathering called in Allegheny, Pennsylvania, to unite railroad workers like John Siney's AMA united miners. Ammon's vision echoed Siney's: "The purpose and object of the Trainmen's Union was to get the trainmen—composing engineers, conductors, brakemen, and firemen, on the three grand trunk lines of the country—into one solid body."[97] He planned to "combine into one body all the men, at a certain hour on a certain day, if the railroad magnates did not accede to our demands we would strike, and leave the trains standing just where they were, and go home."

After he signed union card no. 1, Ammon became the union's "grand organizer" then fanned out to enlist members. A month later a detective estimated the union had recruited 1,200 from thirteen railroads including the Pennsylvania and New York Central.[98] Ammon found "they talked most loud at Martinsburg, but I thought it was all wind."[99] Events in Martinsburg worried B&O head John Garrett because a strike at this key hub could have crippled his system.1[100] After strikers occupied the roundhouse, local militia failed to oust the workers, largely because they sympathized with them. Garrett lobbied for federal troops.

Pres. Rutherford Hayes, who pulled troops that were protecting African Americans in the South, had no problem using them against organized labor. In one of the era's worst decisions, Hayes firmly put a finger on the scale of justice. His July 18 proclamation featured a sleight of hand even Franklin Gowen would have admired, as the strike became an "insurrection": "The laws of the United States require that in all cases of insurrection . . . whenever it may be necessary, in the judgment of the President, he shall forthwith, by proclamation, command such insurgents to disperse and retire peaceably to their respective abodes within a limited time."[101] Federal troops left Fort McHenry (of "The Star-Spangled Banner" fame) for Martinsburg, with the government paying the B&O for transport. The reaction was subdued save for a few, like the *New York Sun*, which reported: "The injustice of this scheme of a national army police is monstrous."[102]

Days after the troops quelled the Martinsburg rebellion, Baltimore erupted in rioting that left 10 dead and untold wounded. Crowds blocked national guard troops from boarding trains headed for Cumberland, where the governor ordered them to put down a different railroad strike at Garrett's request. The storm broke when striking tin can makers, sawyers, and box makers joined others in tearing up rails, sabotaging switches, and torching rolling stock. Among those killed when troops fired on the crowds were a sixteen-year-old photographer trying to protect a woman stepping off a streetcar, a fifteen-year-old newsboy, a forty-year-old tinner standing perplexed as a mob surged around him, and a salesman trying to calm his sisters.

Meanwhile, the strike moved to other rail systems, including one run by the nation's toughest railroad boss: the Pennsylvania Railroad's Thomas Scott. He had served in the Lincoln administration and then reputedly brokered the Hayes-Tilden compromise that resolved the deadlocked 1876 presidential election. Hayes received the telegram notifying him of his election while ensconced in Scott's private railroad car. Wendell Phillips remarked that as Scott "trailed his garments across the country, the members of twenty legislatures trembled like dry leaves in a winter's wind."[103]

In an 1877 letter to the *North American Review,* Scott presented a too-big-to-fail argument: "Upon these [railroads], is borne traffic so essentially national, so closely interwoven with the interests not only of our own but other countries, that it demands the most efficient and speedy protection against all unlawful interference."[104] Scott recommended troops be stationed "at prominent points, large cities, and other great business centres" to protect the railroads. His letter pinpoints a systemic issue behind what Michael Bellesiles labels "America's year of living violently."[105] Because the nation's transportation arteries were in private hands, it all but guaranteed the government would have to protect them.

By mid-July, protests and rioting coalesced into what has become known as the Great Railroad Strike. The *Pittsburgh Leader* invoked a familiar metaphor: "This may be the beginning of a great civil war in this country, between labor and capital."[106] Tom Scott agreed, saying, "The insurrection presents a state of facts almost as serious as that which prevailed at the outbreak of the Civil War."[107] Dealing with the "insurrection" would not be easy at Scott's headquarters in Pittsburgh, where budget cuts had laid off half the patrolmen.

Like disease epidemics, riots are governed by the potency of the virus, its transmission, and people's susceptibility. Pittsburgh made transmission easy, with every street corner an information hub. The virus was potent, as witnessed by the damage. Susceptibility was high because, as a Pennsylvania legislative committee found, "citizens had a bitter feeling against the Pennsylvania Railroad Company."[108] The committee explained why shopkeepers supported the strikers: "The tradesmen with whom the trainmen dealt also had a direct sympathy with the men, for [the strike's] results would affect their pockets."

The Pittsburgh rail yard held two thousand railroad cars filled with goods people had seen in store windows, stoking the instant gratification of rioters drunk on the consumer culture. Melting ice identified the much-coveted meat and produce. A witness described the scene: "I saw a woman dragging a sack of salt, another woman a bag of flour in a wheelbarrow, and a great many others carrying leaf tobacco and some rolling pieces of lard."[109] Free liquor fueled a bacchanal, where axe handles were staffs of authority, grain alcohol the communal liquid, and fire the baptismal stream. Cars carrying oil turned into rolling incendiaries. Heat-twisted rails mutated into hellish shapes. When it was over, steaming iron wheels marked phantom railroad cars.

When national guardsmen sought to protect Scott's assets, everything came to a head at Twenty-Eighth Street. Pressed by demonstrators, the troops opened fire, killing twenty-two. The coroner described the victims: "There was [*sic*] some of all kinds, painters—some railroad men among them, there was [*sic*] some rolling-mill men, I think."[110] Rolling-mill men were steelworkers, which means other unions supported the strike, at least informally.

Across the river in Allegheny, "a boy of twenty-seven in side whiskers and with the appearance of a bank clerk" captured a dispatcher's station, where he coordinated actions by telegraph.[111] "Such a thing never occurred before, save in time of war," remarked one newspaper. The Pennsylvania committee investigating the violence termed Robert Ammon's performance "extraordinary . . . to control the men he did, and to keep the passenger trains running regularly without accident."[112] A reporter was as star-struck as everyone else: "The railroad magnate was sitting at the telegrapher's desk, and about him were a mingled group of engineers, brakemen, and firemen. They were hurrying in for orders and out to execute them. The commands of Ammon being given curtly and always verbally."[113] In Pittsburgh, strikers and city officials began enforcing order. In the aftermath, a Pennsylvania legislative committee trying to understand the violence observed, "It is in the power of the capitalist . . . [to provide] fair, frank, and just treatment of his employee, but also in looking after their social and educational interests."[114]

The Point of Origin

The Railroad Strike has dominated discussions of 1877, but to towns like Ohio's Bellaire and Doylestown and Massachusetts's Natick and Neponset, local strikes were as important as what had occurred in Pittsburgh. If railroad riots lit the fuse smoldering under the wreckage left by the Panic of 1873, the number of strikes demonstrated the breadth of that anger. In 1877 the Bureau of Labor Statistics recorded thirty-seven strikes in cigar-making, glass-blowing, steel, and other industries.[115] David Stowell notes many involved local grievances.[116] Hearing of them, Karl Marx wrote Friedrich Engels: "This first explosion against the associated oligarchy of capital which has occurred since the Civil War will naturally again be suppressed, but can very well form the point of origin of an earnest workers' party."[117]

The strikes spilled blood in more cities and towns than any other American civil conflict and involved workers in over a dozen states. Casualties totaled at least 100 dead, most of them victims of indiscriminate gunfire by troops. The headline "Slaughter" in the *National Republican* covered dispatches from Chicago, Toledo, Philadelphia, St. Louis, San Francisco, Syracuse, Albany, Detroit, Louisville, and cities such as Elmira and Poughkeepsie in New York, Mount Airy, Maryland, and Easton, Pennsylvania. The destruction is difficult to compute, but the Pennsylvania legislative committee listed Pittsburgh's losses at $5 million. According to union members, it could have been worse: strikers had amassed a large cache of arms but chose not to use it.

Several strikes illustrate the difficult position of working women. In Newark, New Jersey, women walked out when a shirt manufacturer hired men to work in the formerly all-female ironing unit. A reporter explained, "They considered ironing their special work, and thought if men were introduced into the factory they would soon take the place of female ironers."[118] Cincinnati cigar workers protested adding women because they took jobs from men.[119] On New York's 42nd Street, women weavers struck when the owner lowered their wages to $3 a week.

A little-noticed confrontation at a carpet company in Philadelphia's Kensington area symbolized women's situation. In the 1870s a carpet was essentially a rug and no place made more of them than Philadelphia. Like other skilled trades, carpet makers faced the machine process. As handlooms became extinct, machines allowed women to do what had been men's work for lower wages. By the late 1870s, 45 percent of Philadelphia carpet weavers were women, whose frequent strikes symbolized a grim reality: people came cheap; machines did not. A Murkland weaving machine cost $1,000; the average annual wage of carpet weavers was $335.53.[120]

Grace Palladino emphasizes that after 1877, industrialists commanded the coercive power of the state "to protect their particular economic interests and to disrupt and discredit organized labor."[121] The Molly Maguire executions in 1877 raised questions about whether the country's institutions could handle the problems brought by the machine process. "It seemed as if the whole social and political structure was on the very brink of ruin," wrote one account.[122]

For the Discontented, the strikes were a learning experience. They had to be. The decade's most revealing statistic came when its first year marked the first time most Americans worked for wages. They might find themselves with a boss who could be some sawed-off punk with a Napoleon complex bent on making work a living hell, illustrated by the many complaints about supervisors triggering wildcat strikes. Workers also were whipsawed by corporate consolidations like Gowen's cartel.

If the unrest has a pattern, it is that multiple 1877 strikes involved skilled trades that had been eclipsed by the machine process. They were devastated by the ego-draining change from working with their hands in ways that required practiced, subtle movements, to turning a screw or pulling a lever over and over. It is little wonder workers often referred to themselves as slaves. An Ohio report a year after the strikes offered this assessment:

> They struck as strong men in agony, they struck against conditions that they were not considered worthy of being consulted upon, they struck against a contract to which they were no party. The [railroad] strike was costly to both parties, as well as to the State, but if its result is to be that railroad employés will be looked upon and treated in the future as men by railroad managers then the loss of all parties in July 1877 will prove their gain for many years to come.[123]

John Siney shows how the Discontented were not an undisciplined rabble, but a populace woven together from connections made by people like him. In 1869 he served on the mining committee of the NLU convention in Philadelphia. At the 1870 Cincinnati meeting, delegates appointed him to the Committee on National Political Organization. He was elected temporary chairman of the National Labor Reform Convention in 1872. Three years later he presided as president at the Workingmen's Conference. Siney also worked with the Greenback Party, where he connected with leaders such as Joseph Osborn of the Wisconsin Grange and M. M. Hooten of the Illinois Farmer's Central Association.

While workers endured many dictatorial bosses, what made the mini-Mussolini of Schuylkill County so frightening was how Gowen's demagoguery destroyed the miners' political power. Historian Barbara Freese believes "it would be hard to find another single proceeding in American history where a single corporation, indeed a single man, had so blatantly taken over the powers of the sovereign."[124] Gowen defended his actions with the classic authoritarian ploy pointed out by Hannah Arendt and others: those against me are against the fatherland.

Despite problems, workers made considerable strides in the 1870s. The Pennsylvania mine safety law, with its restrictions on child labor, said that contrary to the nullification-like views of corporate executives, government had a right—and an obligation—to intervene in corporate affairs. The other legislative achievement of the WBA was the passage of a law granting workers the right to form unions. Upon those two rocks—government oversight and union representation—the Discontented built an impressive structure.

For some, the ensuing years were not kind. The name of Robert Ammon appears on the police blotter more than anywhere else. No doubt he was blacklisted, but his response was to float schemes like an Eldorado gold mine. Franklin Gowen and John Siney clashed again. On May 9, 1877, the Wadesville Mine faced its own Avondale when an explosion killed six men. After Siney convinced survivors to testify, a jury concluded the mine was being run "in violation of the law" and convicted an inspector of negligence and fined the mine Gowen owned.[125]

Three years after the Molly Maguire executions, Franklin Gowen sent the Reading into receivership. By 1886 J. P. Morgan had enough of Gowen's antics and bought the Reading during a second receivership. Three years later authorities found Gowen in a Washington, DC, hotel room with a bullet in his head. Although ruled a suicide, his death inspired conspiracy theories. A Morgan henchman offered an epitaph: "He is an able and brilliant man and, in some respects, a veritable Napoleon, but he is no railroad manager."[126]

By 1878 black lung disease was choking John Siney; the man who had devoted his life to fighting for miners had ingested too much coal dust. A reporter noted, "John Siney, who once had a salary of $1500 as president of the Workingmen's Benevolent (even though he could scarcely write his own name), is dependent upon charity for his daily bread." He was only forty-eight when he died in 1880. A mile-long procession followed his body to the St. Clair cemetery.[127] Frank Warne of the Bureau of Labor Statistics penned an epitaph: "It was mainly through his leadership that the anthracite mine worker enjoyed his high estate."[128] Kevin Kenny states that Siney and the WBA gained "recognition for labor as the fundamental constituent of industrial society."[129] The future tested that recognition.

CHAPTER SEVEN

FROM SOME LOFTY HEIGHT OF VISION

After next voting day,
When the sons of toil have sway,
They'll wipe the frauds away,
With more Greenbacks.
From "The National Greenback Rally,"
National Greenback Campaign Songs, 1878

Ignatius Donnelly was deemed "radioactive" decades before anyone knew what that euphemism meant. People worried this dangerously unstable bundle of contradictions might set off a chain reaction. Historian John Hicks calls him "erratic," "impractical," "a political nuisance," a man of "many idiosyncrasies," and, paradoxically, "a parliamentarian of extraordinary skill and a born politician."[1] Propelled by his ego, the power of his ideas, and the magnetism of his rhetoric, Donnelly held more leadership roles over a longer time than any other late nineteenth-century major political figure. Some whispered that he might have been president had he remained in one place long enough to cultivate and harvest the goodwill of a major party. As Hicks notes, he admitted, "I ran upon the platform of Ignatius Donnelly. I still regard it as a good, sound, substantial platform, but there isn't enough to make a party of." Between writing speeches and editorials for his newspaper, he wrote bestsellers that proved—at least to his satisfaction—that the lost city of Atlantis and the Flood were real and that Shakespeare never wrote his plays. Of all the causes that seduced Donnelly, none was more alluring than the quest for the political holy grail of a farmer-worker alliance. You can almost hear the sigh when historian Barton Shaw describes how Populists "dreamed of a union between the toilers of the country and city."[2]

Donnelly's radioactive character was appropriate for a leader of one of this country's most radioactive political parties. In the 1870s he and thousands of others who worried about the tilt of the playing field gathered in places like Toledo, Ohio, and Indianapolis, Indiana, where they briefly touched immortality. Their vehicle was variously known as the Independent Party, the National Party, the Greenback Party, and the Greenback-Labor Party. Over time the shorthand label of the Greenback Party has been applied to them all, which is unfortunate because it emphasizes monetary concerns and diminishes the party's broader economic and social aims. Garnering little more than a passing reference in histories of the 1870s, it fit under its tent both John Siney and the Molly Maguire prosecutors who opposed him. It replayed the feud about rural politics between the Grange national office and Oliver Kelley and Caroline Hall. Most of all it stirred up the racism and antisemitism lurking in the shadows.

The Great Problem

Without Abraham Lincoln's profile on its left side, the greenback resembles a piece of play money. The writing on the back, in bold capital letters, gives its purpose away: "This note is legal tender for all debts public and private except duties on imports and interest on the public debt and is receivable in payment of all loans made to the United States." Similar bills show Treasury Secretary Salmon P. Chase, Alexander Hamilton, George Washington, an eagle, and a sculpture of Lady Liberty. Some say "Receivable for United States Stamps," others read "This note is exchangeable for United States notes." Today one of these uncirculated greenbacks can bring over a thousand dollars, a value that may not be out of line in terms of their historical significance, because during and after the Civil War they determined the fate of presidents and congresses.

Greenbacks came to preoccupy the Discontented to the point that some complained they distracted from more important business, while others made them a litmus test of orthodoxy. Two agendas whipsawed the Greenbackers from one direction to another, depending on which faction had control. One focused on a narrow monetary program; the other on social and economic reforms where monetary issues were less a crusade than a flag of convenience. Those favoring currency concerns tended to be lawyers and businessmen, while those backing a reform agenda were Grangers and union members. Within those two groups some favored incremental change while others advocated radical action. Hanging in the balance was the nation's future.

The title "father of the Greenback movement" goes to former steel mill supervisor Alexander Campbell, who authored *The True American System of Finance* (1864) and *The True Greenback* (1868). He drew his ideas from New York merchant Edward Kellogg, whose currency reform proposals first reached the public through Horace Greely's *New York Tribune* newspaper and were published in book form in 1849 as *Labor and Other Capital.*

In an era when ads filling newspapers touted elixirs like "the elegant combination beef, wine and iron . . . for children and delicate ladies," Campbell sold a concoction that promised to conveniently resolve multiple social and economic ailments.[3] If he was a second-rate economist, he was a first-rate writer, as witnessed by a diagnosis that foreshadowed Henry George: "Look where you will upon society, you will see those who build palatial residences living in hovels, those who manufacture the finest cloths clothed in the coarsest fabrics, those who produce in abundance the most wholesome and delicate food subsisting on the poorest diet, and all to a great extent destitute of the ordinary comforts and conveniences of life."[4] Campbell's cure was disarmingly simple: business and financial institutions had commandeered the government's power of overseeing the nation's currency and it needed to be changed.

In the years following the Civil War, everyone from banks to municipalities printed money, but no one was under obligation to accept any of it. This glut of paper caused massive inflation and increased anxieties. Campbell stipulated only the federal government could issue "legal tender" that would be "interconvertible," meaning it could be exchanged for government bonds having an interest rate set by the government. Supply and demand would govern the bonds and greenbacks: if too many greenbacks, exchange them for bonds; if too few greenbacks, exchange bonds for them. Although far-fetched, it was a big idea around which to build a third-party that could challenge the hard money loyalties of the two major parties.

Three boosters of the greenback idea, one in Ohio and two in Indiana, sought to construct just such an alternative. One of them, James Buchanan, testified, "Leaders it has none; for the lack of proper guidance it has gone astray here and there; but it is from the people, and it will succeed in the end."[5] Both states were Grange strongholds, with Ohio reaching a peak of 1,246 local granges in 1876 and Indiana topping that the same year with 2,036. These militant granges were not afraid to risk conflicts with the national office, avowing, "We create the wealth, and the wealth builds the cities and is the incentive to all improvement; yet we hold it not, it is enjoyed by others who manipulate it to their own advancement."[6]

In Ohio, Sen. George Pendleton became one of the first of many ambitious politicians who grasped that the greenback idea might enhance the prospects of someone with a checkered history. Pendleton was a Copperhead, a northerner who openly sympathized with the South during the Civil War. When the war ended he became an outspoken foe of Reconstruction, especially of giving African Americans the vote.[7] Pendleton also had the White House bug. After an 1864 run as vice president for Gen. George McClellan's 1864 Democratic Party, he coveted a place at the top of the ticket. His version of Campbell's plan came to be called the "Ohio idea." While he succeeded in adding it to the 1868 Democratic platform, Pendleton lost the presidential nomination. A year later he lost a close race for Ohio governor. The Ohio idea exited, but the vision was very much alive.

It received a boost from two unexpected sources and one of history's supreme instances of bad timing. Two more Midwesterners, *Indiana Farmer* editor E. A. Olleman, and James Buchanan, a lawyer who also invented the pneumatic stacks for threshing machines, picked up the pieces of the Ohio idea. Both men held strong opinions salted with personal eccentricities. A former cabinetmaker, Olleman used his sharp pen to agitate for social and economic reform. Buchanan's ambitions were as outsized as his three-hundred-pound frame. He specialized in brash predictions, like the new party "will elect the next President."[8]

President Grant's signature on the Coinage Act of 1873 proved to be one of history's more shortsighted decisions because five months later came Black Friday, September 19. Never had our government so restricted currency so close to a major depression. As the panic raged, even the dimmest soul connected currency contraction and hard times. To people like those in Ottawa, Illinois, the solution seemed obvious: "In every point of view, give us the greenback."[9] With greenback supporters needing a Moses to lead them out of the wilderness, James Buchanan figured he was born to play the role. To convince skeptics, he chiseled the equivalent of a stone tablet by packaging Campbell's ideas into what became known as the Indiana Plan.

In June 1874 he and Olleman convened a meeting in Indianapolis to discuss a third party, attracting fifty delegates from Indiana, New York, New Jersey, Connecticut, Illinois, Michigan, and Kentucky. The gathering was notable because delegates with ties to the former National Labor Union had met with advocates of the Ohio Plan and a healthy contingent of grangers. Labor representatives included Richard Trevellick, Industrial Congress president Robert Schilling, and *Workingmen's Advocate* editor A. C. Cameron, whom William Sylvis had sent to the 1869 Congress of the International Working Men's Association in Switzerland. Also present was the father of the greenback idea, Alexander Campbell. The *Chicago Tribune* viewed it as largely a rural gathering, reporting that "the Farmers' Convention at Indianapolis yesterday was a failure in point of attendance, but, for the most part, a success in respect of declaration of principles."[10]

Those principles began with the preamble's reaffirmation of the principle of a level playing field: "We desire a proper equality, equity, and fairness; protection for the weak, restraint upon the strong; in short, justly distributed burdens, and justly distributed powers: these are American ideas, the very essence of American Independence."[11] In its eagerness to be accepted, the platform itself suggests a newcomer trying to avoid stepping on too many toes. It made sure to point out "we are not enemies of railroads" and that class legislation "is wrong and subversive." In criticizing the two major parties as "engines of oppression, crushing out the lives of the people," the platform was notable in going beyond currency reform to condemning "banking and monied monopolies," "consolidated railroads," "land, commercial and grain monopolies," as well as recommending cutting taxes and restricting "the abuses of the liquor traffic."

In March 1875 the efforts of Olleman and Buchanan came full bloom in Cleveland, Ohio, at a meeting the *Chicago Tribune* termed "the National Convention of Workingmen and Grangers."[12] The workingmen included a star-studded list: Richard Trevellick, A. C. Cameron, and Robert Schilling, along with current Industrial Congress president J. H. Wright and John Siney of St. Clair, Pennsylvania. Farm activists included Michigan scientific farming advocate Lysander Woodward, Illinois Granger Law proponent M. M. Hooten, and *Carthage Press* editor and Missouri farmer A. W. St. John. Pennsylvania congressman William "Pig Iron" Kelley spoke to an August 1875 meeting.[13]

In early March, Cleveland, Ohio, can be an uncertain place when the wind blowing off the lake might carry stinging sleet or bring a mild day when the gulls screech of a false spring. With an election year looming, there was talk that the new party could hold the balance of power. Gathered beneath a banner proclaiming "The Republic of Washington and Jefferson—Down with Monopoly," delegates crafted a more resolute platform than the one from the year before, probably due to additional representation and better planning.[14] A phrase in the document's preamble signaled the change, declaring "a legal representation of their right to control the products of their hands."[15] The resolutions that followed, while similar to those of the previous year, were pruned and refined. Gone was the reference to the "liquor traffic" and the cloying "we are not enemies of railroads." Remaining were the people's right to public lands and corporations' subservience to the "rights of the people." The convention also added calls for government improvement of rivers and harbors and equalizing bounties paid to soldiers.

The Time Has Come

In 1876 the country crackled with the promise of political realignment. The farmer-worker intersection of the Greenbackers was becoming the place to be if you wanted to reinvent a country in danger of losing sight of its fundamental principles. Writing in his *Anti-Monopolist* under the headline "The Wonderful Growth of the Independent Party," Ignatius Donnelly heralded "a revolution."[16] He went on to proclaim, "This is purely a people's movement. The politicians stand amazed at the popular enthusiasm and cannot account for it."

When Greenbackers convened in Indianapolis on May 17, the conversational topic they could not avoid was the race riot that had occurred just two weeks before. The spark that touched off what has become known as the Election Day Riot is unknown, but the reason for it is not: white citizens sought to intimidate African Americans from voting. On election day African Americans had gathered in numbers at the polls, determined to protect their franchise. In the words of the *Chicago Tribune*, a "state of volcanic quietude" prevailed, "not to be trifled with."[17] A mob the *Tribune* referred to as "unshaven, unkempt Irishmen" sought to prevent them from voting. Police intervened on the side of the Irish, who were shouting, "Damn the ——, shoot the ——! What right have they to vote?" An officer even handed his revolver to a rabble-rouser. After attacking those waiting to vote, the mob careened through the city. At this point the thrust of the riot was no longer about voting; it was pure, unadulterated hatred. The brutality was as perverse as it was savage: the mob disemboweled one victim with a Bowie knife and slashed another in the groin with a razor. According to the *Tribune*, the carnage left one dead, two near death, and at least five wounded.

The convention began with Ignatius Donnelly's stem-winding welcome speech. He did his best to set off a chain reaction, reminding them the current House of Representatives contained 1 mechanic, 14 farmers, and 185 shareholders of national banks. He explained: "Just so surely, my friends, as the English aristocracy have diverted all the powers of government to strengthen their class and oppress and impoverish the many, just so certainly must like causes produce like results in this great land of ours."[18] The strongest applause came when he proclaimed, "This is a people's country and we need a people's party." The name "People's Party" was picked up over a decade later.

The 1875 convention had seemed to signal the Greenbackers were moving toward an agenda of social reform, but in 1876 the currency faction seized control and eliminated the previous reform agenda. After much debate and what one observer termed "great confusion," delegates selected New York industrialist Peter

Cooper as the US president nominee and California senator Newton K. Booth as his running mate.[19] A wealthy eighty-five-year-old New York City industrialist, Cooper was a compromise choice who had made his fortune manufacturing iron rails and his fame for the 1830 design of the Tom Thumb, America's first locomotive. Cooper sported one of history's strangest beards: a white wreath stretching horizontally from his chin like the collar of a medieval burger. Cooper merited the honor of being selected because of his longtime support for workers, including the 1859 founding of the Cooper Union, which included Richard Trevellick among its alums. At first Cooper declined, but party officials convinced him to change his mind, replacing Booth with Ohio congressman Samuel Cary, who was known for his support of temperance and as the author of one of the first Congressional greenback bills.

The convention also created local greenback clubs to provide grassroots connections. Historian Matthew Hild reports that Texas alone had seven hundred of them by 1878.[20] Unfortunately, the Greenback Party's chosen coordinator of the clubs was the ambitious and controversial editor Marcus "Brick" Pomeroy, an appropriate nickname for a man whose nasty editorials were like bricks thrown through a window (although the accepted story is that it referred to the late nineteenth-century term for a wise guy). Buffalo Bill Cody became wealthy by doing in excess what anyone else able to pull a trigger could accomplish—kill buffalo; while Brick Pomeroy made money by doing in excess what any soused barfly could do—insult people.

Before the "yellow" journalism of Joseph Pulitzer and William Randolph Hearst, Pomeroy used insults to sell newspapers. The problem with excess is that it fades, so Pomeroy kept inventing more despicable things to say about Abraham Lincoln, until in 1864 he wrote, "If he is elected for another four years, we trust some bold hand will pierce his heart with dagger point for the public good."[21] After Booth pulled the trigger, Pomeroy barely escaped a lynching.

Pomeroy's rise to dominate a key element of the new party marks a troubling trend that plagued it and other reform movements. Delegates to the 1876 Greenback Convention were certainly well aware of his views, especially because he delighted in irritating people with them. During the Civil War he proclaimed, "We will not be forced into a fight to free the Negroes."[22] "White Men Must Rule," announced an ad for Pomeroy's smoking tobacco.[23]

Brick Pomeroy's ascension is a prime example of the unholy alliance between racism and business that John Harlan would later point out in his *Civil Rights Cases* decision. The same Copperhead-business alliance that scuttled the reforms of the 1875 platform and nominated businessman Peter Cooper selected

Pomeroy to head the Greenback clubs. One should not forget that reformers like Donnelly acquiesced to Pomeroy's selection. In many ways the 1876 Greenback Party reflected Donnelly's stance: someone who espoused equality but whose perspective always came with a qualifier. He wrote, "To the white race I would preach mercy and charity. . . . To the black race I would preach patience and wisdom."[24]

The racist, anti-reform turn of the Greenbackers in 1876 would reverberate nationally and through history with the November election. The contest between Republican Rutherford B. Hayes and Democrat Samuel Tilden ended with Tilden winning the popular vote and the electoral college in turmoil, leaving a bipartisan electoral commission to sort out the mess. The Greenbackers could have held the balance of power, but the total popular vote for Cooper was disappointing, in part because the party had abandoned the 1875 platform. Indirectly, the Greenbackers influenced the outcome. Five held the balance of power in the Illinois legislature, where they provided the deciding votes to elect Supreme Court justice David Davis to the Senate. This prevented Tilden supporter Davis from becoming chair of the commission tasked with finding a solution to the deadlock.

The 1876 results suggest many Greenbackers sat out the election or voted for one of the major parties. The criticism noted in the *Grange Advance* suggests the depth of the anger, as it asked, "Is it not those unprincipled shysters who assumed control of the reform movement for the purpose of advancing their own political fortunes? Who have sold the party out on every occasion when an opportunity offered, and who will hereafter claim their reward from the democratic or republican [*sic*] organizations?"[25]

Two years later, when the Greenbackers again met in Toledo, Ohio, the party's two factions squared off again. Toledo in February 1878 might be best described as an almost city at an almost time of the year. Tucked in the northwest corner of Ohio, its citizens dreamed of equaling the industrial might of nearby Cleveland and Detroit. As a city with one foot in the consumer culture of an industrial future and the other in the staples society of an agrarian past, Toledo seemed an appropriate choice to host the national convention of a political party that sought to reconcile factory and farm.

By 1878 Brick Pomeroy had become a major problem because it seemed he could not resist throwing gasoline on the fire of racial and partisan conflict. At the center of the controversy were packets he sent to the local Greenback clubs bearing names like "Hot Drops, No. 1," "Hot Drops, No. 2," and so forth, and spiced with words like "cowardly, sneaking, dishonest, treacherous, false-hearted, avaricious, mercenary."[26] Pomeroy, who had never fought in the Civil War, urged members to master the manual of arms, turning the clubs into paramilitary forces, with each club having "a drill master." When that idea left people uneasy, in typical Pomeroy fashion he escalated: "We, the people, propose to have our rights peaceably, and by means of the ballot, if possible, by the bayonet, if we must." Leave it to Pomeroy to issue the ultimate threat: "If this government of ours will not protect us, the TAX PAYING PEOPLE, then we owe it no allegiance ... we had better unite the west and the south, secede from a Union that benefits only eastern bond holders."

Republicans quickly took advantage of the situation. Under the guise of the Honest Money League, Republican sympathizers circulated a slim treatise titled *Communistic, Inflammatory & Treasonable Documents Circulated by the National Greenback Party*, consisting largely of Hot Drops excerpts. Reporters followed the Hot Drops back to Pomeroy's Copperhead history. The *Emporia News* reminded readers, "Pomeroy sympathized with the rebels and made no secret of his Copperheadism."[27] By 1880 papers equated Pomeroy's control of the clubs with the Greenback Party, charging, "The Greenbackers, in fact, are nothing more than disguised Copperheads."[28]

Certainly the connections were there. We know the anti-draft militancy of some workers, such as the Schuylkill County coal miners', put them in the Copperhead camp. The Pennsylvania Democratic Party also had a copper tinge. In the Midwest the prime Greenback states of Ohio, Indiana, and Illinois were also former Copperhead hotbeds. During the Civil War, Judge Advocate General Joseph Holt claimed the strength of third-column movements was centered in those states, with a force in Indiana "from 75,000 to 125,000; in Illinois, from 100,000 to 140,000; in Ohio, from 86,000 to 108,000."[29]

A second obstacle growing out of the events of 1877 compounded the problems presented by Brick Pomeroy. The presence of former Molly Maguire prosecutor Francis Hughes and his nephew and law partner, Francis Dewees (who authored an anti-Molly book), must have raised eyebrows.[30] The same year that Gov. John Hartranft delayed signing the death warrant for John Kehoe until after the election, Hughes, who prosecuted alleged Mollies, ascended the steps of the rostrum in Toledo to preside over the convention. His 1877 summation in the trial of Patrick Hester, Patrick Tully, and Peter McHugh still hung over the coalfields: "It is better that five, ten, or five hundred Mollie Maguires should be suspended by ropes from the gallows, than that civilized society should disappear."[31]

Already weakened by black lung disease, John Siney summoned the strength to deliver a scathing address to the Toledo delegates, declaring, "There are but two parties in this country, the skinners and the skinned, the robbers and robbed."[32] He then took his seat with Francis Dewees among the Pennsylvania delegation. What they said to each other is not recorded, but the fact that two men on opposite sides of the coalfield wars sat together in the same delegation shows the appeal—and tensions—of the Greenback Party.

Francis Hughes epitomized the devil's bargain behind the 1876 election. He landed on the podium at the 1878 Greenback national convention in part because he possessed the same checkered history as former Copperheads Pendleton and Pomeroy. During the Civil War he was the chief spokesperson for the Pennsylvania Democratic Party. After the war he served as chairman of the committee on resolutions at the 1875 state convention, where he set off a near riot by proposing a resolution favoring greenbacks. This prompted the *New York Herald* to refer to Hughes and fellow Pennsylvania Democrats as "the old Bourbon Copperhead politicians, the tramps, and vagabonds who nourished during the war."[33]

A year later Hughes had switched parties, becoming the Pennsylvania spokesman for the Greenbackers, no doubt due to his state convention resolution. His party shift may have resulted from the political realignment of Schuylkill County in which the Ancient Order of Hibernians played a role, since 1875 was the year Governor Hartranft supposedly cut a deal with John Kehoe to deliver the Irish vote. Hughes's role as a prosecutor in the Molly Maguire trials is more problematic when placed in the context of Schuylkill County politics where, according to Dewees, "in every election they [the Mollies] have exercised a corrupting influence."[34] Although Hughes was among the national Greenback convention delegates endorsing the ticket of Peter Cooper and Samuel Cary in 1876, late in the campaign he switched support to Samuel Tilden and Indiana governor Thomas Hendricks, a former Copperhead who had opposed the Thirteenth, Fourteenth, and Fifteenth Amendments. Two years later Hughes was holding the gavel in Toledo and twenty miners were dead at the hands of Pennsylvania executioners.

The other delegate with connections to the Mollies was Richard Trevellick, who, along with William Sylvis, had attempted to organize the National Labor Union in anthracite country. In that capacity Trevellick certainly became aware of the leadership of John Siney, Patrick Hester, and John Kehoe, although it is unclear if he met them. Three days before he died on the gallows, Hester told a reporter, "Politics are at the bottom of it. That was the starting of it."[35]

The Most Effective and Available Means

Despite the obstacles, the Toledo delegates repudiated the narrow focus of 1876. Although Hughes held the gavel, the dream of a farmer-worker alliance was once more alive and reached its Greenback apogee in the Toledo platform, in the national platform of 1880, and in the New York and Connecticut state platforms of 1878. The two state platforms are interesting because they appeared after the national convention. What swung the pendulum back from the focus of 1876 was the reinvolvement of labor. John French notes that in Pennsylvania's Allegheny County, which encompassed the Pittsburgh steel mills and was still reeling in the aftermath of the 1877 strikes, the majority of the delegates to the Greenback Party county convention "were from the mines, mills, and workshops."[36]

Through the 1878 and 1880 Greenback national conventions, along with the two state conventions, a series of core resolutions were remarkably similar, forming a systemic response to the machine process and other aspects of industrialization. Currency reform remained, but the game had changed since 1876. A push by the increasing power of western silver mining interests and cries about the "crime of 1873" resulted in the passage of the Bland-Allison Act of 1878. It required the US Treasury to purchase silver each month and put silver coins back in circulation.

The Greenback Party's response was to reaffirm its commitment to currency reform. Resolution No. 4 in the 1878 platform represents the preeminent statement of that objective; it required Congress to provide enough currency to enable "the full employment of labor, the equitable distribution of its products, and the requirements of business" and continue "regulating its volume . . . so that the rate of interest will secure to labor its just reward."[37] The other Greenback platforms used slightly different language and added unique provisions, like placing silver coinage on the same basis as gold. How authors of the resolution expected the government to print enough money to provide "full employment" and "secure labor its just reward" is a brew of economic alchemy. Notably missing from the laundry list of ailments this elixir could cure are farm-related items, suggesting the text came from labor leaders.

Rural Americans exercised their muscle in the resolutions covering western lands. The idea of homesteading as a safety valve may be controversial for historians and economists, but farmers felt it was critically needed. The 1878 Connecticut Greenback platform offered the most eloquent statement of that support: "The public lands, belonging to all the people, should sacredly be held in trust for the homes of American citizens."[38] This resolution also strikes at the policy of providing the railroads with free land, which they sold to settlers.

Added to the emphasis on public lands and currency reform was concern over business concentration. A year after the 1877 Railroad Strike, Greenbackers focused on the sins of the railroads, which by 1880 had expanded to include condemnation of "gigantic land, railroad, and money corporations."[39] The 1878 national platform calling for state railroad commissions by 1880 had changed to a proposal to bring "all lines of communication and transportation" "under legislative control." This was not an idle comment, when words like "socialist" were applied like anathemas to suggestions of government intervention.

Voting rights and education represented a third concern. In 1880 delegates endorsed a suffrage resolution presented by Susan B. Anthony, but watered it down to a mere condemnation of efforts made "to restrict the right of suffrage."[40] The 1878 Connecticut platform included the most comprehensive resolution supporting education with its demand in Article 9 for "a thorough reform in the system of public school education, so as to establish agricultural and mechanical schools in addition to our Common Schools."[41] As an article in the *New York Herald* pointed out, Article 9 also was concerned about textbooks, presaging a fight that raged in the 1890s: "All books should be procured at the expense of the State government, and that not less than one lecture per week be delivered upon the dignity of labor and its paramount importance in the affairs of men in every walk of life."

Notable among other resolutions passed by Greenback conventions were recommendations for a national bureau of labor statistics, an income tax, and abolishment of the convict labor system. William Sylvis observed in 1865, "The science of statistics is to political economy what steam is to the steam engine."[42] Sylvis's idea of a bureau of labor statistics appears most notably in the 1878 platform, when delegates proposed "obtaining reliable statistics … on labor questions" such as the "hours of labor and causes which throw workmen out of employment."[43] This recognizes the growing belief that maintaining a level playing field required valid information, not anecdotes, skewed self-reports, and rumors. Initiatives like the Grange lecturers and scientific farming, along with the WBA's and the NLU's signing sliding-scale contracts and demanding information about wages and prices, helped to spur this change.

Of all the resolutions, Resolution No. 3 from 1880 remains the most complete and succinct statement of workers' rights by a political party in the late nineteenth century: "That labor should be so protected by National and State authority as to equalize its burdens and insure a just distribution of its results."[44]

The specifics may be unclear and open-ended (such as defining "just distribution"), but the principle was firm: government was the only institution that could ensure a level playing field.

What is especially significant about the 1878–80 Greenback Party resolutions is that we can follow their footprints in platforms and resolutions dating back to the Baltimore labor congress of 1866. Among the footprints were those of Centralia, Illinois, strawberry farmer and Granger M. M. Hooten, who had served as a Union Army surgeon at Kennesaw Mountain, where a quarter of his regiment was killed, captured, or wounded in less than thirty minutes. An advocate of scientific farming who backed the Granger Laws, in 1871 Hooten shipped 557 crates of strawberries, netting $3,820. Another footprint was that of cowboy-hatted cattle raiser Solon Chase of Maine, who attended the 1876, 1878, and 1880 conventions. Known as the "farmers' friend," his phrase "them steers" became a campaign slogan after he explained how two cows he bought for $100 fetched only $90 two years later.[45]

Hooton and Chase are two examples of those who attended Greenback conventions. Analyses of delegate lists from 1875–80 show over half (51 percent) came from the Midwest, no doubt influenced by the fact that most of the major Greenback Party conventions took place in that region. In contrast to the major parties that funded delegates attending national conventions, some Greenback delegates paid their own way. The percentage of midwestern delegates ranged from a high of 76 percent in 1875 to a low of 37 percent in 1880. The second-place East had 22 percent, with 13 percent coming from the South and 7 percent each from the West and border states. The number of midwesterners essentially made the Greenback Party a regional party with national aspirations. Members hailing from New York, Pennsylvania, and New Jersey outnumbered southerners, the latter of whom were evolving into a single-party system dedicated to segregation.

Ignatius Donnelly's 1878 preamble captures the tone of the platforms agreed upon by delegates like Chase and Hooten. Note the inclusion of the subject of starvation: "The value of real estate is depreciated, industry paralyzed, trade depressed, business incomes and wages reduced, unparalleled distress inflicted upon the poorer and middle ranks of our people, the land filled with fraud, embezzlement, bankruptcy, crime, suffering, pauperism, and starvation. . . . This state of things has been brought about by legislation in the interest of and dictated by money-lenders, bankers, and bondholders."[46] The flurry of verbs in the first two lines—"depreciated, paralyzed, depressed"—assaults us today as it must have assaulted listeners of the time. In line 4 Donnelly shifts from verbs to nouns such as "fraud, embezzlement, bankruptcy" to provide a sobering list of the impact of the crisis. What is remarkable is how Donnelly's words echo the words found in the 1866 labor congress preamble, which read, "The growing and alarming encroachments of capital upon the rights of the industrial classes of the United States has rendered it imperative they should calmly and deliberately devise the most effective and available means by which the same may be averted."[47]

These two preambles written for different audiences and in different circumstances share an extraordinary similarity. In 1866 it was "growing and alarming encroachments . . . upon the rights of the industrial classes." By 1878 that diagnosis had become a list of ailments: "Real estate is depreciated, industry paralyzed, trade depressed, business incomes and wages reduced." The 1866 preamble blames "capital"; the 1878 platform is more specific: "legislation in the interest of and dictated by money-lenders, bankers, and bondholders." The parallels suggest that despite the twelve-year gap, grievances remained remarkably unchanged. There is one difference, though. Donnelly uses the word "money lenders," a term that in the late nineteenth century reverberated with anti-Semitic undertones.

The Greenback Party's 1878 and 1880 platforms produced its electoral high-water mark. In 1878 nine states elected fourteen Greenback congressional representatives. The party endorsed eight Knights of Labor members, including Knights founder Uriah Stephens and future head Terence Powderly. Powderly was elected mayor of Scranton; Stephens lost his race for Congress. With Solon Chase traveling with two live versions of "them steers," the Maine Greenbackers piled up almost a third of the vote, sending 32 members to the upper house and 151 members to the lower house. In Texas the Greenback vote reached almost 25 percent, followed by Iowa with 22 percent, Kansas with 19 percent, and Illinois with 15 percent.[48] Had this occurred two years earlier, we might be a different country.

If reports from the *Red Cloud Chief* are any indication, the Greenbackers were strong in 1878, then declined rapidly. An 1878 notice of a mass meeting of the Red Cloud Greenback Club connects the Nebraska city to Brick Pomeroy, a man it had lauded in 1876, when a biography in the paper concluded, "He has a charming family, and is doubtless the hardest working and best-abused man in the United States."[49] In 1879 the paper commented on the founding of a new Greenback paper, *The Portfolio*, in Omaha: "Like all other ventures of its kind, it is started to supply 'a long felt want.'" By June of that year it was observing, "The conviction is growing that the Greenback repudiation craze is dying out."[50] A year later, on the eve of the 1880 election, it noted, "The Greenback meeting held at the court house in this burg last Friday night was rather slimly attended."[51]

One reason for the decline may be a feisty message published by local Republicans urging people not to throw away their votes: "Every Republican who bolts the straight ticket and supports an independent candidate or votes a mixed ticket, virtually casts a ballot for the disorganization of the Republican party."[52]

In Pennsylvania, Terence Powderly, Uriah Stephens, and John Siney played roles in the 1878 state convention, with Siney serving on the committee on permanent organization along with a mine owner who testified against Franklin Gowen in 1871, J. A. Cake. The absence of the coalfield Irish, whose political activities figured in the Molly Maguire trials, testified to Gowen's success in purging people like John Kehoe, whom Francis Dewees described as a "fiend" with an "appalling and inconceivable" disregard for human life.[53] Voting data compiled by Paul Kleppner shows that in Pennsylvania the strongest support for the Greenback Party came from Schuylkill County.[54] Ralph Ricker writes, "The ineffectiveness of the campaign and of the election results caused many Greenback-Labor supporters to start dropping out of the movement after the election."[55] Terence Powderly was one of them. Craig Phelan believes those who had little empathy for industrial workers assumed more control of the party.[56]

In 1880 Greenback presidential candidate James B. Weaver received three times as many votes as Peter Cooper had in 1876, but many expected better. Weaver, not William Jennings Bryan nor Harry Truman, ran the first whistle-stop campaign, eventually traveling 20,000 miles.[57] He was an authentic Civil War hero who had risen from private to general while serving in several of the war's bloodiest battles. He later served as a Greenbacker congressman until 1889, then as the 1892 Populist presidential candidate. If he had run in 1876, he certainly would have out-campaigned Cooper.

Weaver's ideals are expressed in his acceptance letter, acknowledging the Greenback Party had succeeded in realizing the dream of a worker-farmer alliance that had captured the imaginations of Ignatius Donnelly, William Sylvis, and others. He congratulated delegates for "the great work accomplished, in the unification of the various Greenback and Labor elements, into one compact organization."[58] Then he attacked the two major parties: "With fifty million people looking them in the face and pleading for relief, they utter not one word of promise or hope. Their leaders and platform makers are in the toils of the syndicate, gigantic bank corporations, and railroad monopolies, and have neither the disposition nor the courage to strike one generous blow for industrial emancipation." Taking a cue from the platform's denouncing "every attempt to stir up sectional strife," Weaver reassured southerners: "One of the grand missions of our party is to banish forever from American politics that deplorable spirit of sectional hatred." This echoed Resolution No. 12 from the 1866 labor congress that called for "speedy restoration of the agricultural interests of the Southern States."[59]

Weaver never abandoned these beliefs, although they were sorely tested. A congressional speech he delivered in 1886 called for an "adequate, permanent financial system," using a pointed analogy when he attacked the banks: "The rebellion was overthrown, but this conspiracy never has been; and it will require all the power of the country, now happily reunited, to uproot it."[60] Campaigning as the 1892 Populist presidential candidate, the former Union general's hope for sectional reconciliation received a rude reception from southerners, who pelted him and Mary Lease with vegetables and other indignities. At his 1912 funeral, a minister summed up his life: "From some lofty height of vision or inspiration he came down to plead for the men who toiled, the true homemakers of America. The causes he advocated were in the interest of that class which has no great lobbyists, no strong organizations, no skillful friends at court."[61]

The intersection that began in the person of William Sylvis and grew into the Greenback Party is now overgrown with weeds. Few histories cite Ellis Usher, who wrote in the party's first history, "The first organized and pointed criticisms of corporations and the earliest demand for their control by the Government, came from the Greenbackers."[62] One could compile an impressive list of Greenbackers who played major roles in the future People's Party, including Weaver and the man many believed should have become the 1892 Populist presidential nominee, Leonidas Polk. The Knights of Labor contributed leaders such as Terence Powderly and Robert Schilling (who was also prominent in the People's Party). The Grange and Farmers' Alliance had multiple Greenback connections. John McLuckie, who served as Homestead's mayor during the lockout, cut his political teeth as a Greenback Party candidate, as did Daniel McLaughlin, a United Mineworkers leader and mentor to future UMW president John Mitchell. Clarence Darrow's father was a Greenbacker, as was Florence Kelley's. No other intersection at the time brought together leaders from such varied backgrounds to collaborate in improving their country.

Collaboration is not an abstraction; it is a living thing that changes with circumstances. We too easily forget the real value of the Greenback Party was as a catalyst that taught people how to work together. Accounts show it was not an easy thing to do. Uniting farmers and workers meant dealing with sometimes conflicting needs. More difficult to overcome were the lingering animosities of the Civil War that made the party a haven for former Copperheads like Brick Pomeroy, who brought along their toxic racism.

The Greenback Party was the perfect home for people like Ignatius Donnelly. His combination of ambition, ego, opportunism, and political skill emulated the likes of George Pendleton and Brick Pomeroy. As former Copperheads Pendleton and Pomeroy had nowhere else to go that could offer them a chance at higher office. A great example is Francis Hughes's experience with a Pennsylvania Democratic Party that found his views too radical.

What separates Donnelly and others in the Greenback reform faction from the Pomeroys and the Pendletons was their views on race. The putrid stench emanating from the diatribes of so many former Copperheads arose out of their unequivocal hate for people of color. Hatred is a potent, irrational drug that erases empathy and warps natural curiosity. Rational people do not openly call for assassinating presidents.

Where Copperhead influence becomes most intriguing is in the internal struggle in the Greenback Party between the monetarists and the reformers. The Copperheads formed a large part of the faction that sought to steer the party away from the social and economic agendas of people like John Siney, Richard Trevellick, and Ignatius Donnelly. Brick Pomeroy hated African Americans; Donnelly hated monopolists. For every Pomeroy there were dozens of Americans who did not want to be told they had to sell goods to African Americans or rent them apartments or hotel rooms or, like those in the Indianapolis riots, allow them to vote. This was the fear Joseph Bradley related in his *Civil Rights Cases* decision, when he said government could not enforce rules for "the conduct of individuals in society towards each other."[63] This fear lurked behind the Hayes-Tilden resolution supported by Tom Scott. It is hard to believe it was not behind the monetarists' attempts to curb the scope of Greenback social reforms.

Both the eccentric Donnelly and the Greenback Party did have a center: a commitment to a level playing field. They both may have wavered on this, particularly over the rights of women and people of color, but the principle was there. Donnelly's preamble attests to that.

As control of the Greenback Party lurched from one faction to another, the country lurched along with it, still unsure about industrialization, the heritage of the Civil War, the rights of newly freed enslaved, and the growing impatience of women. In the next decade the nation continued to lurch, but this time it had the map sketched by the Greenback Party, the Grange, the NLU, and the WBA, along with the history of how that map was made.

THE 1880s

CHAPTER EIGHT

In All Things Essential

Oh come ye jolly farmers,
And join our legal band,
That ye may share the profit,
Of the labor of your hand.
—*From "Spread the News,"*
music and lyrics by Mrs. J. T. Kellie, ca. 1890

It is said there are two kinds of preachers: dreamers and damners. Central Texas raised both, including one of America's supreme dreamers. Young C. W. Macune sat on Abraham Lincoln's knee, but the path from Lincoln's knee to leadership was rough. He was thirteen months old when his father died traveling to the California goldfields. Forced into the world at an early age, Macune wandered in the wilderness as a farmhand, a pharmacist, a circus roustabout, a cowboy, a painter, a hotel manager, an editor, a lawyer, and a minister.

In 1881 he finally settled down with his wife and family as a physician in Cameron, Texas, where he built a practice among immigrant Czech and German farmers whose languages he spoke. There he found his calling, not in the pulpit but in politics. He rose rapidly after county Democrats elected him party secretary in 1885. Annie Diggs described what made him a formidable leader: "To watch him in debate, and notice his straight-from-the-shoulder blows, his tenacity, and his coming up fresh after every round, is to lead one to exclaim, 'Here is an intellectual pugilist who will quit the field a victor.'"[1] Diggs omits that in 1874 Macune started a newspaper, pledging that Texas was a "white man's state," a crucial fact in understanding why he was so controversial.[2]

Macune walked out of the wilderness at a critical time. He found his calling when ideas flowed across the land like rivulets after an intense thunderstorm, nurturing groups like the Farmers' Union, the Agricultural Wheel, and the Brothers of Freedom that all arose as Grange membership declined. While these groups were short-lived, they served as the crucial transition between the Grange and the next national rural organization.

Farm movements are as much a part of the American landscape as wind and rain, and like them, result from atmospheric disturbances. During the 1880s it did not take a farmer's nose for the weather to detect something unsettling about the climate. In 1881 farmers received $1.20 per bushel of wheat; in 1884 they earned 65¢. Cotton prices plummeted more than 20 percent from their 1881 late nineteenth-century high.[3] It was as if a mysterious disease had withered their crops. In 1918 Elizabeth Barr remembered, "Farmers sold their corn, which . . . cost 21c per bushel to produce, for ten to fifteen cents per bushel. The grain speculator received forty-five to sixty cents per bushel for the same corn, and before it reached the laboring man who must buy it for food, the price was considerably higher."[4] Then came bad weather. From 1887 to 1897 some counties experienced only two years with enough rain for a full crop.[5] A Nebraskan wrote, "One could drive whole days across beautiful, level land, every acre of it a claim of some kind or other, and find nothing but crumbling sod walls and untilled fields."[6] By 1889 manufacturing had succeeded farming as the largest generator of national income.[7]

Historians tend to agree with Robert McGuire's contention, "The uncertainty in late-nineteenth-century agriculture stemmed from the fact that yields, prices, and incomes were influenced by numerous factors in an unpredictable or random manner from one year to the next."[8] Douglass North, Robert Higgs, and Anne Mayhew identify some of those factors, including production (Higgs), commercialization (Mayhew), and the impact of world markets (North).[9] Comparing graphs that depict wheat prices and GDP helps us understand the farmers' plight (see figs. 8.1 and 8.2). Wheat, by the way, is the crop McGuire most associated with a high degree of farm unrest.

The GDP graph demonstrates the reality gap for farmers who experienced leaps in technology and saw town-dwellers living in nice houses and wearing the latest fashions. Together the graphs also illustrate the paradox of record production and social misery identified by Robert Fogel, Henry George, and others. Note how the steep drop in wheat prices parallels the rise of farm unrest: the dramatic decrease with the Panic of 1873 coincides with the rise of the Grange; a similar decline in the late 1870s corresponds with the ascendency of the Greenback Party.

A Kansas study showed striking differences in wheat crop profits earned by various farms.[10] In Harvey County a farmer planted 34 acres of wheat for a

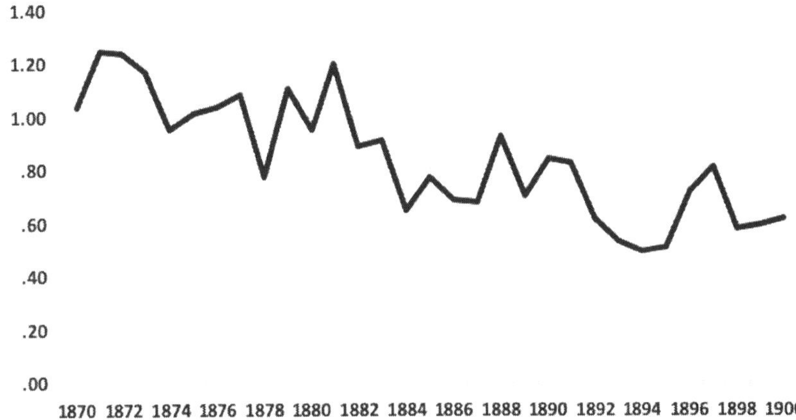

Figure 8.1 Wheat Price per Bushel

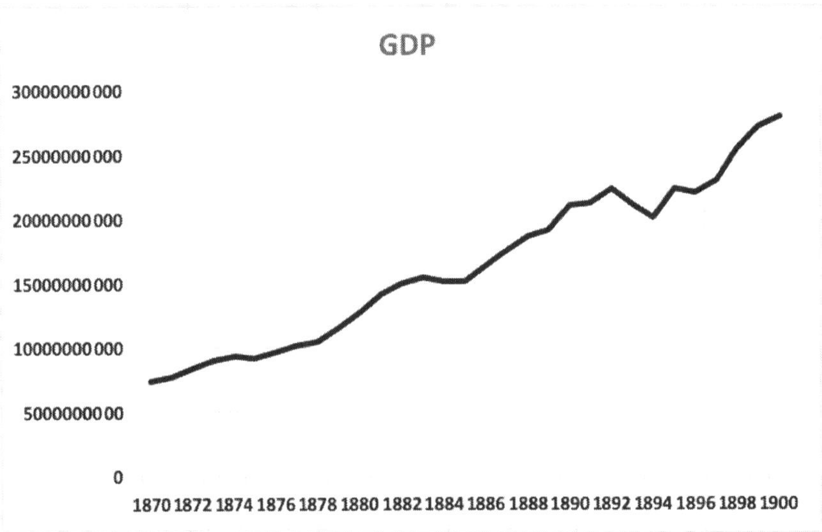

Figure 8.2 GDP 1870–1900

profit of $833.45; another planted 40 acres but received only $385.00. The lowest profit was earned by a farmer who made only $22.20 on 12 acres; the highest was $11,138.92 on a mammoth 1,065-acre farm. Without further information we do not know what influenced these differences. The author contrasted two farms: "One man had fifteen bushels of wheat per acre while his neighbor with the same kind of land had less than two bushels," but the one with a higher yield used a disc harrow and the other did not. The sobering aspect of this study is that the median acres planted among 163 farms was 34.5, with a median profit of only $282.47. Even added to the food they raised for themselves, this amount put them near poverty level.

Instead of blaming the weather, farmers believed their plight had more to do with Wall Street than the clouds. In his wanderings, Walter Wycoff met an Iowan who condemned "an incalculable power which took on vague form in his mind as a conspiracy of the rich, who seemed to him not to work and yet to have unmeasured wealth, while he and his kind could hardly live at the cost of almost unceasing toil."[11] The *Red Cloud Chief* warned: "American railway monarchs wield greater power and exercise more power arbitrarily than any King or Emperor in all Europe. If this power goes unchecked another decade the great body of American people will be reduced to abject vassalage and their government instead of being for the people, by the people, will be for the monopolies by the corporation kings."[12]

No one expected what arose in Lampasas County, Texas, though. In this region of towns named Bee Cove, Ding Dong, and Nix, they formed the Farmers' Alliance in 1877, paying their debt to the Grange by adopting its motto word for word: "In all things essential, Unity, and in all things Charity." Historian Solon Buck claimed the Alliance "sprang from the soil, as it were, and, like Topsy, 'just growed' instead of being deliberately planned and put into operation by a group of founders."[13] Buck's words echo James Buchanan's explanation for the genesis of the Greenback Party, affirming the bottom-up nature of the Discontenteds' revolt.

Members struggled, causing one Alliance historian to lament, "No cause unaided by God could have withstood the mistakes, bad management, vicious foes, and traitorous friends, and come out purified, stronger, and better for the ordeal, as has the Alliance."[14] In 1879 W. T. Baggett revived the struggling organization, chartering it with the state in 1880. To enlist recruits, the reborn Alliance hired S. O. Daws in 1884, giving him the title of "traveling lecturer." Daws was a self-taught farmer from Springtown, a community north of Fort Worth that today advertises itself as a place where "ideas begin that set trends for other small cities." For Daws, this was amply true. A Texas history describes his "vigorous strength," an attribute he put to work crisscrossing the state.[15]

Termed the "first Populist" by historians Lawrence Goodwin and William Holmes, Daws found a kindred spirit in redheaded farmer and natural-born organizer William Lamb, whose dogged efforts recruiting Alliance members had attracted attention.[16] The two complemented one another like Caroline Hall and Oliver Kelley with the Grange. Daws was the more conservative, while Lamb had a more expansive vision.

Together they brought a formula but not a prescription. Suballiances were free to develop solutions. The results were mixed, but there were enough successes to attract new members. One innovation was "bulking," where members pooled crops and then sold them at auction. Lawrence Goodwyn notes a bulking sale in Fort Worth netted 5 percent more than what an individual farmer earned. These actions increased the number of alliances from five hundred in 1885 to twenty-two hundred in 1886.[17]

That year members from eighty-four counties sent delegates to a convention in Cleburne, Texas. Located south of Fort Worth, between Coyote Flats and Bono, this town, named after a Confederate general, hosts museums honoring two-thirds of the American tryptic: one for *Gone with the Wind*, the other for the Chisholm Trail. The Industrial Narrative put the town on the map as host to the biggest Santa Fe Railroad shops west of the Mississippi.

Five years after the first train arrived, an unusual number of strangers stepped onto the station platform with a determined look in their eyes. Among them was C. W. Macune. They carried no sidearms but had the manner of those who meant business. Their determination reflected a desire to resolve the hornet's nest of issues they faced, most stirred up by the Grange, the Greenback Party, and the National Labor Union. In Texas, Greenbackers sent a scare into the major parties when in 1882 gubernatorial candidate George Jones polled the largest popular vote ever by a losing candidate.[18] The vote made Democrats wary of anything resembling a third party.

The biggest issue looming over the delegates was the Southwest Railroad Strike. Called by the Knights of Labor against Jay Gould's Texas and Missouri Pacific Railroads, the strike exploded into one of the country's largest and most violent labor conflicts, splitting Texas communities. Seeking to cooperate with the workers, Lamb urged Alliance members to boycott Gould's trains. In a replay of the battles between Oliver Kelley, Caroline Hall, and the Grange national office, Lamb's strategy angered the Texas Alliance state office, particularly its president, Andrew Dunlap, who declared it illegal. In response, an open letter from Lamb declared, "We think it is a good time to help the Knights of Labor in order to secure their help in the near future."[19] Goodwyn believes Lamb's letter signals a major shift in consciousness among farmers, as they came to think of themselves as workers. They demonstrated their solidarity with the striking Knights by donating food and financial support.

With the dispute over the boycott festering, Alliance leader Daws proposed a compromise. The official Alliance position resembled that of the Grange: no support for candidates or parties. Echoing how Caroline Hall and Oliver Kelley finessed the issue of Grange political involvement, Daws offered the subtle but important change that members could "call each neighborhood together and organize anti-monopoly leagues"[20] and nominate candidates. It was an astute move because it committed the Alliance to becoming a political force without making them an official registered party.

A Greatly Expanded Role

When delegates stepped off the train in Cleburne the Alliance was at a crossroads. Historians like Donna Barnes have framed the moment as the stage for a battle between conservatives insisting on limited economic self-help strategies and insurgents who also wanted political action.[21] But far more was happening. Once again the Discontented faced the issue of control that had bedeviled the Grange, the Greenbackers, and the National Labor Union: would it be a loose federation or controlled by a central office and agenda?

Besides farmers recruited by Daws and Lamb, the Knights sent a large contingent to Cleburne, hoping to craft resolutions reflecting their dissatisfaction with how industrialization was tilting the playing field. Workers worried that a missed paycheck, sudden injury, or unexpected shutdown could drive them into starvation; farmers feared a lost crop, abrupt foreclosure, or unpredicted swing of the market. All dreaded becoming one of the uncounted and unknown, dying as alone and friendless as Mary Hennessey.

To calm a potentially combative meeting, the Alliance formed a committee to draft resolutions that became known as the Cleburne Demands, a name reflecting both the farmers' anger and their desire to "secure to our people freedom from the onerous and shameful abuses that the industrial classes are now suffering at the hands of arrogant capitalists and powerful corporations."[22] Seventeen demands covering several subjects—land use, railroads, currency reform, labor, and corporate abuse—followed words resonating with the Declaration of Independence. In six of the first seven demands, which dealt with public lands, one can hear an echo of the farmers who had gathered in Lampasas almost a decade before. Demands three and four called for taxing "large bodies of land held by private individuals or corporations for speculative purposes" at the same rate as those "offered to purchasers on credit," as well as forbidding aliens from acquiring land. The latter had become important to Texans, as European aristocrats were buying ranches and farms. Demands five and seven prohibited "the dealing in futures of all agricultural products" and the removal of "fences by force if necessary from public or school lands unlawfully fenced by cattle companies." The latter refers to the fence-cutting wars that raged through Texas in 1883, as ranchers indiscriminately strung barbed wire on public lands. Demand six required that "all lands forfeited by railroads or other corporations immediately revert to the government and be declared open for purchase by actual settlers."

The labor demands reflected the hand of the Knights. Calls for a bureau of labor statistics and the abolishment of convict labor were long-standing labor issues. Coming on the heels of the Southwest Strike, number thirteen demanded "the enactment of laws to compel corporations to pay their employees according to contract in lawful money for their services and the giving to mechanics and laborers a first lien upon the product of their labor to the full extent of their wages." The final labor demand called for something Terence Powderly had desired: a national labor conference reminiscent of what William Sylvis had organized in the 1870s.

The sole demand related to corporations was relatively mild and vague, perhaps reflecting the Alliance's hopes for forming partnerships to benefit the cooperatives. It merely asked the state "to compel corporations to pay the taxes due the State and counties." More pointed were demands aimed at the railroads during a year the Southwest Strike increased animosity. One required "railroad property shall be assessed at the full nominal value of the stock on which the railroad seeks to declare a dividend." Another called for an interstate commerce law that "shall secure the same rates of freight to all persons for the same kind of commodities according to distance of haul without regard to amount of shipment and preventing pooling and rebates." The most controversial provisions revived the Greenback idea, recommending "the rapid extinguishment of the public debt of the United States by operating the mints to their fullest capacity in coining silver and gold." Another echoed Alexander Campbell's 1868 proposal for the federal government to issue paper money, with "the substitution of legal tender treasury notes for the issue of the national banks."

The convention approved all the demands, but the vote was fairly close, 92–75. Robert McMath believes delegates "anticipated a greatly expanded role for the state in protecting the rights of farmers and laborers."[23] That role dates to the 1860s. The call to abolish convict labor first arose at the 1866 NLU convention and subsequently again at the 1873 Labor Reform and 1878 Greenback conventions. William Sylvis advocated for the creation of a bureau of labor statistics in the 1870s, and a call for it appears in Article 2 of the 1881 Knights of Labor Constitution and the 1878 Greenback convention. Provisions for reserving public lands for settlers along with abolishing railroad ownership of said lands weave through the 1866 NLU convention, through platforms of various Greenback conventions, and in the Knights' constitution. The 1880 Greenback platform contained a plank stating, "It is the duty of Congress to regulate interstate commerce."[24] The Cleburne language resembles a bill Texan John Reagan introduced in Congress. Although there are slight differences in language, the Cleburne currency demands also echo language used in various Greenback platforms.

Parallels with Greenback Party platforms suggest Greenback ideas were still alive in Texas. McMath points out that the birthplaces of the Texas Alliance were also Greenback strongholds.[25] National Greenbackers lost support in Texas when in 1884 they nominated for president Benjamin Butler, a former Union general and author of the Ku Klux and Civil Rights Acts.

What is notable about the Cleburne language is that the demands are missing the 1880 Greenback calls for an income tax and a provision denouncing "as most dangerous the efforts everywhere manifested to restrict the right of suffrage."[26] You will not find anything in the Cleburne Demands similar to the anti-corporate provision of the 1880 Greenback platform (number seven): "We denounce as destructive to prosperity and dangerous to liberty, the action of the old parties in fostering and sustaining gigantic land, railroad, and money corporations and monopolies invested with and exercising powers belonging to the Government and yet not responsible to it for the manner of their exercise."[27] The real value of the Cleburne Demands lay in what they promised. Somehow farmers and workers joined to draft a common agenda for the country. The language also fits the larger pattern of the Discontented: a conservative movement dedicated to restoring the country to the principles of the Declaration and the Constitution.

Actions at Cleburne also revealed the rift over race that plagued the Greenbackers. In what was becoming a one-party state dedicated to upholding segregation, Democrats worried the Alliance might spawn a new party. As an early Alliance history ominously puts it, "Their fear, was then the same as now, that it might 'go into politics,' and that if it did, some one might get injured."[28] This was one of the few examples of understatement during an era when people exacted retribution with terrible finality. Three years before Cleburne, fifty masked men barged into a saloon in McDade, dragged away a suspected burglar and two bystanders, and lynched them. Relatives of those murdered returned to town the next day seeking retribution, setting off a gun battle that left two more dead. At that point, the governor called out the national guard.[29]

Fears the Alliance might "go into politics" were behind the next moves by those who perceived Cleburne as a coup by the Lamb-Daws forces. They immediately announced plans for the new Texas Alliance. This critical chess game threatened to tear the Alliance apart just as the fledgling organization was flexing its wings. Enter Macune, who had vaulted to the front of the Alliance's leadership by helping to secure passage of the Cleburne Demands.

Macune convened a restructuring meeting at Waco designed to heal the differences. From the discussions emerged a resolution about political involvement that found its way into the constitutions of state alliances: "[The Alliance is] to labor for the education of the agricultural classes in the science of economical government, in a strictly nonpartisan fashion."[30] Macune also received the green light to expand the Alliance. The new organization adopted the title National Farmers' Alliance and Cooperative Union of America, but it became known as the Southern Alliance when it rapidly spread, bringing colorful characters under its umbrella.

Two who represent the variety of personalities attracted to the Alliance were South Carolina's Ben Tillman and North Carolina's Leonidas Polk. Known as "Pitchfork Ben" for threatening to skewer Grover Cleveland with a pitchfork, the one-eyed Tillman possessed a sinister stare that reinforced the unabashed racism he had exhibited in the Hamburg Massacre and by quashing the Knights' attempts to organize African Americans. A Kansas paper noted he relished "white supremacy . . . in the good old South Carolina way."[31]

Progressive Farmer editor Leonidas Polk was a scientific farmer like Oliver Kelley. A southern reporter described him this way: "From his eyes darts the spark of intelligence, knowledge of the world and of men . . . with a glint of genial good nature and hospitable intent toward all, and by his gracious manners and frank, open speech captivated all whom he met."[32] Polk's "hospitable intent" built a formidable state farm organization, which he merged with the Southern Alliance after reading the Cleburne Demands. By 1890 North Carolina had 2,147 suballiances and 90,000 members, twice the number of the state's 43,957 Confederate veterans.[33]

The Northern Farmers' Alliance

There were attempts to form a Northern Farmers' Alliance in places like New York, but generally historians credit *Western Rural and American Stockman* publisher Milton George with bringing to fruition the idea.[34] Tufts of a beard barely under control personified the feistiness needed to overcome the difficulties George faced. "Although the plan of organization of the new Alliance . . . was so simple that anybody, learned or unlearned, could effect an organization," he wrote, "no one seemed ready to take the initiatory step."[35] Finally, where suburban Chicago tract houses now sprawl, one of the nation's largest farm organizations arose in the offices of George's newspaper at the same time that C. W. Macune was getting his feet wet in Texas. Officers A. B. Smith of Kentucky, J. J. Fass of Michigan, J. E. Colby of Iowa, and the new president, Matt Anderson of Wisconsin, show the initial reach of the Northern Alliance. The constitution approved by Northern Alliance No. 1 stated their aims:

> To unite the farmers of the United States for their protection against class legislation, and the encroachments of concentrated capital and the tyranny of monopoly. . . . To oppose . . . the election of any candidate to office . . . who is not thoroughly in sympathy with the farmers' interests; to demand that the existing parties shall nominate farmers . . . and to do everything in a legitimate manner that may serve the benefit of the producer.[36]

The endorsement of political action boldly contrasted with what had emerged in Cleburne. The Northern Alliance even allowed local suballiances to nominate candidates. Without a central office controlling them, locals were free to create programs to benefit only their members. Dakotans offered crop insurance. Kansans marketed cattle. While this independence appealed to individualistic farmers, collaboration was difficult, which explains why historians continue to wrestle with defining the alliances.

Contrary to some portrayals, there never was a single monolithic Farmers' Alliance. Instead, there were alliances, not merely Northern and Southern, but local alliances that pulled in different directions. An alliance in Edgefield, South Carolina, differed markedly from one in Broken Bow, Nebraska. Southern farmers largely grew cotton and toiled under a feudal crop lien system that at "settling-up time" often left them owning more to "the man" than the year before. Meanwhile, Northern farmers grew wheat and corn, which put them at the mercy of bankers, seed suppliers, grain elevator operators, and the railroads.

A year after the formation of Northern Alliance No. 1, the *Red Cloud Chief* boasted, "The *Lincoln Globe* says that Nebraska now has nearly three hundred Farmer's Alliance clubs and before fall there will be three hundred more."[37] Remember, the Southern Alliance hired Daws two years *after* the Northern Alliance arrived in Nebraska. How, within a year, George's idea had surfaced hundreds of miles away shows the depth of people's anger and the Alliance's appeal.

The local alliances resembled a series of prairie fires. Lightning would strike in one community, then randomly hit another a hundred miles away in another state. There was no pattern save seething discontent. Ill winds, like those after the Panic of 1873, pushed isolated farmers together as they sought common ground with others in pain. If hard times were the catalyst, the wonder is how rural Americans came together without telephones or automobiles.

Credit the explosive growth of newspapers. According to US Census data, the number of daily papers grew from 574 in 1870 to 2,226 in 1900.[38] This growth was especially dramatic in the Midwest. Rowell's *American Newspaper Directory*, which tracked circulation, reported that in 1870 there were approximately 280 dailies, weeklies, and quarterlies in Iowa, Kansas, and Nebraska. By 1893 there were ten times that many. Lincoln, Nebraska, boasted more papers in 1893 than the entire state had in 1870. Topeka, Kansas, claimed 32 papers with a total circulation of more than sixty-five thousand—exceeding the population of the entire Shawnee County. Smaller towns like Columbus, Nebraska, and Salina, Kansas, had half a dozen papers. Some were foreign-language publications that spoke to new immigrants filing homestead claims.

To subsidize this growth, the government provided reduced postage for newspapers and allowed papers to exchange copies for free, facilitating a rural mind-meld between communities. Without this aid it is doubtful the alliances would have expanded as widely or quickly as they did, another early example of government helping to level the playing field. The telegraph also enabled local papers to access the latest stories and spread them further. The largest growth of telegraph messages occurred between 1880 and 1884, paralleling the expansion of the alliances.[39]

A letter to the *Red Cloud Chief* reveals the importance of local papers in this expansion: "We do not know much about the Alliance but think there must be something good in it as the *Chief* is in the advance." The *Chief*'s editors replied, "It is gratifying that the farmers all over the land are already wide awake and rallying for mutual protection."[40] Like its dalliance with the Grange, the *Chief*'s flirtation with the Alliance was brief. The last mention is of an 1884 meeting in Kearney.[41]

In the Remotest Degree Repugnant

In 1886 the US Supreme Court nudged the Northern and Southern Alliances together through its decision in *Wabash, St. Louis & Pacific Railway Company v. Illinois*, which overturned *Munn v. Illinois* and the Granger laws it upheld. The 6–3 court majority bluntly stated, "It is not and never has been the deliberate opinion of a majority of this Court that a statute of a state which attempts to regulate the fares and charges by railroad companies . . . is a valid law."[42] Dissenters, including John Harlan and *Munn* author Chief Justice Waite, responded, "The making of railroads and regulating the charges for their use is not such a regulation of commerce as to be in the remotest degree repugnant to any power given to Congress by the Constitution, so long as that power is dormant and has not been exercised by Congress."

By reversing *Munn*, the court had moved the goalposts. *Munn* held that since the federal government declined to regulate railroad rates, individual states could act. *Wabash* said railroads were a federal concern. As *The Nation* perceptively editorialized: "The decision . . . utterly demolishes the pretensions of State legislatures and railroad commissions to regulate the rates of freight and fare on goods and passengers passing through the States, or from one State to another."[43] What *The Nation* did not state was how, since the 1870s, the Discontented were instrumental in convincing states to form bureaus of labor statistics, railroad and factory commissions, and regulations like the Granger Laws. Moving the goalposts meant passing new reforms and required cross-country coordination, favoring those with the resources to harness the telegraph's cryptic codes while handicapping those with fewer connections.

For the alliances, the impact came to a head at the December 1890 Ocala, Florida, national meeting. The *Ocala Banner* announced, "All eyes are turned on Ocala . . . and we must be equal to the occasion."[44] On the surface the alliances appeared strong. Over half of all eligible people in Arkansas, Mississippi, Florida, and Georgia were Southern Alliance members, along with 40 percent in Alabama, North Carolina, South Carolina, Texas, and Tennessee.[45] The Northern Alliance had 400,000 members in 1889.[46] To show how far the Farmers' Alliances penetrated community life, Omaha fielded an alliance baseball team.

Two issues faced the delegates: a proposal called the subtreasury plan and the question of a third party. A Macune idea, the subtreasury would offer loans to farmers using their crops as collateral to be "banked" and drawn on when needed. Like many Macune ideas, it had a southern tinge, since the cotton farmers of the South could more easily store crops than Northern wheat and corn growers. At Ocala, Macune agreed the land itself could also be used as collateral, securing the votes to pass the measure. The idea went no further because of congressional opposition.

Macune also negotiated a compromise on the third-party issue similar to what he proposed in 1886. Before Ocala, Kansans had formed a new political party with a platform "based on four fundamental ideas—land, labor, transportation, and money," in the words of William Peffer, an Alliance leader famous for his prophet's beard and feisty editorials in the *Kansas Farmer*.[47] They called it the People's Party. "Neither the conditions nor the proposed remedy was new, but the Kansas method of handling them was novel," wrote Elizabeth Barr.[48] Kansans wanted to apply "the method" to the country. Macune's compromise postponed a decision until 1892, handicapping any organizing since it meant a new party would have to gear up during a presidential election year.

While the subtreasury idea never left the ground and delegates tabled the third-party issue, they did reach consensus on other resolutions, some dating to the 1870s: an income tax, removing high tariffs, direct election of senators, and government control of the railroad and telegraph systems. Although the delegates did not know it, they were attending something of a funeral. Ocala marked the high point for the alliances.

It Was a Religious Revival

In 1908 Annie Diggs perceptively explained the difference between the alliances and the Grange: "The Grange was full of poetry; the Alliance was full of politics."[49] Barr described the enthusiasm as "a religious revival, a crusade, a Pentecost of politics in which a tongue of flame sat upon every man, and each spake as the spirit gave him utterance. . . . The dragon's teeth were sprouting in every nook and corner of the State."[50]

Barr's characterization is not out of place because Bible readings and prayers were a part of many local meetings. Diggs described the meetings this way: "The solemn prayers, the fervid exhortations full of stories of the distressed, the homeless and the helpless everywhere, made the majority of the meetings more like religious revivals than like unto any ever before known in the realm of politics."[51] The religious tilt also reflects the experiences of farmers who underwent the equivalent of a conversion experience, where the light came suddenly for some while for others it dawned gradually, transforming how they saw themselves and their world.

Dragon's teeth sprouted spontaneously from rural communities. In 1882 the

Red Cloud Chief predicted, "It is more than probable [Alliance members] will make their influence felt by the time the election of 1882 rolls round."[52] A sample ballot featured a Red Cloud resident as a Farmer's Alliance legislative candidate. The 1886 meeting of the Minnesota Alliance declared, "The alliance, while not a partisan association, is political in the sense that it seeks to correct the evils of misgovernment through the ballot-box."[53] Leading the charge to correct those evils was the feisty Ignatius Donnelly, who thundered, "There are really two parties in this state to-day—the people and their plunderers."[54]

In nearby North Dakota the Alliance recommended raising sorghum and supported equal rights for women, saying "He who would refuse equal rights and respect for his best friend, is not as good a man as he ought to and might be."[55] The South Dakota Alliance pushed open the doors to the US Senate by helping elect future Populist James Kyle. Faced with the South's evolving political climate, most Southern Alliance members opted to unite with the dominant party. One southerner bragged, "We took possession of the Democratic Party."[56] In 1888 the North Carolina Alliance pushed a contest for governor at the state Democratic Convention to thirty-two ballots, then successfully elected an Alliance member as House Speaker. A listing of petitions filed by 145 Nebraska alliances in the March 31, 1890, *Congressional Record* demonstrates their political power: the list contained the signatures of 6,395 members—an average of 44 per alliance and representing 4 percent of the state's total population.[57]

Firebrands with colorful nicknames fanned this zeal. There was Texas Alliance lecturer "Cyclone" Davis, a lawyer whose histrionics were legendary. Iowan "Calamity" Weller was never far from the latest ruckus. Kansan Mary Lease acquired monikers like "Mary Yellin," as she rose to become the most incendiary speaker of her time. Medicine Lodge, Kansas, town marshal "Sockless" Jerry Simpson earned his nickname when he mocked his opponent as "Prince Hal": "His dainty person is gorgeously bedizened, his soft white hands are pretty things to look at, his tender feet are encased in fine silk hosiery, what does he know of the life and the toil of such plow-handlers as we are?"[58]

Simpson was a prime example of how alliance passions could manifest themselves in those who found their calling in giving voice to the Discontented. He worked as a Great Lakes sailor, dabbled in the lumber business, and ran a cattle ranch. The lumber business killed his daughter when an errant log crushed her. The ranch did well until a bad winter took most of his stock. Diggs perceptively grasped her friend's rapid rise: "There was no miracle or mistake about the fame that came to Jerry Simpson; it was merely that the man was ready when the time arrived."[59] The uneducated Simpson was ready because he was an "eager and thorough student" of the lecturers and publications of the Grange and the alliances.[60]

This man who "ain't afraid to get up and say what he thinks," never forgot where he came from, often lapsing into his characteristic drawl: "Many a feller went down into his pocket and gave me a quarter who didn't have hardly another to rub agin it."[61] Simpson could also craft moving poetry. Asked why he came to Kansas, he answered, "The magic of a kernel, the witchcraft in a seed; the desire to put something into the ground and see it grow and reproduce its kind."[62] Simpson was one of the Kansans who called for a national people's party not long after delegates left Ocala, carrying gift boxes of lemons and oranges courtesy of local merchants.

After Ocala, the Farmers' Alliance faded, as more leaders devoted their energies to the new party. As historian John Hicks observes, "The public was left to infer it was no longer possible to be a good Alliance man unless one were a good Populist."[63] The climactic blow occurred as the 1892 Alliance meeting in Memphis, Tennessee, faced a considerable decline in attendance. Macune blamed it on the Alliance's dalliance with a third party while he commanded the charge to revive nonpartisanship. Delegates favoring a third party united behind South Dakota's J. L. Loucks, who argued that losing members was an inevitable "winnowing" process.[64]

The Memphis gathering exposed the simmering Northern-Southern split. Southern delegates stayed away because they thought the third party was a fait accompli. Macune was under fire for possible financial irregularities and for supporting Democratic candidates. In addition, a rule change stating delegates could only vote as individuals allowed Loucks forces to select him to head the national alliance as the alliances morphed into the People's Party.

It Is a School of Education

Lost in debates over a third party was what Alliance historian Nelson Dunning calls "the foundation stone of the order."[65] In Ocala, L. L. Polk eloquently described it:

> If asked what is the greatest and most essential need of our order, as contributing most to its ultimate and triumphant success, I should unhesitatingly answer, and in one word—Education; education in the mutual relations and reciprocal duties between each other, as brethren, as neighbors, as members of society; education, in the most responsible duties of citizenship; education, in the science

of economical government; education, for higher aspiration, higher thought, and higher manhood among the masses; education, in a broad patriotism, which should bind the great conservative masses of the country in the strongest ties of fraternity and union.

Note Polk's definition of education as "mutual relations and reciprocal duties" and his characterization of the alliances as a conservative movement. Just as it nourished the Grange, education fed the farmers' efforts. If farmers were going to be cheated, it would not be through ignorance.

The lecturer idea borrowed from the Grange was crucial. "The lecturer holds the most important office in our order," according to Virginian J. H. Robertson.[66] With a nose for the next political opportunity, Ignatius Donnelly astutely maneuvered to become the Alliance state lecturer for Minnesota, which became his stepping stone to a state senate seat from which he immediately began raising hell. Mary Lease, the woman Diggs describes as hurling "sentences as Jove hurled thunderbolts," became an alliance lecturer in 1889.[67]

At their peak the alliances had as many as 40,000 lecturers in the field. While many represented the educated and professional classes, their chief requirement was the ability to think on their feet.[68] Like their Grange counterparts, lecturers rode a circuit, depended on communities for food and lodging, and engaged in lively discussions around meals or coffee.

The alliances' broad view of education served as a catalyst for establishing newspapers that spoke for farmers. Annie Diggs found her voice writing for the *Kansas Liberal* and the *Lawrence Journal*. The *Southern Mercury* became the chief organ of the Texas Alliance, with a circulation of at least 40,000. Kansas had almost two dozen papers with "Alliance" on their masthead. At Macune's urging, alliance papers formed an alternative to the Associated Press—the National Reform Press Association—which grew to a thousand members and a circulation in the hundreds of thousands.

For those who paid a fee, Macune bundled articles like Kelley and Hall had once mailed to local granges. "Want to start a paper for the good of the cause," claimed an advertisement. "We issue pages as follows: Illustrated, correspondence, fashion, humor, science, sporting, theatrical, sensation, novelty, agriculture, short stories, etc., etc. Our non-illustrated features include straight miscellany, paragraphs, camp-fire, youths, ladies, etc. Ready prints and plates furnished from all of our offices as follows: Chicago, St. Louis, Omaha, Denver, Kansas City, Des Moines, Lincoln, Winfield, K., Dallas, and Detroit."[69] Note the reach of these offices. Media historian Patrick Garry writes that Macune's association "stood as a monument to the democratic intensity of the agrarian crusade and provided the adhesive for the populist movement."[70] When asked to stand if they subscribed to a reform paper, those attending a Texas Alliance meeting all rose as one.[71]

Like podcasts of today, late nineteenth-century papers could be started with a small amount of capital and function as alternatives to the mainstream press. The letters they published provided rural Americans an opportunity to connect with larger audiences. Norman Pollak gives examples of dozens of letters attesting to rural Americans' high literacy level. When writing about the Homestead Lockout, one asserted, "We condemn anarchy, but we detest the causes that produce it even more. These evils are all the legitimate children of the oppression of capital."[72]

Alliance papers also served as the nation's first systematic source of media-assisted education. As editor of the *National Economist*, Macune created the "Economist Educational Exercises," which included teaching techniques, sample lessons, and reading lists designed to empower farmers to form their own "schools." Macune outlined his aims: "The National Economist is strictly a *peoples' paper* . . . calculated to educate the masses in Social, Financial and Political Economy. . . . Its teachings are calculated to be a source of gratification to the aged, of emulation to those in the prime of life, and of instruction to the youth."[73]

By linking education and leadership training, the alliances became a thousand-mile laboratory for rebuilding America, delivering a message shouted by a national chorus. The *Cherokee Scout* in Cherokee, North Carolina, praised these efforts: "As an educational organization, the Alliance surpasses that of any this Country has ever known. Men who were totally ignorant on public questions are now enlightened and familiar with them. . . . Such an organization . . . should receive the encouragement and support of fair minded, liberal, and honest men in every section of the country."[74] Goodwyn terms this a "movement culture," putting stress on the word "culture" because it depended on a support network resembling a rural barn raising.[75]

The *Economist* was critical to this process. Macune crammed its sixteen pages with more news, analysis, and practical information than found in most television newscasts of today. Front pages featured current news, such as the capture of the Dalton Gang or the death of Alfred Lord Tennyson.[76] Other pages covered scientific discoveries or offered advice on tending hogs or weeding cotton.

Macune's most radical contribution was what he called "the lessons," a formidable mix of education and consciousness-raising that had farmers doing calculations or reading aloud from books and articles. Added to the *Economist*'s base circulation of 100,000 was the probability that copies were shared by friends and neighbors, raising the number of pupils in Macune's "classroom." As much as Macune strove to keep politics out of the lessons, though, historian Robert McGrath says their value lay in creating a "political culture."[77]

The alliances also built an economic network of exchanges that Goodwyn and others view as the heart of their leaders' efforts. The Fort Worth *Weekly Gazette* described one: "The Farmers Alliance Exchange of Texas will be a chartered corporation with a capital stock of $8,500,000 . . . to purchase any corn commodity needed by the order from the factories and sell the same at actual cost."[78] A central part of the alliance store was its return to the barter system of the staples society: "The stockholders mostly wanted it [the store] to be for farmers or the working-type people . . . where they could bring in . . . wheat or grain or stuff to swap for sugar and coffee and so forth like they used to."[79]

This alludes to a critical dimension of the alliances and other reform efforts of the Discontented. As much as they rebuilt the country, they did so while striving to preserve what they saw as the best of the past. Farmers and workers envisioned a world where the staples society coexisted with the consumer culture. State agents estimated that in 1890 the exchanges conducted $10 million in business.[80] The Northern Alliance also created cooperatives. One study estimated fifty-three stores in New England brought in $2 million.[81] The South Dakota Alliance had a capitalization of over $200,000 in 1887.[82]

Recognized and Treated as Human Beings

If women represented the heart of the Grange, they were the soul of the alliances. Research by Mary Jo Wagner on Nebraska alliances from 1890 to 1894 discovered women comprised 31 percent of suballiance membership. Where the Grange had a low glass ceiling, 26 percent of suballiances had female officers and 14 percent had a majority of women members. In North Carolina one-third to one-half of alliance members were women.[83] Mary Lease described her liberation: "The doors of the Farmer's Alliance were thrown wide open to the women of the land. They were invited into full membership, with all the privileges of promotion; actually recognized and treated as human beings. And not only the mothers, wives and daughters, but 'the sisters, the cousins and the aunts,' availed themselves of their newly-offered liberties, till we find at the present time upward of a half-million women in the Alliance."[84] The alliances enabled Lease to become "the first important female politician in [nineteenth century] America," according to biographer Richard Schiller.[85] But she was only one of many female leaders. Texan Bettie Gay affirmed, "The Alliance has come to redeem woman from her enslaved condition, and to place her in her proper sphere."[86] The self-confidence this instilled resulted in the invigoration of "the entire being." Gay exuded this spirit in a penetrating analysis:

> The reason why so many people are found occupying unnatural conditions is because of the violation of the principles of justice and right, by the government allowing the few to monopolize the land, money, and transportation, which deprives a large portion of the people of their natural right to apply their labor to the gifts of nature. Under such conditions, the people become dependent, hopeless slaves, a condition which drives the last spark of manhood and womanhood from their bosoms, and they become outcasts and criminals, and fill our jails and penitentiaries and other places of shame.[87]

The unified Farmers' Alliance did not flinch from loudly declaring support for equal rights. In 1891 the national convention passed a strong resolution affirming that "women have the same rights as their husbands to hold property" and declaring: "We are in sympathy with any law that will give our wives, sisters, and daughters full representation at the polls."[88]

That is not to say the alliances did not have a glass ceiling. A Texas Alliance history offers one example: "From its inception, women were admitted as members of the Alliance. As it grew in numbers, the social feature became a strong bond of union."[89] Even feisty Alliance members like Bettie Gay could speak in ways that revealed the complexities of women's lives. Gay wrote that women's participation helped "to control the strong tempers of many members, and [placed] a premium on politeness and gentility."[90]

While the alliances opened horizons for women, their attitudes toward African Americans was another matter. Most Blacks toiled in the South under the new slavery of the tenant farm system. Because the tightening coils of segregation excluded them from the Southern Alliance, they formed the Colored Farmers' Alliance (CFA). While its origins remain clouded, the white Southern Alliance probably played a role in the 1886 creation of a separate Colored Alliance in Houston County, Texas.[91]

In one of the era's stranger developments, a former Confederate officer became the head of the CFA. R. H. Humphrey was a complicated man. He once voiced his prejudices against a race "which, from long endurance of oppression and chattel slavery, had become increasingly besotted and ignorant."[92] Yet he became head of an African American organization when white-robed myrmidons did not take kindly to anyone who aided people of color in any way. Historian Floyd Miller claims African Americans needed Humphrey to front the organization: "For black farmers, organization beyond the local level was impossible without some conduit to white support."[93] Inevitably, the relationship between Humphrey and the African Americans on the CFA governing board became an uneasy compact.

The CFA was received "as a sort of second emancipation."[94] Cooperatives provided capital to buy a stock of bacon or pay off a mortgage. In 1889 the CFA started a newspaper, which quickly circulated through the South and beyond. Two years later the CFA numbered over a million members, making it the largest nonreligious African American organization of the time. Its 1890 declaration reflected the realities of a time when the doors to freedom were slamming shut: "To be more obedient to the civil law and withdraw attention from political partisanship."[95]

Meanwhile, the clash between African American aspirations and segregation generated sparks. As the CFA grew, Blacks began opposing southern measures to restrict their rights. The inevitable came in 1891 when Memphis plantation owners cut the wages of African American cotton pickers. CFA head Humphrey tried to convince members to call a general strike, but they refused. Among those opposing him was Andrew J. Carothers, founder of the National Colored Alliance, which had merged with the CFA. Carothers warned it "will engender a race feeling, bitter and deep and lasting, and one which may result in riot and bloodshed."[96]

Humphrey went ahead with his plans by forming the Cotton Pickers League. He then issued a foolish ultimatum: "The biggest agricultural strike in the history of the world is imminent."[97] It never happened, but a spark did catch fire in Arkansas, where Ben Patterson organized a wildcat strike that began on September 20. During a confrontation, strikers killed two field hands, touching off vicious retribution. By the time it was over, a posse had lynched nine strikers, killed six others (including Patterson), and jailed an additional six. The strike is usually viewed as a low point for the CFA, yet it showed that consciousness and confidence-raising had reached the point where Patterson was willing to take on the white establishment. That came with a price, because after the strike the Colored Farmers' Alliance lost members and influence.

The CFA's tragedy was that it came of age just as the shackles of Jim Crow tightened around African American ankles. It brought people together by offering hope and reinforced the work of institutions such as churches. In this sense it was one of the most important African American institutions of its time because it picked up the pieces left by the Hayes-Tilden election and sought to remake them into something to sustain African American life. As a bridge from slavery to freedom, the CFA told African Americans they mattered, even as those measuring skulls, singing coon songs, and parading in bedsheets sought to break them.

Among the People

Today the narrow stairway to the second story of Oliver Kelley's Minnesota house is blocked by a "No Admittance" sign. Much as Kelley's second floor remains a mystery to tourists, farm movements remain a mystery to many Americans. How could farmers who traveled by foot and horse form organizations like the alliances without telephones or the internet? Consider a counterintuitive explanation: they organized *because* they were isolated. True, they could congregate at local institutions, especially churches, but the rush of rural Americans to the Grange, the alliances, and farm organizations like the Wheel tells us they hungered for another kind of interpersonal contact. Churches might fill their spiritual hunger, but could not fill their material hunger.

Second "stories" also can hide secrets. The alliances never generated violent battles like the Southwest Railroad Strike, but their members were as angry and determined as members of unions. Workers clashed with local mine and factory supervisors, while farmers fought more distant foes. When they wanted to fence their land, they faced the barbed-wire trust; when their homes needed repair, they faced the hinge and bolt and nut trusts. When they wanted to bathe they faced the soap and sponge trusts. When they died there were the casket, burial, and tombstone trusts. Mary Lease used all of these for ammunition: "Wall Street owns the country. It is no longer a government of the people, by the people, and for the people, but a government of Wall Street, by Wall Street, and for Wall Street."[98]

Like the Grange stores, alliance ventures faced pushback from the local merchants who found themselves in an uncomfortable situation. Storekeepers could side with either those who supplied them with merchandise and finances or the alliances. In Tennessee, corporations blackballed alliance cooperatives.[99] For African Americans, the pressures could get them killed. In Laflore County, Mississippi, vigilantes stirred up by white merchants murdered alliance leaders who dared to set up a CFA store.[100] Donna Barnes states that by 1890, the economic strategies of the alliances had been exhausted as they faced corporate pressure.[101]

The other not-so-secret problem for farm movements was the lingering animosity of the Civil War. Although the Kansas Alliance collaborated with southern counterparts, the relationship inspired considerable controversy, which is not unexpected in a state once known as "Bleeding Kansas" for its bitter battles that made John Brown a national figure. The *Saline County Journal* accused the Southern Alliance of being "a Democratic contrivance, originated in the South, by southern Democrats, for the purpose of dividing the Republican party of the North, so that the Democrats may win an easy victory."[102] The *Thomas County Cat* quoted New York Farmers' Alliance president John Livingston's charge, that he could "prove conclusively" Southern Alliance leaders "are . . . in with the railroads."[103]

Southerners also had strong feelings about the alliances, especially its slow dance in forming a third political party. Commenting during an 1891 alliance convention in Waco, C. W. Macune told the *Fort Worth Gazette* that he "regrets very much the outcropping here of a third-party spirit."[104] The *Gazette* then reminded readers that the majority of Texans were "true Democrats." The Charleston *News and Courier* was adamant: "Certainly no Democratic farmer will be driven by his threats into an independent political organization which would be necessarily hostile to Southern interests and Southern sentiment." These remarks received circulation in Northern papers, where readers viewed them as more examples of southern intransigence.[105] While thoughtful southern leaders like Leonidas Polk labored to heal regional tensions, agitators like Ben Tillman actively worked to make them worse.

Like other groups that made up the Revolt of the Discontented, farmers confronted organizational issues. Where the national Grange office drove away its two most important leaders, Caroline Hall and Oliver Kelley, by yanking too hard on their short leashes, the alliances went in the opposite direction, allowing suballiances much autonomy. As a result, they had no way of enforcing discipline. Still, some complained. The Topeka *Dispatch* charged, "The entire line of Alliance leaders has managed during the past twelve months to draw from the farmers of Kansas over $500,000. Each one of these apostles of liberty and social freedom have drawn from $10 to $30 a day for lecturing and stump speaking. . . . In addition, they have sold books, papers, pamphlets, ribbons, and relics that were all profit."[106]

Hovering over the tensions was what some historians have seen as the chief problem of late nineteenth-century reform efforts: the holy grail of a worker-farmer collaboration. Dating to Cleburne, the Knights of Labor sought to forge a partnership with the Farmers' Alliance. Knights officials even drew up a formal agreement in St. Louis, specifying, "The legislative committee of both organizations shall act in concert before Congress for the purpose of securing the enactment of laws in harmony with the demands mutually agreed."[107] Knights leader Terence Powderly commented, "We have met the Farmers and we are theirs or they are ours."[108] As the alliances moved toward a third party, Powderly dug in his heels. "The Farmers' Alliance would like us to start the ball rolling [for a third party] and wreck us so there would be but one industrial organization existing."[109]

Lawrence Goodwyn identifies the chief obstacle between farmers and workers as an inability to speak each other's language. Even more, they had little understanding of each other's *worlds*. Rural newspapers covered strikes, but publications like the *Locomotive Firemen's Magazine* and the *Cigar Makers Journal* devoted little space to subjects relevant to rural America. Few workers had seen the flat treeless landscape of the prairie, any more than farmers had seen the black muddy alleys of mining towns in eastern Pennsylvania. Workers' fates lay in the tension between labor and management; farmers' fates lay in the caprices of nature and the whims of Wall Street. Company towns and tightly managed factories handicapped workers; distance and ghostly institutions handicapped farmers.

Despite the difficulties, the alliances had a lasting impact. Goodwyn believes they generated "a new way of looking at society, a way of thinking that represented a shaking off inherited forms of deference."[110] They brought together people isolated by more than miles. Alliance educational activities paralleled a dramatic drop in national rates of illiteracy, from 20 percent in 1870 to only 10 percent by 1900. Even though they were denied the opportunity of public education in much of the country, illiteracy among African Americans decreased from 80 percent in 1870 to 44.5 percent in 1900. Schools, churches, and the CFA also contributed to this increase in an educated populace, which belies the stereotype of submissive African Americans facing the rise of Jim Crow. Cooperatives turned farmers into an economic force, teaching them business skills and rescuing those who might have joined the Great Retreat. Macune's astute lessons and Farmers' Alliance lecturers helped farmers understand concepts such as compound interest. This played a role, albeit difficult to calculate, in lowering foreclosures and bankruptcies. Ironically the alliances' most important contribution may have been political. Elizabeth Sanders believes movements like the alliances "constituted the most important political force driving the development of the American national state in the half-century before World War I."[111]

To farm families, the alliances provided assets they could not buy: skills, knowledge, and, most of all, self-confidence. Looking out over fields of rustling cornstalks in the moonlight, they no longer needed to think of themselves as victims. For women, role models like Mary Lease and Annie Diggs dared speak of equality. Rural families looked forward to an alternative future in which people were not passive purchasers but could bargain for the best deal.

1. John Mitchell, the Miners' Champion, Library of Congress, LC-DIG-ppmsca-46655.

2. The Breaker Boys, Library of Congress, LC-DIG-det-4a16385.

3. Grange poster, Library of Congress, LC-USZ62-53913.

4. Sweatshop, Library of Congress, LC-USZ62-35877.

5. Leaders of the Knights of Labor, Library of Congress, LC-USZ62-9466.

6. Women and machinery in New England cotton mill, Library of Congress, LC-USZ62-41434.

THE GREAT STRIKE—BURNING OF THE ROUND-HOUSE AT PITTSBURGH.—From a Sketch by J. W. Alexander.—[See Page 630.]

THE GREAT STRIKE—A FUNERAL AMONG THE RUINS AT PITTSBURGH.—Drawn from a Sketch by John W. Beatty.—[See Page 626.]

7. The 1877 strike in Pittsburgh, Library of Congress, LC-USZ62-61643.

8. The importance of education, Library of Congress, LC-USZ62-15542.

9. View of the Great Railroad Wreck, Library of Congress, LC-USZ62-108552.

10. Homes of the poor, Library of Congress, LC-USZ62-75197.

11. Steel mill scenes, Library of Congress, LC-USZ62-108121.

12. In the wheat field, Library of Congress, LC-USZ62-40411.

CHAPTER NINE

To Help and Assist All Employed and Unemployed

Storm the fort, Ye Knights of Labor,
Battle for your cause;
Equal rights for every neighbor,
Down with tyrant laws.
—*From the labor movement song "Storm the Fort," ca. 1880*

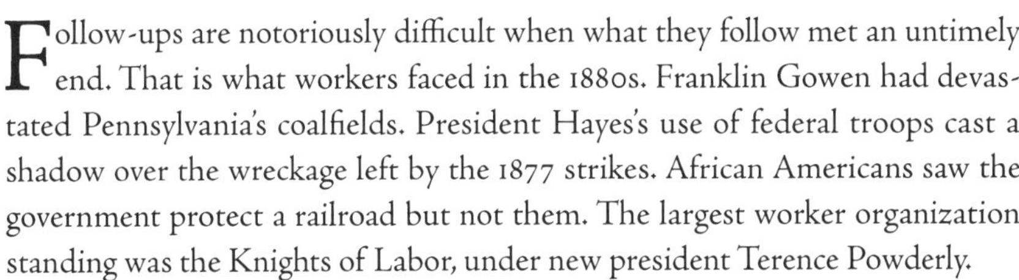

Follow-ups are notoriously difficult when what they follow met an untimely end. That is what workers faced in the 1880s. Franklin Gowen had devastated Pennsylvania's coalfields. President Hayes's use of federal troops cast a shadow over the wreckage left by the 1877 strikes. African Americans saw the government protect a railroad but not them. The largest worker organization standing was the Knights of Labor, under new president Terence Powderly.

Dating to Selig Perlman's view of the Knights as an "association of idealistic cooperators," the Knights have been a mirror reflecting a variety of perspectives. Kim Voss traced their European roots; Herbert Gutman their religious roots. Others have examined their organizational style (William Birdsall) and their culture (Robert Weir).[1] Dominating that mirror, even in the case of those who sought to gaze elsewhere, is Terence Powderly.

Powderly was a master illusionist during the golden age of illusion. Harry Houdini was perfecting his escapes, séances were fashionable, hucksters sold cures in a bottle, and evangelists offered salvation in crowded tents. *The Trades* describes "Terry" as a man who, "when you shake his hand, you can feel a chord of sympathetic feeling run all the way up your arm even into your heart."[2] This came six months after Powderly had incited a mob by telling them "Benedict Arnolds deserve summary justice." Not surprisingly, these contradictions have generated contrasting opinions about Powderly's leadership. Samuel

Gompers reviled Powderly's "contemptible conduct to the labor movement in general and the trades unions in particular." Labor historian Norman Ware considered him "a windbag whose place was on the street corner rousing the rabble." And the editor of his autobiography, Harry Carman, thought he was "a person of far greater stature than he has been credited with being."[3]

Powderly wanted to be a poet, but instead he authored his grand illusion: his autobiography. While autobiographies often smooth over rough edges, Powderly's creates an alternate reality. A prime example is the event he views as a turning point, John Siney's Avondale speech. Although he wasn't in attendance, Powderly fabricated a story about how witnessing it was a conversion experience (while omitting his attempts to curry favor with business leaders).

He began as an apprentice to mechanic James Dickson, repairing engines for the Delaware, Lackawanna, and Western Railroad, joining the Scranton Machinists and Blacksmiths' Union in 1871. When the world came crashing down during the Panic of 1873, Powderly found himself caught in the wreckage. The bosses he had cultivated ignored his desperate pleas for help, so he walked from Scranton to Canada, picking up odd jobs, including playing nursemaid to a herd of pigs for 75¢ a day.

After wandering for several years in places like Oil City, Pennsylvania, he returned to Scranton and joined the Knights of Labor. With typical hyperbole he wrote, "After September 6, 1876, I knew no waking hour that I did not devote, in whole or part, to the upbuilding of the Order."[4] A young cigar maker named Samuel Gompers underwent the same initiation ritual, whose oath bound members to "defend the life, interest, reputation, and family of all true members of this Order."[5] Like a shaft of light penetrating a tangled forest, the order's pledge to "help and assist all employed and unemployed, unfortunate or distressed members" recognized that many were alone and lost, scratching just to make it to the next day.

The Knights were the brainchild of another nineteenth-century original, Uriah H. Stephens. In a history of the Knights, Carroll Wright described Stephens as "a man of great force of character, a skilled mechanic, with the love of books which enabled him to pursue his studies during his apprenticeship."[6] In 1869 the man who became affectionately known as "Old Man Stephens" convened fellow garment workers in his Philadelphia house to form a secret union modeled after Freemasonry. Stephens undoubtedly knew about the Working Men's Benevolent Association and probably also Oliver Kelley's idea of modeling the Grange after the Masons.

Like Kelley, Stephens believed the fellowship and solidarity of shared rituals was an elixir for people craving stability. Contemporary works such as Franz Boas's 1889 study of the Indigenous people of British Columbia affirmed this need. Boas hypothesized: "I believe the source of the ritual . . . must be looked for in the advantages and the prerogatives which the membership of secret societies gives."[7] United Steelworkers founder Clinton Golden used more direct language to describe the Knights. "Their ritual, the secrecy with which their meetings were conducted, the signs and symbols that gave notice to their members as to when and where meetings were to be held, fired my interest and imagination."[8] Robert Wier, who authored a study of the Knights, believes the group's rituals created a sense of community.[9]

Stephens envisioned the Knights as an order with secret handshakes, meeting locations, and rules. In Philadelphia, five stars chalked onto the walls of Independence Hall announced meetings.[10] To prevent blacklisting, members pledged not to reveal the names of those attending. The Knights' playbook, the mysteriously named *Adelphon Kruptos*, reflects Stephens's reputation as a by-the-book stickler for detail. It included detailed illustrations for rituals like the "Sign of Obliteration: Do not bring the hands together with a slap or noise—an error in some locals. Do not hold the hands higher than the elbows. In separating the hands do not throw them out sidewise beyond a line with the body."[11] For Stephens, ritual may have created solidarity, but requiring members to rigidly follow such instructions echoes the industrial machine process, where workers had to follow supervisors whose penalties for disobedience were harsher than the Knights'.

Yet Stephens's penchant for detail also had a positive side, leading him to insist the Knights become one of the first organizations to employ a statistician years before Carroll Wright took up his post in Washington, DC. The *Adelphon* description of rituals includes a requisite sign: "The symbol of the Statistician is a Hook and Flash of Lightning, and signifies 'Light, knowledge, and power.' The Statistician shall collect from the members and all other available sources, all information attainable concerning the condition of the laboring people in the locality, and shall faithfully report the same to the District Assembly Statistician, at least once a month."[12]

To Secure to the Toilers

If we follow the custom of Indigenous Americans—and some historians—to assign a name to a portentous year, then 1878 might be termed the Year of Promise, when the Knights of Labor met to assess their future and the Greenback Party issued its most comprehensive platform. The most pressing issue for the Knights was a widening rift caused by the Catholic Irish, who strongly objected to the inclusion of Protestant scripture in the rituals. There was more than religion behind the friction. Anti-Irish elements had become more vocal during the Molly Maguire conflicts. Powderly resigned from his post as Grand Master Workman of the Scranton Knights to protest inclusion of anti-Irish agitators in the order, then helped heal the wounds.

At the 1878 meeting, the Knights formed a committee to "exercise supervision over the organization."[13] One member was Samuel Gompers of 85 Columbia Street, New York City. With the shadow of the Molly Maguires hanging over organized labor, the Knights dropped their secrecy and rewrote their governing documents. What emerged in parallel with the Greenback convention is fascinating, especially given the involvement of Knights like Powderly and Stephens in the new party. Section 3 of the Knights' new preamble states: "The alarming development and aggressiveness of great capitalists and corporations, unless checked, will inevitably lead to pauperization and hopeless degradation of the toiling masses. It is imperative, if we desire to enjoy the full blessings of life, that a check be placed upon unjust accumulation, and the power for evil of aggregated wealth."[14] The 1878 Greenback platform began: "Throughout our entire country the value of real estate is depreciated, industry paralyzed, trade depressed, business incomes and wages reduced, unparalleled distress inflicted upon the poorer and middle ranks of our people, the land filled with fraud, embezzlement, bankruptcy, crime, suffering, pauperism, and starvation."[15] The Knights' proposals included health and safety laws, banishment of child labor, government ownership of the railroad, telegraph, and telephone systems, reserving public lands for settlers, an eight-hour day, and binding arbitration. Through the rest of the century the country attempted to check them off, one by one. The language of Principle 2 represents the heart of the Knights' appeal: "To secure to the toilers a proper share of the wealth which they create; more of the leisure that rightfully belongs to them; more society advantages; more of the benefits, privileges, and emoluments of the world; in short, all those rights and privileges necessary to make them capable of enjoying and appreciating, defending and, perpetuating, the blessings of good government."[16] Principle 13 promised "To secure for both sexes—equal pay for equal work." The Knights' resolutions confirm the strong connections among the Discontented. Provisions about convict labor, public lands, and a bureau of labor statistics parallel Greenback Party resolutions from 1878 and 1880. The connection between the two groups became even stronger when Stephens resigned to run for office on the Greenback ticket and the Greenbackers helped elect Powderly mayor of the town he had left in disgrace.

Stephens recommended two successors; one was the thirty-year-old Powderly, who won in a landslide. Unlike his idol, John Siney, Powderly stressed control, which may be why Stephens saw him as a worthy successor. How far this went is conveyed in a tale Powderly told during his second career as an immigration official. He wondered whether "I might, as Commissioner-General of Immigration, be obliged to deport [his father]."[17]

While Siney was a humble man, Powderly believed himself superior to those he led. Significantly, he hung a portrait of the crucified Jesus behind his desk. Those who saw an after-shift beer as a worker's communion must have rolled their eyes when Powderly preached: "The number of those who have been reduced to poverty through strong drink is far greater than those who have been made drunkards through poverty."[18] The Knights' temperance oath became known as the "Powderly Pledge."[19] Powderly's defense of the oath reveals his obstinacy: "My position on the question of temperance is right. I am determined to maintain it and will not alter it one jot or tittle."[20] Powderly endeavored to keep the reins tight. When he learned locals planned a symbolic May Day strike, he responded like an adult berating an unruly child: "No assembly of the Knights of Labor must strike for the eight hours system on May first under the impression that they are obeying orders from headquarters, for such an order was not, and will not be given."[21]

The playing field had tilted substantially since John Siney chartered the WBA. "Americans confronted a new form of centralized power for which at first they had no institutional response," observes Paul Starr.[22] Nothing aided the power of corporate empires more than the telegraph. British economist Alfred Marshall described its importance in his influential 1891 book, *Principles of Economics*, with a sentence that has appeared in the works of contemporary economists. Explaining why people could amass fortunes previously not possible, Marshall states, "The development of new facilities for communication, by which men, who have once attained a commanding position, are enabled to apply their constructive or speculative genius to undertakings vaster, and extending over a wider area, than ever before."[23]

A prime example was the rise of the Associated Press, a news subscription service built on the brilliant idea of employing the telegraph to allow reporters to file stories instantaneously, courtesy of a sweetheart agreement with one of the country's biggest monopolies: Western Union. In 1872 the AP served over two hundred newspapers and paid Western Union $200,000. By 1880, 30 percent of the country's daily papers were AP members, netting Western Union $392,800.[24] Small-town papers used the AP to get as much as 80 percent of their copy.[25] Local papers faced a dilemma like the storekeepers whose ads they published: shoppers wanted the latest fashions and readers wanted the latest news. As demand increased, the AP became an exclusive club with a New York franchise reputedly worth $250,000.

An 1884 congressional hearing pulled back the curtains on the AP–Western Union relationship: "They offered to give you this service of thirty-five hundred words a day for $30 a week, provided you took your news from a certain association. . . . But if you obtained your news from any other source you were required to pay $105 a week? Answer: That is it exactly."[26] The *Detroit Evening Journal* editor Lloyd Breezee corroborated how the AP curtailed competition": "*The Post and Tribune*, the *Free Press* control the afternoon franchise of the Associated Press in Detroit, and we can neither buy nor lease it."[27] AP president William Smith's defense of the setup evoked social Darwinism when he told the committee it was not his policy "to make weak newspapers, but to make strong newspapers."[28] The committee responded by writing that "Telegraphic news is the breath of life of the daily press, and to receive such news practically at the will of one company is an intolerable condition, degrading to the newspapers and alarming to the country."[29]

Probably no other leader suffered from this communications imbalance more than Terence Powderly. On assuming his new post he expanded the Knights' educational offerings, including providing reading rooms and libraries for members and following the Grange system of traveling lecturers. In 1885 more than 800 people a week used the newspapers in Knights union halls.[30] The Knights also organized cooperatives to purchase items. One source estimated capitalization at $5 million, although this is unconfirmed.[31]

Her Brother's Equal

The Knights' stance on equal rights attracted women, such as labor organizer Mother Jones and Hull House's Alzina Stevens. A Kansan whose writing resembles that of Knights member Mary Lease wrote:

> Her faith and patient industry
> as willing, useful worker,
> Will strengthen earnest workingmen,
> Check doubter, growler, shirker.

Here she's her brother's equal quite,
she votes as well as he,
Therefore our Order's rightly blessed,
with much prosperity.[32]

The numbers tell a different story. The Knights attracted an estimated 65,000 women, but they represented only 10 percent of the membership, far below the number of women members in the Grange or the Farmers' Alliances.

The Knights' most powerful woman's voice was its chief investigator for women's work, Leonora Barry. One Knight wrote, "She . . . reaches the hearts of all—to stir each to a sense of his or her duties. She talks straight to the point and shows that she means all she says."[33] Barry connected with workers because she had lived a hard life, beginning with a family chased to a hardscrabble New York farm by the potato famine, where she grew up to become a teacher, marrying when she was twenty-two. Her husband's sudden death in 1880 sent her into the mills. She was thirty-one. "I was left without knowledge of business, without knowledge of work, without knowledge of what the world was, with three fatherless children looking to me for bread" she told an audience at the International Council of Women.[34] When starvation wages had forced workers into a strike they eventually lost, Barry landed on the blacklist. She channeled her anger into the Knights. Her talents enabled her to rapidly rise to become its highest-ranking female member. In that position she saw her duty was "to educate her sister working-women and the public generally as to their needs and necessities."[35] A charismatic speaker, she tirelessly traveled America, enlisting workers and exposing deplorable working conditions.

In one interview Barry commented on why her appointment was so important: "When our organizers were men, the women were loth [sic] to appeal to them, but to me they told some very pitiful things." In sentences veiled by Victorian conventions, Barry reveals why the union needed female organizers: "I am daily called upon to interfere between some poor girl who has been grossly insulted by some male boss or underling, and who fears discharge if she resents it. What makes the matter more difficult of remedy is, I am sorry to say, that some of the girls do not resent these attempted familiarities."[36]

Barry's veiled language about girls being "grossly insulted" reveals a side of industrialization that remains largely unmentioned in most histories, especially those employing the Industrial Narrative: the sexual harassment of working women. *The Sun* reported Knights of Labor leader T. B. McGuire told a rally for William Jennings Bryan, "There were 60,000 working girls in New York, and that these girls were urged daily to desert the path of virtue."[37] Like Barry's, the few narratives we have about women factory workers hint at the depth of the problem.[38] Elissa Isenberg found that "an extensive examination of newspaper articles reveals that seduction, breach of promise, and general unwanted sexual attention were real and pervasive issues in the workplace, and that young female workers often were unaware of how to prevent such behavior."[39]

Recent historians have documented the exploitation of enslaved women, but similar acts by workplace supervisors and owners have received less attention. Even more than today, these "gross insults" (the polite label for describing a variety of assaults on women, from verbal harassment to physical assaults) were unreported in part because of a double standard: talking about such things was vewed as immoral and reporting them were evidence of the victims' own moral failure.[40] Yet, as Rosemarie Skaine notes in her history of sexual harassment in this country, "Sexual harassment occurred frequently during this period."[41]

Barry also addressed other abuses. In an 1887 report she skewered a corset factory for imposing fines for "eating, laughing, singing or talking, of 10 cents each."[42] She goes on to describe the intolerable conditions in another workplace:

> Women are compelled to stand on the stone floor in water the year round, most of the time barefoot, with a spray of water from a revolving cylinder flying constantly against the breast; and the coldest night in winter as well as the warmest in summer those poor creatures must go to their homes with water dripping from their under-clothing along their path because there could not be space or a few moments allowed them wherein to change their clothing.

With a no-nonsense manner and a voice that cut through the pandemonium of machines or the din of a crowded union hall, Barry became the Knights' best speaker, giving over five hundred speeches in her first three years alone. She described workdays that began before the sun rose, a lunch grabbed in spare moments, and the awkward problem of dealing with bathroom breaks. Barry deliberately used her native Irish brogue:

> Pat had lately come to this country. He was asking Mike, who had been here many years, the meaning of the 5–20 bonds, and the 7–30 bonds, and the 10–40 bonds. "Vell," says Mike to Pat, "thim has one meanin' for the rich and another for the likes of us; but take it for all in all, the size of it is about this—it means that we shall get up at 5:20 in the mornin' and work till 7:30 in the evenin' in order that the rich may lie in bed till 10:40 in the day."[43]

What drained Barry was not so much the demands of her job as the stress of holding the Knights accountable. Like Caroline Hall, she felt undervalued, especially given the Knights' hypocrisy about women's rights. Always someone who spoke her mind, she charged:

> If those who pledged themselves to the support of [equal pay] do not resolve to trample under foot their selfish personal ambition and for a time turn their attention to the poor down-trodden white slave, as represented by the women wage-workers of this country, then let us here and now withdraw the twenty-second plank out of our platform, and no longer make a farce of one of the grandest principles of our Order.[44]

Ultimately the Knights' refusal to listen caused Barry's resignation in 1890, costing the union crucial support at a critical time.

Industrial Disturbances Belong to Modern History

During the years from 1881 to 1884, when it appears the Long Depression was on vacation, strikes were at their lowest level. However, some wondered if the apparent harmony could last. Those fears proved true when panic again hit the nation in the mid-1880s, bringing a new word to America's vocabulary: "anarchist." As the economy again faced a downturn, strikes increased, from 645 in 1885 to 1,432 in 1886 and remaining above 1,000 every year for the rest of the century. Known as the Year of Upheaval, 1886 found 750,000 workers on strike. Chicago experienced over 300 strikes by everyone from lumber workers to messenger boys. On May Day, 80,000 marched in favor of the eight-hour day.

The economic downturn was serious enough to become the first studied by Carroll Wright's new US Bureau of Labor Statistics. Wright estimated a "loss of consumptive power of at least $1,000,000 per day, or a crippling of the trade of the country of over $300,000,000 per year."[45] Business failures increased by nearly 20 percent between 1883 and 1885;[46] state bank suspensions reached levels similar to the worst years of the previous decade. Wright notes the industrial world had brought something new: "The regularity and contemporaneity which characterize commercial, financial, and industrial disturbances belong to modern history."[47] Faced with the realities of this pessimistic analysis, Americans struggled to find answers.

Following the pattern of the Grange and the Farmers' Alliances, membership in the Knights increased substantially during the downturn, rising from 74,000 in 1884 to 730,000 in 1886.[48] Explanations include the Knights' involvement in the eight-hour movement and the union's victory over Jay Gould in the 1885 Wabash Railroad Strike. The victory brought thousands: over 650 local assemblies formed in the four months after the strike's settlement.[49] The *Princeton Review* termed it "the *greatest* demonstration of the power and the weakness of the Knights of Labor."[50]

The *Review* was right: the Knights lacked a strategy to deal with a large membership increase. Locals grew so chaotically that Powderly saw villains everywhere. "Designing and unscrupulous persons flocked into the order from all parts of the country."[51] Twisting about in this widening gyre, Powderly and the Knights were blindsided by events in Chicago's Haymarket Square and at the Sedalia, Missouri, headquarters of Knights' District Assembly (DA) 101.

Like many tragedies, the Haymarket affair began when an event took a wrong turn. Crucial gaps in the official story, unreliable witnesses, and the city's volatile atmosphere complicate the ability to determine what happened. We do know that by the 1880s, Chicago had become a late nineteenth-century version of Concord, Massachusetts, nurturing a "flowering" of talent that brought together entrepreneurs of new ideas, including Clarence Darrow, Louis Sullivan, Florence Kelley, Frank Lloyd Wright, John Dewey, Jane Addams, Thorstein Veblen, Henry Demarest Lloyd, and Franz Boas.[52] Of course, Chicago also contained the vices plaguing other American cities. In *If Christ Came to Chicago* journalist William Stead cataloged them: blackmail, boodling, bribery, and multiple forms of bamboozling. The biggest sinners, though, were businessmen who showed "an almost total lack of ordinary business honesty in the transaction of the city's business."[53]

Questions of honesty buzzed loudly around the city's newspapers. The collusion between business leaders and the press was an open secret, capped by Marshall Field's $10,000 loan (assisted by silent partner Andrew Carnegie), which enabled Joseph Medill to buy the *Chicago Tribune*. Feeding the collusion was the Citizens' Association formed by business leaders during the 1877 strikes, when they collected $27,515 to buy 599 muskets, 50,000 rounds of ammunition, and a Gatling gun.[54] By 1886 Chicago had become one of America's most paranoid cities, as newspapers amplified fear of a labor uprising. An annual report from the Citizens' Association shows how close the city came to being run by millionaire vigilantes: "During those days of terror and excitement we had daily meetings — they might almost be called continuous—for the purpose of agreeing upon a plan of action in case the necessities of the situation should demand our intervention in any way."[55]

In 1886 Chicago workers were in an ugly mood following a lockout by one of the city's largest employers, the McCormick Harvester Company, whose workers were represented by the Knights of Labor. On May 3, after police fired on a crowd, killing four, some called for revenge. One was Albert Parsons, a former Civil War cavalryman, newspaper editor, Reconstruction official, and Knights member who gained notoriety during the 1877 strikes when he declared, "It rests with you to say whether we shall allow the capitalists to continue to exploit us."[56]

The anarchist International Working People's Association (IWPA) had printed flyers announcing a rally at Haymarket Square on May 4, 1886. One flyer closed with the phrase "Workingmen Arm Yourselves and Appear in Full Force."[57] Luckily *Arbeiter-Zeitung* editor August Spies caught the inflammatory language and revised it, but too many flyers were already on the streets. As a swarm gathered for the rally, everyone feared the worst. After circulating through the crowd riding his distinctive white horse and smoking his trademark cigar, Mayor Carter Harrison told officers in the nearby Desplaines Street police station they had nothing to worry about. A chilling breeze picked up as stray raindrops brushed shivering onlookers. Shortly after the rally concluded, policemen ran into the station house shouting that the last speaker had called for workers "to throttle it, kill it, stab it."[58] The officer in charge, "Black Jack" Bonfield (nicknamed for his preferred method of suppressing demonstrations), ordered his men to break up the rally. As officers stood in formation, something sparkled through the air like a Fourth of July firework: the blast from a crude bomb killed seven officers and four protestors.

Unable to identify who was responsible, prosecutors charged eight men with conspiracy, including Spies and Parsons. Although no evidence connected them to the bombing, prosecutor Julius Grinnell stretched the law in a way that Franklin Gowen might have approved, telling jurors: "The question for you to determine is … not only who did it, but who is responsible for it, who abetted it, assisted it or encouraged it?" When Judge Joseph Gary said the attack on Fort Sumter was nothing compared with "this insidious, infamous plot to ruin our laws and our country secretly in this cowardly way," the verdict was predictable.[59] Gary sentenced seven people to death.

This miscarriage of justice inspired a movement to save the defendants from the gallows that included former Lincoln law partner Lyman Trumbull and author William Dean Howells, but they were fighting a growing public outrage that was threatening to become a national lynch mob. Ever the perceptive one, Hull House's Florence Kelley saw a connection: "The only trial closely resembling it in any considerable degree [is] that of the Molly Maguires."[60] One voice missing from the cries about the miscarriage of justice was Powderly, whose concern about distancing the Knights from the riot left him silent about the defendants.

Their lives were now in the hands of Governor Richard Oglesby, a popular figure who was at Lincoln's deathbed and accompanied the president's body to burial at Springfield. After one defendant committed suicide, Oglesby commuted the sentences of two defendants to life in prison. The remaining four went to the gallows on November 11 in a grisly hanging that may have been deliberately botched, prompting protests after graphic accounts appeared across the country.[61] In 1893 Governor John Peter Altgeld summed up Haymarket: "Until the state proves from whose hands the bomb came, it is impossible to show any connection between the man who threw it and these defendants."[62]

The Haymarket affair exposed the growing power of mass communications to influence public opinion. *Inter Ocean* editor William Penn Nixon reflected, "Every incident was magnified, every speech exaggerated; sensation piled on sensation, and in this way, step by step Haymarket was reached."[63] A prime example was a *Wichita Daily Eagle* headline: "Demons of Hell!!"; the double exclamation points resembled bullets.[64] The hysteria caused Powderly to write, "The sound of a bomb did more injury to the good name of labor than all the strikes of that year."[65]

It was one of Powderly's more disingenuous statements because the Knights were a crippled union, severely wounded by one of the century's largest strikes. The bomb and the strike were what his orderly mind hated: spontaneous events driven by the irrational. A deranged mind had thrown the Haymarket bomb. By the time the Southwest Railroad Strike was over Powderly probably wondered if it too was the product of a deranged mind.

The strike began in March, two months before Haymarket, bringing Powderly the nightmare he feared when the Knights' membership ballooned: a wildcat strike led by a hotheaded official. The Southwest Railroad Strike involved over 14,000 men and 5,000 miles of track running through places like Atchison and Parsons, Kansas; Marshall and Big Springs, Texas; Sedalia and Moberly, Missouri; Alton and East St. Louis, Illinois; and Little Rock and Hoxie, Arkansas.[66] In these towns, where the railroad was a lifeline and a life's work, the strike split neighbors, families, and congregations.

As with the 1877 Railroad Strike, a disgruntled worker triggered the Southwest Strike. The Texas and Pacific Railroad (T&P) abruptly fired the absent union organizer Charles Hall, who had been given permission to attend a union meeting. Part of the "Gould system" with lines in Kansas, Missouri, Texas, and

Arkansas, the T&P was in court-ordered receivership under former Tennessee governor John C. Brown and former New Mexico territorial governor Lionel Sheldon. Anyone searching for a link between racism and laissez-faire capitalism need search no further than ex-Confederate general and Klansman Brown, who was T&P's vice president from 1876 to 1881 and chief attorney for the Gould system from 1882 until he became a receiver. In New Mexico Sheldon took a hands-off stance with the "Santa Fe Ring" of businessmen controlling the state. The congressional committee investigating the Southwest Strike elicited from him the comment that he was fighting for "the preservation of the independence of American manliness."[67]

At the center of the strike was the Knights' DA101, headed by Martin Irons, a man who resembled a riverboat card sharp more than a machinist—but maybe that is appropriate, considering the strike was a gamble. Headquartered in Sedalia, Missouri, midway between Kansas City and St. Louis, DA101 was a classic example of the Knights' runaway growth. Formed only the year before by bringing together five local assemblies, by 1886 it encompassed more than thirty locals with 3,200 members.

Like Robert Ammon, Irons walked out of obscurity onto the front pages. After arriving in this country in 1844 when he was fourteen, Irons endured what the Texas Historical Society termed "years of wandering" as he bounced from New York to New Orleans.[68] In another example of cross-fertilization among the Discontented, he even became a Grange member. In 1884 Irons landed in the Sedalia machine shop of the Missouri Pacific, where he organized DA101.

By dismissing Hall, the railroad intended to provoke a union response. In testimony before the congressional committee, Irons explained why he had fallen into the trap: "I aimed to embody all the grievances, to bring up the general thing and settle it all at once."[69] The siren song of an all-or-nothing solution is a powerful lure but is usually neither wise nor feasible. Irons compounded his error by not consulting the national office. If you are going to bet everything on a single Hail Mary play, you best let your coach know what you're doing. Certainly Irons must have known of the Knights' success against Gould in the Wabash Railroad Strike and an earlier victory in an 1884 strike led by Joseph Buchanan against the Union Pacific.

The matchup between Gould and Irons resembles the Tom Scott–Robert Ammon scenario of 1877, except that Gould was no Scott and Irons was no Ammon. Jay Gould was the figure people evoked as the classic robber baron and on hearing of his death, the New York *Sun* wrote, "By the great majority he has long been viewed as the incarnation of all that is evil and mischievous in his sphere of activity, and his removal will, therefore, be hailed as a blessing."[70] Negative opinions date to when Gould attempted to take over the Albany and Susquehanna Railroad. In a scene resembling a Looney Tunes cartoon, a locomotive carrying Gould's army of Bowery toughs crashed head-on into a train carrying rival troops in the Long Tunnel outside Binghamton, New York. The results were not funny: ten died. Although such incidents contributed to the view of Gould as out of control, supporters saw him differently. Typical was the son of Western Union president and Cornell University founder Ezra Cornell, who said, "As a business man he was the most far-sighted man I have ever known. He was the soul of honor in his personal integrity."[71]

Gould and his lieutenant who headed the Missouri Pacific, H. M. Hoxie, wanted an all-or-nothing settlement as much as Irons did. According to the State of Missouri's official account, "There was the grim, unswerving fixedness of purpose of H. M. Hoxie. The time had come, he said, when the question had to be decided whether he should run his own railroad or have the Knights of Labor run it."[72] His attitude contributed to a spiral of escalation made worse by misunderstanding, creative interpretations of the contract, and T&P receivers.

On hearing Hall's story, the DA101 executive board was furious but followed protocol by sending a request on February 17 demanding his reinstatement. Meanwhile, Irons and others gathered eyewitness testimony corroborating that Hall's supervisor gave him permission to be absent. The receivers promised to investigate but did nothing. DA101 executive board member T. J. Burnett telegraphed George Noble, an agent for the receivers, "Please come to Marshall immediately, to settle trouble in shops."[73] Noble replied that he knew of no trouble and was too busy to travel, an explanation that stretches credibility. It was clear, if it had not been before, the owners wanted to break the union.

Irons was growing frustrated. He wired Noble on February 28 saying that if he did not hear from him by 2:00 p.m. on March 1, he would call a strike. Noble was silent to that and another wire Irons sent at the eleventh hour. In congressional hearings, the T&P later claimed it did not know Martin Irons, although he signed the telegram "Chairman Executive Committee K. of L."

The Southwest Strike hinged on what happened next. Standing at the edge of the precipice, Irons could have stepped back and consulted Powderly. He chose not to. In congressional testimony he implied that the national union had no jurisdiction over DA101: "The district assembly is composed of all the locals in a certain district, taken up in a certain territory, *subject to have their own government and laws*."[74] Faced with a strike, railroad officials gave employees until March 4 to return to work. Technically the strike was now a lockout. Meanwhile, neither the receivers nor the railroad attempted to contact Irons. Had they had the courtesy to reply, events might have ended differently.

On March 6, DA101 extended the strike to the Missouri Pacific. Two days later, an angry Hoxie issued a circular condemning the union:

> There has never before been an act so arbitrary, useless, and uncalled for as that of last Saturday, whereby a few men, to whom you have voluntarily given the power, are depriving many thousands of their collaborators of their accustomed wages, divesting this company of the capacity to pay its employees for their services, shutting up the avenues of traffic in four States, and preventing some 4,000,000 of people from obtaining their customary supplies and the necessities of life.[75]

Irons replied, but after Hoxie's impassioned argument, he was losing the battle in the press. He never chose to use the words he spoke to the congressional committee, "That the strike was not in the interest of one man, but for a principle involved; that the contract between the employees and the railroad made through the mediation of the governors of Missouri and Kansas one year ago, had been violated."[76] He was right, but those wanting to break the union didn't care.

In the tinder-like atmosphere, the strike spread quickly. Many walked out because of loyalty—a significant statement—but did not know why. Asked the reasons for the strike, one worker said, "I never heard."[77] Given the lack of organization, it is not surprising that the strike quickly ran off the rails (pun intended), as violence and destruction sprang up randomly, as they had in 1877. Workers also began disabling locomotives. Locomotive engineers had refused to honor the strike, prompting the Knights' local publication to call Locomotive and Fireman's Union president Lloyd McBride an "insolent traitor dude."[78] To prevent "insolent traitors" from running trains, the strikers crippled their locomotives. They claimed the disabled engines could be restarted but risks ranged from malfunctioning controls to every engineer's nightmare: exploding boilers. It was a divisive, dangerous, and ultimately stupid action.

It remains a blot on DA101 that Powderly learned of the strike through the newspapers. If nothing else, it must have felt like a severe blow, because Powderly had more than he—or anyone else—could handle. One day provides an idea of the pressures he faced. On March 9 alone the Knights were involved in a cotton strike in Galveston, Texas; they had just settled an eighteen-month boycott with the Fuller Warren Company of Troy, New York; and they had fended off rumors of organizing a political party and attempting to unionize police. With the union threatening to split at the seams from the glut of new members, the national office directed state organizers to quit organizing for forty days and concentrate on instructing assemblies.[79]

With the Knights threatening to break apart, Powderly sent an urgent telegram to receiver Brown, asking to discuss the strike. Brown replied, "I do not see any good that arbitration with the committee of the Knights of Labor could accomplish."[80] Brown's words, so in keeping with the nullification view of many late nineteenth-century corporations, sealed the strike's fate. Powderly called an emergency meeting to discuss a strike that no one appeared able to control. During the meeting Martin Irons whispered to Powderly a plot worthy of a dime novel: a masked intruder surprised him as he worked at his desk, pointed a gun at his head and demanded that he order the strike. This story has troubled historians for decades. Maybe Irons manufactured it because he was afraid to tell Powderly the truth. There is another possibility: Powderly invented the story with Irons's collusion, thus removing both from a jam.

On March 28 Powderly convinced Gould to discuss the matter and ordered the strikers back to work. Gould told Hoxie to allow all workers to return to their jobs, an order he never carried out. Negotiations continued through April with no resolution; talks did not stop the escalating violence. The *Labor Herald* from Richmond, Virginia, weighed in: "The Knights of Labor who, as an organization, are not responsible, find that their leaders are powerless to control the unreasoning masses."[81] Rioting in East St. Louis mirrored Pittsburgh in 1877. On April 9 a train guarded by hired "deputies" used Winchesters to break through a mob blocking the tracks. When the train reached the city, police attempted to arrest the deputies, but they threw the train in reverse and opened fire, leaving six dead. The continuing violence of the Southwest Strike prompted a congressional investigation, which in turn prompted an ending to the strike on May 4, the day the bomb exploded in Haymarket Square. According to the congressional committee, railroad property damage totaled $2.8 million and strikers lost $900,000 in wages. It cost the Knights everything.

If the Movement Is Successful

The same year as the Haymarket affair and the Southwest Strike, the man who saw himself as an equalizer attempted to organize African Americans in the South. The Knights were not the first to try forming a multiracial labor organization. Richard Trevellick and William Silvis had sought to diversify the National Labor Union but failed when African Americans formed their own union after a fight over delegates. By the 1880s the Knights were swimming against the growing apartheid in the South, as African Americans became entangled in a bewildering web woven of impenetrable laws, bizarre customs, white sheets, and knotted ropes.

The Knights began organizing the South in earnest in 1883, increasing membership to 21,208 in 1888.[82] This represented only a fraction of the total union membership but resulted in a disproportionate amount of support. The same year as Haymarket, Powderly made a gambler's decision to go all in even though he lacked the chips to cover his bet, wagering on a strike in Charleston, South Carolina. While the Knights were involved in several multiracial strikes in the South, Charleston was critical.

Charleston membership in the Knights had exploded in parallel with the national increase, growing to 4,000 members and four locals by 1886. A significant number were African Americans in a city where they were a majority. Then came one of those serendipitous events around which history often pivots. On August 31, 1886, a massive earthquake hit Charleston, killing nearly sixty and leaving the city with too much to do and not enough workers to do it—or at least not enough willing to work for minimal wages. Assuming they were in the driver's seat, the Knights made an ill-advised power play by asking the city to give the union a portion of the relief funds pouring in from all over the country. The relief committee politely declined, although one member said those who signed the request ought to be "hung to a lamp post."[83]

African Americans, who realized the crisis made their labor valuable, decided to leverage the situation. Church leaders urged workers not to settle for less than they were worth. Recognizing they needed help, Charleston union members asked the Knights' national office to send a Black organizer. Instead, the national office left strategy and tactics in the hands of W. P. Russell, the white Grand Master Workman for South Carolina, who had a checkered reputation.

Russell proceeded to inflame the situation when he sent a letter to the press stating, "The laborers in the rural districts of South Carolina are to be used as the lazy, intolerant men in these districts choose to dictate."[84] Newspapers relayed Russell's message and its inevitable pushback: "Some papers advise the farmers to 'spot' all white men like Russell if they try to organize negro Knights of Labor, and to run them from the neighborhood," read one story.[85]

One citizen ignited by Russell's words was Ben Tillman, who relished playing the role of a backcountry redneck with a tongue like a bullwhip. Tillman made his mark as a leader of the notorious 1876 Hamburg Massacre, when terrorist "Red Shirts" summarily executed African American members of the local militia, leaving a carnage the governor described as "a darker picture of human cruelty than the slaughter of Custer and his soldiers."[86] Whites like Tillman were not about to let Russell cause trouble, quickly passing a state law making it a conspiracy to recruit "negroes" to join a union. Offenders risked six months in jail and a fine of $200. Despite the Knights' attempts to soldier on, Tillman had won.

That All in Harmony May Live

By the time the Knights' national convention met in Richmond, Virginia, on October 4, Terence Powderly had experienced a year of tribulation. A poem by "Toiler" expressed the convention delegates' hopes:

> We organize that wealth no more
> Shall rich and poor divide;
> That all in harmony may live
> And labor side by side.[87]

It took an African American New Yorker named Frank Ferrell to show how tilted the playing field had become. Ferrell is often referred to as a mechanic, but he was a classic Yankee tinkerer, eventually holding a dozen patents on steam valves.[88] As a delegate from District Assembly 49 of New York City, Ferrell was one of about twenty African Americans attending the meeting. The Knights' largest and one of its most radical locals, DA49 militantly opposed the newly founded American Federation of Labor. Before leaving the city, district officials concocted an audacious plan to confront southern racism in the former Confederate capital.

The Knights chose Richmond because they naively believed they could unite Black and white workers in the face of Jim Crow. On a long trip through the South in 1885, Powderly stated his aim was "to educate both [Black and white] and elevate them, bringing them together."[89] During that trip he organized Richmond's first African American local.

The DA49 delegation reserved rooms in Murphy's Hotel, but when they arrived they were told Ferrell was not welcome. It is tempting to find metaphorical significance in the alternative lodging they chose—Harris Hall—which was above a funeral parlor. Other African American delegates chose not to challenge the color line except for Baltimore's Joseph Ward, who stayed with his white comrades at the St. Charles.[90] For the delegates, Harris Hall proved hospitable, with Ferrell serving as skillful a diplomat as he was an inventor.

DA49 master workman James Quinn met with Powderly to propose that Ferrell should introduce Virginia governor and former Confederate general Fitzhugh Lee. The nephew of Robert E. Lee and grandson of Revolutionary War general "Lighthorse Harry" Lee, Fitzhugh Lee led the last cavalry charge before Appomattox, where he initially refused to surrender. When Powderly opposed Quinn's idea, saying it would not be "an act of courtesy," Quinn had an alternative: Ferrell could introduce Powderly. *Frank Leslie's Illustrated Newspaper* captured the moment that Powderly rose from a chair next to Lee.[91] Looking distinguished in a frock coat, Ferrell extends a hand to Powderly, while in the other hand he clutches his speech. The bearded Lee looks directly at Ferrell, but we cannot read his expression. Ferrell's words link the Knights with justice: "One of the objects of our Order is the abolition of those distinctions which are maintained by creed or color. I believe I present to you a man above the superstitions which are involved in these distinctions. My experience with the noble Order of the Knights of Labor and my training in my district, have taught me that we have worked so far successfully toward the extinction of these regrettable distinctions." Speaking next, Powderly explained why he asked Ferrell to speak. In one of his finer moments, he stated, "I made the selection of that man from that delegation to introduce me during the address of his Excellency, Governor Lee, so that it may go forth from here to the entire world that 'we practice what we preach.'"[92] The evening tested his words.

The next morning, after Ferrell attended a performance of *Hamlet* at the segregated and prestigious Richmond Academy of Music, the city was in an uproar. A group called the Law and Order League announced that an armed patrol would "guard" the theater to prevent a repeat of the "outrage." Hearing of threats to disrupt the Knights' meeting, Powderly went to the police chief to demand protection. Then he issued an open letter, quoted at length here, because to do otherwise would be to distort its power:

> The negro is free; he is here, and he is here to stay. He is a citizen, and must learn to manage his own affairs. His labor and that of the white man will be thrown upon the market side by side, and no human eye can detect a difference between the article manufactured by the black mechanic and that manufactured by the white mechanic. . . . Our principles will be better known, if not to-day it may be tomorrow; they can bide their time, and will some day have the world for an audience.[93]

Unfortunately, by the time this appeared the Knights were gravely wounded.

The final word on the Knights' fateful year came from the congressional report on the Southwest Railroad Strike. Issued shortly after Congress passed the Interstate Commerce Act, the committee's findings brought America back to fundamental principles:

> There can be no doubt that the concentration of wealth and power, and the oppressions which have occurred, as shown in the evidence taken, may have promoted the unrest of labor, as is painfully apparent. Whatever remedy will give the proper protection to the capital invested in the railroads of the country and at the same time protect their employees from injustice and oppression, your committee propose that they shall together, as a single instrument of our interstate commerce, be looked upon as the servants of the people of the United States, and as such be regulated and protected by law.[94]

The Knights struggled on for several more years. Viewing it as an opportunity to reinvigorate the organization, Powderly seemed to be everywhere during the 1892 Omaha People's Party convention. At one point he was seen walking into the main hall arm-in-arm with eventual presidential nominee James Weaver, accompanied by resounding applause. His overtures came too late. The involvement of Powderly and the Knights suggests some tantalizing if-onlys about the People's Party. Had the Populists emerged when the Knights were stronger, it might have come closer to fulfilling the promise of an 1890s farmer-labor coalition along the lines of the Greenback Party.

By 1894 Powderly had been eased out of the Knights' leadership and become a Republican. Reflecting on what had happened to him, he commented, "You know it makes a decent man smell to be pissed on by a skunk."[95] He eventually became an immigration official, a post suited to his officious ways. After Martin Irons died in poverty, union members commissioned a statue in his honor. A solicitation by the woodworkers' union assessed the strike Irons had led: "It was the first great labor battle in the Southwest and as such it laid the foundation for the labor movement in the Southwestern states."[96]

If 1886 was a year of upheaval for America, it was more than that for the Knights of Labor. The Haymarket affair, the Southwest Strike, the Charleston earthquake, and the annual convention were all tainted by rogue elements. The Haymarket rally wasn't even organized by the Knights, who had even less connection to the murders than those who wrongly paid the price for them. The Southwest Strike began as a wildcat action that went out of control. DA49 instigated the controversies at the convention. The Charleston debacle resulted from decisions made by someone who should have never been in charge.

In addition, Terence Powderly's frenetic schedule and the Knights' explosive growth would tax the best of organizers, even in our Internet-centered world. One contemporary remarked, "During that year it spread like wild fire and there was not a city of importance in the Union nor a good-sized town in the North that did not contain from a few to several thousand members of the order."[97] By 1893 the Knights' membership had declined to 75,000. Andrew Carnegie termed the Knights "one of those ephemeral organizations that go up like a rocket and come down like a stick. It was founded upon false principles, viz., that they could combine common or unskilled labor with skilled."[98]

In the end the Knights organization collapsed from its own systemic weaknesses. Powderly was everywhere, which was his problem. Organizing African American workers in the Deep South would have been difficult for an organization with far more resources than the Knights, but attempting it while managing the McCormick and Southwest Strikes, along with the other actions occurring at the time, amounted to organizational suicide.

Robert Weir and Craig Phelan are among those who have pointed out the Knights' organizational difficulties. Weir states, "Left with unclear lines, too many individuals and assemblies were left to 'improvise.'" Phelan says the Knights' organization was "too fragile."[99] It is true that Powderly was fighting tendencies not even he could manage. Control was central to the dynamics of the late nineteenth century, but it had multiple interpretations. "Control" to workers on a steel mill shop floor meant something different than it did to mill owners and union officials hundreds of miles away. In the transition from staples society to consumer culture, workers resented anyone telling them what to do, whether it was a shift boss or Terence Powderly.

From a systemic perspective the Knights' were a loose federation built around common principles in which local assemblies held the balance of power. Even as he struggled to exert control, Powderly had little leverage over the likes of Martin Irons. In turn, Irons had little power to rein in rioting workers. Wildcat strikes stemming from negative reinforcing loops, once set in motion, have no internal brakes to keep them from careening out of control.

People at the time recognized the Knights' organizational problems. An 1888 New York report blamed one strike on conflicts between two district assemblies, one of them DA49.[100] Connecticut reported, "A considerable number of strikes have been ordered during this period by local assemblies of the Knights of Labor which have not been authorized by the Executive Board of the District Assembly."[101] Powderly did not like these actions, as his comment about a wildcat strike in San Pedro, California, illustrates: "A strike entered upon so recklessly without the sanction of higher authority within the organization, with no proper effort having been made by peaceful negotiation to settle differences, did not deserve and could not expect a successful issue."[102] Yet he could not prevent such actions.

From the perspectives of community organizing and strategic planning, Powderly's Knights made a classic mistake: they had admirable goals, some borrowed from the NLU and Greenbackers, but they never articulated the steps nor actualized them, nor measured their progress. National meeting minutes betray this weakness, with most discussions focused on policy rather than structure and implementation. The intent of DA49 to press the race issue in Richmond was admirable, as was Frank Ferrell's courage to carry it out, but something so crucial should never have been decided at the last minute.

The federation structure did have the advantage of allowing local assemblies to make some of the Knights' most lasting contributions. Analysts like Richard Oestricher have detailed some of these efforts in cities like Detroit.[103] For trades like bakers, who were not under the thumb of monopolies, local assemblies made adroit use of boycotts to bring recalcitrant owners to the bargaining table. These were successful because they could boycott a particular bakery while allowing patrons to purchase bread from establishments down the street. This worked for brewers, textile workers, and others, but you could not boycott Jay Gould.

The Knights' most important local success stories come from agitating for bureaus of labor statistics and various state inspection laws. Their lobbying for the national bureau was so great that Powderly expected to receive the post that went to Carroll Wright. An 1887 Pennsylvania report reflected on the Knights' role: "Bureaus of Industrial Statistics . . . are to a considerable degree the result of efforts made by members of the order."[104] In return, the Knights aided the new bureaus, earning a thank-you from one in Iowa, who said, "Many of the Statisticians of the Knights of Labor Assemblies have extended kind cooperation and to them I am grateful."[105]

Other measures also reflect organized labor's influence. In 1877 Massachusetts approved the nation's first workplace health and safety law, followed in 1879 by the appointment of three inspectors to enforce work hour limits and working conditions. Other states followed. In 1897 Michigan's Department of Labor noted, "In the five years of factory inspection there has been a gradual and substantial reduction in the number and character of accidents."[106]

The Knights brought a potent mixture of pride and hope to individual workers being overwhelmed by industrialization. Treated as interchangeable parts by owners, in countless meetings they developed a sense of solidarity. When you engage in repetitive, backbreaking, and dangerous occupations, it is easy to feel the weight of every dawn-to-dusk day with little hope that life might improve. Individuality and the joys of the human spirit are as much casualties of this system as any physical injury a worker might suffer. The only way to lift this weight, which is far too heavy for any individual to move, is to seek common cause with fellow workers and together lift the burden. A Connecticut report had a different opinion than Carnegie about the Knights: "It has represented labor as a whole in its contests against capital as a whole. It has taken men from all ranks of life and made them work together."[107] For the Knights and others dealing with the Age of Discontent, their efforts finally reached fruition at the end of the decade.

CHAPTER TEN

THE REINVENTION OF AMERICA

Come join our reform, and enter the field.
The numbers are ours, the power we wield.
Our armor is bright and our weapons are strong.
—*From "Call to Arms," a Farmers' Alliance song*

How a former Confederate postmaster general became the catalyst for one of America's most significant pieces of legislation remains one of history's stranger tales. John Reagan lived most of his life in Paradise, an idyllic Texas town north of Dallas. In photographs he is easy to identify because of a meticulously combed, wave-like sweep of hair on his left side that exemplifies his penchant for control. As postmaster general his insistence on efficiencies led the postal service to earn a profit. Uncomfortable with post–Civil War violence, Reagan urged Texans to support Emancipation, although he warned of "the dangers of universal negro suffrage."[1]

In the 1870s Reagan held various offices before landing in the House of Representatives in 1876. At that time the Grange was becoming a force in Texas politics. His biographer says, unequivocally, "Reagan was a Granger."[2] Reagan believed "the Granger movement was a protest against robbery by monied power. The national party, greenback party, Farmers' Alliances, and the labor party, or Knights of Labor, were all so many forms of protesting against class legislation, tending to enrich the few at the expense of many."[3]

In the late 1880s and early 1890s those forms of protest became instrumental in passing a series of laws designed to alter a playing field Americans believed was perilously tilted. The Interstate Commerce Act of 1887 (ICA) asserted federal regulatory authority. That year, congress also approved the Hatch Act, establishing federal funding for agricultural extension stations. Three years later Congress passed the Sherman Antitrust Act and the Second Morrill Act.

Finally, in 1893 came the Safety Appliance Act mandating automatic couplers and air brakes on trains. Together they reinvented American democracy.

A Pressure So Great

When John Reagan presented his first interstate commerce bill in 1878, he anticipated John Harlan's *Civil Rights Cases* dissent: "Railroads receive their franchises from the public for the public good as well as for the profit of the stockholders. Railroad corporations are in an important sense public corporations, and are always recognized as quasi-public corporations."[4] Reagan's leadership over the next decade is why Elizabeth Sanders terms him the "father" of the Interstate Commerce Act.[5] A Louisiana newspaper explained, "His inter-state commerce bill, whether it ever becomes a law or not, has made the name of John H. Reagan a familiar one from one end of this country to the other."[6] In 1879 the Grange urged members to petition their congressional representatives to support "Reagan bills."[7] A newspaper commented: "The Reagan bill was drawn by the National Grange, and placed in the hands of Mr. Reagan. . . . Through the instrumentality of the National Grange this bill was industriously pushed and a pressure so great brought upon members of Congress, that they acknowledged that they must obey or answer to their constituents."[8]

Despite the Grange national headquarters' distaste for politics, local granges fought to control a runaway railroad business. During the 1870s, what an observer termed "the Granger tornado" of legislation emerged to deal with the abuses of the railroads.[9] Iowa, Wisconsin, and other states formed railroad commissions and passed regulations like the Granger Laws.[10] Six state constitutions added prohibitions against pooling—a cartel-like arrangement whose members collaborated for greater efficiencies and leverage.[11] Pressure continued in the 1880s, as the Discontented continued demanding railroad regulation.

Richard Bensel analyzed state party platforms favoring government regulation or ownership of railroads and found that they were strongest in plains states, with the West a close second.[12] As Thomas McCraw and others have pointed out, single carriers dominated in the South and Midwest, leading to concerns about monopoly power, while in the East many roads competed for customers.[13] The South and Midwest were also strongholds of the Greenback Party and Farmers' Alliances. This southern-midwestern "McCraw pattern" became a political force in the late 1880s legislation.

During the 1880s the Wild West characterizing the railroad business caused conservative executives to wonder if an interstate commerce law might tame the outlaws. Their loudest voice was Charles Francis Adams Jr., the grandson of President John Adams and president of the Union Pacific Railroad. In 1869 Adams created the Massachusetts Board of Railroad Commissioners, whose "sunshine" approach publicized transgressions while relying on the courts to punish them. That same year Adams also wrote *A Chapter of Erie*, criticizing the tactics Jay Gould and Jim Fiske used to gain control of the Erie Railroad. Taking a cynical tone, Adams wrote, "It would be no difficult task to make the cunning civilization of the nineteenth century appear but as a hypocritical mask spread over the more honest brutality of the twelfth."[14] Against this background, Reagan explained why he continued bringing forward his interstate commerce bill: "There was a general depression of business, and the great body of the people had been driven away from commercial centers. The people have been compelled to make great efforts to meet the increased burdens imposed upon them, to pay their taxes and preserve their rights and property from grasping monopolists."[15]

In 1884, as Reagan's newest bill moved through the House, railroad interests with competing agendas fought to shape it. Major players like the New York Central wanted to preserve their dominance; speculators like Jay Gould wanted to make money. Local and regional lines feared being gobbled up. Then there were the pools. German immigrant Albert Fink showed the power of pooling when he created the Southern Railway and Steamship Association in 1875. Historian Richard White writes that Fink "studied railroads the way Darwin studied evolution," a talent he used to create innovative accounting methods.[16]

The coalition backing Reagan was neither bipartisan nor national. In sixteen votes taken on the bill from December 16, 1886, until final passage, of the 51 members who supported Reagan on all but three votes, 39 were from southern and border states, along with three each from Indiana and California, two from Illinois, and one each from Michigan, Delaware, Nevada, and Pennsylvania. All were Democrats. Because this Reagan bloc was insufficient to pass the bill, it needed Republican support.[17] In the end 28 Republicans crossed the aisle to pass the bill, most from the Midwest, including 7 from Kansas, and 4 each from Minnesota and Indiana. This southern-midwestern McCraw combination characterized support from the Discontented. Faced with the Reagan bloc and Republican allies, opponents attempted to stall the bill by offering amendments punctuated by constant interruptions designed to filibuster. A frustrated Reagan exclaimed, "It seems I can not read a sentence without some gentlemen rising to interrupt me."[18]

Several amendments raised the issue of accommodations, showing the *Civil Rights Cases* decision was still festering. North Carolina Republican representative James O'Hara, one of two African Americans in Congress, offered the following amendment: "Whenever any person purchases a ticket or pays an amount of money as fare to the officer or agent of any railroad corporation in the United States for a continuous passage from one State to another, that person shall be entitled to the same facilities, privileges, accommodations, and advantages that any other person or persons holding the same class of ticket is accorded and entitled to."[19]

Among those defending O'Hara's amendment was Charles Brumm, a Greenbacker from Schuylkill County, Pennsylvania. Growing up in Pottstown, the hometown of Franklin Gowen, Brumm knew corporate abuse firsthand. Because the 1884 Greenback platform regulated interstate commerce and condemned pooling and discrimination in rates and charges, Brumm would have been expected to support Reagan's bill.[20] His speech supporting O'Hara explains why he did not:

> I saw in the cars passing through South Carolina Southern women coming in who chewed tobacco and spat over the floor, and I saw well-dressed Southern ruffians come in who were allowed to sit in the same cars with white men, and when a colored man came in he was compelled to take a seat in another car. I was interested to know why, and followed him into the other car. I said to him, "Please let me see your ticket." He showed me the ticket, and it was exactly the same ticket sold to and held by those in the same car we were in and from which he was expelled.[21]

In response, Arkansas representative Clifton Breckinridge offered a separate but equal solution, anticipating the 1896 *Plessy v. Ferguson* decision.[22] After a series of dueling resolutions, the House settled on the following: "No discrimination is made on account of race or color; and that furnishing separate accommodations, with equal facilities and equal comforts, at the same charges, shall not be considered a discrimination."[23] It is little wonder Brumm and many northerners opposed the final bill. Despite their opposition, the bill passed on January 8, 1885; it required public posting of schedules and rates, equal rates for long- and short-haul shipping, and a prohibition against pooling, rebates, and drawbacks. The battle then moved to the Senate.

Reagan's Senate counterpart was Shelby Cullom of Illinois. Cullom had once approached Abraham Lincoln to study law, but the future president declined because of his many obligations. Cullom found others to mentor him and, after passing the bar, became active in politics, serving as city attorney, congressional representative, and governor, entering the Senate in 1882. Cullom was neither the Senate's brightest bulb nor its most feared orator. His methodical mind moved slowly, but his dogged persistence and attention to detail earned the respect of his colleagues. While senators like Nelson Aldrich were known as "railroad men," Cullom worked with all factions.

Cullom's previous interstate commerce bills died like Reagan's. All revolved around a national commission resembling the one in Charles Adams's Massachusetts. In 1884 Cullom sponsored a new bill that ran on parallel tracks to Reagan's House bill. He explained: "In undertaking to frame any legislation upon this subject we must constantly bear in mind the fact that the interests of the railroads and of their patrons and of the whole people are identical."[24] The bill faced a scrum of lawyers, complicated by the presence of eleven former Confederate generals.

By January a Senate still debating Cullom's bill faced the radically different Reagan bill that had recently passed the House. The House had enacted restrictions with the courts to enforce them, while Cullom proposed a commission with investigative but not enforcement powers. Sen. Charles Van Wyck (Nebraska-R) declared, "The bill passed in the House known as the Regan bill is infinitely better. It declares offenses, affixes penalties, directs the prosecution, and allows the citizen to select attorneys and a State or Federal Tribunal. The Senate bill denies all these privileges, and makes the latter end worse than the first."[25] Termed "an honest, fearless, and able representative in the stronghold of the monopolists" by a Grange paper, Van Wyck was a former Civil War general who had survived an assassination attempt after giving a rabid antislavery speech.[26] In 1892 he ran for governor as a Populist.

Cullom's solution was as ingenious as it was inflammatory. He brought Reagan's bill to the floor, then amended its entire text with his bill. That did not sit well with Van Wyck and others who responded, "It will be an unfortunate day when a Republican Senate declines to accept a measure adopted by a Democratic House in the interest of the people."[27] After a vigorous debate, the Cullom bill passed 43–12 on St. Patrick's Day. Understandably, when the Cullom bill came back to them with their text completely erased, the House tabled it.

Cullom had another card to play. To build support for his bill, he formed a committee to "investigate and report upon the subject of the regulation of commerce among the several States."[28] In hearings that began May 20 in New York and ended November 18 in Atlanta, the committee heard 163 witnesses who generated fourteen hundred pages of testimony. The largest number of those testifying were merchants (40), followed by railroad commission members (17), railroad owners and managers (15), and business owners (15). No witnesses represented the Grange, the Farmers' Alliances, or the Greenback Party, but the committee did hear from Charles Adams, meatpacker Gustavus Swift, department store magnate Marshall Field, and mill owner Charles Pillsbury. Although Cullom had successfully locked out the Discontented, there was testimony about their grievances from people like Minnesota farmer Datus Meyer: "The people are absolutely feeling that their rights are being jeopardized; and there is an idea taking possession of them that unless there are some steps taken to mitigate or regulate the condition of things in some way a feeling will spring up that will be dangerous at times. If there were a failure of the crops the people might become violent."[29] Despite hearing mostly from business owners, the committee rejected a laissez-faire approach. Conceding the tendency "to throw the control of the commerce of the country more and more into the hands of the few," the report affirmed, "the State possesses the right to supervise and regulate the administration of such imperial power [of the railroads] upon the broad ground of public policy."[30]

With the report as ammunition, Cullom's committee reintroduced an interstate commerce bill in February 1886, which finally passed the Senate then the House with amendments necessitating a conference committee. The Senate bill enjoyed a better reception in the House because the 1886 election cost the Democrats sixteen seats; Reagan lost eleven members of his coalition. With the Supreme Court's *Wabash* decision hovering over them, the discussions produced the fragile final compromise.

The twenty-four sections of the Interstate Commerce Act contained enough ambiguity to provide long-term employment for a horde of attorneys. To grasp the frustration it caused, the five-hundred-word, comma-weighted sentence that opens Section 16 is worth reading. And Elizabeth Sanders's response to it is apt: "One could not, because of the less precise wording, be sure what was outlawed."[31] In its convoluted language, the ICA prohibited railroads from pooling, from charging different rates for long- and short-haul routes, from providing discounts based on volume, from distributing free passes, and from giving special rates. It required railroads to "print and keep for public inspection" records of fares and other charges. A five-member Interstate Commerce Commission (ICC) appointed by the president regulated its use by investigating and hearing cases but lacked enforcement powers.[32]

It seems ironically appropriate that much of the country learned about the passage of the ICA on Groundhog Day. After the act passed, Congress and the courts kept rewriting it, trying to get it right, like the Bill Murray character in the movie *Groundhog Day*. Someone found a typo, causing amateur lawyers to wonder whether the mistake killed the bill. Lobbyists worked overtime to convince Pres. Grover Cleveland to veto the bill. After Cleveland signed it on February 4, 1887, the maneuvering began to place people on the new commission.

The tortuous clauses of the ICA have become a deep pool, reflecting the views of those peering into it while revealing little about the churning waters beneath its surface. The most controversial interpretation came almost a century later when Gabriel Kolko created a tempest by making the ICA the centerpiece of his theory that "business control over politics (and by 'business' I mean the major economic interests) rather than political regulation of the economy ... is the significant phenomenon of the Progressive Era."[33] Kolko proposed railroad regulation was "political capitalism for the sake of the railroads."[34]

Historians have largely debunked the Kolko interpretation, pointing out its misuse of sources and misinterpretations of the bill's provisions.[35] Shelby Cullom brings those lost in the thickets of the ICA back to the forest: "The great object achieved by the passage of the Interstate Commerce bill was the assertion of the power of the national government to regulate internal affairs."[36] Cullom also reminds us that the ICA maintained we are a nation, not a confederation of states, and as a nation we must assert principles that bind us together for the greater good.

Conduct Original

The ICA wasn't the only major legislation emerging in 1887. Passage of the Hatch Act provided states with "such sums as Congress may from time to time determine to be necessary" to "conduct original and other researches, investigations, and experiments ... as have for their purpose the development and improvement of the rural home and rural life and the maximum contribution by agriculture to the welfare of the consumer."[37] These aims were tied to the land grant colleges and universities approved by Congress in 1862. The man most responsible for that law was a Vermonter who believed this country needed an option to the elitist colleges mainly serving the upper class. Described as "a complex man who did not fit into any rigidly-defined niche," Justin Morrill entered Congress in 1853 and served six terms in the House, followed by six more in the Senate, where colleagues bestowed on him the highest term of respect: "Father of the Senate."[38]

In 1858 Morrill proposed his idea for colleges "to broadcast that knowledge which will prove useful in building up a great nation."[39] His inspiration was academies like the Agricultural College of the State of Michigan (now Michigan State University), funded by the state in 1855. In advocating similar institutions, Morrill invoked the level playing field:

> Pass this measure and we shall have done—
> Something to enable the farmer to raise two blades of grass instead of one;
> Something for every owner of land;
> Something for all who desire to own land;
> Something for cheap scientific education;
> Something for every man who favors intelligence and not ignorance;
> Something to remove the last vestiges of pauperism from our land.[40]

Ironically, the bill Abraham Lincoln signed, funding what became known as "land grant" colleges and universities, would not have passed before the Civil War because southern states opposed it.

The Morrill Act provided states with 30,000 acres for each senator and each representative "in order to promote the liberal and practical education of the industrial classes in the several pursuits and professions in life."[41] By the end of the century California had 2 million acres in Morrill lands. Land grant researchers produced more than two thousand farm-related books and pamphlets between 1852 and 1877.[42] Despite this, they suffered from funding problems.

College officials and agriculture researchers periodically discussed plans to rationalize the system, but the first bill to federally fund agricultural experiment stations came from a former Iowa pig farmer turned university professor. Raised on a New York farm, Seaman Knapp taught in Poultney, Vermont, after graduating Phi Beta Kappa from Union College. Then the rug was pulled from under him when an accident left him permanently disabled. Physicians urged him to move west, following the well-worn path of those hoping a new start might bring stability. He bought a sheep farm, but a blizzard destroyed his herd. Like others, after hitting bottom Knapp had a conversion experience, reinventing himself as a scientific farmer. His expertise in raising pigs brought him to Iowa State University.

Knapp was a creative and discerning borrower who carried with him ideas about the experiential learning he received at Union College. These eventually germinated into his conviction that the best way to teach agriculture was through demonstration. Like Oliver Kelley, Knapp also wanted to make it possible for farmers to learn from the best. Kelley's lecturers were one way to share that knowledge; Knapp took a different direction, perfecting the idea of using test plots to identify the best varieties and how to cultivate them.

Knapp is known as the "father of cooperative extension" and "schoolmaster of American agriculture" because he expanded his test plots into a blueprint for a national system of extension stations, funded by Washington but controlled by the states.[43] Connecticut's Wilbur Atwater and colleagues, who founded experiment stations in the 1870s, had dreamed of networking their work. Knapp gave their ideas concrete form. Publisher Walter Page called Knapp's efforts "the greatest single piece of constructive educational work in this or any age." Further words of Page's tribute capture Knapp's commitment: "It was no part of his great work to lead armies, guide political parties, or write essays on the theory of government and the rights of man. His achievements were greater. He sought freedom and independence in the soil, and he found both, and gave them to the world."[44] Knapp was leading a symbolic army. Discontented farmers who endured hardships after the Panic of 1873 had begun changing their outlook. Prodded by Grange and Farmers' Alliances members with a thirst for education, leaders like Leonidas Polk stepped up agitation for what Polk termed a "system of practical technical training."[45]

During an 1882 gathering convened by Agriculture Commissioner George Loring, Knapp drafted legislation to "establish national experiment stations in connection with the agricultural colleges in the various states."[46] Carried by Iowa Representative C. C. Carpenter, the bill died in committee. At a second convention a year later that included Justin Morrill, a committee with Knapp and four representatives of extension stations and agricultural colleges was appointed to work with Congress in reintroducing an extension bill. It also died. As it became clear that passage of the bill required determined lobbying, the Grange and Farmers' Alliances turned up the heat. Congress received petitions for funding experiment stations from California, Illinois, Maine, Michigan, New Jersey, North Carolina, Ohio, South Carolina, Texas, and Wisconsin.[47]

A thousand miles east of Knapp's Iowa, new Pennsylvania State University president George Atherton saw the Knapp bill as an opportunity to revive his struggling institution.[48] Atherton's skills lay in meticulous preparation and keeping his eye on the objective of not separating the stations from the universities. At the same time, he knew the bill could not pass without satisfying all factions. Atherton assumed the leadership of the committee of college and extension officials as efforts revved up in 1886.

In 1887 the bill gained a new champion: Rep. William Hatch, a Missouri

Democrat who had reached the rank of lieutenant colonel in the Confederate Army. Fresh from supporting John Reagan's Interstate Commerce bill, Hatch joined Atherton to patch over disputes among alliance, Grange, and university representatives over the bill. Like the argument over interstate commerce, the dispute was about control.

The Alliances and Grange had become increasingly distressed by land grant institutions neglecting farmers' needs, instead opting for a "classical education." Their anger surfaced during the 1887 Grange national meeting: "Many of the colleges that availed of the land grants made by the act of 1862 have failed utterly to meet its provisions . . . they realized large sums of money from the sale of lands given with the purpose of encouraging agricultural and mechanical education and made little attempt to meet obligations imposed by the laws."[49] A Minnesota Farmers' Alliance meeting turned ugly over "charges made against the management of the [test] farm and of the state university."[50] A proposed resolution to support "farmers' institutes" passed only after inserting language mandating the Alliance's management of them.

Michigan State Agricultural College president Edwin Willits described what happened in the Senate: "In the three days' discussion . . . the whole bill was sadly mutilated, not from intent, but from a desire to harmonize conflicting demands."[51] The legislation that emerged was a tribute to the work of leaders like Atherton and Knapp and the relentless pressure of the Grange and Farmer's Alliances. As Willits put it, the Hatch Act came about "by dint of hard work." It provided additional funding for the stations and strengthened their link to higher education.

The result was a uniquely American solution whereby agricultural researchers held the prime responsibility in partnership with government. Because of the Hatch Act, during their first decade extension services grew from thirty-eight stations to fifty-six, staff increased from 402 to 693, and income went from $710, 000 to $1.1 million.[52] Historian Charles Rosenberg reminds us, "as much as any single factor," the stations are responsible for the growth of productivity in twentieth-century American agriculture.[53]

At the semicentennial of the Connecticut Experiment Station, E. W. Allen used words paralleling Shelby Cullom's defense of the ICA: "This Nationwide subsidizing of research in agriculture was evidence of change which had come in the conception of the relationship of the Federal Government and the States. It was a recognition of a joint responsibility in developing the industry of agriculture on a high stage of efficiency, and it was a new expression of what the general Government may do under the Constitution for the promotion of public welfare."[54] Roger Williams credits the Hatch Act with providing a "precedent" that "the federal government could use institutions of higher education as instruments of national policy."[55]

The year 1887 is a watershed because it strengthened the principle of a level playing field by formalizing powers for government that would be challenged but not relinquished. The Discontented achieved leverage in large part because of efforts by the Grange, the Farmer's Alliances, the Greenback Party, and the Knights of Labor. All played a role in act 2 of the reinvention of America.

Let Us Have Such Colleges

George Atherton had no sooner finished working on the Hatch Act than he faced another crisis precipitated by the legislation that had aided his institution. Justin Morrill had seen his act as primarily funding vocational education, but many institutions broadened their offerings, adopting variations on what was called the "classical curriculum" modeled after Ivy League schools. Evidence gathered by the Grange and the Farmers' Alliances shows that colleges following the classical model downplayed agriculture, with some not even offering degrees in it. Caught in the middle were faculty agricultural researchers expected to fulfill the triad of teaching, research, and service. Many felt they had little time left for research.

In the years since the passage of the land grant bill, Morrill grew increasingly dissatisfied, in part because of inadequate funding. He was also disturbed by the actions of southern states, whose land grant institutions systematically denied access to African American students. Although it was not until 1901, when Tennessee became the first state to make it illegal for Blacks and whites to share the same classroom, the practice was already unofficially in place. In response, Morrill proposed funding institutions solely for African Americans. The bills he introduced failed. He continued modifying his legislation, but its fate was similar to John Reagan's.

If the time was right for the ICA and the Hatch Act in 1887, by 1890 everything aligned for what has become known as the Second Morrill Act. Spurred by the Grange and Farmers' Alliances, supporters mobilized to work on the legislation. Aiding them was the Association of American Agricultural Colleges & Experiment Stations, a group Atherton helped found after the passage of the Hatch Act, to link college and extension station leaders. "Senator Morrill . . . expressed a wish to have it well supported," recalls an account.[56] Association members rallied to support Morrill:

Gentlemen went to Washington from Maine and Florida, Kansas and Dakota, and from numerous States between these limits to help on the good work. One made journeys of 1,000 miles each five times during the season. Another visited Washington eight times, occupying at least three days on each trip. Several practically surrendered their summer vacation and held themselves in readiness to respond to the call of the committee for work either at Washington or in their respective States.[57]

During the debate, congressmen invoked organizations lobbying for the bill. Michigan representative James O'Donnell recited a long list of them:

I have here, Mr. Speaker, letters from the ex-master of the National Grange, the present master of that body, the master of the Mississippi State Grange, the Ohio State Board of Agriculture, the Schoharie County [New York] Farmers' Association [fourteen hundred members], the farmers of Niagara County, New York, all demanding, in the interest of agriculture, that this amendment be made a part of the bill. I also have a petition to the Committee on Education, signed by the officers of the National Grange, Patrons of Industry, and four college presidents of the National Association of Agricultural Colleges, asking for the insertion of the amendment."[58]

The opposition grudgingly noted the contributions of these groups: "They have haunted the halls of this Capitol with their presence. They have buzzed in your ears, sir, and in yours, and in the ears of every member of this House. It has been an organized, strong, combined lobby for the benefit of the agricultural colleges of the country."[59]

The story of the Second Morrill Act lies in the congressional debates surrounding it, particularly the House session of August 19, 1890. Congressional debates of that era can make for compelling reading, giving further evidence of how far removed we are from that time. When stump speaking was an art form everyone took seriously, it was rare for a representative or senator to not be an accomplished orator. Whether flamboyant in their actions, what made reputations was the ability to engage in rhetorical duels, where survival depended on an ability to think on your feet and find the right words.

Mr. GEAR. I never knew one of my Democratic friends who could not find a warrant in the Constitution for anything.

Mr. CARUTH. And I never knew one of my Republican friends who regarded the Constitution of this country as our fathers made it.[60]

The record shows ruthless combat, depending on the intensity of the principles at stake. The unofficial titles assigned to political leaders—"judges" and "colonels"—describe the two main styles. Masters of law and logic, judges pulled precedents and obscure cases out of the air like a magician conjuring a coin from behind someone's ear. Colonels wielded words like a Winchester rifle, ambushing opponents before they knew what hit them.

Justin Morrill was a different kind of leader. He succeeded through grit and force of character. Like John Reagan, he brought bills back again and again, convinced each year they would succeed. This forever linked Morrill to higher education as it linked Reagan to interstate commerce. The strength of that association is seen in Morrill Halls at the universities of Idaho, Illinois, Maryland, Minnesota, Nebraska, Nevada, North Dakota, Tennessee, and Vermont, along with Iowa State, Oklahoma State, and Cornell.

For obvious reasons, states' rights defenders like Kentucky representative Asher Caruth opposed the Second Morrill Act. A Louisville attorney and Kentucky "colonel," Caruth made his position clear: "I am unwilling to undertake by any legislation we may adopt to carry the authority of this Government into the various States of this Union and, by a proposition of this character, make our Government an educational institution."[61] Race was the unspoken subtext, but budget hawks also opposed the bill. New York representative Charles Turner cleverly melded regional antagonism with fiscal concerns: "I can conceive no good reason why a million dollars a year should be appropriated to teaching the sons of farmers agriculture any more than a like sum should be appropriated to teaching the sons of the men in my district bricklaying or carpentry or any other useful employment."[62]

As always, there was the old quarrel between big states and little states. "Under this bill, the State of New York, with thirty-four Representatives, would get only $25,000, while the State of Delaware, with one Representative, the State of Rhode Island, the State of Vermont, each with two, would get $5,000. . . . There is no justice in any such legislation."[63] This opposition met the astute management of Maryland representative Louis McComas, a lawyer who had supported Reagan and later served on the District of Columbia Supreme Court.

We often forget there were two Morrill acts. The critical difference is that the second extended the benefits of land grant colleges and universities to people of color. Four states, Virginia, Kentucky, South Carolina, and Mississippi, established institutions for people of color using funds from the first Morrill act, but in other southern states the doors of land grant colleges and universities were open to whites only. The 1890 act provided:

No money shall be paid out under this act to any State or Territory for the support and maintenance of a college where a distinction of race or color is made in the admission of students, but the establishment and maintenance of such colleges separately for white and colored students shall be held to be a compliance with the provisions of this act if the funds received in such State or Territory be equitably divided as hereinafter set forth.[64]

Although the law intended to stress agriculture and mechanic arts, what became known as the 1890 institutions came to focus on teacher training, enrolling twice as many students in the "education curriculum" as in agriculture and mechanical arts combined.[65] For African Americans, the Second Morrill Act was yet another partial loaf. On the one hand it recognized that the South excluded Blacks from land grant access; on the other it enshrined what became known as "separate but equal" from the *Plessy* decision. Constantly fighting for funds, these institutions survived through the hard work and ingenuity of administrators, faculty, and staffs.

Besides opening the door for African Americans, the Second Morrill Act required land grant presidents to submit annual reports to the secretary of education. Various state legislatures such as Ohio cited a key portion of the act :

Regarding the condition and progress of each college, including statistical information in relation to its receipts and expenditures, its library, the number of its students and professors, and also as to any improvements and experiments made under the direction of any experiment stations attached to said colleges, with their cost and results, and such other industrial and economical statistics as may be regarded as useful, one copy of which shall be transmitted by mail free to all other colleges further endowed under this act.[66]

The wording in the last part of this provision, stressing "industrial and economical statistics as may be regarded as useful," elevates it from a simple oversight requirement to a collaborative enhancement of knowledge.

Undergirding that collaboration was a provision broadening the mission of land grant institutions by providing "instruction in agriculture, the mechanic arts, the English language and the various branches of mathematical, physical, natural and economic science, with special reference to their applications in the industries of life, and to the facilities for such instruction."[67] The words following the first "and" changed this nation. They laid the intellectual foundation of this country for the next century by enabling the comprehensive research universities that remain the envy of the world.

The language emerged from a negotiation session between the Grange and the Association of American Agricultural Colleges & Experiment Stations. Representatives included Atherton, Ohio State University president William H. Scott, University of Massachusetts at Amherst president Henry Goodell, and Maryland Agricultural College president Henry Alvord. Crucial consequences can hang on a few words, which is why we need to remember the names of the people who drafted the law. When we celebrate the expansion of higher education that helped make America a world power, we should remember those names.

This Feeling of Injustice

At the same time the Second Morrill Act was wending its way through Congress, the Sherman Antitrust Act was taking an equally tortuous route as the cross-currents of politics came together with a determination to do something about trusts. The halls of Congress echoed with cries of "unconstitutional," punctuated by tales of evil deeds and accompanied by the requisite biblical allusions, but it is telling that no one made an unqualified defense of trusts.

To read the Sherman Act debates is to enter a thicket full of prickly brambles and impenetrable brush that can easily upset one's sense of direction. This pertains even to the bill's name. Missouri senator George Vest, who sought to derail the bill, declared John Sherman had no more to do with the "misnamed Sherman Act" "than the inhabitant of another planet."[68] The person who delivered Sherman's eulogy, Massachusetts senator George Hoar, admitted, "I suppose he introduced it by request. I doubt very much whether he read it. If he did I do not think he ever understood it."[69] When Sherman died, his obituary omitted mention of the antitrust act.

John Sherman continues to dwell in the shadow of his more famous brother, Gen. William Tecumseh Sherman. John was neither a gifted orator nor known for quick thinking. Despite his shortcomings, he had presidential ambitions, which he pursued doggedly. Hoar explained how a man of limited abilities rose to leadership: "In him sound judgment and common sense, better than genius, better than eloquence, always prevailed and sometimes seemed to rise to sublimity which genius never attains."[70]

Sherman was also a man of deep principles and courage, as shown by a debate about southern suppression of voting rights that occurred while the Senate considered his bill. Someone else might have tempered his remarks to attract support for antitrust legislation, but Sherman was not that kind of man. He plunged into turbulent waters, reminding fellow senators, "[If] the Southern people had performed one half of their duty . . . there would have been the end of the controversy."[71] He also explained why northerners were angry about voter suppression: "This feeling of injustice does prevail in the North that by your own act in depriving these people of their representation you yourselves exercise an undue power in this Government." Mississippi's James George and South Carolina's Matthew Butler took offense. Butler lectured: "I will tell the Senator from Ohio another thing, whenever he carries out his threat which I understood to be a threat of a crusade upon the South through United States supervisors and States marshals to dominate elections in that region, he will hear a fire in his rear from those very men from the North who have their money and invested it there." Butler's speech is remarkable for revealing the degree of southern intransigence and the corporate ties that helped sustain it. It must have been a tense moment. Butler all but invited another civil war if the North moved to enforce the rights that Congress had granted to African Americans. With former Confederate officials in the Senate firmly entrenched around what some called the New South, a similar intransigence shaped the antitrust debate.

Like Reagan's interstate commerce bills, the antitrust bill Sherman introduced in December 1889 underwent debate and re-debate, amendment, and re-amendment, until Pres. Benjamin Harrison signed it into law on July 2, 1890. Sherman stated his intent several times during the debates: "The object of this bill as shown by the title is to declare unlawful trusts and combinations in restraint of trade."[72] The senatorial wrangling makes for engrossing reading because it reflects the concerns the Farmers' Alliances and the Knights of Labor held regarding tariff policy.

The main opposition came from states' rights defenders who opposed federal intervention in Jim Crow's kingdom and northern corporations' dedication to keeping government out of the boardroom. The same alliance had killed the Civil Rights Act. Their strategy borrowed from the ICA opposition: delay the bill until it drowned in a morass of amendments.

On December 4, 1889, Sherman introduced his bill as Senate No. 1. It contained three sections. In a long sentence full of commas that recalls the ICA, the first section prohibited "all arrangements, contracts, agreements, trusts or combinations between persons or corporations made with the intention to prevent full and free competition" and "all such arrangements, contracts, agreements, trusts or between persons or corporations intended to advance the cost to the consumer." Section 2 allowed anyone injured by such combinations to sue for damages "in any court in the United States." Section 3 states "that all persons entering into any such arrangement" shall be guilty of a misdemeanor and "subject to a fine of not more than $10,000 or to imprisonment in the penitentiary for a term of not more than five years or to both."[73]

The Senate referred S.1 to the finance committee and, after some tweaking, Sherman moved for its adoption on February 27. After introducing his bill, he yielded to Mississippi's James George. A former Confederate colonel and slaveholder, George was one of the Senate's most ardent defenders of states' rights, searching under the bedsheets of any legislation for any offending clause. An unreconstructed racist, George also was a skilled debater and brilliant legal scholar.

In a long speech he left Sherman's bill in tattered shreds, ripping its shortcomings with phrases like "worthless," "a sham," "fanciful," "ambiguous," "a delusion," and "an abortion."[74] The man who at the time was leading the rewriting of the Mississippi constitution to prohibit voting by African Americans argued, "What is lawful by the State regulation can not be made unlawful by the United States." George concluded with a flourish: "If we pass it we do not only a vain and useless thing; we do a wicked thing. We give to a suffering people, as a remedy for a great wrong, that which will not only prove utterly inefficient but will prove an aggravation of the evils."

It was by all accounts a masterful performance that exposed the problems with the bill. The language "any such arrangement" could include unions and the Grange. "Advance the cost to the consumer" implies that any move to raise prices was illegal. Suing "anyone" in "any court" muddied jurisdiction. Suing for damages plus adding criminal penalties opened the prospect of double jeopardy. The use of the term "intent" raised multiple issues. George pointed out that the language of the bill would allow corporate executives to form trusts outside the United States, "so the bill is a sham so far as the real criminals are concerned, the men whose wealth enables them to fleece and rob the people."[75]

It was not until late March that the Senate again took up antitrust legislation. In the intervening weeks, Sherman had worked with the Finance Committee on modifications in response to George's objections. Section 1 inserted a clause that included arrangements made in foreign countries. Another made clear jurisdiction lay with circuit courts. Section 2 clarified offenses as those "defined in the first section of this act."

No sooner had Sherman introduced the revised bill than Texas senator John Reagan, who once fought hard for the Interstate Commerce Act as a House member, introduced an amendment. It is hard to believe Reagan, who had a long memory, did not realize he was doing to Sherman's bill what the Senate had done to him a few years before. Reagan proposed striking out everything but the title and substituting his language defining trusts and adding stricter penalties.

After the clerk read the Reagan amendment, Sherman rose to speak, saying he had not intended to do so, but now felt compelled to defend his bill. He hit the right chords: "The popular mind is agitated with problems that may disturb social order, and among them all, none is more threatening than the inequality of condition, of wealth, and opportunity."[76] He reminded his colleagues, "Such a combination is far more dangerous than any heretofore invented. . . . If we will not endure a king as a political power we should not endure a king over the production, transportation, and sale of any of the necessaries of life."

Over the next few days senators conducted themselves like football players scrambling to recover a fumble, piling on Sherman's bill while making sure to throw a few well-placed jabs at colleagues. At one point before a vote, New Hampshire's Henry Blair blurted, "There is so much confusion that I do not know what the question is."[77] Two votes provide perspective. The first proposed sending the bill to the Judiciary Committee, but arguments like those of Alabama's John Pugh and North Carolina's Zebulon Vance defeated it. Vance used a colorful analogy: "I never have a bill in which I feel any interest referred to this grand mausoleum of Senatorial literature, the Judiciary Committee without feeling that I have attended a funeral."[78] The second vote was on Reagan's "amendment." It passed, along with another lengthy amendment by Kansas senator John Ingalls about trading in futures. In effect, one bill had become three.

Comparing the votes helps clarify what happened and why the Sherman Act emerged in its final form. The core of Sherman's support came from fellow midwesterners, with help from the Northeast and some southern votes. They supplied twenty-four of the twenty-eight votes that defeated the first attempt to send the bill to the Judiciary Committee. Of the fifteen voting to "deliver the child for nurture to the persons having the most interest in its death," there was only one midwesterner, with a majority of the votes coming from southern and border states.[79]

Many who supported sending the bill to the Judiciary Committee voted for the Reagan and Ingalls amendments, and introduced others, creating an unwieldy mess. Sherman repeatedly tried to counter them with the same forthrightness he had shown in defending voting rights: "The amendments which have been put upon this bill in the last few minutes are such as simply bring it into contempt and the manner in which this has been done tends to bring the whole bill into contempt."[80] At one point Ingalls became so frustrated by states' rights advocates repeatedly stating they were defending the constitution that he angrily retorted, "If I recollect aright those gentlemen spent a considerable portion of time in endeavoring to destroy the Constitution."[81]

The opposition destroyed Sherman's bill, resulting in the passage of a second vote to send it to the Judiciary Committee. Sherman biographer Winfield Scott Kerr describes the events in saying, "It was loaded with amendments, both limiting and extending its provisions, until it became a legislative monstrosity, an unskillful piecing together or hitching on of other bills or party measures which had little or no connection with or relation to trusts."[82]

Despite being condemned to a mausoleum where two senators, George and Vest, had already announced they intended to bury the bill, it was clear even the most diehard opponents felt compelled to do something about trusts. Vest admitted, "No one can exaggerate the importance of the question pending before the Senate or the intensity of feeling which exists especially in the agricultural portions of the country in regard to it."[83] Numerous references to the Farmers' Alliances and others representing the Discontented show this intensity. Colorado senator Henry Teller defended the Alliances when he claimed, "No organizations in this country can be more beneficial in their character than Farmers Alliances and farmers associations."[84] Others like Vest testified to the Alliance's impact: "The Farmers Alliance are cooking now and there is no dish that can be put on this Senatorial table which will not go down with a gusto that will astonish any gourmand from the restaurants of Paris."[85]

Senators debated whether language about combinations applied to groups like the alliances and unions. Senator George argued, "Under the original bill . . . every farmer belonging to one of these alliances would be liable to a civil action and to the recovery of double damages against for being a member of that organization the tendency of which is to increase the price of his farm products."[86] No one argued that any part of the bill *should* forbid combinations by farmers and workers.

When the mangled Sherman bill reached the Judiciary Committee, the wrangling became intense. After he drafted an alternative, George Hoar remembered, "There was a good deal of opposition to it in the Committee. Nearly every member had a plan of his own. But at last, the Committee came to my view."[87] What emerged was not to everyone's liking, but after surviving the gauntlet of a conference committee it passed overwhelmingly.

The final bill has a change from the first section, and reads, "Every contract, combination in the form of trust or otherwise, or conspiracy, in restraint of trade or commerce among the several States, or with foreign nations, is hereby declared to be illegal."[88] Section 2 lowers misdemeanor penalties to $5,000 and/

or a year in jail. Section 3 extends Section 1 to apply to US territories. Section 4 places jurisdiction in circuit courts. Section 6 allows the seizure of property involved in illegal activities as specified in Section 1. Section 7 allows injured individuals to sue for damages plus attorney's fees. Section 8 contains the bill's most far-reaching assertion, giving corporations the status of persons.

Seen in the context of the late nineteenth-century desire for a level playing field, the Sherman Act joins the Interstate Commerce, the Morrill, and the Hatch Acts as an assertion of government's authority. Before this legislation one could argue that *in principle* government should regulate the economy, but after enactment of the new laws, this country was *by law* committed to it. Historian William Letwin's interpretation is on target: "If not the most powerful instrument of economic policy in the United States, the Sherman Act is its most characteristic."[89]

Sworn to Serve

One more piece completed the reinvention of American democracy. The man who made it possible raised shorthorn cattle with names like Gloster Beauty, Airdrie, and Prince Gem, near Fort Dodge, Iowa. Lorenzo Coffin was content to live his life tending his herd, until a chance accident changed it. A year after the 1873 Panic, he observed a brakeman coupling a car when the man fell, his shrieks piercing the air. Despite the cries, he was one of the lucky members of America's second most dangerous occupation. He lost a couple of fingers. Lorenzo Coffin found a cause.[90]

When inquiring about the fate of that worker, he discovered, "These cases were of such everyday occurrence, it was taken as a matter of course that the men must of necessity be maimed and killed."[91] That troubled him so much that he spent the next nineteen years seeking justice: "I began to feel that I was not doing my duty as a sworn officer of the State, if I did not try in some way to lessen the great loss of life, and the suffering sustained by these railroad men, who were our fellow citizens, and whom I was equally sworn to serve."

Known as the "railroad crank" for his zeal about safety, Coffin threw himself into an 1883 appointment to Iowa's railroad commission with the attention to detail and determination he showed raising cattle. In a photograph his angular face with a Ulysses Grant–style beard and haircut leans toward the camera, as if to make a point to the world. Coffin needed Grant-like leadership to secure passage of the Safety Appliance Act, requiring railroad air brakes and safety couplers. Contrary to what laissez-faire capitalism advocates believe, government regulation of railroad safety was no new socialist experiment. As early as 1839, New Jersey required engineers to ring a bell when approaching a crossing [early engines lacked whistles].[92]

In the 1880s various state commissions noted the need for better couplers to reduce accidents to railroad brakemen. In 1885, Illinois railroad commissioners advocated this by asking, "Should not an automatic coupling be adopted by the railroad companies, the use of which might tend to save the lives and limbs of employees."[93] By 1890, growing dissatisfaction with train wrecks moved Interstate Commerce Commission secretary Edward Moseley to advocate for railroad safety. At Boston's Faneuil Hall Moseley told listeners: "There is something appalling in the statement that more hard-working and faithful railway employees in the United States went down in sudden death last year than all Union dead [over 2,200] at the Battle of the Wilderness."[94]

Moseley sometimes receives credit for the Safety Appliance Act, but Coffin was the real hero. In 1885 he arranged the first systematic tests of railroad brakes. The editor of *Engineering News* remembers the tests themselves scared many observers, but not Coffin, who always chose to sit in the train's most dangerous place. "As a result, he knows as much about power brakes and automatic couplers as the average general manager of our railroads," wrote the editor.[95] Coffin used "press, platform, pulpit" to pursue the cause. "Wherever there were great official gatherings of the different denominations and religious bodies, I would try to get a hearing," he wrote.[96] By 1888 he had shepherded a railroad safety act through the Iowa legislature.

The bill became the template for the Safety Appliance Act. In Washington, opponents cleverly fought his bill in a battle that lasted two congressional sessions. Opponents proved to be their own worst enemies: "N——s were cheaper than automatic couplers and power-brakes," said one southern railroad executive, who probably had never heard of Andrew Jackson Beard or his safety coupler.[97] Hollywood could not have more melodramatically staged the bill's final passage. Delays and maneuvers by opponents left Coffin with only three days to gain passage before the session ended.

While a fierce storm raged, the coughs of a bad cold punctuated his late-night efforts to pen a pamphlet supporting the bill. Early on February 27 he rushed it to a printer so he could place copies on every congressman's desk. As opponents raised objections, the bill's sponsor rose in indignation. Coffin describes Virginia representative George Wise as a tall man with long arms and a "nervous manner," but his words were forceful: "Sir, I will stand here till eternity comes before I will turn my back on these deserving men."[98] The *Railroad Trainmen's Journal* celebrated the act's passage: "This slaughter of American workmen is about ended. A national law, the expression of the Congress of the United States, has called a halt to the heartlessness or heedlessness of railroad companies, and it has been decreed that an army of men shall no longer be offered up as an annual sacrifice to corporate greed."[99]

In recognition of Coffin's generalship, the Brotherhood of Railroad Brakemen awarded him a gold shield embossed with a red and green flag, a red lantern, a ticket punch, and a coupling link. It was well deserved. The number of railroad men injured by coupling cars fell from 7,155 in 1891 to 4,698 in 1898, and the number killed falling from trains fell from 467 in 1891 to 325.[100] Today Coffin's grave sits behind a chain link fence nestled amid weeds and scrubby forest. Nature is held at bay by railroad workers who tend the site in honor of his contributions. That grave reminds us that the reinvention of this nation took the tireless efforts of extraordinary people.

As with the other initiatives of the late 1880s and early 1890s, the real value of the Safety Appliance Act was its destruction of the pretexts of laissez-faire capitalism and its affirmation of government's role in keeping the playing field level. The Discontented wrought, through five pieces of legislation—the Hatch Act, the Second Morrill Act, the Interstate Commerce Act, the Sherman Act, and the Safety Appliance Act—a third and necessary American revolution. In the second revolution, the constitutional amendments produced by the Civil War did away with the notion African Americans were not citizens and states could nullify laws they did not like. The third revolution did away with the idea that corporations could decide which laws they would obey. The country emerged from these revolutions stronger and more unified. We were one people in law and in spirit.

When Lawrence Goodwyn notes the efforts of the Farmers Alliances were "the most massive organizing drive by any citizen institution of nineteenth-century America," he could also be describing the work of the Discontented.[101] The initiatives their organizing helped to pass add up to a systematic development strategy consisting of four ingredients: broadening and improving education, providing supply-side aid for railroads and telecommunications, priming the demand side to increase discretionary spending, and ensuring a fair and competitive marketplace. These ideas, not the machine processes of industrialists, laid the foundations for modern America. Those foundations were built by the Discontented, whose protests, lobbying, and gathering evidence laid the groundwork for legislation that remade this country. Like all transformations, it was an imperfect evolution, but that is the nature of transformations. We must continually reaffirm them to meet new challenges or they will grow stale.

PART THREE

THE LEGACY OF THE DISCONTENTED

CHAPTER ELEVEN

WIDENING THE GATES OF OPPORTUNITY

> Come listen awhile I'll sing you a song,
> Concerning the times it will not be long,
> When everybody is striving to buy,
> And cheating each other, I cannot tell why.
> —*From the folk song "Hard, Hard Times"*

Willa Cather is the perfect guide to the systemic dimensions of late 1880s and early 1890s legislations and other initiatives propelled forward by the Discontented. She understood her generation with an artist's sense of the epic importance of the everyday. In 1883 a ten-year-old Cather huddled in a wagon taking her from the Red Cloud, Nebraska, train station to her grandfather's homestead. The girl who once roamed the Virginia woods was devastated by the flat new land. "As we drove further and further out into the country," she reflected, "I felt a good deal as if we had come to the end of everything—it was a kind of erasure of personality."[1] She called herself Willie, wore her hair like a man, and was a crack rider. She destroyed most of her papers, leaving scholars to puzzle over her life.[2] The Cather enigma also encompasses her critical reputation. Granville Hicks argues, "[She] has been barred from the task that has occupied most of the world's great artists, the expression of what is central and fundamental in her own age."[3]

Today we know less about her than about the town of Red Cloud, which she renamed Sweet Water, Frankfort, Black Hawk, and Hanover in her novels. Much remains in her hometown from when as a child she signed her name Wm. Cather, M.D. and accompanied doctors on house calls. The railroad depot where she had disembarked, along with twenty other buildings related to her life, constitutes the largest national site dedicated to a single author. Gazing out of the single floor-length window in her childhood bedroom, with its original wallpaper she bought with money saved by working in the local drugstore, forces us to examine the connections between fiction and history. Cather's Red Cloud experiences spawned two important novels about the Age of Discontent: *My Ántonia* and *O Pioneers!* Their power comes from an unflinching honesty that colors indelible portraits of two homesteaders, Antonia Shimerda and Alexandra Bergson. Marilee Lindemann describes Cather's attitude toward the land with words that also describe her perspective towards her times: "Shame and terror; power and passion."[4]

Rather than avoid her times, Cather's novels wade into their bleakest realities, which is why they make a fascinating guide to the economic impact of the Discontenteds' playing field initiatives. Although current disciples of William Graham Sumner cling to the belief that welfare coddles the lazy, their comments are usually less direct than Sumner's, employing code words like Ronald Reagan's "welfare queen." This speaking in tongues runs through long-running feuds over social spending and regulation versus tax cuts for the wealthy. For laissez-faire capitalism advocates, legislation such as the Interstate Commerce, Sherman, Hatch, Second Morrill, and Safety Appliance Acts are a drag on the economy rather than a contributor to it. Cather knew better. Her novels intuitively grasp the feedback between the four dimensions of the Discontenteds' efforts: educational access, aid for infrastructure, priming the demand side, and ensuring fair markets.

A Great Aid

It is possible to read *O Pioneers!* as a not-too-thinly-veiled endorsement of the agricultural extension stations and the Hatch Act's steady source of funding. In the novel, the transition from generations-old farming practices to research-based agriculture underlies the tension between Alexandra Bergson and her brothers, Lou and Oscar. Alexandra has become wealthy by buying land and farming it with new methods.[5] This angers her brothers, who believe "the property of the family belongs to the men of the family . . . because they do the work."[6] When they tilled the fields and harvested the grain, their exertions gauged their productivity. Alexandra's work required an unfamiliar calculus, especially for Lou, who plants his corn on the same date every year, "whether the season were backward or forward."[7]

Cather grew up on the "Nebraska Divide," a jagged region where the land twists and turns on itself to throw up a jumble of ravines and streambeds. A 1923 survey of Webster County (Red Cloud is the county seat), observes, "Both soil and climate, called for new crop varieties and special farming systems."[8] With help from university experts, Alexandra learned how to farm this land. In a spirited exchange with Lou and Oscar, she reminds them that when she first sowed alfalfa, "You both opposed me, just because I first heard about it from a young man who had been to the University. You said I was being taken in then . . . but you know as well as I do that alfalfa has been the salvation of this country."[9] They also laughed when she planted wheat, a crop that in reality has made Nebraska a highly ranked state in wheat production.

The impact of the stations' efforts on the wheat crop is best told by the gnat-sized Hessian fly, named because it supposedly hitched a ride in the straw used for bedding by Revolutionary War German mercenaries.[10] Fly larvae that destroyed young wheat plants worked their way west, reaching the plains simultaneously with the homesteaders. Experiment stations found that farmers could reduce crop damage by delaying planting until after the fly larvae had matured. Because optimal planting dates varied, stations borrowed Seaman Knapp's idea of test plots to determine them. Agriculture Entomology Bureau chief L. O. Howard described how they took the sting out of the fly: "The entire community delayed their sowing until after [agents] decided would probably be a safe date. The result is that . . . in no case is there sufficient fly to cause the loss of a bushel of grain in this neighborhood."[11]

Three agronomists explain the probable fate of those who refused to follow this advice: "Those farmers would not have had a wheat crop worth harvesting."[12] Alan Olmstead and Paul Rhode believe that if farmers had not adopted strategies like those used to battle the fly, by 1909 wheat production would have been 46 percent lower.[13] Because lower yields have a larger impact on marginally producing lands, over a quarter of these lands would have become unfarmable, resulting in a loss of 20,477,000 acres or almost 341,000 sixty-acre farms.[14] At an average value per farm between $1,704 and $2,786, the national economy might have lost as much as $950 million, not including the decrease in land and crop values.[15] For comparison, in 1900 the profits of the world's biggest company, Carnegie Steel, were $40 million, meaning the Hatch Act led to yields worth more than twenty years of steel profits.[16]

With their test plots demonstrating new ideas, the extension stations began winning over skeptics like Lou and Oscar. Alfred Charles True, the director of the stations from 1893 to 1915, boasted, "The stations have secured the confidence and respect of practical men to a remarkable extent."[17] They accomplished this by borrowing a page from Jacob Riis. Riis used photographs to convince skeptics about the problems on Mulberry Street; the stations used photos in bulletins and flyers sent to farmers to show successful crops.

The Oklahoma experiment station issued free bulletins documenting the experiences of successful wheat growers and the work of researchers. Ohio and other states printed maps showing the dates for beneficial sowing of wheat in different areas. Along with instructions on combatting the Hessian fly, the Purdue University experiment station asked farmers to "UNITE to combat this pest of the wheat field."[18] The bulletins also recruited farmers for institutes held by the stations, where they could personally connect with researchers and each other. True estimated that in 1898–99 there were two thousand institutes held in thirty states, with an estimated attendance of half a million.[19] Farmers who attended brought with them experiences with Grange and Farmers' Alliances meetings.

Skeptics like Lou and Oscar might have asked, "What is the economic return?" One answer comes from Olmstead and Rhode's 46 percent difference in wheat crop production. From 1888 to 1900 it totaled 7.4 million bushels, which, at an average price of 85¢ per bushel, yields a total value of $6.29 million. Had that crop been 40 percent lower, its total value would have dropped by $2.5 million. The system-wide shock would have set off a cascade of lost store revenues, fewer merchant orders for goods, production cuts, and, most ominously, higher food prices.

The stations also influenced the production of other crops. According to True, "the work done by the Montana Station in promoting the use of better varieties of barley and demonstrating their value for malting led to large exports of barley."[20] Montana barley production more than doubled from 100,902 bushels in 1889 to 216,000 bushels in 1899.[21] The Nebraska station was "a great aid to the extension of agriculture" by "bringing about the establishment of three sugar beet factories" and planting new crops like alfalfa (thereby verifying Cather's story).[22] A New York Agriculture Department report commented on the impact of Alexandra's alfalfa: "Alfalfa has done more to project [Kansas and Nebraska] into the center of the map and has sold more land at higher prices than any other one growth, commodity, or influence. Raw lands, supposedly unproductive, with almost no buyers before, and considered a burden at a $5 valuation, have been quick sales at $40, $75, and sometimes $100 per acre when seeded to this wonderful forage."[23] The fabled North Carolina tobacco crop and Wisconsin's "cheese heads" owe much to the work of the experiment stations. True's assessment of Vermont's maple sugar industry could apply to other stations as well: "As a result of the station's work[,] many times the expected number of persons drew bounties, bringing many thousands of dollars into the hands of farmers."[24]

Lou and Oscar might have viewed the stations differently had they seen the data on average wheat yield per acre, but they probably did not need to because they witnessed it in the wagons pulling up to the grain elevator. Farmers achieved yields as high as 20.5 bushels per acre after the Hatch Act was passed—something unheard of in the 1870s and 1880s.[25] Corn and cotton farmers also experienced yield increases amounting to 7.6 percent for the 1890s over previous decades. As a result, gross farm output in the 1890s outpaced that of the previous two decades, from 18 percent in the 1870s to 27 percent in the 1890s.[26] Mechanization, weather, and other factors undoubtedly influenced these numbers, but it is also hard not to see the hand of the extension stations in them.

Willa Cather puts a human face on these numbers, accompanied by an artist's eye for telling details, including unpleasant ones. A field hand falls into machinery, a farmer ignores his appendicitis, and there are the suicides of the despairing. For all her realism, however, Cather reminds us the Nebraska Divide was a "fortunate country," ready to receive hearts like Alexandra's and "give them out again in the yellow wheat, in the rustling corn, in the shining eyes of youth."[27]

The Best Prophesies of Success

Willa Cather would be pleased to know analyses confirm the role of knowledge-building in this increase, with the number of conferred college degrees showing a strong relationship to increasing wheat yields. She was among the 528,954 students awarded degrees from land grant institutions between 1870 and 1900.[28] Others taking advantage of those opportunities included Clarence Darrow, Frank Lloyd Wright, John Dewey, John Muir, Florence Kelley, and Mary Baird Bryan. "The reports sent from these colleges reveal ... a certain fresh interest, a spirit of youth, a new enthusiasm," wrote the federal commissioner of education, "which, when intelligent and enduring, is one of the best prophesies of success."[29]

That enthusiasm sparked a doubling of the degrees awarded from an average 130,000 in the 1870s to 260,000 in the 1890s. What is impressive is the tenfold growth in the number of doctorates awarded, from 282 in the 1870s to 2,936 in the 1890s. These new PhD-certified educators swelled the number of faculty, from 5,553 in 1870 to 19,151 in 1900.[30] Allan Nevins recognizes this effect:

[Land grant institutions] established a connection between the national government and the academic world which provided an apparatus for research and for the rapid general diffusion of scientific discoveries, unparalleled elsewhere. Widening the gates of opportunity, it made democracy freer, more adaptable, and more kinetic.[31]

Stanley Lebergott seconds Nevins in affirming that what was decisive in America was "the unprecedented acceptance of novel ideas."[32]

The graduates appreciated the value of their diplomas. Historian Scott Key asserts the Morrill Act was "fundamentally concerned with economics not education" because the act "promised to increase agricultural production, which would increase consumption and, in turn, increase government revenue."[33] Detractors of public education should ponder that sentence because it illustrates the same systemic truth as the Hatch Act: education increases wages to purchase more consumer goods whose profits go to increasing production.

Some attempted to determine the earning power of these degrees. In 1903 Bowdoin College estimated its graduates earned $3,356.[34] Based on data collected about its almost 60,000 schoolchildren, Boston Public Schools determined a single college graduate earned as much as twelve mill hands.[35] A third estimate comes from the 1890 US Census, which divided workers into three categories: 1) pieceworkers, 2) operatives skilled and unskilled, and 3) officers, firm members, and clerks. The average annual wage for the latter was $850 versus $455 for the first.[36]

Those benefits also accrued to graduates of African American colleges funded by the Second Morrill Act. W. E. B. Du Bois was well aware of the importance of these degrees. His study of African American business shows 150 out of 181 businessmen attended colleges, public schools, or night, normal, or grammar schools.[37] Statistics show a significant number of students from historically Black colleges and universities became teachers, not farmers.

A valuable role performed by what became known as the 1890 Colleges was creating the equivalents of African American think tanks, where earnest discussions could occur in the privacy of dorm rooms and faculty offices. In assessing the importance of the Second Morrill Act for African Americans, historian Lee Craig concludes, "Without this investment on the part of the 1890 land-grant colleges and their graduates, the subsequent road of economic development would have been steeper and the gains even slower than actually experienced."[38]

For the Support of Schools

Those who think federal aid to education is a new idea will be surprised to learn it was the Founders who had the foresight to build it into the Ordinance of 1785 by requiring a section of every township be reserved "for the maintenance of public schools."[39] It was a stroke of genius to link education funding to our greatest commodity: land. Thomas Jefferson famously saw education as democracy's foundation, writing, "Whenever the people are well-informed, they can be trusted with their own government; that, whenever things get so far wrong as to attract their notice, they may be relied on to set them to right."[40] What became known as school trust lands "have been wheel, ballast, and lever of our states' systems of free schools," wrote Fletcher Swift in 1911.[41] "They set those systems in motion and kept them going. They maintained the equilibrium. They lifted them to higher and higher levels."

There may be no more eloquent testimony to the resolve of the Discontented amid hard times than the increase in public school enrollments, from 6,872,000 in 1870 to 15,503,000 in 1900. This contrasts with the Great Depression of the 1930s, when enrollment fell from 29.9 million in 1932 to 28 million in 1940.[42] The growth allowed schools to increase the number of teachers, from 170,000 in 1870 to 436,000 in 1900, while those in "other professional services" grew from 140,000 to 500,000.[43] The increase in college enrollments would not have occurred without the enrollment increase in K–12 education or the new teachers farmed by land grant institutions.

Congress continued its commitment to public education by requiring Ohio to include school trust lands as a condition for admission to the Union in 1803. When the country admitted more states, only four did not receive trust grants: Texas, Hawaii, West Virginia, and Maine, the first two because they had been independent nations prior to the Union and the other two because they were created out of existing states. Unfortunately, many states squandered their trust lands, otherwise today's schools might not be holding bake sales to purchase teaching supplies.

In 1875 Congress became so disenchanted with trust land mismanagement they tightened the rules, requiring trust lands "shall be disposed only at public sale and at a price not less than two dollars and fifty cents an acre, the proceeds to constitute a permanent schools fund."[44] Computing the impact of this legislation would be impossible without Swift's diligence in gathering facts from Maine, New York, Indiana, Florida, Massachusetts, and Connecticut. From them he calculated the trust funds of those states earned a total of $3,116,329 in the years 1885, 1895, and 1905.[45] Extrapolation over three decades yields an estimated $90 million total.

Claudia Goldin and Lawrence Katz comment that, regarding salaries, "There was a substantial occupational wage premium from the 1890s to the 1910s for both men and women and . . . the implied return to a high school education was substantial."[46] Education allowed people to move from unskilled, manual labor jobs into positions where the return was "extremely high for both males and females." Some idea of that return can be grasped by noting the Census calculation of the average manufacturing wage from 1890–1900 was $421.45 while the average clerical wage was $941.45.

It is important to recognize that during the late nineteenth century, over half of high school graduates were women.[47] In a lively debate on coeducation at the 1893 Columbian Exposition, a French minister of education remarked, "Of all the features which characterize American education, perhaps the most striking is the coeducation of young men and young women." Still, some worried that if coeducation "is not remedied there will soon be a race of women capable of being doctors, journalists, advocates, architects, engineers; in one word, everything except wives and mothers."[48]

Local granges and alliances enlisted support for education by building the knowledge, confidence, and support of rural Americans. Only meetings with neighbors could soften the skepticism of the Lous and Oscars who clung to the old methods and distrusted "book learning." They thought their children needed to be working in the fields, not conjugating verbs using squeaky chalk. An unsung contribution of the Grange and the Farmers' Alliances was helping to change attitudes by enhancing people's abilities to acquire, access, and analyze information. Because many of the lecturers were farmers or community members themselves, they enjoyed a higher level of credibility than university researchers miles away. At a time when the dominant pedagogy included educators leading pupils in rote recitation, lecturers stressed learner-centered learning.

While we cannot account for all the systemic impacts of public education, we can assess one: patents registered. The growth in education funding stimulated the late nineteenth-century technology explosion. Since 1646, when Joseph Jenks received the first patent awarded in North America for a scythe, registered patents have propelled productivity and education has propelled patents.[49] A 1902 report on patents offered a guided tour of inventiveness, including over eleven thousand patents for plows alone.

Researchers determined the annual production value of industries that resulted entirely from patents in 1870, 1880, 1890, and 1900 was $622,672,933—or just over $155.5 million per year. That adds up to $4.6 billion from 1870 to 1900.[50] Because that number only includes industries resulting from specific patents, this amount is likely just the tip of a large iceberg. By 1900 virtually every industry could attribute its success to improvements generated by patents. A 1902 study noted that for iron and steel, "a prohibition of the use of the patented inventions of the last half century would stop every one of these establishments."[51]

The One Real Fact

Railroad trains wind through Willa Cather's novels, touching towns like Black Hawk and Hanover, where they become metaphors.[52] In her third novel, *The Song of the Lark*, a major character describes people as gamblers playing for small stakes, but "the railroad is the one real fact in this country."[53] That observation may be one of Cather's most insightful.

Growing up in Red Cloud, she knew the multiple dimensions of that reality. A steaming locomotive brought her family to join fellow townspeople during a heavy snowfall to watch the night train arrive at the station, its headlight slashing through swirling flakes. A railroad system celebrated by an Ohio judge as the lifeblood of America allowed a local merchant to advertise fresh oysters in the town paper, which editorialized, "American railway monarchs wield greater power and exercise more power arbitrarily than any King or Emperor in all Europe."

Cather's "real fact" recognizes that the railroads remain one of the greatest paradoxes of the Age of Discontent. Alfred Chandler views the railroads as the cogwheel of American industrialization, while Richard White reviles them as a prime example of the era's economic and moral corruption. Chandler terms them "the nation's first modern business enterprise"; White views them as "a Gilded Age extravagance that rent holes in the political, social, and environmental fabric of the nation, creating railroads as mismanaged and corrupt as they were long."[54] The paradox is that despite all the faults, from a systemic perspective, in a territory as vast as the United States, only by providing supply-side aid for transportation and telecommunications could the map's empty spaces be bridged, especially across the prairies and in the mountains. Without its train depot, Red Cloud might have been a ghost town. The problem was how to lay the miles of track that linked the country.

Cather also hints at one of the supreme ironies of the Age of Discontent: it wasn't the golden age of laissez-faire capitalism; it was the golden age of corporate welfare. J. Bradford DeLong estimates tariff subsidies amounted to a minimum of $2.3–$4.2 billion, though those subsidies brought little return to the rest of the citizenry. According to DeLong, "Postbellum U.S. history thus lends little support to the view that tariff protection improved the living standards of American workers."[55]

No one benefited from corporate welfare more than the railroads. Fred Shannon estimates the value of railroad land grants and loans at half a billion dollars.[56] Lloyd Mercer believes "available" land was probably the best stimulus for laying the railroad and telegraph lines, because the government had a lot of it to give away and it was the most politically feasible alternative.[57] Of course, much of that land was home to Indigenous nations who resisted violations of their treaty rights. An 1883 report of the commissioner of railroads estimated the total land grant to the Union Pacific Railroad Company at 19,100,000 acres. The Central Pacific held another 12,882,400 acres, the Southern Pacific 11,964,100 acres, and the Northern Pacific 31,323,053.70 acres, or 63,305,453 acres between the four companies. If we add acres held by other railroad lines referenced in the report, by 1883 railroad lands totaled almost 93 million acres.[58] A 1901 report calculated total railroad land grants covered 137 million acres, or enough to make the railroads the third-largest state.[59] If we use the school trust land sale value of $2.50 per acre, the value of those lands was at least $342.5 million. An additional $64.6 million in bonds brings the railroad subsidy to $407 million—close to Shannon's half a billion.[60]

There is little question that the railroad subsidies, the rampant speculation they fostered, and the conspicuous consumption of those who profited from it amply demonstrate the tilted playing field that provoked the Age of Discontent. For one thing, the acreage granted the railroad barons exceeded (by 13.4 million acres) all the acres granted to homesteaders from 1870 to 1900. Another boondoggle lies in the sixty-plus pages of figures from the 1883 report covering regional lines, such as the Choctaw, Oklahoma and Gulf; the Portage, Winnebago & Superior; and the St. Louis and San Francisco (which never made it farther west than Oklahoma City). Together they received 16,114,543 acres, an area approaching the size of Maryland and Massachusetts combined. Henry George vented his indignation: "Twenty years from now the lands of the company will have sold for or will be worth an average of at least $20 per acre. . . . A sum more than half the national debt. . . . And for what? For building a road which cannot cost more than eighty millions, and for building it for themselves!"[61] Remember this corporate largesse came at a time when Philip Sheridan refused to release surplus rations to starving farmers and President Cleveland vetoed a bill to aid others who were starving because, "Federal aid, in such cases, encourages the expectations of paternal care on the part of the government and weakens the sturdiness of our national character."[62]

George is one of many over our history who have recognized the extent to which extravagant infrastructure subsidies and benefits can tilt the playing field. The interstate highway building mania that gathered pace after the Second World War ran as roughshod through African American neighborhoods as the railroads had done through Indigenous lands. The zeal to prop up the internet generated the infamous Section 230 of the Communications Decency Act of 1996, which protects tech giants like Facebook as surely as the Supreme Court protected the railroads.

During the late nineteenth century the Discontented acted as a brake on the profligacy, sometimes causing the rails to squeal in protest. Between 1870 and 1890 the Discontented offered alternatives to corporate welfare in the form of proposals that would today feed an army of trolls decrying them as "communist plots." The National Labor Union, the Farmers' Alliances, the Knights of Labor, and the Greenback and People's Parties at varying times and in various forms advocated government ownership of the railroad and telegraph systems, but their proposals never received a serious congressional hearing.

Many of those platforms also called for government lands to be given to settlers and not the railroads. Their authors sensed what research has since confirmed: railroad land grants were not a bargain for settlers. In his 1893 study of a Nebraska township, Arthur Bentley found the average debt of homesteaders holding mortgages was significantly lower than those who bought land from railroads or private parties. Half of all homesteaders were entirely free from mortgages. Bentley states that "the great majority of prosperous farmers are to be found" among those who settled government land.[63] A century after Bentley's study, James Stewart discovered late nineteenth-century farmers in Marshall County, South Dakota, paid "only a fraction of the land's actual worth" because of homestead laws. "The transfer or sale of valuable public land at a fraction of its market worth," observes Stewart, "enriched landholders instantly and created opportunities for future wealth."[64]

The fact that proposals nationalizing the railroads or offering land to settlers did not receive congressional support does not mean they had no impact. During a time when a mere whisper of socialization was enough to cause corporate executives sleepless nights, the threat to push the nationalization of the railroads from organizations like the Knights and the Greenbackers exerted subtle pressure on the railroads to acquiesce to less radical solutions.

The Discontented were such a powerful force because, like Sarah Murray and so many others, when hit with a setback they picked themselves up and kept moving forward as they sought to contain the dangerously fluctuating steam gauges of the railroads. Their agitation created the Granger laws, along with state railway commissions like the one on which Lorenzo Coffin served and which required state inspection of factories and railroads. The creation of state bureaus of labor statistics fulfilled what those who proposed them had hoped: drawing back the curtain on the realities of industrialization. Together those commissions, inspection laws, and a system to monitor them remain some the Discontented's most valuable contributions.

Inevitably these proposals morphed into federal legislation, such as the creation of the national Bureau of Labor Statistics. Two critical pieces of the Discontented's legislation of the late 1880s and early 1890s were the Interstate Commerce Act and the Safety Appliance Act. Historians who fault the ICA point to its erratic enforcement. Between 1887 and 1906 the US Supreme Court upheld ICC decisions in only one of sixteen cases brought before it, turning the bill into what Charles Beard calls a "scarecrow."[65] The consensus is that the ICC was not very effective until the passage of the Hepburn Act in 1906.

This does not mean it had no impact. Bruce Blonigen and Anca Cristea claim, "The post-ICA period is characterized by significant price stability compared to the prior decades."[66] In 1895 the Interstate Commerce Commission reported that the ICA did more than stabilize prices: "Only from an extended inquiry would it be possible to accurately estimate the total reductions effected since the passage of the Act to Regulate Commerce, but that it has been very considerable is well known."[67] The report includes tables demonstrating that in 1890 the cost per ton for freight was $.604; two years later it was $.582. According to the ICC, "if the average receipts per mile for 1888 had been maintained during the subsequent five years, it appears that the public would, in such case, have paid for freight and passenger transportation by railroad from 1889 to 1893, inclusive $525,459,587 more than was actually paid for such transportation during that period."

The impact of the Safety Appliance Act is no better gauged than in a 1925 tribute to Lorenzo Coffin that appeared in the *Santa Fe [Railroad] Magazine*. Commenting on a proposal to erect a monument to Coffin, the railroad acknowledged, "By hastening the evolution of the railroad, which in its turn made possible the more rapid growth of the nation with consequent prosperity, Coffin placed the whole country under obligation to him." The tribute included a glowing appreciation: "Every man who works for a living should honor the memory of Lorenzo S. Coffin, because he was the pioneer in safety work."[68] What the *Santa Fe* does not mention is something that would have been anathema to those who ran the railroad in 1890: how the Safety Appliance Act established the principle that in maintaining a level playing field, the government has a right to regulate working conditions.

One overlooked impact of the Safety Appliance Act is that it increased the efficiency of the railroads. Safer rail travel meant fewer accident claims by workers and passengers, reduced breakdowns and delays, and more consistent overall operation. It also revealed the absurdity of corporate nullification. Companies resisted measures that could benefit them in the name of not allowing government tell them how to run their businesses, the true definition of an obsession. Instead, the initiatives of the Discontented reinforce Lloyd Mercer's main point: "Society's well-being was improved by government intervention."[69]

The Top Wire of a Barbed Wire Fence

Another Discontented model of infrastructure development has largely escaped the attention of historians. Willa Cather recalled that when the first telegraph message reached Nebraska, the dignitaries who were gathered in a log cabin removed their hats "as if they were in church," when the key clicked the message: "Westward the course of empire makes its way."[70] Thomas Edison even named his daughters Dot and Dash. But the telegraph was used mainly by corporations and the wealthy. Unlike most European countries, the United States never made the telegraph accessible to ordinary people. In 1884 the head of Western Union testified, "Not more than 500,000 persons, or less than 1 per cent of the people of the United States use the telegraph."[71] This contrasts with Belgium and Switzerland, where 55.1 percent and 61 percent, respectively, of the telegrams were about "family and social matters."

In one of the most critical defeats for the Discontented, efforts to change the telegraph system failed. In 1890 farm organizations and unions generated a petition with 540,000 names, calling for placing telegraph terminals in post offices with local carriers delivering telegrams. In Baltimore the *Manufacturer's Record* notes the poor private service experienced in the South: "Southerners send important messages in an expedited letter, because the probability of immediate delivery is greater by that mode of conveyance than by the wires."[72] The *Chicago Tribune* spoke for city dwellers: "There is perhaps not one of our readers who have not found that it took as long to get a message delivered a short distance in the city or in the suburbs by telegraph as it would have taken him to walk with it to its destination."[73] The *Review* in Denison, Iowa, argued the case for rural America: "There is no word in the English language sufficiently strong to express the contemptible character of the local telegraph service."[74]

Despite wide support, pro-business Republicans and Bourbon Democrats killed the plan. The *Washington Herald* saw the lesson: "A country that leaves its most vital means of intercommunication . . . in the grasp of a Jay Gould, deserves to have a strike every week . . . until it learns sense in the school of experience."[75] Gould, who gained control of Western Union in 1881, had an answer: "The telegraph system, of all other business, wants to be managed by skilled experts, while the Government is founded on the idea that the party in power shall control the patronage. If the Government led it, the general managers' heads would come off every four years and you would not have any such efficiency as at present."[76]

Although the postal telegraph bill failed, the Discontented used collaboration and organizing skills learned from the Grange and Farmers' Alliances to pull off one of the country's most fascinating technological achievements. When the telephone arrived in Cather's Red Cloud in 1899, a quiet revolution was occurring in the delivery of rural phone service that serves as an inspiration for what collective action can accomplish in the face of daunting problems. The story begins with the 1894 expiration of the Bell System patents. Before then, the telephone, like the telegraph, was a monopoly that showed little interest in serving ordinary people. When the patents expired, independent phone companies formed across America, some hoping for a quick profit.

The catalyst for rural phone systems was the discovery that although they lacked the clarity and reliability of corporate lines, barbed wire fences could carry the human voice. One story credited "farmers who think" as the originators:

> One of these, living on one of the wide Illinois prairies where there were no telephone poles to be cut, conceived the idea that, after all, the top strand of his barbed fence was wire—wire much the same as that stretched on poles in the cities. He insulated the wire at the posts, bridged connections over roads and fences by using uprights, or ran them under ground by using the ordinary drain tiles. He hitched on his instruments. Of course, it "talked."[77]

A farmer could even hang a portable phone on a nearby fence wire, making it possible to deliver "rush letters" in the fields. The *Red Cloud Chief* had a warning: "During thunder storms no calls can be sent as the wires are grounded or shut off at such times for reason of safety."[78]

The *Scientific American* explained how to build barbed wire phone lines, while J. A. Williams's classic *Manual of Rural Telephony* detailed how to organize a phone company. As farmers created their own systems, they developed a way to finance them that harkens back to the Grange and Farmers' Alliances. They organized cooperatives into which members could contribute money, labor, or materials to own their shares.

These efforts lowered the average cost of rural lines to as little as $3.50 a year, a fraction of the $10.00–$18.00 charged in urban centers.[79] With communities in the grips of "telephone fever," cooperatives formed as fast as farmers could organize them. Their names expressed their origins: Citizen Telephone Company, Enterprise Telephone Company, and Farmers Mutual Cooperative Telephone Company. In 1902 these systems linked more than a quarter of a million people through 5,979 rural phone co-ops.[80] Five years later there were 1.5 million rural telephones and 18,000 cooperative systems.[81] The *American Telegraph Journal* proclaimed, "To the people themselves, working through independent companies, is due the reduction in rates and improvement in service and business methods which have resulted in such an enormous expansion of the telephone industry."[82]

Willa Cather stressed the telephone's social impact, but the impact it had on leveling the economic playing field was also critical. One survey showed farm families made half or more of their calls for business purposes.[83] Phone cooperatives wired farms into a mutual support system that undoubtedly kept more people on the land. A mother going into labor, a child whose illness took a sudden turn for the worse, or a farmer injured by an accident were but a phone call away from a doctor. Farmers could share ideas about seed varieties and cultivation, equipment repairs, and problem solving. The telephone brought closer the dreams of the Grangers and Farmers' Alliances for collective action. While the barbed-wire phone model obviously would not have worked for railroads, it does remind us that infrastructure improvement does not need to be a centralized, top-down process, something we might have learned when interstate highways ran unchecked through inner-city communities much like they did through Indigenous lands.

Her Sole and Separate Property

Willa Cather came of age at a time the number of female sole traders increased from 52,344 in 1880 to 197,378 in 1890, suggesting a lot of women were plowing their own channels.[84] "Sole trader" is a nineteenth-century term applied to a business owned by women. In 1848 New York became the first state to permit married women to hold property in their own names. By the 1870s similar laws existed in most states. Many followed New York's lead in allowing women to collect their own earnings and share custody of their children.[85] Some states also passed laws that permitted women to own businesses.[86] Cather's Nebraska had one of the most liberal sole trader laws: "A woman may carry on any business or trade or perform any labor or services on her account, and her earnings shall be her sole and separate property, and may be used and invested in her own name."[87] Those words enabled Alexandra Bergson to buy and sell land, along with giving Cather the plot for a novel.

B. Zorina Khan argues that laws like Nebraska's brought a surge in inventive activity, because "women were directing their efforts to devise and promote patented inventions."[88] Khan employs a playing field argument when further writing, "The experience of women patentees supports the arguments of economists who emphasize the role of institutions such as legal and property rights systems in eliciting and encouraging the growth of markets." The names of some of these inventor-entrepreneurs have come to us through court cases. Mrs. Bonesteel patented a way of making pavements that became the Nicholson Pavement Company, of which she owned 1,145 shares. After inventing a drive screw and starting a company, Mary Fetter won a court case concerning her right to assign the patent.

There were no fair trader laws for African Americans. Over 4 million newly freed enslaved no sooner celebrated their freedom than they found the industrialization of the North passed over them in favor of the Europeans and Chinese brought to this country to work in factories and mines and on the railroads. In the South, some never left the plantations they had dreamed of escaping. Even the statistical studies conducted by Carroll Wright's Bureau of Labor Statistics intentionally ignored the work of African Americans. Wright had proposed a study of African American families, but his superior, former Confederate officer, secretary of the interior, and future Supreme Court justice Lucius Lamar told Wright that if Southerners discovered he had authorized a Northerner to make the report, "there would be the devil to pay."[89] As with much else during the Age of Discontent, African Americans had to conduct such studies themselves.

Besides the 1893 Columbian Exposition study, there was the work of W. E. B. Du Bois, who authored *The Negro in Business* for the Fourth Atlanta Conference on Negro Problems in 1899. "Physical Emancipation came in 1863," wrote Du Bois in his introduction, "but economic emancipation is still far off. The great majority of Negroes are still serfs."[90] Du Bois defined a "business man" as

OCCUPATION	NUMBER	TOTAL WEEKLY WAGES	AVG WEEKLY WAGE	TOTAL WEEKS WORKED	AVG YEARLY WAGE
Merchant	26	688.5	26.48	1776	1808.79
Physician	4	96	24.00	208	1248.00
Contractor	8	187	23.38	345	1008.26
Mail Carrier	4	71.13	17.78	208	924.56
Teacher	14	208.25	14.88	560	595.20
Bricklayer	14	183.16	13.08	496	463.41
Clergy	21	266.34	12.68	1082	653.32
Mason	10	112.5	11.25	415	466.88
Barber	21	201.5	9.60	1008	460.80
Carpenter	47	437.33	9.30	1854	366.86
Butcher	5	46	9.20	260	478.40
Longshoreman	6	54.5	9.08	297	449.46
Hack Driver	8	69	8.63	363	391.59
Painter	20	168.5	8.43	778	327.93
Fireman	11	88	8.00	568	413.09
Iron Worker	7	54.5	7.79	318	353.89
Janitor	15	116.75	7.78	756	392.11
Porter	50	373.9	7.48	2415	361.28
Teamster	35	255.6	7.30	1696	353.74
Railroad	46	330.44	7.18	2066	322.48
Blacksmith	15	103.5	6.90	734	337.64
Coachman/Driver	22	144.61	6.57	1127	336.56
Quarryman	5	31.5	6.30	190	239.40
Laborer	195	1209.91	6.20	8750	278.21
Drayman	20	121.5	6.08	982	298.53
Shoemaker	7	42	6.00	355	304.29
Lumber	12	70.5	5.88	556	272.44
Boarding House Owner	4	23.4	5.85	298	435.83
Waiter	28	154.7	5.53	1365	269.59
Farmer	5	20	4.00	252	201.60
Nurse	10	39	3.90	365	142.35
Seamstress	14	52.1	3.72	534	141.89
Cook	55	154.38	2.81	2480	126.71
Laundress/Launderer	115	301.15	2.62	5762	131.27
Servant	15	37.33	2.49	719	119.35
	894	6514.48	7.02	41938	455.17

Figure 11.1 Select Wages for African American Wages

someone who had invested at least $500 ($19,000 in 2017 dollars). Focusing on the South, his tables detailed $8,784,637 in investments.[91] It testifies to African American grit that they established 60 percent of those enterprises after the end of Reconstruction.[92]

Speaking for those he interviewed, Du Bois lamented, "Large industry, the department store, and the trust are daily making it more difficult for the small capitalist."[93] He went on to explain, "A Negro can today run a small corner grocery with considerable success. Tomorrow however, he cannot be head of the grocery department of the department store which forces him out of business." In this study Du Bois viewed education as the key to overcoming the inequities of race and class.

Du Bois's study came two years after Carroll Wright's bureau finally published *The Condition of the Negro in Various Cities*, focusing on eighteen businesses, all in the South except for one in Cambridge, Massachusetts. The table in figure 11.1 compiles these data for the first time.

Accounting for actual hours worked, the table shows 53 percent of African Americans earned less than $300 per year; according to Aldrich, the national average annual wage at the same time was $442. That almost a fourth of African American workers earned less than $200 a year shows their grim condition.[94]

A Gatling Gun on Paper

Creating fairer markets was the purpose of the Sherman Antitrust Act, but its fate after it passed was even more problematic than the ICA's. The sharpest legal mind of his generation, Oliver Wendell Holmes, viewed the Sherman Act as "a humbug based on economic ignorance and incompetence."[95] An 1893 attorney general's report was not as harsh: "It is not surprising, therefore, that different judges who have been called upon to put a legal meaning upon the statute have found the task difficult."[96] It does seem harsh to condemn the legislation in light of the lax enforcement of pro-business presidents, corporate attorneys general, and a Supreme Court inclined to make laissez-faire capitalism the law of the land.

Neither has this prevented critics, especially those representing the Industrial Narrative, from hijacking the intent of the bill. Prominent among them is rejected Supreme Court nominee Robert Bork, who advanced a novel interpretation of the Sherman Act as being focused on consumer welfare and efficiency. In his stated view, if we get what we want and it is delivered satisfactorily, then it does not matter if a company controls the market. Bork claims his interpretation is "originalist" because it relies on the contemporaneous debates over the bill. As several critics have pointed out, the *Congressional Record* shows the absurdity of this position.[97] The main references to consumer welfare in the debates over the wording in the act are in Sen. George's February 27, 1890 speech *opposing* the bill.

It is telling that one of the first applications of the Sherman Act was not to break up a trust but to break a strike. Even though the recorded debate over the bill clearly asserts that it did not apply to groups like the Farmers' Alliances and the Knights of Labor, Grover Cleveland's clever attorney general, former railroad counsel Richard Olney, thought otherwise. During the 1877 railroad strike the government had left Robert Ammon and union officials alone, but during the 1894 Pullman Strike, Olney used the Sherman Act to prosecute officers of the American Railway Union (ARU) for conspiracy. During the trial of those officials, Clarence Darrow pointed out that John Sherman had affirmed, "combinations of workingmen . . . are not affected in the slightest degree, nor can they be included in the words and content of the bill."[98]

Sparked by eighteen-year-old labor organizer Jennie Curtis, the ARU had initiated a boycott of Pullman cars. Olney's restraint of trade injunction against union leader Eugene Debs was so broad, a judge termed it "a Gatling gun on paper." In response *The Arena* charged that the action was "tantamount to a declaration that labor unions are illegal," since "any organization that may interfere with or inconvenience corporations" was viewed as a conspiracy.[99] Darrow effectively argued the Debs case by quoting from the debate over the bill, but the Supreme Court ruled against him.

After sending Debs to jail, the court further crippled the Sherman Act with its Sugar Trust case decision. The facts of *United States vs E. C. Knight* are simple and a clear violation of the Sherman Act's intent. The American Sugar Refining Company moved to acquire the E. C. Knight company and three other companies, enabling it to control 98 percent of the sugar market. The Cleveland administration sued to prevent the acquisition as a violation of the Sherman Act.

The opinion by Justice Melville Fuller began by recognizing the obvious: the American Sugar Refining Company "acquired nearly complete control of the manufacture of refined sugar within the United States."[100] He then penned a sentence that still has scholars scratching their heads: "The monopoly and restraint denounced by the act are the monopoly and restraint of interstate and international trade or commerce, while the conclusion to be assumed on this record is that the result of the transaction complained of was the creation of a monopoly in the manufacture of a necessary of life."[101] Then he added another head-scratcher: "The tentacles which drew the outlying refineries into the dominant corporation were separately put out, therefore there was no combination to monopolize." Finally, the last nail in the coffin: "The relief of the citizens of each state from the burden of monopoly and the evils resulting from the restraint of trade among such citizens was left with the states to deal with, and this Court has recognized their possession of that power." In short, the opinion allowed the merger to continue for three reasons: it dealt with a "necessity of life," the companies acquired by the trust did not conspire to form the combination, and the prosecution of such acquisitions was a state matter.

The absurdity of these arguments is readily apparent. Necessities of life should be kept from monopoly control lest a company hold people's lives hostage, as Sen. Amy Klobuchar affirms in a story about the predatory pricing of the heart drug indomethacin, which opens her book on antitrust legislation. Whether they conspired or not, the merger produced a near-monopoly. Referring the matter back to the states is strange in light of the *Wabash* decision overturning *Munn*. Despite these problems, seven justices sided with Fuller, leaving the dissenter in the 1883 *Civil Rights Cases*, John Harlan, as the sole dissenter in the *Sugar Trust Case*.

Harlan's opinion included numerous citations, but like his *Civil Rights Cases* dissent, it relied on a common-sense argument. It made no more sense for African American passengers to have to change cars at the Mason-Dixon line than it did for a sugar company to control 98 percent of the market for an important commodity. "This view of the scope of the [Sherman] Act leaves the public, so far as national power is concerned, entirely at the mercy of combinations which arbitrarily control the prices of articles purchased to be transported from one state to another state," Harlan wrote.[102]

The *Sugar Trust* and *Debs* cases unwittingly reveal the paradox of laissez-faire capitalism. On the surface, proponents favor minimal interference in corporate affairs, yet underneath, they make the opposite case by saying they need government protection to prevent that interference. This contradiction runs throughout the late nineteenth century, which is why it ranks as one of our most intensive periods of corporate support, whether through welfare, like the tariff and railroad subsidies, to the actions of pro-business supreme courts and presidential administrations. The more corporations insisted on their rights, the more they called on government to protect them, and the more government protected corporations, the more people came to view the playing field as tilted. This created a classic feedback loop that produced the corrections advocated by the Discontented.

By Which Alone Truth Can Be Found

A century after the American Revolution, the country had to extensively remodel what the Founders had created because the Declaration of Independence and the US Constitution were in mortal danger from forces never imagined by Thomas Jefferson or John Adams. Because the Discontented were reinventing American democracy on the fly, the wonder is that they got so many things right despite the race and gender bias, and this remains their tragic flaw. Even more amazing is that they accomplished so much against overwhelming odds. The defenders of corporate nullification had far more money, far more communications resources, and far more firepower.

History is never neat and no revolution is perfect. Left behind most revolutions is the unfinished business resulting from imperfection. And, despite efforts to cage history in generalizations, it escapes between cracks in the evidence that widen under the stress of time. Yet all groups need historical narratives to help them function. The difficulties come when the imperfections of those narratives become too burdensome to ignore. As we struggle to deal with our current problems with the American tryptic, we might do well to learn from a generation that also faced a world shifting beneath them.

The original sin of slavery tainted the first American Revolution, but the infamous three-fifths clause, which sought to mollify the South by counting the enslaved as partial persons for purposes of allocating congressional representation, resulted from deeper forces. Of course, one was racism, but the other was the perverted notion of property rights, which would resurface in Chief Justice Taney's *Dred Scott* decision. We should not be surprised that this unholy alliance between racism and property rights overshadowed the Age of Discontent.

Rather than dwell on the imperfections of the Discontenteds' actions, however, it is wise to remember what they did right. This begins by acknowledging they saw themselves not as radicals but as conservatives dedicated to holding this country to its ideals. Chief among them was the principle that a chief function of government is to ensure a level playing field. The more corporations insisted on their notions of nullification to justify everything from unsafe workplaces to outright murder, the more the people pushed back. The initiatives they fostered are the result. The Age of Discontent is unique because in no other period did so many diverse people and agendas come together to achieve goals. The melding and the legislation may have been imperfect, but their reforms have never been repudiated. They showed the country how to make the constitution relevant to an industrial world.

We have seen how those efforts contributed millions to the economy, but what those estimates cannot calculate are the resulting systemic dynamics. Their beauty is that they reinforce one another, increasing their impact. Education may have increased production, but without the infrastructure to assure distribution and regulations to oversee the marketplace, the country would have squandered that production. What the country needed was fuel to stoke the emerging consumer culture in the form of increased discretionary spending. A West Virginia railroad engineer helps us understand how that happened in the next chapter.

The education initiatives of the NLU, the Knights, the Grange, and the Farmers' Alliances—as embodied in the Hatch Act and the Second Morrill Act, plus school trust lands—remain their most significant achievements. Corporations contributed little to these efforts, and oftentimes they opposed them. Expanded public education provided the brainpower to engineer factories, increase farmers' yields, provide security against marginal years, and ensure a more equitable nation by giving people a chance to improve their lives. Economist Thomas Piketty has affirmed, "U.S. economic leadership came from mass education, not from a small elite of billionaires."[103]

What emerged in this country in the twentieth century would not have been possible without the initiatives of the Discontented. This is seen in the life of the man who gave this country the New Deal. The birth that nearly killed Franklin Delano Roosevelt and his mother occurred the same year John D. Rockefeller formed the Standard Oil Trust and Congress passed the Chinese Exclusion Act. During FDR's first year, Willa Cather moved to Nebraska and Buffalo Bill inaugurated his Wild West Show. When Franklin was four, the house must have buzzed about Henry George's audacious run for mayor of New York City. In the year of Haymarket, Grover Cleveland patted FDR on the head as he silently wished the youngster would never become president. Roosevelt was peddling a bicycle through Germany when William Jennings Bryan delivered his "Cross of Gold" speech.

From the estate Franklin's parents built on the Hudson River he saw J. P. Morgan's black yacht prowling the Hudson. He heard of his father's visit to a tenement, where he found "half a dozen nearly nude and hideously dirty children, a man toiling by the flame of a candle, a woman lying ill abed, all in this pestiferous and dingy den."[104] It is not too much to say that modern America was born in the Age of Discontent.

CHAPTER TWELVE

How Much You Can Buy

Along came the F.F.V., the fastest on the line,
A running on the C. and O. road, thirty minutes behind time.
As she passed the Sewalls it was quarters on the line;
And they received new orders to make up some lost time.
—*From the railroad song "The Wreck on the C&O"*

Drizzle and downpour alternated under the shroud of an October night in 1890 when George Washington Alley climbed into Engine #134 at Hinton, West Virginia.[1] With his Wyatt Earp mustache and coal black hair, this ramrod-slim engineer appeared chosen by central casting to make up lost time for the Chesapeake and Ohio's premier train, the Fast Flying Virginian (FFV). Barely thirty, Alley starred on a team of crack engineers who earned double the average wage by braving hairpin turns and wagon-sized boulders suspended over the three-hundred-million-year-old chasm of West Virginia's New River. Completed at a cost of 100 lives and $24 million, the route moved a reporter to describe it as a "marvel of engineering," unequaled in "wildness, grandeur, and picturesqueness."[2]

Trained by his engineer father, Alley belonged to a distinguished railroading family unmatched in its "long and faithful service with the same railroad."[3] That was saying a lot in the days when stories and songs memorialized those who had mastered the power of locomotives. People knew the whistle "signatures" announcing the hand controlling the throttle.[4] It was said the wail of a skilled engineer could pierce your soul.

When Mark Twain wrote that a riverboat pilot had to learn that "more than one man ought to be allowed to learn" he might also have been describing railroad engineers like Alley.[5] Lives hung on their ability to make exacting, split-second calculations at high speeds, like those described in a textbook for engineers: "Driver C goes in for 140 lbs. from the start to the finish, not a pound less; works with the regulator full open, and with the reversing-lever in No. 1 notch (next to the centre of the sector), expanding the steam until it can scarcely rise over the chimney top when it swoops down on the boiler, and in the face of the driver."[6] Engineers who understood knew that if they miscalculated the settings on the maze of gauges, valves, and levers crowding the cab, they risked a hellish death by steam and fire. C&O engineer Billy Richardson momentarily lost his concentration and was decapitated by a mailbag swing near Hinton.

Engineers were not the daredevils sometimes portrayed in story and song. According to one respected railroad manual of the time, daredevils were not wanted.

> He, above all men, must be practical, conservative, possessed of an apprehensive mind, anticipating always what is before him. He must not only be alive to his own duty but alert to that of others. There must be nothing of the braggadocio about him, nothing of the pyrotechnical or spectacular. He must be a conscientious man, taking the safe course not because the rules tell him so, but because it is his nature. Such is the true engineer.[7]

Alley had a special responsibility because the FFV was the country's most opulent and technically advanced train, the first to "boast all vestibuled cars, electric lighting, steam heat, and electricity throughout."[8] Ads hyped a journey similar to one combining the Alps and the Rhine in "the elegant Day Coach with Smoking Saloon and Lavatories. . . . Dining Car cooled with Electric Fans and Pullman Sleeping Cars."[9] Under the glow of crystal chandeliers passengers dined on baked apples and cream, boiled sea fish, sirloin steak, spring lamb chops, and a delicacy called Saratoga Chips—known today as potato chips.[10] In 1903 two Ohio bicycle mechanics chose the FFV to carry them and their their flying machine.

When George Alley took over Engine #134, he was well aware of another side of the FFV. According to railroad historian Thomas Dixon, "The FFV was not only famous for her luxury and speed but also renowned for her train wrecks."[11] In January 1890 a disastrous accident in the New River Gorge left 10 dead and "about a score injured."[12] Alley may have read the newspaper headline, "An Unusual Number of Train Wrecks," as he waited to take over the eastbound FFV after bringing the westbound from Clifton Forge to Hinton that morning. A Cincinnati tunnel collision had killed 10. A crash in Kansas City left 9 injured and 1 dead. An Alabama engineer had reversed his engine to retrieve a conductor left at the station, forgetting the freight train barreling toward them. The railroad accident rate for the month of October 1890 totaled 288 collisions and 100 fatalities, or 9.2 wrecks and 3.2 deaths per day.[13]

If George Alley was a star engineer piloting the country's most advanced train, many regarded the man who built the route as one of the country's premier railroad executives. A colleague called Collis P. Huntington "the most remarkable man we have had on Wall Street."[14] At age eight he got his start hauling wood with an ox team, then rose to become one of the Big Four overseeing the Central Pacific's conquest of the Sierra Mountains in the Far West by combining nitroglycerin with cheap Chinese labor. Huntington then took on the New River Gorge. His scouting expedition became the second party to conquer its formidable rapids (Chief Justice John Marshall led the first). Huntington's plans employed steam drills and leased convicts to lay track. Among those who died from breathing the silicon dust stirred up by the drills was an African American convict named John Henry.[15] Perhaps because he knew railroads, Huntington had a phobia: he refused to ride night trains.[16]

At 5:30 a.m. on October 23, 1890, the C&O's best engineer, its most advanced train, and its foremost financier became entangled in one of America's most famous train wrecks. According to the *Hinton Independent*, "Going round a curve near the mouth of the Greenbrier River, [the FFV] ran into a rock that had fallen from the cliff, and the engine, tender, baggage car and postal car were derailed."[17] Pinned inside the overturned engine, George Alley cried out, "Are they coming?" as rescuers tried to free him while his family rushed to the scene. His obituary saluted "a brave and noble Christian spirit" who left "a noble example of unselfish devotion to duty and principle" by ordering his crew to jump then saving the train and its passengers from plunging into the gorge.

Because the C&O had no insurance "of any sort," Alley's only death benefits were the $103 raised by passengers to support his wife and four young children. Other than attempts by the C&O to bring Alley's family to the wreck site, it offered little else, recalling Franklin Gowen's perverse offer to ship the bodies of the Molly Maguire defendants he had had executed. Alley's courage inspired one of America's classic railroad ballads, recorded by Johnny Cash, the Carter Family, Joan Baez, Doc Watson, Ralph Stanley, and others. The earliest known text of the song, appearing in 1913, included a chorus absent from recordings.

> Many man's been murdered by the railroad, railroad,
> Many man's been murdered by the railroad and lain in his lonesome grave.[18]

The author of that chorus was not the first to blame the railroad. Immediately after the wreck, the Hinton paper charged, "The railroad . . . should have extra watchmen at the points of the road where land slips are likely to occur, in such weather as we had last night."[19]

Recordings lacking this specific chorus fault Alley for "trying to make up lost time." Given that the curve where the train derailed was not far from Hinton, it is highly unlikely that he had gone roaring out of the station to his death. No contemporary reports mention speed as a factor, which means sometime after the wreck an alternate version of events developed. Norm Cohen provides a hint about when and why that might have occurred: "Public attitudes towards rail-roads remained predominantly negative until 1920," which is when the original lines disappeared.[20] A song about a train wreck also clashed with the C&O ad campaign introduced in 1933 featuring the mascot Chessie the Kitten and the slogan "Sleep like a kitten."[21]

Collis Huntington could not supply enough watchmen to prevent the wreck after he ran into a boulder of his own, losing the C&O in 1888. A former exec-utive described it at the time as a "physical and financial wreck."[22] J. P. Morgan and William K. Vanderbilt snapped up the bankrupt company, giving Morgan control of 60 percent of the country's railroads. Morgan upgraded the FFV, but the list of repairs mentioned in the company's 1890 annual report did not include the wreck site.[23]

There was another potential factor contributing to the story about the wreck. Some locals did not like the C&O. An article reported the capture of an outlaw who two weeks before George Alley's death sabotaged a switch. The C&O even hired a detective to investigate attempts by "a gang of train wreckers . . . prin-cipally directed against the Fast Flying Virginian."[24] While it is unlikely train wreckers pried loose a boulder in the rain, it does support the Hinton paper's charge that the C&O should have been alert to the danger.

The fates of George Alley and Collis Huntington are sobering reminders of how late nineteenth-century forces could unexpectedly take anyone from progress to poverty. The Alley family fell from the middle class to the brink of destitution in a fateful ten seconds. Huntington was more fortunate: he became president of the Southern Pacific the year George Alley was killed.

How People Can Live

Many of the legislative initiatives fostered by the Discontented arrived too late to save the FFV. The Sherman Act did not pass until after Collis Huntington had squandered the C&O. The Interstate Commerce Act was in its infancy. The Safety Appliance Act was still Lorenzo Coffin's dream. The December 1890 edition of *Locomotive Engineer's Monthly Journal*, which contains a tribute to George Alley, also features a paper read by H. H. Westinghouse at the annual meeting of the American Railway Superintendents' Association. The treatise claimed that the company's new triple valve system "effected a reduction in the time of application of the brakes on a train of 50 cars from 18 to 2 seconds."[25] Those brakes might have saved Alley's life.

In a larger sense the FFV wreck speaks about the ambivalence of history. The FFV story resonates with themes that have wound through these pages: ambivalence about the limits of technology, the avarice of grasping corporations, the cruelty of unnecessary industrial accidents, and blaming others for them. But it is the different versions of the story, one blaming Alley and the other the railroad, that elevate the story to a far larger and more important example about our use of history. The stories we choose to preserve about the past, the lessons we draw from them, and how we apply those lessons to policy decisions and other aspects of our lives shape our characters. The whitewashing of the C&O in many recordings evokes the larger theme about the Industrial Narrative: how it has whitewashed our views of the Age of Discontent. George Alley did not cause the accident when trying to make up lost time. He saved the train, its passengers, and its crew by staying at his post to slow the train. Corporate executives did not save this country; they were directly responsible for the discontent and the miseries brought into the lives of so many, including resisting the very safety measures that might have saved the train. Instead it was people like George Alley, people like Lorenzo Coffin and Leonora Barry, who rescued this country. The dimensions of that rescue and an important refutation of the Industrial Narrative can be found in two government reports almost as forgotten as the true story of George Alley. The author of both reports, conducted twenty-eight years apart, is the person who answered many late nineteenth-century questions: Carroll Wright.

The first is an extensive 1875 study of wage earners for the Massachusetts Bureau of Labor; the other is a 1903 study published by the federal Bureau of Labor Statistics as the *Eighteenth Annual Report of the Commissioner of Labor*. Wright acknowledged both studies' limitations. The first had only 397 subjects, some of whom were recruited from people the enumerators had met on the street. The second omitted farmers because of difficulties gathering data. And Wright adds a third qualifier: "Schedules were secured from quite a number of colored families, but their facts are not shown separately."[26]

Wright's Massachusetts report remains the main analysis of consumer expenditure patterns in the 1870s. The Aldrich Report attempted to compute prices and expenses for the decade, but its data came with a warning label from the committee's minority: "No accurate or reliable approximate conclusion as to the movement in prices can be reached by comparing the movement in prices of a few articles at one period with the movement of many and dissimilar articles at another period."[27] There are also embarrassing discrepancies between Aldrich expense data and other sources. Aldrich states that families spent $262.42 on food in 1890, but Wright's 1903 study reports 1890 food expenses were $318.28—a significant difference.

Despite these limitations, the rows and columns of Wright's two studies offer an alternate perspective on late nineteenth-century American economic development. It revolves around one key variable: the cost of food. According to Wright's data, food expenses amounted to 57 percent, or $422.16 for an average 1875 family, but only 42.6 percent, or $312.92 by 1903.[28] Two other expenses fell during that time: rent costs went from 16.7 percent ($123.84) to 12.9 percent ($99.49) and fuel from 6 percent ($43.91) to 4.2 percent ($32.23). Given their small percentages and changes, their decline had less of an impact than the cost of food.[29]

The almost 15 percent drop in food expenses was the equivalent of a wage increase for every family, no matter what their income. In simple terms, it meant they had more to spend on discretionary purchases, but the calculus of lower food expenses reverberates far beyond that. In homes that typically got by on gruel and other unappetizing fare, it meant they could enjoy better meals and larger portions, making starvation less likely and increasing life expectancy. No numbers can capture how more and better food expanded their horizons.

Carroll Wright would have made a good storekeeper. His 1903 "ledger" included over one hundred pages of tables tracking thirteen years of prices for salted and fresh fish, lard, beef steaks and roasts, evaporated apples, prunes, vinegar, and other foodstuffs in towns like Racine, Wisconsin; Pittsfield, Massachusetts; Ottawa, Illinois; and Saginaw, Michigan. Had he not cast such a wide net, our knowledge of food prices would rely on sources like a frontier newspaper that stated, "We are essentially a hungry beef-eating people," no doubt with the blessing of ranchers.[30]

Technology affected the American diet before 1890. There were attempts to design refrigerated cars before the Civil War, but it wasn't until after 1880, when Chicago meatpacker Gustav Swift formed his refrigerated car line, that transportation of fresh food became widespread. Canning dates to the early nineteenth century, but it was a notoriously slow—and dangerous—operation to hand-solder the lids. That changed in 1888, when J. D. Cox perfected the canning machine, earning him credit as "the man who lifted the canned foods industry out of hand work to the dignity of mechanical production."[31] Given this evidence, it is hard to attribute the decline in food prices to changes in technology alone. The reason for the decline becomes clear if we investigate what people ate.

The 1883 edition of *Mrs. Lincoln's Cook Book* preached, "Nothing in the whole range of domestic life more affects the health and happiness of the family than the quality of its daily bread."[32] This was especially true of low-income workers who, based on various state reports, ate bread as the main staple of their diet, often without meat or cheese. In Wright's 1903 tables, flour and cornmeal accounted for 22.1 percent of family food consumption, with bread adding another 10.1 percent. The only other items with double-digit consumption were milk (13.8 percent) and beef (12.7percent);[33] but only wheat prices declined. At the end of the nineteenth century, beef prices reached their highest level in thirty years. Estimating the cost of milk is more difficult because of the introduction of canned evaporated milk in 1885, but Wright's tables show its cost *increased* by 5 percent. The price of wheat flour declined 64 percent from $10.21 in 1875 to $3.59 in 1903.[34]

In the world of ragtime and movie space, the benefits from lower food prices flowed unevenly. In extensive tables detailing the prices of items such as sugar and baking powder in over fifteen hundred towns during the 1890s, the 1900 Industrial Commission affirmed the price of a gallon of Mr. Rockefeller's heating oil ranged from 7¢ in Detroit, Chicago, and Cortland, Ohio (pop. 520) to 35¢ cents in Park City, Utah, and Virginia City, Montana.[35]

Wright's tables show a similar variation in the price of a one-pound loaf of whole wheat bread. Consumers in Troy, New York, paid 5¢ cents for it, while people in Bethlehem, Pennsylvania, must have wondered if their town name brought them good fortune because a loaf cost them only 4¢. Buttering that bread cost 30¢ a pound in Birmingham, Alabama, but 37¢ in Atlanta, Georgia.[36] In the big picture, the average prices declined, causing advertisers to shift their pleas from cost to quality. Ads in *American Kitchen* showcased awards. Push Leaf Lard touted a Columbian Exposition medal. The Washburn and Crosby company cleverly named its flour Gold Medal.

One factor contributing to the decline of wheat and bread prices is that there was no bread trust to control it. Although there were big mills like Washburn and Crosby, and speculators played a role in prices at the Chicago Board of Trade, thousands of local mills existed and no one controlled the bakeries. Where many cartels and trusts centered on controlling distribution, no one could control the wheat supply itself. This left bread in an unusual situation in comparison to other foodstuffs like sugar, meat, or other necessities.

An Advantage and a Blessing

The reduction in food prices bought working families a cushion against uncertainty. Those on the margin were less likely to suffer the fate of Mary Hennessey. John Sherman understood this, pointing out that low food prices were the main reason for immigration, followed by the Homestead Act and education. "This is an advantage and a blessing which the poor man enjoys in no other country," he said.[37] The *Locomotive Fireman's Magazine* agreed: "The effective earning or productive power of man is greatest, in the United States, where the supply of food is most abundant."[38]

Identifying the causes of price shifts can be challenging, especially when data are scarce and sometimes unreliable. Costs for raw wheat, milling, transportation, and even the cost of the barrel could influence the price of a barrel of wheat flour. Scholars have mixed views of the reduction in freight rates noted by the 1901 ICC report. Robert Higgs demonstrates that railroad shipping rates remained horizontal before 1897. James Stewart claims "Real rates (railroad rates relative to the prices farmers received for their output) were highly variable between 1865 and 1900."[39] Other variables, like milling costs, are even more difficult to compute as they varied by the mill and the type of flour produced. The factor having the highest correlation with the price of flour is the amount of wheat production.[40]

Contrary to the belief that raising wheat was largely a specialty of the wheat belt that today runs from the Dakotas through Nebraska and Kansas, four of the top ten wheat-producing states for the late nineteenth century lie to the east of there: Ohio, Illinois, Michigan, and Indiana. During the late nineteenth century Michigan achieved the highest yield per acre, 20.5 bushels, just beating the 20.0 achieved by Kansas. One wheat producer lay far to the west: California. Missouri, Iowa, and Minnesota, plus the traditional wheat belt states of Kansas and Nebraska, round out the top ten. Although they are now big wheat-producing states, the Dakotas are not included because they did not become states until November 1889.

If the final *Jeopardy* question asked which state led the nation in wheat production in the late nineteenth century, most people would guess Kansas or Nebraska, but it was Minnesota. Together the Wheat Ten accounted for more than two-thirds of the nation's wheat acreage and almost three-quarters of the wheat harvested.[41] In the 1870s the eastern four states contained the most acreage and generated the most production. By the 1890s the center of wheat production had moved west, as settlers filled in the map of the Wheat Belt.

The wheat crop also experienced dramatic increases in production during the late nineteenth century. The standard explanation attributes this to mechanization.[42] While there is little question that technology altered farming after the Civil War, tractors were not a major part of that shift. Even at the beginning of the Great Depression, only 17 percent of Minnesota farms owned tractors.[43] Improvements to John Deere's self-polishing steel plow and the 1875 invention of the Gilpin sulky plow influenced production, but most farmers were already using the first, and the use of the second is difficult to determine.[44]

For wheat, the game-changing machine was the reaper, whose use became widespread after the Civil War. Tinkerers added improvements, the most important being the binder, which eliminated the labor-intensive task of tying threshed stalks. An 1891 Kansas report testifies to this change: "I need scarcely call the attention of intelligent farmers to the fact, that a boy of sixteen, driving a span of horses attached to a binder, can do the work it took ten strong men to do less than fifty years ago and do the work far better."[45] A US Senate committee study headed by Kansas Populist William Peffer was more skeptical:

> It is doubtful whether the cost of producing grain on small farms is much less now than it was before the use of machinery became common. The object of using machines is to save labor; hence if no labor were displaced there would be no gain. Where one man with his family can perform all the work required on his farm he would lose and not gain by the use of machines, because he would have to pay money for them and he is able to do the work without them.[46]

One setting where machinery had produced a major impact is America's first factory farms, the "bonanza farms" of the Dakotas and California. Encompassing as many as 100,000 acres each, these farms employed gang plows, planters, and reapers supervised by military-style management. In California, plows and seeders pulled by eight horses could turn over 6 acres a day and seed 20. Today's most advanced tractor, the $300,000 Challenger MT775, can cultivate 150 acres per day.[47] Peffer's committee described a North Dakota bonanza farm:

The plan adopted by Mr. Dalrymple and all the other "bonanza" men is to divide the land into tracts of 6,000 acres each, and these are subdivided into farms of 2,000 acres each. Over each 6,000 acres a superintendent is placed, with a bookkeeper, headquarters building, and a storehouse for supplies. Each subdivision of 2,000 acres is under the charge of a foreman, and is provided with its own set of buildings, comprising boarding houses for the hands, stables, a granary, a machinery hall, and a blacksmith's shop, all connected with the superintendent's office by telephone.[48]

Despite their size, the impact of bonanza farms was limited. During their heyday the average acres per farm in the Dakotas was only 200–300.[49] The dry years of the 1890s ended the bonanza farm. Fred Shannon observes, "The large-scale grower found it hard to compete with the smaller farmers."[50] By 1896 the Dalrymple farm was gone.

The best data about mechanization comes from the US Census Bureau, whose broad definition of "farm machinery" included hand tools and implements like wagons and carts. It is no surprise that in the Wheat Ten, the total farm machinery value per farm grew from $132 in 1870 to $201 in 1900.[51] The standard theory about the impact of machinery is that in the case of a crop like wheat, machinery would enable a farmer to plant and harvest more acres in less time. Yet the acres cultivated per farm grew only slightly, from 185 to 191. The 53 percent increase in spending on machinery raised the acres cultivated per farm by a mere 2 percent, providing support for Peffer's assertion. Absent more data, it appears machines were not the main cause of increased wheat production.

The size of the wheat crop is a function of two factors, acreage and yield. A farm with many acres and low yields may produce a smaller crop than one with fewer acres and high yields. During the 1890s, the crop was 2 billion bushels higher than in the 1870s and 1 billion bushels higher than in the 1880s. In the first decade after the Civil War, yields averaged 12.4 bushels per acre; in the 1890s the average was 13.6. Wheat Ten yields averaged 13.4 bushels per acre in the 1870s and 14.1 in the 1890s.[52]

While factors like weather influenced yields, it is not hard to see the impact of the experiment stations, along with the support provided by the Grange and Farmers' Alliances. The increase in the 1890s is especially impressive if we factor in the drought that hit Kansas and Nebraska in the early 1890s, the one Stephen Crane portrayed in his article that pictured bodies lying in the fields. During that time Kansas yields fell from 18 bushels per acre in 1892 to half that the next year and stayed that low for the next three years; Nebraska's yields plummeted from 13.5 to 8.5 bushels per acre over the same time period.[53]

The drought perplexed the experiment stations. The Kansas station admitted, "The disastrous drought of 1894 made the results of nearly all field experiments so meager and uncertain as to preclude publication."[54] Still, scientists continued searching for solutions. The Kansas station issued periodic reports with titles like "Experiments with Wheat," detailing the benefits of tilling with manure, using hot water to kill smut, following plowing dates, drilling versus tilling, and methods of conserving soil moisture and using the best varieties. The Nebraska station's work on soil treatment for orchards in drought even reached New Jersey.[55] Despite the drought, the 1890s median yields in Kansas and Nebraska were higher than in any other decade, suggesting the experiment stations played a role.

The other factor influencing wheat production is acreage. The wheat acres planted in the Wheat Ten increased from 12.8 million to 33.7 million from 1870 to 1900.[56] The obvious question is what role did the Homestead Act play in this increase. A comparison of wheat acres to homestead acres in the Wheat Ten shows total homestead acreage was 59 percent of all wheat acres, but data about homestead acres planted in wheat is unknown. We do know Nebraska, Kansas, and Minnesota, plus the land that became North Dakota and South Dakota, accounted for 70 percent of all homestead acres registered in the 1870s, 60 percent in the 1880s, and 46 percent in the 1890s.[57] In reviewing the story of wheat growing, a Minnesota publication found that "much of the wheat was planted by farmers taking advantage of incentives like the Homestead Act of 1862."[58] A great deal of the scholarly discussion about the Homestead Act has focused on its role as a "safety valve," but statistics about the number of homesteaders in the Wheat Ten indicate a strong likelihood the act played a role in reducing the price of wheat for everyone. Definitive confirmation awaits a more intensive county-level study of wheat and homestead patterns.

The Best Varieties to Sow

Railroad engineers like George Alley stayed in touch with the latest research through the *Locomotive Engineers Monthly Journal* and similar publications, which presented technical articles complete with diagrams for addressing problems, like how best to slow a train. Just as engineers who did not keep up with research were more likely to die, farmers who did not seek advice were more likely to fail. This was especially true in the Wheat Belt. When people landed on the prairie, they left behind the trees and shrubs of their homelands for a flat, brown region where temperatures can vary by as much as 120 degrees and a tornado can pick up a house. There they had to relearn how and what to plant. If they were stubborn or stupid, they probably busted, but some, like Alexandra Bergson who were open to experimenting and new knowledge, adapted.

The prairie demanded what Alan Olmstead and Paul Rhode term "biological innovation."[59] Making what some still called the American Desert bloom required new varieties, new cultivation techniques, and new ways of combatting diseases and pests. In the northern tier of Minnesota and the Dakotas, farmers found success with a wheat variety called Red Fife, developed in Canada. Farmers in the southern tier of Nebraska and Kansas had another lesson. They learned to plant their crop in the fall, an idea that must have seemed even more fantastic than flying monkeys and melting witches. Eventually the winter wheat brought by European immigrants caught on. In 1919 Department of Agriculture researcher O. C. Salmon looked back and concluded that without winter wheat "the wheat crop of Kansas today would be no more than half."[60]

The conclusion James Malin reached in his pioneering 1941 study of winter wheat has become widely accepted: "The spread of the hard winter wheat throughout Kansas was almost entirely, if not altogether, a folk phenomenon, the common people following their instincts even against the advice of experts."[61] While this perspective certainly fits the Frontier Narrative—and not coincidentally helps Malin support his barely concealed rant against the New Deal's Agricultural Adjustment Administration—it focuses on only part of the equation.[62] Malin ignores the dynamics of that "folk phenomenon" and the transmission lines of the Grange and Farmers' Alliances.

Countering Malin's view are numerous newspaper stories showing the experiment stations played a role in improving wheat varieties, planting techniques, and disseminating results. One editorialized: "A gentleman said to us the other day that he had tried Turkey or Russian wheat, for four years, simultaneously with Red May and some other varieties, and that Turkey was superior to all the others. What is the testimony of other farmers as to the best varieties to sow? Let us hear from you, friends of the farm."[63] An article touting the Ohio stations' experiments with fertilizer appeared in Kansas and Maryland. North Dakota and Minnesota papers discussed the proceedings of an 1899 convention of grain growers from three states held in Fargo, North Dakota, that included multiple presentations by experiment station researchers. Suggestions that emanated from the Kansas experiment station appeared in Idaho, Oregon, Iowa, and Montana. The Topeka *Advocate* printed suggestions by C. C. Georgeson for the Kansas station's seed purchases. Editors often endorsed these findings, giving them added weight. Reporting on seed planting practices, the *Western Kansas World* noted advice "has been used for the past three years and always with advantage at that station."[64]

Two other channels of transmission were the cooperative stores and the lecturers of the Grange and Farmers' Alliances. Because the Grange and the alliances sold seeds and tools, they served as an intersection where farmers could trade information. If nothing else, if farmer Svendsbye brought in a record yield, word about it traveled quickly. The *Grange Advance* of Red Wing, Minnesota, reports farmers asking, "What kind of crops should be cultivated, and in what proportion on a farm of 120 acres?" A Michigan grange endorsed a particular strain of wheat.[65] Olmstead and Rhode claim this biological revolution was the agricultural equivalent of "the steam engine, the Bessemer process, and electricity [that] revolutionized the structure and location of industry."[66] Given the relationship between food prices and wheat, it is reasonable to conclude that new varieties like Red Fife and Turkey Red, along with the activities of the experiment stations, influenced the price drop of food.

Hands of Every Description

If the falling price of food provided people the equivalent of a wage increase, how did they spend this income? Help comes from a curious source. In *A Connecticut Yankee in King Arthur's Court*, Mark Twain writes, "It isn't what you get [paid], but how much you can buy with it that's important."[67] Wright made "how much you can buy" a key part of his two studies. In his 1875 study, he proposed to determine the health of the economy (and by implication American society) not using production data, but with consumption data. His conclusion echoed economist Richard Ely's theories about the importance of consumer purchasing power:

No one should receive such small compensation for his toil, that even when expended with economy and prudence, it fails to pay for his necessary cost of living; rendering him an involuntary debtor, subjecting him continually to the demands of creditors who wish pay for the necessaries of life he has consumed; obliging him to overwork his wife with home and outside duties; forcing him to deprive his children of education, that he may supply by their labor their cries for bread; finally, bringing him to the poor-house.[68]

The first revelation concerns expense categories. In 1875 Wright divided expenses into subsistence, clothing, rent, fuel, and "sundries." In both the 1900 US Census and Wright's 1903 report, subsistence becomes "food." The more interesting change is in sundries: the Census Bureau references that in 1875 it included items "although not absolutely necessary for the life of the body, are, in their way, an imperative necessity in a man's social life." Examples were furniture, carpeting, books, religion, charity, recreation, and travel;[69] in the 1900 census and Wright's 1903 table, the term "other expenses" supplants sundries; by 1910 expenses for specific items had become the norm.

According to Wright's tables, the reduced food expenses due to lower prices raised discretionary spending from 6.3 to 20.6 percent of annual household income.[70] This increase opened doors to the plumed hats and billowing dresses in department store windows and connected rural consumers with the precise line drawings of intricately stitched parlor chairs and sinuously curved hay rakes advertised in mail-order catalogs. It also led searching eyes to newspaper advertisements for fur-trimmed coats and lace gloves. In turn, these purchases increased demand and stimulated production.

Like much else during the Age of Discontent, the increase in discretionary spending did not occur incrementally, but instead followed the uncertain, syncopated rhythms of the Long Depression. Lacking more complete yearly data on all consumer spending, one can grasp this dynamic by tracking annual silk imports for consumption. Why silk? Jerry Simpson's crack about his opponent's silk socks is a reminder that silk was synonymous with an upscale lifestyle. For Simpson and most of his contemporaries, buying silk was the equivalent of someone today splurging for an upscale pair of jeans. In this sense silk purchases act as a handy stand-in for discretionary consumer purchases. Anecdotal evidence suggests silk became more widely available by the end of the century. In 1890 a fashion maven ranted, "On paper, the [silk] mitts are always placed on white and shapely hands; on the street, unfortunately, they are permitted to encase hands of every description."[71] A look at silk imports provides a rough verification of that fashion trend. As the graph in figure 12.1 shows, silk imports rise through the 1890s, but that rise is an uneven one, with sharp declines following increases.

A second graph helps demonstrate the uneven rise in silk imports. Business failures are a rough gauge of the country's economic health, rising in bad times like the panics and falling as times get better. A graph of business failures compared to the silk graph shows that in years where failures were high, like 1893 and 1896, silk imports were low. When failures were low, such as in 1892 and 1895,

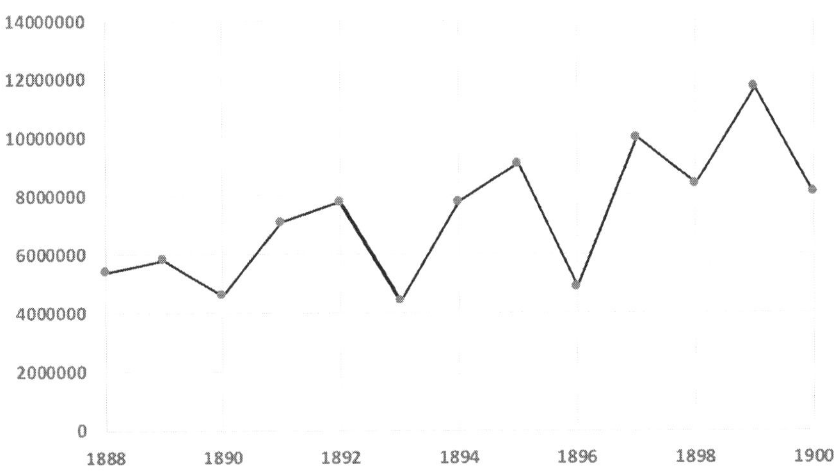

Figure 12.1 Silk Imports, 1888–1900

Figure 12.2 Business Fails, 1883–1900

imports were high. The highest year for silk imports, 1899, was one of the lowest for business failures.

The rise of the consumer culture and with it the modern American economy was not a steady climb, but rather a series of jerks not unlike what ripples through a freight train as it starts out of the station. This helps explain why with the rise in discretionary spending came so much social unrest. People would realize they had more discretionary spending one year that only disappeared the next. One minute they were getting ahead and the next those gains were snatched away as if by some force that demanded a name. This may explain why currency concerns reverberated through the Age of Discontent.

We Must Prepare

The most fascinating part of Wright's 1903 tables is that they peek into parlors and kitchens, where people decided what to do with their increased discretionary spending. In a sense, when they sat down to decide what to buy, they were also sitting in a voting booth, because their economic decisions had political consequences. Wright's numbers demonstrate that consumers made sensible purchases with the 14.4 percent increase in income they gained from lower food prices. They invested in the new vehicles of property and life insurance marketed by innovators like composer—and insurance executive—Charles Ives, who told his employees there was no more important service than selling life insurance.[72] While contributions to charity were small (only 1 percent), they represent a rejection of Charles Sumner's belief that charity encourages laziness. People gave double that amount to religious causes.[73]

Two items are notable. One is union dues, which amounted to 2 percent of expenditures in Wright's 1903 table. Since the days of the Workingman's Benevolent Association, negotiating a settlement could resemble a high-stakes poker game. Unions hoped they could stay in the game long enough to draw the equivalent of an inside straight. In 1879 cigar makers began the first strike fund. Union president Samuel Gompers explained, "We have found that if we are desirous of gaining anything in a strike we must prepare in peace for the turbulent time which may come."[74] A decade later, Gompers's *American Federationist* made the same case: "Workers who fail to organize and, in their organizations, pay reasonably high dues to create a defense fund, and funds which shall stand them in good stead in all the vicissitudes of life, simply pay ten-fold into the coffers of their employers in the shape of lower wages and longer hours and win the contempt of their employers, their friends, and fellow-citizens."[75]

For unions and their workers, the decline in food prices was pivotal because they desperately needed an infusion of resources. In Wright's 1903 table, individual expenses for union dues were 88¢ per month. Multiplying that figure by the 3.73 million total union members at the time yields a war chest for all unions of $3.28 million. An 1899 Bureau of Labor Statistics study notes that lower food prices enabled strike funds to stretch further: "It will be observed that the average cost per member for strike benefits has been very much less since 1888 than previously."[76]

Increased spending for union dues played a role in increasing the winning percentage of strikes in the 1890s. From 1895 to 1899 unions won in 61 percent of strikes, including a record 72 percent in 1899. The variable with the highest correlation to the number of strikes is the price of wheat flour. As the price of wheat flour decreased, more strike fund money was available and the number of strikes increased. The price of wheat flour also has a strong relationship with the number of workers on strike.

The other notable statistic in Wright's 1903 table confirms the hunger for knowledge that characterized late nineteenth-century Americans. Instead of splurging on plumed hats, people set aside 1.9 percent for books and newspapers. Let today's readers feel smug about their intellectual superiority, the amount spent on newspapers and books in 1970 was 1.4 percent and has fallen since.[77] Spending on books expanded the publishing industry, with new titles increasing from 2,076 in 1880 to 6,356 in 1900. In 1880 there were 971 daily newspapers in the United States; in 1900, there were 2,226.[78] Many of these newspapers supported the Grange and Farmers' Alliances. As debates over the nation's future enlivened rural dinner tables and inner-city taverns, people had more money to support those papers. Since that money likely went to papers whose editorial stances were supported, the lower price of wheat also helped to level the publishing playing field.

What is impressive is that these expenses increased from 1875. That year 66 percent of families bought books and newspapers; by 1903, an overwhelming 96.5 percent did so. This fact verifies the value of increased education funding plus the efforts of the Grange, the Farmers' Alliances, and the Knights of Labor. That within three decades virtually every family in Wright's survey purchased books and newspapers demonstrates how widespread literacy had become.

The cumulative impact of increased discretionary spending reverberated through the economy. Those reverberations answer many questions about the late nineteenth century, not the least of which is the rise of the middle class. The still-prevalent explanation used to justify corporate subsidies and tax cuts for the rich claims that production is key. While there is no question the "machine process" of industrialization provided jobs and consumer goods, its impact is tempered by data suggesting wages were capricious for most workers.

As Richard Ely pointed out over a century ago, production goes nowhere if no one can buy the goods produced. The shift in food expenses largely attributable to wheat offers an alternative explanation for the rise of the middle class and the blooming of the American economy: increased consumer spending that came with lower food prices helped jump-start the consumer culture. Had discretionary spending remained at 1870 levels, demand for consumer goods would not have risen. This process is evident in several other studies Wright conducted between 1875 and 1903. Spaced at approximately eight-year intervals are an 1883 Massachusetts follow-up to the 1875 study, and investigations into the cost of living for employees in the steel, glass, cotton, and wool industries issued in the early 1890s.

In the 1883 study, Wright added comparative statistics from Illinois and Great Britain. In Massachusetts annual expenses for food fell to 49 percent and in Illinois to 41 percent. Expenses for sundries increased to 11 percent and 15 percent, respectively. In Britain, expenses were 53 percent for food and 12 percent for sundries, although British rent costs were 6 percent less than in Massachusetts and 4 percent less than in Illinois.[79]

The 1891 Seventh Annual Report shows those working in cotton and wool manufacturing spent 44 percent of their income on food as opposed to 36 percent for glass workers and 42 percent for those working in iron, steel, and soft coal. Thus cotton and wool workers spent 19 percent on sundries, glass workers 30 percent, and iron, steel, and coal workers 21 percent. Their European counterparts spent more on food and less on sundries. European wool and cotton workers spent 47 percent on food and 21 percent on sundries; glass workers budgeted 46 percent on food and 19 percent on sundries, while those in the iron, steel, and soft coal industries had the highest food expense of 50 percent and the lowest sundry budget of 17 percent.[80]

These data about food costs and other expenses and their role in increasing strike success, in seeding a growing literacy, and in spurring discretionary consumer spending suggest that wheat farmers and legislation like the Hatch Act helped lay the foundations for America's rise as a world power. Larger increases in discretionary spending than those occurring in other countries played a role in that rise, as did the multiplier effect of other Discontented initiatives.

The Final Quality

As far as we know, George Alley was not an active participant in any of the initiatives of the Discontented, although the tribute by his union suggests he was an active member. Still, in sacrificing his life to save the passengers of the FFV he personifies the principles of those efforts. This becomes clear if we take a closer look at the wreck itself. According to *Railroad Gazette*, the average locomotive headlight in 1890 illuminated 300 to 500 feet. The FFV required almost double that length to come to a stop. The *Gazette* states: "[Distances illuminated by the headlight] are traversed by a train running at 40 miles an hour in 5 sec. and 8 sec., respectively, and at 60 miles an hour they are covered in about 3 and 5 sec., respectively."[81] Those numbers show the Westinghouse air brake might have saved the train.

It was essential for each engineer to know how long it would take to stop a specific locomotive traveling at various speeds and carrying various loads. Alley knew he could not bring the FFV to a complete stop before it hit the boulder; all he could do was minimize the impact. Had he decided to save his own life, the entire train might have derailed, sending cars into the river and killing or injuring dozens. J. P. Morgan would have paid the settlements, but a major accident would have stained the reputation of the FFV and the C&O, perhaps ruining the financier's investment.

Alley's action offers an insight into why the Discontented succeeded. His decision came from the same source as those of Lorenzo Coffin, Leonora Barry, and Seaman Knapp, and from the same place as the many initiatives (legislative and otherwise) that lowered the price of wheat and the price of food, thus increasing the amount available for discretionary spending. Stephen Crane captured this source when he saluted the survivors of the 1894 drought: "The final quality of these farmers who have remained . . . is their faith in the ultimate victory of the land and their industry."[82] Crane may not have been a social scientist but saw why the Discontented succeeded.

In the time it takes to snap your fingers, George Alley had to decide whether to save the FFV or save his own life. He had little time to think; his decision-making had to have been all instinct. Instincts, especially in life-threatening situations, are not built up overnight; they are sculpted by history and by habit. Given the number of train wrecks during the late nineteenth century, many engineers faced the same decision. Because of sketchy accounts it is difficult to draw generalizations, except that those who stayed with their engines, like George Alley, and

Casey Jones, who died in a similar accident in 1900, earned immortality in our shared story. In trips George made with his father, he certainly was taught that engineers, like ship captains, stayed on the bridge till the end.

Collective and national instincts are also shaped by history and habit, especially in times of crisis. For most of the last century the Industrial Narrative—along with the Plantation Narrative and the Frontier Narrative—honed those instincts, influencing crucial public policy decisions. The Industrial Narrative has remained strong because, unlike the other two, we have lacked the evidence and the willpower to refute it. For the other two, evidence has existed, but we could not see it, much like the truths found in the narratives of enslaved people "rediscovered" by Henry Louis Gates Jr. and Charles T. Davis or the Western gunfights as recounted by Richard Maxwell Brown.

While there is no denying the influence and power of late nineteenth-century industrialists, especially their technological achievements, people like Mary Hennessey, Sarah Jane Geary, and the family of George Alley can testify that life under what Thorstein Veblen termed the machine process was far from the benign world portrayed in many textbooks. The sins of the tycoons went far beyond the financial manipulations generally cited by "robber baron" critics. Wages were often barely enough to keep people alive. Working conditions in this country were far worse than those in other industrializing nations. Most of all, what passed for a safety net relied on donations like the $103 chipped in by FFV passengers for Alley's family.

When necessary, the tycoons hired thugs to enforce their edicts and break strikes, supplying them with the latest weapons as they did in Lattimer, Pennsylvania, in 1897. In less time than it takes to listen to a single CD track, 100 "deputies" armed with new, sixteen-shot Winchesters gunned down at least 19 unarmed marchers and wounded another 36. Perhaps because it clashes with the Industrial Narrative, the Lattimer Massacre does not appear in most history texts, even though the shots reverberated across the Atlantic.

Despite the wishes of some contemporary apologists for laissez-faire capitalism, most of us would not want to go back to the so-called Gilded Age, forced to work in the coal mines beside John Siney or eke out a homestead like Willa Cather's Ántonia. We have the Discontented, not corporate America, to thank for the fact that we do not live in such conditions. By affirming the Founders' beliefs that government's role is to ensure a level playing field, the Discontented did more than bury the dubious economic principle of laissez-faire capitalism. As a systemic strategy, their initiatives improved millions of lives by bringing enhanced opportunities and a higher standard of living. Despite their faults, the

Discontented left the country a better place than they found it and this is all we can ask of any generation.

George Alley's experience shows that significant change is built one life at a time, one action at a time. Democracy requires everyone to make sacrifices. If we do not believe enough in ourselves to make those sacrifices, we do not believe in democracy. If we lack the courage to defend it, we lose it.

A SECOND EMANCIPATION

Be sure to stick to Mitchell boys
Your faithful president,
For he's the one who won for you
The gain of ten percent
—*From the folk song "Be Sure and Stick with Mitchell," ca. 1903*

Although he was barely over thirty, John Mitchell had seen more than his share of the Age of Discontent. As head of the country's most powerful union, Mitchell held the country's fate in his hands during what Samuel Gompers termed "the most important single event in the labor movement in the United States": the 1902 Anthracite Coal Strike.[1] Along with the US Supreme Court's *Northern Securities* decision, the strike was the result of decades of suffering, protest, and action.

Much had transpired for the Discontented in the 1890s. The decade following the legislative victories of the late 1880s and early 1890s was a difficult lesson in understanding that hard-won gains must continually be renewed. If anything, corporate America had become more organized and more determined in its defense of nullification. The Supreme Court decisions in the *Debs* and *Sugar Trust* cases exuded such determination, as plaintiffs sought to weaken or even kill reinvention legislation. The dead bodies of the Homestead Lockout, the Pullman Strike, and the Lattimer Massacre revealed how far they would go.

The Panic of 1893 upended lives with the same swift devastation as the 1873 Panic had done. The *Washington Star* reported, "Men [are] pleading for food who have never before been compelled to seek aid."[2] In response, ten of the nation's largest cities abolished outdoor relief and others reduced it.[3] Hundreds enlisted in an "army" commanded by Ohio gravel merchant and horse breeder Jacob Coxey, then marched on Washington to demand action.

Trust had become as rare as a Klondike nugget; truth as elusive as the fabled northern pass to the Pacific. Anyone needing confirmation could ponder the nearly four thousand strikes involving over a million workers occurring between 1892 and 1894. As strikes multiplied and the rhetoric of prairie firebrands flared, compromise became a casualty of fevered minds. In Lawrence Goodwyn's words, "In the late nineteenth century and on into the twentieth, the courts, the press, the National Guard, governors, legislatures, and the Pinkertons all worked in harmony to defeat workers at the pivotal moment."[4]

Hope came from an unexpected source in the form of one of those periodic American "awakenings" that attract uncertainty like moths to a flame. People by the thousands opened their eyes to find themselves kneeling in the uncompromising white light of God with nowhere to hide, save under the forgiving mantle of faith. As hard times continued, clerical vestments and academic gowns became uniforms in a struggle that tied justice to theology by proclaiming that the way to save souls was to save society. The intellectual streams of the social gospel flowed through America beginning in the late 1880s, reaching flood stage with the Panic of 1893 and continuing into the New Deal, ebbing and flowing with the economic and political climate. Among those enlisting in the cause was the reed-thin charismatic preacher George Herron, who held the endowed position of professor of applied religion at Iowa College. Herron's jeremiads thundered across the Midwest to Wall Street, as audiences hung on every word of his high-pitched voice. "There is not one kind of right for God and another for man; one for the church and another for the market; one for the individual and another for the state; one for men acting singly and another for men acting collectively as a commonwealth or a financial corporation."[5]

As they had so many times, the Discontented picked themselves up, dusted themselves off, and kept walking. Frustrated by the inaction and indifference of the two parties, they gathered in Omaha in 1892 to nominate ex-Greenbacker James Weaver for president under the banner of the People's Party. Ever one to seize an opportunity, Ignatius Donnelly recycled the Greenback agenda into the preamble of the new party's platform. The People's Party flamed out after the 1896 election, when they backed the candidacy of William Jennings Bryan, but not before Bryan articulated the central principle of the Discontented in his "Cross of Gold" speech: "There are those who believe that, if you will only legislate to make the well-to-do prosperous, their prosperity will leak through on those below. The Democratic idea, however, has been that if you legislate to make the masses prosperous, their prosperity will find its way up through every class which rests upon them."[6]

By the end of the decade optimistic signs began to appear. During 1898 and 1899 bank suspensions fell to the lowest recorded level since 1870–71. In 1899–1900 the business failure rate was under one hundred for two successive years for the first time since 1881–82. Silk purchases reached an all-time high in 1899. Farmers saw four years of wheat yields above twelve bushels an acre. It seemed the playing field initiatives had matured. Those earning college degrees increased from 20,000 to nearly 30,000 in the 1890s. Historian Mary Furner comments that by 1903, "Laissez-faire [capitalism] collapsed as a creditable basis for policy and the failure reopened discussion of the proper role of government."[7]

Me Johnny Mitchell Man

John Mitchell absorbed these developments as he tried to cope with this shifting world. Born in 1870, he suffered a childhood that even Charles Dickens could not have imagined, and on some "Days I used to consider my self [sic] the most unfortunate being on Earth."[8] His home was Braidwood, Illinois, a boomtown created by coal speculation. After his father died in a mining accident, Mitchell lived with a stepmother who liberally applied the "sting of the cat-o-nine-tails."[9] At age ten he took the one step open to abused children during those years: he ran away. He worked on a farm for two years, then slunk home. Whatever happened on the farm must have been terrible enough to make him return to his stepmother's discipline and the mines that killed his father.

Mitchell became one of the boys who operated the doors separating underground coal chambers, sitting alone with his imagination between blasts echoing in the shafts. The mine where he worked drew attention from the Illinois Bureau of Labor Statistics when a February 16, 1883, disaster flooded several shafts, killing 69. Thirteen-year-old Mitchell carried decomposing corpses through bone-chilling water. Someone saw him limping across a frozen field, his unshod feet bleeding from cuts made by the ice.

In the next years Mitchell wandered to the West as if trying to escape bad memories. In Colorado he found a mentor in Dan McLaughlin, who tutored him in union organizing. Mitchell returned to Spring Valley in 1890, becoming an early member of the newly founded United Mine Workers. At that time the community was reeling after a lockout by the Spring Valley Coal Company. The resulting eight-month standoff prompted Henry Demarest Lloyd to author several articles that became the book *A Strike of Millionaires Against Miners*. He echoed the local paper:

That the wives and children of miners are dying of starvation, right in ... the center of the "land of the brave and home of the free," is not a very consoling spectacle for a Christian country to present to the world.... When such suffering, poverty, and death are the result of an attempt of coal operators ... to starve laborers into submission ... the sight ... should forever damn the system and the soulless capitalist that it protects.[10]

By December, with families starving, the miners capitulated. Arriving after they trudged back to work, Mitchell found his calling—servant to fellow citizens—earning the board of education presidency. He also found another mentor in Fr. John Power, who continued the education Dan McLaughlin had begun. During a violent 1894 strike, the union enlisted Mitchell as an organizer.

By 1900 the former tunnel rat had become the president of the country's largest—and arguably most important—union, the UMW. The frontispiece portrait of his book, *Organized Labor: Its Problems and Purposes*, resembles a priest, not an organizer: dark eyes, neat black hair parted on the left, high white collar. "There is mildness in his eyes," wrote a contemporary, "the eyes of a dreamer or poet rather than of a man of action—that gives little indication of the great power and the strength of will that lie behind."[11] Sometimes he wore a western duster that when combined with the clerical-like collar gave the impression he was a man of the cloth.

At the height of his power, miners listened to John Mitchell as religiously as those who dispensed confession. Robert Reynolds, who interviewed miners about the 1902 strike, noted parlors often displayed pictures of Jesus Christ and "Johnny d'Mitch."[12] This uncommon common man earned their adulation because he was one of them. A year after the 1902 strike he offered his thoughts about a miner's life through a novelist's eye for detail:

[They] delve in the bowels of the earth; removed from the sight of their fellow beings; obscured from the rays of the sun; with hundreds, oftentimes thousands, of feet of rock between them and all that is dear to them; in a place which teems with dampness and danger; where not a day goes by without recording the death, by falls of rock, coal or slate, of more than one unfortunate miner; and where, at frequent intervals, by the explosion of gases which are permitted to accumulate in the mines, there are accidents by which the nation is appalled, humble homes are made desolate, wives made widows and children orphaned.[13]

Nothing captures Mitchell's charisma more than a photograph of him riding in an open carriage as boys run after him, jostling to touch their hero. No doubt these boys knew of Mitchell's fight to include them in union meetings. Watching them bent over while sorting coal, he said, "As I saw those eager eyes peering at me from eager little faces; the fight had a new meaning for me; I felt that I was fighting for the boys, fighting a battle for innocent childhood."[14]

Some thought his ascension smelled unsavory, but Mitchell was a genius who quoted figures about production and costs as if the pages sat open in front of him. He also had a way of disarming all but the most hard-hearted opponents. During the 1902 strike one mine owner characterized him as "a very fair and conservative man"; another admitted, "I am beginning to like him."[15] Andrew Roy, who knew most of the union organizers, stated, "There is no more intelligent and broad-minded leader."[16]

In consolidating power Mitchell could be tough, but he would not have succeeded without this principle: The coal you dig is not Slavic coal, or Polish coal or Irish coal. It is coal.[17] He backed up his words by hiring multilingual organizers and admitting Slavs and other ethnic groups into the union. He told organizers to "speak positively to the men, to abstain from name-calling and to treat immigrants as equals."[18] One key ingredient of his leadership was the journeys he made to the patches and hollows to visit miners. The young president found his way into song:

> Righta here I tell ya,
> Me no scabby fella,
> I'm a good union citizen,
> I'm 'a Johnny Mitchell man.[19]

Amazons

It wasn't Mitchell but women who kept the union going in the days after the 1897 Lattimer Massacre. Their leader, clay-pipe-smoking Irish miner's widow Martha McCrone, spoke to a curious reporter about why she had organized the resistance: "I ain't doin all this because I like to raise a fuss. No, sir. I want the men to win and know they can't if any of them go back."[20] She explained her decision to rally women to keep mines from reopening was a combination of psychology and necessity, "Ain't the women as much interested as the men? Devil a sight more, I do think, 'cause if there is low pay and poor work, for sure the women folks and the children suffer more than the men."[21] In the same article

McCrone voiced a distaste for immigrants, saying, "The white folks, them as speak English, I mean, are all right, furriners are just like animals."[22]

The women confounded troops who had no idea how to deal with them. They outflanked the national guard by moving south to Carbon County, where the military had no jurisdiction. A lurid *Los Angeles Herald* story "Raids of Amazons" related: "Over a hundred men reported at Monarch colliery for work when a band of Amazons armed with sticks and stones swooped down upon them, but violence was avoided by the men promptly going out."[23] They drove out replacement workers at the Bunker Hill and Honey Brook mines by creating a diversion that allowed a larger force to close them down. Then they shut down mines in McAdoo and Audenried. The climax fittingly occurred at Lattimer, where the women intercepted miners attempting to return to work. National guard commander Gen. John Gobin, who had had enough, ordered his troops to fix their bayonets. Accounts of soldiers with their bayonets glinting in the sun opposing women armed with rolling pins, broomsticks, and fire pokers worked on readers.

After the women's strike, the battle was no longer—if it ever was—a battle between mine owners and their workers. Instead it became a struggle between owners and the *community*. The women dramatized that jobs were not about wages; they were about the survival of families. Despite the ineffectiveness of their strike, the women's actions revived the union, which gained 10,000 members in Pennsylvania alone after the strike.

In the coalfields, echoes of the Lattimer Massacre Winchesters and cries of the wounded and dying on that September day in 1897 refused to go away. The grass that grew over the graves was still young; the bitter perfume of flowers was still fresh. In 1900 the miners again went on strike. Following Daniel McLaughlin's arbitration strategy, Mitchell sought to bring owners and workers together. When employers refused to bargain, the workers walked. The public sided with the workers, perhaps because of Mitchell's ability to talk to the press.[24]

With Republicans campaigning to reelect William McKinley in a replay of the 1896 contest against William Jennings Bryan, Mitchell bet they would not prolong the strike. McKinley advisor Mark Hanna convinced owners to accept a 10 percent pay increase on October 29, in time to avert a winter shortage of coal. Mitchell biographer Craig Phelan states the workers' "new found unity and discipline represented the real victory."[25] Designated as "Mitchell Day," October 29 became a holiday in the anthracite region.

The settlement brought attention to another player: the National Civic Federation (NCF). Founded in 1893 by Ralph Easley of the *Chicago Inter Ocean* newspaper, the NCF's mission was to "serve as a medium of sympathy and acquaintance between persons and societies who pursue various and differing vocations and objects, who differ in nationality, creed and surrounding [and] who are unknown to each other."[26] That vision is seen in a description of one NCF annual dinner: "The sack coat of the work-a-day world and the evening garments of convention were there in about equal numbers, and bankers and truckmen, college professors and carpenters, mine owners and mine laborers sat shoulder to shoulder."[27] The 1900 strike wasn't the first involvement of the NCF in a labor dispute. Easley and founding member Jane Addams had offered the federation's services to mediate the 1894 Pullman strike but were rebuffed by management.

David Montgomery credits the NCF with offering a less-hazardous means of settling disputes, and one that resulted in 118 agreements in 1902–3 and 156 in 1905.[28] Labor historian Philip Foner disagrees: "The big employers and the trade unions" reached what "would come to an implicit agreement," he writes. "The unions would make no real effort to organize unskilled workers (especially the foreign-born and Negro workers)" and in return "the corporations would make certain concessions to the craft unions."[29] One key to the federation's mindset lies in its publication, the *Review,* with article titles like "The Assault by Socialism," "Socialism and Revolution," and "Socialists Seek to Inflame the Mind of American Youth."[30] The federation's executive committee included Harvard president Charles Eliot, three lawyers, a banker, two business executives, a former interior secretary, and Grover Cleveland.

Impressed with Mark Hanna's role in the 1900 strike, the federation offered to him the presidency in 1901. Contrary to his image as a scheming ideologue, Hanna preferred collaboration to confrontation, respect to rancor, and dialogue to divisiveness. He acknowledged, "We ... forgot that two factors contributed to the prosperity of our nation,—the man who works with his hands and the man who works with his head—partners in toil who ought to be partners also in the profits of that toil."[31]

At that time Hanna was mourning the assassination of his close friend, William McKinley. He termed their relationship "an affection that cannot be explained."[32] The man Hanna never wanted as vice president was now sleeping in the White House. Biographer Herbert Croly admits "the dislike which President McKinley and Mr. Hanna felt towards Mr. Roosevelt as Vice-Presidential nominee was natural."[33] The only positive side was "the incarceration of a very promising political career in [the vice presidential] cold storage box." When Roosevelt emerged from that box, the nation wondered how the man with a reputation for impulsive actions would alter the sober efficiency of McKinley's presidency. When Hanna accepted the civic association post there was talk about a fight for the 1904 nomination. Croly wrote that in 1902 Hanna and Roosevelt "had the good sense and the good feeling to recognize what the situation demanded and both proved capable of acting up to its needs."[34]

The Proper Role of Government

Five years after Lattimer, six owners controlled 96 percent of Pennsylvania's anthracite production. A miners' advocate described the situation: "The anthracite industry has been organized into a huge combination, a monopoly very similar in structure to an octopus. Its head and body are a very small group of banking interests. Its entwining arms are seven railway systems which control at their extremities the anthracite mining operations of the country."[35] At the center was J. P. Morgan, with his interlocking directorships and Byzantine alliances. He was interested in coal because he knew it determined the wealth of nations. Britain had long claimed the title of superpower, but in 1899 America eclipsed it as the world's greatest coal producer. Morgan also knew that the strategic importance of America's "black diamonds" meant that when instability hit the mines, it rebounded through the economy. Morgan did not tolerate disorder, especially the kind brought on by intoxication. If Puritanism insisted nothing occurs without reason, Morgan represented a reincarnation of eighteenth-century Puritans Cotton Mather and his father, Increase Mather. With a mind nearly as sharp as Cotton's, who graduated from Harvard at fifteen, and convictions as firm as Increase's, who chronicled examples of God's judgment, Morgan had an unshakable need for control. The 1902 strike tested that need.

The protagonists in this unfolding drama were known simply as "The Six." Each company leader owed his position to Morgan, giving their social Darwinist views a certain tinge of hypocrisy. Their leader was George Baer, who held Franklin Gowen's old position as head of the Reading Railroad and its affiliated mines. Baer had served as counsel to Gowen and the Reading through the Molly Maguire trials and the violence of 1877. His views of the union might have come from Gowen: "We are asked to permit the officers of labor organizations who may belong to other trades and ignorant of our business to determine all questions relating to the management of our railway shops."[36]

The other five owners were equally militant. W. H. Truesdale of the Delaware, Lackawanna, and Western was a career railroad executive who came to his post after serving as head of the Rock Island Railroad. After the strike, he wrote in the *New York Times*, railroads contributed "more largely than any other one interest to the growth and development of the country."[37] Eben Thomas of the Erie Railroad had only recently purchased the Pennsylvania Coal Company and the Hillside Coal and Iron Company, instantly becoming a major player in the anthracite region. He told the US Industrial Commission that the greatest danger came from unrestrained competition.[38] The senior member of the group, R. M. Olyphant of the Delaware and Hudson, had served as its president since 1884. Franklin Roosevelt's father was the D&H vice president.

Olyphant, Thomas, Baer, and Truesdale had ties to Morgan, who had created a new version of the anthracite cartel similar to the one Franklin Gowen formed in the 1870s. Morgan controlled the stock of the Reading (and Baer) and was the board chair of the Erie. In addition, "the output of the Delaware and Hudson, a road usually credited with Vanderbilt affiliation, was largely handled by the Erie Railroad, controlled by Mr. Morgan," writes historian Eliot Jones.[39]

As 1902 dawned, the pressing issue was renegotiation of the 1900 contract, The Six signaled their intent by protecting their mines with versions of the fort Henry Frick had employed in the Homestead lockout. These preliminaries had all the trappings of the union-busting of Homestead and Pullman. Breaking the United Mine Workers would deal a deep, if not mortal blow to its parent, the American Federation of Labor. Their battle plans centered on starving the workers into submission and provoking them to engage in violence. However, the winds had shifted: Theodore Roosevelt was not William McKinley and the UMW was in far better shape, due to an increased war chest from union dues. Most of all, the country had changed. The Muckrakers' arrows were hitting their targets, increasing general worry about trusts.

When Mitchell wrote to The Six on February 24, asking for a joint conference, Baer lectured him like a schoolboy: "There can not be two masters in the management of business. The objection to your proposition is not alone the impracticability of forming a uniform scale of wages, but it is to the divided allegiance it creates. Discipline is essential in the conduct of all business."[40] E. B. Thomas was equally feisty: "It is the inalienable right of a man to labor, and this without regard to nationality, creed, or association. To seek to prevent it is a crime, and we can not, even by implication, sanction such a course." These are not the words of those seeking a settlement; they are declarations of war. The *Indianapolis Journal* agreed: "Kill the union is the watchword of the operators."[41]

Reflecting on the replies he received, Mitchell wrote, "There is growing up in these United States a small body of multi-millionaires, men exorbitantly rich and tremendously powerful, but apparently without those ideals of free and democratic government which should be the distinguishing characteristic of every American citizen."[42] Mitchell knew the owners' letters' could help create a stronger relationship with Hanna and the Civic Federation. As he pondered his next move, the owners planned a public relations campaign. Still steaming over the 1900 settlement, they believed they held a winning hand.

Peace or War

The wildcat strikes that had always plagued the coalfields broke out in 1902. Near Shamokin, Pennsylvania, Hickory Ridge mine workers struck because a clerk had overcharged for supplies. Nearby at the Colbert Colliery the breaker boys left their jobs because they wanted owners to fire their boss.[43] The situation could have quickly escalated as in 1897, but the union kept everyone calm. The 150,000 miners, their families and friends, plus other UMW members added up to half a million people in thirty states.[44] This total gave 1902 a far more ominous tone than 1877 and 1886.

The next few months tested union solidarity as The Six declined every proposal put forth by the union. Meanwhile, Mitchell followed a difficult path. By offering concessions he hoped to show that the owners were unreasonable. At the same time, he had to contend with militants whose desire for an immediate strike would have undermined his plan to enlist Hanna and the federation.

A headline captured what was at stake during a March 18–24 union meeting in Shamokin: "Peace or War?"[45] The city was the first town to combine mining and electricity, having enticed a young Thomas Edison to build the Edison Electrical Illuminating Company there in 1882. It was also home to one of the country's largest silk mills.[46] If Shamokin could combine electricity, mining, and silk, perhaps it might unify the disparate factions of the union. After much maneuvering, delegates voted to contact the owners one more time. When Mitchell requested a meeting, Baer answered, "Always willing to meet our [individual] employees to discuss and adjust any grievances. I had hoped that my letter clearly expressed our views."[47]

At the eleventh hour Hanna convinced the owners to meet with him and union representatives, but he only extracted an agreement to extend the previous settlement for a month. Observing that it had taken "all the resources at the command of the committee" to set up the meeting, Ralph Easley characterized the owners as "forty years behind the times in their attitudes towards organized labor."[48] Mitchell revealed his frustrations in a letter to his friend Harry Taylor: "I oft' times wished I were constituted differently, and could, after working hours, forget the troubles and cares of my office."[49] In 1900 those "troubles" had almost hospitalized him.

As the clock continued ticking, Hanna brought the parties together again on April 26. Mitchell was conciliatory, cutting the union's original offer of a 20 percent raise to 10 percent. He found the right words, saying this tactic "was dictated not by fear of losing the strike, but in order to avert the terrible suffering which, it was clearly foreseen, would inevitably result from the desperate conflict."[50] The owners dismissed that offer and his follow-up one of only 5 percent. Finally, they rejected arbitration. Baer lectured: "Anthracite mining is a business, and not a religious, sentimental, or academic proposition."[51] He added, "I could not, if I would, delegate this business management to even so highly a respectable body as the Civic Federation."

The UMW met in Hazleton on May 12, not far from the site of the Lattimer Massacre. Beneath a front-page photograph of anxious breaker boys waiting for news of the outcome, the *New York Tribune* quoted one delegate in bold-faced type: "If John Mitchell advises us to strike it will be a unanimous vote. If he says no, then there will be a fight in convention, but there will be no strike."[52] Outside the opera house where the delegates were meeting, miners, some with coal dust on their clothes, milled about discussing possibilities. At a quarter past six Mitchell appeared on the front steps, heightening suspense as he waited for reporters. His eyes betrayed nothing. He then announced the workers had voted to strike by a vote of 461¼–349¾.

The owners had succeeded in forcing a strike. They believed the public would now view the union as responsible for whatever occurred. Mitchell wrote later that he had hoped to avert a strike, but underestimated the impact of fruitless attempts to convince the owners to arbitrate. Like two gunfighters on a dusty street, both sides appeared headed to the confrontation historian Perry Blatz termed "one of the titanic industrial struggles in American history."[53] Theodore Roosevelt used a familiar metaphor: "The coal strike in the anthracite regions threatened our nation with a disaster second to none which has befallen us since the days of the Civil War."[54]

On June 8, Roosevelt sent Carroll Wright to the coalfields on a fact-finding mission. The president kept the report private until pressure forced its release in August. Wright endorsed much of what the union asserted, admitting, "They had a slight hope that the strong prejudices of the anthracite coal operators might be softened by meeting them frequently."[55] Page after page cited the owners' contempt for Mitchell, whom they saw as an uneducated soft coal worker who knew nothing about anthracite. Wright summed up the situation: "Mine owners too often have regarded the average miner as unreasonable, and likely to be unruly when occasion offered. The miner has come to regard the average owner as greedy and ready to do anything which will take advantage of him. Long-continued conditions on this basis of suspicion make the question one of great difficulty."[56] In one of the few times he went beyond orders, Wright recommended forming a separate union of anthracite miners, which may explain why Roosevelt tried to keep the report private.

As the strike continued into June, the *New York Times* headlined "Complaints Pouring in to the Board of Health," referring to the crisis created by switching to bituminous coal, which significantly increased pollution. The coal shadow entered the lives of New Yorkers through open windows.[57] Whether because of the fumes or the weather, members of the New York 400 departed for the beaches. The *New York Times* observed that Cape May, New Jersey, "is now as crowded as it was never crowded before this early in the summer season."[58] Among those enjoying ocean breezes were George Baer, retired Pennsylvania Bar Association president Alexander Simpson, House Labor Committee chair John Gardner, and many New York socialites. As the miners settled in for a strike, vacationers enjoyed the new craze of table tennis and "splendid catches of hake, snapping mackerel, and weakfish." The strike threatened the web of interrelationships the nation had been spinning for three decades. For much of this web, anthracite remained the fuel of choice.

Meanwhile, each side waited for the other to make a mistake. Each got their wish. On July 30, strikers besieged Deputy Sheriff Thomas Beddall in a railroad depot as he attempted to escort two scabs to work. When his brother tried a desperate run for help, the mob beat him to death. The owners' blunder came in response to a July 16 letter sent to George Baer, asking him to explain the owners' position. In what became known as the "divine right" letter, Baer asserted, "The rights and interests of the laboring man will be protected and cared for—not by the labor agitators, but by the Christian men to whom God in his infinite wisdom has given control of the property interests of the country, and upon the successful management of which so much depends."[59] The *Typographical Journal* further commented, "President Baer is not insane; he is simply an arrogant ass, clothed with a power which makes his existence one of absolute danger to the community in which he lives." Even more embarrassing was a quote from the article in the meatcutters' journal that showed Baer's words mirrored words uttered by King George III about the American Revolution: "The rights and interests of the American colonists will be looked after and cared for, not by the agitators and rebels, but by the kind Christian gentlemen who, I, as the direct representative of God, have appointed to look after my lands in the western world."

A day after Clark wrote Baer, the national UMW convention met in Indianapolis, where for the first time since the crisis began, anthracite and bituminous workers gathered under one roof. Attendance showed the extent of a battle-scarred membership that had endured multiple strikes and armed conflicts since the Lattimer Massacre. The delegate list totaled 2,253 members, almost half from Pennsylvania (958), followed by Illinois with 391, Ohio with 268, Indiana with 135, and 6 from Indian Territory.[60]

The nation feared these combined forces could shut down the entire coal industry, causing factories to close for want of fuel and locomotives and steamships to lie idle. Only the thin pieces of paper that composed the bituminous contract prevented a crisis that could have dwarfed 1877's. To call a nationwide coal strike required bituminous miners to break that contract. Union leaders found themselves caught between the owners' attempt to break the union and the sanctity of contracts, with the fate of almost half a million workers and their families hanging on the decision. John Mitchell later reflected on the moment: "The effect of such action would be to destroy confidence, to array in open hostility to our cause all forces of society, and to crystallize public sentiment in opposition to our movement."[61] After Mitchell's speech, anthracite region delegates requested a recess until the following morning, to discuss the measure. In the ensuing debate Mitchell noted the union began the year with $130,000 and still had $40,000–$50,000 in its treasury to support the strike, a number which must have given The Six some second thoughts. Declaring "We have faithfully lived up to the letter and the spirit of every contract we have made," delegates unanimously voted against a general strike.

Unlike Martin Irons, who had little to offer the press justifying the Southwest Strike, Mitchell and UMW leadership had drafted a statement explaining their grievances. It struck all the right chords, invoking "the exalted pride of a parent in the wonderful industrial developments of the past fifteen decades" and describing "the dampness we must endure, the foul air we must breathe, and the peculiar rheumatic and lung troubles superinduced by these conditions which we must bear."[62] Explaining the union had "sought to accomplish [its ends] by conciliatory methods," it contrasted the arrogance of the anthracite owners with the willingness of bituminous owners to negotiate a satisfactory settlement.

Recognizing "the care of one hundred and fifty thousand men and their families in a protracted struggle" could cost as much as a million dollars a month, the statement asked the public for contributions. After the vote, Illinois District

12 president W. R. Russell rose to pledge that Illinois workers would contribute $50,000 to the strike fund, setting off a stampede from other states eager to match him. The fact that Russell hailed from Mitchell's old Braidwood district suggests the union leader wanted to ensure he had all the bases covered. The UMW slogan became "He who gives quickly gives twice."[63] Other unions also stepped up to support their comrades with the Garment Workers, the Iron Molders, and the Boot and Shoe Workers each contributing $1,000; the Glass Bottle Blowers added in $5,000. (It's worthwhile to here recall that the source of this aid was the drop in food prices, which allowed workers to contribute 88¢ per month for union dues.)

The other issue facing the delegates was West Virginia. In May the union had called for a work stoppage to pressure a settlement. Mitchell sent Mother Jones and other organizers into the state, backing them with a $400,000 war chest, but injunctions crippled their efforts. When federal marshals attempted to escort Jones to a hotel instead of to jail, she refused: "Did you ever hear of Mother Jones going to a hotel while her boys were in jail?" Responding to the prosecuting attorney's characterization of her as "the most dangerous woman in America," Jones retorted, "I didn't come to court asking for mercy, but I came here looking for justice."[64] By August the West Virginia strike was over.

The situation in Pennsylvania grew uglier as everyone in the stare-down guessed wrong. The mine owners believed the union would collapse. Mitchell believed Hanna could pull off another miracle. Hanna thought the federation could resolve the strike. The man who had charged up Kettle Hill was uncharacteristically reticent. The nation was growing weary. The *Washington Evening Times* ran a story with the subhead "Capitol and Other Buildings at Contractor's Mercy," stating that it required reengineering coal grates to accommodate bituminous nuggets.[65] The Yonkers, New York Board of Education voted to import coal from Wales rather than close its schools.[66] Nebraskans gloated that a "good pile of dry wood" enabled them to view the strike "from a purely sympathetic standpoint."[67]

By September the country was near panic, with the heating season a month away. The *New York Evening World* charged that the operators "have decided to starve their miserable employees into submission no matter how badly the people of the United States may suffer during the process."[68] The *Akron Daily Democrat* took the owners' side, when it blew up a mild confrontation to one involving ten thousand miners attacking forty nonunion men, seriously wounding one.[69] In far-off Honolulu, the *Independent* took a stance no one could dispute: "Statements made by operators and strikers differ widely."[70]

The union had collected over $2 million in donations for the striking miners, with bituminous workers contributing an average of $7–$16 per member, making it the largest union war chest assembled up to that time. When Mitchell made these figures public, Baer and the mine owners knew they had badly miscalculated the miners' ability to weather a long strike. Mitchell later boasted, "There can be no doubt that the contributions would have continued at an increasing rate, had the termination of hostilities been delayed."[71] Coal sellers gloated over potential profits. The *New York Evening World* revealed, "Dealers assert they can get any price they demand if they have the anthracite."[72]

In the coalfields, the standoff escalated when mine owners hired 5,000 additional mine police, equipping many with rifles like those used in the Lattimer Massacre. Among miners, mine police, and the national guard the number of guns in the coalfields probably numbered over one hundred thousand, easily the most armed men ready for combat in Pennsylvania since the Battle of Gettysburg.[73] In the valleys of the coal shadow, people longed for protection when they traveled alone or at night. Given what happened in 1897, everyone showed remarkable restraint.

On September 3 the nation suffered a scare when a trolley hit Roosevelt's carriage, throwing him awkwardly on his leg and killing a Secret Service agent. The injury forced the president to undergo two painful surgeries as Americans anxiously scanned the newspapers, to eventually learn doctors had confined Roosevelt to a wheelchair. The day before the second surgery, Roosevelt wrote Hanna, "I do not see what I can do, and I know the coal operators are especially distrustful of anything which they regard as in the nature of political interference. But I do most earnestly feel that from every consideration of public policy and good morals, they should make some slight concession."[74] Hanna replied, "I . . . will not miss an opportunity to help if I can, but the position of the operators from the beginning has put all efforts of mine in a false light before the public, so I am only able to hold the confidence of the men and serve them if I can." The Six had driven the Civic Federation into the union's corner. At the temporary White House on Lafayette Square—necessitated by renovations to the presidential mansion—Roosevelt's aides and his wife, Edith, tried to prevent the president, who was rolling exuberantly down the hallways, from overexerting himself. Showing remarkable recovery powers, two days after surgery Roosevelt summoned the operators and union representatives to Washington.

On October 3 the mine owners traveled to the meeting in ornate carriages after spending the night in luxurious private railroad cars, while the union team traveled to the meeting aboard streetcars after a night at a cheap hotel. An army of reporters and photographers gathered outside the Townsend House as police struggled to keep order among curiosity seekers who had climbed trees and utility poles to get a better view. Everyone strained to hear voices wafting through the open windows.

Roosevelt began by emphasizing he spoke for the general public. He continued: "The terrible nature of a catastrophe impending over a large portion of our people in the shape of a winter fuel famine" compelled him to act.[75] He emphasized, "The situation imperatively requires that you meet upon the common plane of the necessities of the public." The word "meet" was all Mitchell needed to hear. Before the operators could respond, he complimented Roosevelt, saying, "I am much impressed by what you have to say." Then he went on to ask the president "[to] name a tribunal which shall determine the issues that have resulted in the strike and if the gentlemen representing the operators will accept the award or decision of such a tribunal, the miners will willingly accept it, even if it be against our claims." The operators stewed; Mitchell's words had backed them into a corner. Sensing a confrontation, Roosevelt wisely ordered a recess before they could reply. The president many thought impulsive had shown coolness under fire. He would need it that afternoon.

It was a sign of hope that when everyone returned, white roses, symbolizing peace, had replaced the autumnal asters in the flower bowl by the window.[76] The sweet scent of the flowers did little to calm the owners. Baer turned to Roosevelt and said, "Do we understand you correctly that we will be expected to answer the proposition submitted by Mr. Mitchell?" The president replied, "It will be a pleasure to me to hear any answer that you are willing to make." Baer then began an ill-advised argument over what Roosevelt had said that morning. "I did not say that," the president countered, his high-pitched voice tinged with anger. "But you did, Mr. President," replied Baer, essentially calling the president a liar. A stenographer's confirmation of Roosevelt's version ended the awkward affair.

Without apologizing to Roosevelt, Baer asked to read a statement. Roosevelt agreed. The Six had retreated to their railway cars during the recess, but they could not have composed, edited, and typed their statements in that amount of time, indicating they prepared them before the meeting and, more important, that nothing anyone said had changed anything. As Baer read to the president, he liberally employed words like "wicked," "anarchistic," illegal," "dangerous," "riot," and "rapine" to assert the owners would not bargain with the union. "The duty of the hour is not to waste time negotiating with the fomenters of this anarchy and insolent defiance of law," he read. When Baer accused Mitchell,

Roosevelt looked the union leader in the eye as if warning him against turning the meeting into a shouting match.

Mitchell calmly responded by citing facts and figures contradicting the owners' charges. "The character of these attacks was such as to provoke indignation," he wrote, "but we preferred to disregard them, and I limited my reply to an acknowledgment that there had been some violence, which I regretted, and to the further statement that this violence had been exaggerated."[77] Roosevelt asked the other owners if they had anything to add. Each read a prepared statement, all equally uncompromising. Last was John Markle, who had blood on his hands for purchasing the Lattimer Massacre Winchesters. As he harangued Roosevelt, he thrust a newspaper cartoon in his face.

When Markle concluded, Roosevelt asked if the owners accepted Mitchell's proposal. All declined. The transcript ruefully reports, "At about 5 o'clock the conference was brought to a close, without agreement."[78] Roosevelt summed up the afternoon: "John Mitchell . . . kept his temper admirably and showed to much advantage. The representatives of the operators, on the contrary, came down in a most insolent frame of mind, refused to talk of arbitration or other accommodation of any kind, and used language that was insulting to the miners and offensive to me." Walter Weyl reports the president commented: "There was only one man in the room who behaved like a gentleman, and that man was not I."[79] Roosevelt could barely contain his anger at Baer: "If it wasn't for the high office I hold, I would have taken him by the seat of the breeches and the nape of the neck and chucked him out of that window."[80]

Discontent with the nullification views of corporate executives had reached the White House. Three decades of Baer-like arrogance now extended to even insulting the president of the United States. The path to this juncture wound through the private railroad car of Tom Scott, through New York and Newport mansions, and through the telephone and telegraph-equipped office of J. P. Morgan. Strewn along that path was far too much unnecessary wreckage from the smoldering ruins of the Avondale mine and the Pittsburgh railyard to the skeletal ruins of foreclosed farms in Kansas and Nebraska. Most of all were the countless lives needlessly ruined by those who sought to preserve what they viewed as their feudal privileges.

The press generally approved of the president's conduct. "Instead of the impulsive, strenuous, domineering soldier, it was a quiet, earnest statesman who received the coal barons and pleaded with them to consider the welfare of the people and make peace," said *Public Policy*.[81] Roosevelt was distraught: "I feel downhearted over the result, both because of the great misery ensuing for the mass of our people, and because the attitude of the operators will beyond a doubt double the burden on us, who stand between them and socialistic action."[82]

With winter rapidly approaching, Roosevelt considered employing federal troops to man the mines. "A coal famine in the winter is an ugly thing, and I fear we shall see terrible suffering and grave disaster," he wrote Hanna.[83] Meanwhile, the president approved Secretary of War Elihu Root's plan to meet with Morgan. A close friend of the banker, Root spent October 11 anchored in the Hudson on Morgan's distinctive black yacht. The *Corsair* should have flown the Jolly Roger, because Morgan keel-hauled Mitchell's commission, stacking it with a mining engineer, an engineer corps officer, a judge, a mine operator, and "an eminent sociologist."[84]

When Roosevelt released Morgan's proposal on October 13, it infuriated the UMW. Mitchell complained, "If the operators have a distinctive representative on the commission, a representative trade unionist [should] be also appointed."[85] The president also heard from Hanna:

> I think [Mitchell] feels satisfied with the assurances given him, although, of course, he appreciates the unfairness in the proposition of the operators in not naming an *experienced miner* as a member of the Commission. At his request I sent him a telegram urging the acceptance of the proposition and giving him the assurance that the men could depend on *absolute fairness* at your hands. This, of course, was to show to influential men among the miners.[86]

The letter is a masterpiece of diplomatic language. The words "assurances given" suggest Roosevelt had proposed an alternative . "Experienced miner," "absolute fairness," and Hanna's mention of showing the telegram "to influential men" implied equalizing the composition of the commission.

As Roosevelt, Mitchell, and Hanna continued negotiating, the owners played their trump card by convincing the governor of Pennsylvania to order national guard troops into the coalfields. The owners maintained that the miners would return to work if troops protected them. To demonstrate the miners' solidarity, Mitchell asked them to decide how to meet the threat. He wrote, "On the very day on which . . . every man who desired to work was guaranteed military protection, 150,000 mine workers, without a single dissenting voice, voted to continue the strike."[87] The union held.

To his credit, Roosevelt honored his pledge to Mitchell by making three changes to the commission: he added a priest, plus Carroll Wright as "recorder," and finally Edgar Clark of the Railway Conductors. An angry Morgan sent henchmen George Perkins and Robert Bacon to convince Roosevelt to remove

Clark. Roosevelt and Perkins had once met in the Harvard boxing ring where, as Roosevelt put it, his arms were too short and Perkins's were too long.[88] Since then the president had become a more formidable opponent.

As the two men pressured Roosevelt, they kept the phone lines busy with calls to Morgan's headquarters. In this boxing match they even hit below the belt, presumably with Morgan's agreement, threatening "civil warfare" if Roosevelt did not yield.[89] As the most dangerous assertion of corporate power ever made to a sitting president up to that time, it showed how far Morgan and the mine owners were willing to go to press their views. At midnight Roosevelt had a revelation: "I shall never forget the mixture of relief and amusement I felt when I thoroughly grasped the fact that while they would heroically submit to anarchy rather than have Tweedledum, yet if I would call it Tweedledee they would accept it with rapture; it gave me an illuminating glimpse into one corner of the mighty brains of these 'captains of industry.'"[90] With the stroke of a pen, Clark became an "eminent sociologist." "All that was necessary," commented Roosevelt, "was to commit a technical and nominal absurdity with a solemn face." After Roosevelt outmaneuvered Morgan, the union unanimously ratified the agreement, returning to work on October 23. The next day it was 14 degrees F in Maine; by the month's end it was near freezing in New York City.[91]

With one exception, Roosevelt's commission member choices were well-received. Wright assured solid research supported any recommendations; Brig. Gen. John M. Wilson had recently retired as head of the Corps of Engineers. E. W. Barker was chief statistician of the Coal Division of the US Geological Survey; Judge George Gray was a former Delaware senator; and Catholic bishop John L. Spalding was from Peoria, Illinois.[92] The questionable choice was Thomas Watkins, a former coal company head (and Morgan puppet) who rose to power after the banker purchased his mines and consolidated them with other companies under the Temple Iron and Steel Company. After the sale Watkins gave Baer his proxy.[93] Harvard professor Eliot Jones, who investigated Temple Iron and Steel, noted that, except for the Pennsylvania Railroad, "all of the other anthracite coal roads" were "represented on the directorate of the Temple Iron Company."[94]

We Have Forgotten Why We Are Here

The legal teams representing each side promised high drama. Attorneys for the mine owners included John Lenahan (who defended the deputies in the Lattimer Massacre), Francis Gowen (nephew of Franklin Gowen), and Wayne MacVeagh (the son-in-law of former Lincoln cabinet member Simon Cameron). Attorneys for the miners included Henry Demarest Lloyd, Clarence Darrow, and Louis Brandeis. Lloyd convinced Mitchell to hire Darrow because he thought the hearings demanded a litigator. In a Lincoln-like gesture, Lloyd and Darrow journeyed into the depths of a mine. When Lloyd remarked "it was like the taste of the Inferno," Darrow quipped that his friend had better get used to it.[95]

After the hearings, which included 558 witnesses and produced 10,047 pages of testimony in fifty-one volumes, everyone anticipated closing arguments from Baer and Darrow. Why Morgan chose Baer to deliver the closing is a mystery, since MacVeagh was a better choice.

Baer began on the morning of February 12, with a nod to what he termed "the powerful stimulus individual liberty gives to individual initiative."[96] His case consisted of the mixture of arrogance and threats that had characterized his conduct throughout the affair. In a statement that implied the owners might not obey if the decision did not go their way, he said, "We will not agree to turn over the management of our business to a labor organization because some of our employees belong to it. Our employees, union and non-union, must respect our discipline."[97] After over an hour, Baer concluded by dropping a bombshell: he offered a 5 percent wage increase, the same terms he had rejected in April.

Clarence Darrow followed Baer with one of his most eloquent summations.[98] As always, he made ethics his unspoken subject, forcing commission members to examine their consciences. "We seem to have forgotten this case entirely and what it is about," he began, "and why we are here, and what we are to settle." Darrow wanted the commission to understand—just as the entire era of the Discontented asks us to understand—that corporate insistence on economic nullification creates unnecessary death and misery.

While Baer adopted the lecturing demeanor of a ruler-wielding schoolmaster, Darrow was animated and passionate. Like any good public speaker, he lightened the seriousness with well-placed bits of humor, often at his own expense. Borrowing a tactic from his friend Florence Kelley, who had toured sweatshops with Illinois legislators, Darrow verbally took the commission on the journey he and Lloyd had taken earlier, citing personal testimony from the miners. "There is scarcely one of them who had not been seriously injured, broken bones, eyes lost, some blind, some maimed forever," he reminded listeners. He sounded like John Siney as he pointed to the owners' use of one word, "These operators do love that word discipline . . . as the slaveholder loved it when he raised the lash above the bare back of the slave. . . . These operators had their servants subject to such discipline that the men who went down in the mines and dug up wealth for them were living like pigs and like dogs." He used humorous thrusts (at one time saying "We will give Mr. Baer the benefit of the doubt, he needs it") to set up the flourishes that made him one of the nation's most feared and effective attorneys.

When he spoke of working in the mines, several of the commissioners—certainly Carroll Wright—must have mentally connected Darrow's descriptions with Avondale and other disasters: "When I think of the cripples, of the orphans, of the widows, of the maimed who are dragging their lives out on account of this business, who if they were mules or horses would be cared for, but who are left and neglected, it seems to me this is the greatest indictment of this business that can possibly be made." Turning to Baer his voice conveyed a mix of contempt and outrage as he invoked the mine owners' scorn for their workers: "You thought to bring them to terms by the most cruel, deadly weapon that any oppressor has used to bring men to his terms, hunger and want." He issued a damning denunciation of the use of the breaker boys, turning the eyes of everyone in the room on Baer as he delivered his variation on the progress and poverty theme. "This railroad president," he declared, "was willing to take the earnings of these poor children so he and his family might be richer because of their toil." He could barely conceal his anger about Baer's last-minute offer of a 5 percent wage increase, asking, "Why was all this deferred until 750,000 men, women, and children were brought to the verge of starvation and this country was facing the most terrible fuel calamity it has ever known?"

Darrow's listeners had mentally journeyed with him into the shafts and tunnels of a mine. His final words lifted them out of those depths: "Every advantage that the human race has won has been at fearful cost.... It has come to these poor miners to bear this cross, not for themselves, but that the human race may be lifted up to a higher and broader place than it has ever known before."

The commission's report was as much an assessment of the previous three decades as it was a strike settlement. People in 1902 saw the strike as a watershed, as one commentator observed, it was "the greatest event affecting the relations of capital and labor in the history of America."[99] The commission surpassed Baer's last-minute offer of 5 percent by granting the miners 10 percent, plus reduced hours, systematic weight checking, and a board of conciliation to oversee the settlement. The commission also proposed abolishing the mine police, stating, "The practice ... is one of doubtful wisdom." It reserved its most severe criticisms for child labor: "Infancy should be protected against the physical and moral influences of such employment, and there ought to be a more rigid enforcement of the laws which now exist."

The most memorable sentence in the report asserted: "Where production is controlled despotically by capital there may be a seeming prosperity, but the qualities which give sacredness and worth to life are enfeebled or destroyed." The commission's words stressed that progress cannot be measured solely by production: "That employer who fails to give the same careful attention to the question of his relation to his labor or his employees, which he gives to the other factors which enter into the conduct of his business, makes a mistake, which sooner or later he will be obliged to correct."[100] It is important to remember these words were not George Herron or Mary Lease speaking, but a presidential commission. Their words echoed John Harlan's comments about the "public good" in his *Civil Rights Cases* dissent: "Where a business is of such magnitude, and its physical conditions are such as to constitute a natural monopoly, it is affected with a public interest that can not be ignored by those who control it."[101] The report was not only the vindication of what Harlan had asserted, but a victory for Wright and the use of statistics.

Just as Necessary to Reverse as *Dred Scott*

A year after the strike, John Mitchell invoked a phrase used by William Sylvis three decades earlier: "The recognition of the rights of organized labor should be to the employing class as much a principle as a policy. It is a recognition of the dignity of labor, of the equal rights of men engaged in manual toil. It is a second emancipation, freeing both master and slave."[102] In 1912, while running under the banner of the Bull Moose Party, the man Edmund Morris called "Theodore Rex" had voiced similar thoughts: "The labor problem is a human and a moral as well as an economic problem . . . a fall in wages, an increase in hours, a deterioration of labor conditions mean wholesale moral as well as economic degeneration, and the needless sacrifice of human lives and human happiness, while a rise of wages, a lessening of hours, a bettering of conditions, mean an intellectual, moral and social uplift of millions of American men and women."[103]

After the commission issued its report, the US Supreme Court issued one of its most influential rulings. The *Northern Securities* decision put the full weight of the court behind the principle of a level playing field. In his zeal for control, Morgan and railroad men Harriman and Hill had built a monster "railroad trust" that controlled most railroad traffic, either directly or through linkages to other lines. The court found the trust violated the Sherman Act and ordered it dissolved. A key sentence in the decision stated "The natural effect of competition is to increase commerce. . . . An agreement whose direct effect is to prevent this play of competition restrains instead of promotes trade and commerce."[104]

In justifying Northern Securities, Roosevelt reasserted the federal government's authority to regulate the playing field that it had lost in the *Sugar Trust* case: "It was necessary to reverse the Knight case in the interests of the people against monopoly and privilege just as it had been necessary to reverse the *Dred Scott* case in the interest of the people against slavery and privilege."[105]

The *Northern Securities* decision and the Anthracite Strike Commission report struck a blow to the industrial version of nullification. Today, corporations, unions, and government officials continue sparring, but no CEO would publicly speak as George Baer had spoken. No company would assert that the principles laid out in the US Constitution stopped at the factory gate. It is fitting that the commission's final public session occurred just blocks from Philadelphia's Independence Hall, because the Second Emancipation recognized the fact that industrializing America had demanded the nation reinvent the constitution. This is the meaning behind commission member George Gray's comment, "I have no hesitation in saying that the President of the United States was confronted in October 1902, by the existence of a crisis more grave and threatening than any that had occurred since the Civil War."[106]

The 1902 strike showed an America coming far closer to the edge of the abyss than perhaps many realize. In the film *It's a Wonderful Life*, James Stewart is confronted with a world that would exist as though he had never been born. Imagine an America without the reforms of the late nineteenth century: higher education would be available to the rich only; women, people of color, workers, and farmers would have few if any rights; children would be sent to work instead of school; the world would be a more dangerous place; and we would be stripped of the power to respond effectively to new challenges. If people want to ponder what America could have been like without the Discontented, they need look no further than the police state erected in Schuylkill County by Franklin Gowen or the dictatorship advocated by George Baer.

Even as the commission issued its report and the court announced its decision, the Cripple Creek strike raged in Colorado. The battle over control continued, producing the infamous 1914 Ludlow Massacre, where guards at a mine owned by John D. Rockefeller Jr. set fire to a camp of strikers, killing two dozen. Woody Guthrie later composed a song about Ludlow; presidential candidate George McGovern made it the subject of his doctoral thesis. If race was the unresolved question of the Civil War, the question of how to level the playing field is the not-yet-fully-resolved one of the late nineteenth century.

In recounting 1902, John Mitchell was proudest of the workers' solidarity.[107] In his view of events, the most remarkable aspect of the 1902 strike was not the conduct of leaders like Roosevelt but the actions of 150,000 miners and their families. The most important strike in American history was one of the least violent, even though the coalfields were like dry tinder waiting for a match. Even after The Six brought in the hated mine police, miners refused to be drawn into a fight. The strike also represented an affirmation of the efforts of the Discontented. Their various education initiatives had created a citizenry with increased literacy, knowledge of civic affairs, and critical thinking skills. The growth in newspapers, in part facilitated by increased discretionary income, meant people were up to date on issues. The formation of rural telephone systems had extended the interchange of ideas. Most of all, three decades of agitation for a level playing field had influenced public opinion.

While 1902 was a victory for the miners, it was a fleeting one for Mitchell. Biographer Joseph Gowaskie acknowledges Mitchell became afraid of risks, enamored of press adoration, and addicted to expensive meals and fine cigars. He was forty-nine when he died in 1919. Thousands attended the funeral in Scranton, Pennsylvania, where some anthracite strike committee hearings had taken place. An obituary praised his efforts: "His death is truly not only a great loss to his good wife and children, but the Labor Movement has lost a sterling champion, and the loss is immeasurable. It can only be measured by his wonderful deeds."[108]

Mitchell lived long enough to realize that the Second Emancipation did not end the struggle for a level playing field, any more than Lee's signature at Appomattox ended the issue of racial equality. We continue to learn the chief lesson taught by people like George Alley and John Mitchell: vigilance requires constant attention from everyone, all the time. If we hold up people like Caroline Hall as so extraordinary that we can never emulate their acts of courage, we discount our greatest resource: ourselves. In this sense our very existence depends not on leadership, but followership. What principles do we value so much that, like George Alley, we will make the ultimate sacrifice to ensure them? You may remember ticket agent Kimball who gave Sarah Murray a free ride. His actions lead us to wonder, What if George Pullman, Henry Frick, or George Baer had possessed even a degree of his charity?

If the Discontented leave one message, it is that anything is possible for any one of us. Mary Lease advised, "Keep your eyes fixed on the mark, and don't flinch when you pull the trigger."[109] She and others like Lorenzo Coffin illustrate how we fulfill a dream by acting on it, and by not giving up. That lies behind Thomas Jefferson's imperative, that each generation must apply America's principles to the challenges of a changing world. The late nineteenth century met that test. Now it is our turn.

Note on Sources and List of Abbreviations

A bibliography of sources is available online at press.georgetown.edu on the book's page, under "Additional Resources."

Government Documents Abbreviations

CABLS	California Bureau of Labor Statistics
COBLS	Colorado Bureau of Labor Statistics
CR	Congressional Record
CTBLS	Connecticut Bureau of Labor Statistics
GPO	US Government Printing Office
IABLS	Iowa Bureau of Labor Statistics
ICC	US Interstate Commerce Commission
ILBLS	Illinois Bureau of Labor Statistics
INBLS	Indiana Bureau of Labor Statistics
MABLS	Massachusetts Bureau of Labor Statistics
MIBLS	Michigan Bureau of Labor and Industrial Statistics
MNBLS	Minnesota Bureau of Labor Statistics
MOBLS	Missouri Bureau of Labor Statistics
NJBLS	New Jersey Bureau of Labor Statistics
NYBLS	New York Bureau of Labor Statistics
NYSBC	New York State Board of Charities
OHBLS	Ohio Bureau of Labor Statistics
PBIS	Pennsylvania Bureau of Labor/Industrial Statistics
USBC	US Bureau of the Census
USBL	US Bureau of Labor
USBLS	US Bureau of Labor Statistics
USCO	US Census Office
USDA	US Department of Agriculture
USPO	US Post Office
WIBLS	Wisconsin Bureau of Labor Statistics
WSBCR	Wisconsin Board of Charities and Reform
WVDL	West Virginia Department of Labor

Notes

Preface

W. E. B. Du Bois noted the contribution of the Fisk Jubilee Singers in the "Sorrow Songs" chapter of *The Souls of Black Folk* (Chicago: McClurg, 1903), 252.

1. Ralph Brauer, *The Strange Death of Liberal America* (Westport, CT: Praeger, 2006).

2. Northrop Frye, *Fables of Identity: Studies in Literary Mythology* (New York: Harcourt Brace, 1963).

3. Ronald Reagan, "First Inaugural Address," Avalon Project, Yale Law School, https://avalon.law.yale.edu/20th_century/reagan1.asp, accessed December 28, 2021.

4. Richard Maxwell Brown, *No Duty to Retreat: Violence and Values in American History and Society* (Norman: University of Oklahoma Press, 1994), 44, 92. See particularly the chapter titled "The Gunfighter: The Reality Behind the Myth."

5. Ulrich Phillips, *American Negro Slavery* (New York: Appleton, 1918), viii.

6. Ulrich Phillips, *Life and Labor in the United States* (Boston: Little, Brown, 1929), 197.

7. David M. Kennedy, Lizabeth Cohen, and Mel Piehl, *The Brief American Pageant: A History of the Republic* (Boston: Cengage, 2016), 397; John M. Murrin, Pekka Hämäläinen, Paul E. Johnson, Denver Brunsman, and James M. McPherson, *Liberty, Equality, Power: A History of the American People* (Boston: Cengage, 2016), 535; Larry Schweikart and Michael Patrick Allen, *A Patriot's History of the United States* (New York: Sentinel, 2014), 453; H. W. Brands, *American Colossus: The Triumph of Capitalism, 1865–1900* (New York: Simon & Schuster, 2010), 7.

8. Mathew Josephson, *The Robber Barons* (New York: Harcourt, 1962), 5 (italics in original).

9. Gabriel Kolko, *Railroads and Regulation 1877–1916* (Princeton, NJ: Princeton University Press, 1965), 3.

10. Wally Conger and Samuel Edward Konkin III, *New Libertarian Manifesto and Agorist Class Theory* (Morrisville, NC: Gray Market, 2006), 72.

11. Thomas Ferguson, *Golden Rule* (Chicago: University of Chicago Press, 1995), 22, 49.

12. Nathan Smith, "Bring Back the Gilded Age—Part 2," Foundation for Economic Education, October 8, 2013, https://fee.org/articles/bring-back-the-gilded-age-part-two/.

13. "Remarks by President Trump at the 2019 Conservative Political Action

Conference," White House, March 3, 2019, https://www.whitehouse.gov/briefings-sta tements/remarks-president-trump-2019-conservative-political-action-conference/.

14. There is a large body of literature advancing the notion that economic freedom was the best answer to the COVID-19 pandemic. For example: Vincent Geloso, "Economic Freedom and Resilience: New Evidence from the 1918 Pandemic," Cato Institute, accessed December 2, 2021, https://www.cato.org/pandemics-policy/econ omic-freedom-resilience-new-evidence-1918-pandemic#.

15. Opinion of J. Thomas, *Seila Law LLC v. Consumer Financial Protection Bureau*, 13–14. https://www.supremecourt.gov/opinions/19pdf/19-7_n6io.pdf.

16. Charles B. Spahr, *An Essay on the Present Distribution of Wealth in the United States* (New York: Crowell, 1896), 103, 106.

17. Spahr, 95.

18. David Marchesi, "Thomas Piketty Thinks America Is Primed for Wealth Redistribution," *New York Times Magazine*, April 1, 2022, https://www.nytimes.com /interactive/2022/04/03/magazine/thomas-piketty-interview.html?searchResult Position=1.

19. J. C. Bancroft Davis, *United States Reports, Vol. 109, Cases Adjudged in the Supreme Court at October Term 1883* (New York: Banks & Brothers, 1884), 14.

20. Benjamin C. Howard, *Reports of Cases Argued and Adjudged in the Supreme Court of the United States*, vol. 19 (Washington, DC: Morrison, 1857), 452 (italics added).

21. *Plessy v. Ferguson*, 163 U.S. 537, 16 S. Ct. 1138 (1896), 551.

22. Davis, *Reports*, 48, 42.

23. *Plessy v. Ferguson*, 561.

24. W. E. B. Du Bois, *Black Reconstruction*, ed. Eric Foner and Henry Louis Gates Jr. (New York: Library of America, 2021), 870.

25. *First Annual Report of the Bureau of Labor Statistics, of the State of Connecticut* (Hartford, CT: Case, Lockwood & Brainard, 1885), 13.

26. Callie Oettinger, "Geoffrey C. Ward," https://stevenpressfield.com/2010/08 /geoffrey-c-ward/, accessed April 8, 2024.

27. Richard White, *The Republic for Which It Stands* (New York: Oxford University Press, 2017).

28. Beaumont's use of the phrase appeared in 1890. Lease first used it in an August 1891 speech in Harvey County, Kansas. See "The Bond Mortgage," *Great West* [St. Paul, MN], November 28, 1890, 1; and "Out of the Usual Order," *Wheeling [WV] Daily Intelligencer*, August 8, 1891, 4.

29. Iowa Bureau of Labor Statistics, *Third Biennial Report*, 383.

Introduction

Sheet music available at the Library of Congress website, https://www.loc.gov/item /ihas.100007508/.

1. Terence Powderly, "The Army of the Discontented," *North American Review* 141, no. 341 (April 1885): 371.

2. On railroad ties, see US Bureau of the Census (hereafter USBC), *Historical Statistics of the United States,* "Chapter P: Manufactures," table P231–300, 693–94; on passenger cars and freight cars, 697. This edition has been superseded by the millennial edition, which charges an access fee even though the tables are the same.

3. USBC, *Historical Statistics,* "Chapter P: Manufactures," table P13–17, 667; "Chapter W: Productivity Technological Development," table W96–106, 958; and "Chapter U: Foreign Commerce," table U187–300, 885.

4. Joseph C. Hendrix, "President Hendrix's Annual Report," *United States Investor* 11, no. 36 (September 3, 1898): 1231.

5. USBC, *Historical Statistics,* "Chapter Q: Transportation," tables Q321–328 and Q148–162, 731, 716, respectively.

6. "Massacre of Our Troops," *New York Times,* July 6, 1876.

7. Josiah Strong, *Our Country: Its Possible Future and Its Present Crisis* (New York: American Home Missionary Society, 1885), 4.

8. Mary Lease, "Speech to the Woman's Christian Temperance Union," in *With These Hands: Women Working on the Land,* ed. Joan M. Jensen (Old Westbury, NY: Feminist Press, 1981), 154–60.

9. Connecticut Bureau of Labor Statistics, *Third Annual Report,* 13.

10. New York Bureau of Labor Statistics (hereafter NYBLS), *Third Annual Report,* 537.

11. Iowa Bureau of Labor Statistics, *Third Biennial Report,* 119.

12. Indiana Bureau of Labor Statistics (hereafter INBLS), *Fifth Annual Report,* 221.

13. Powderly, "Army of the Discontented," 369.

14. *Pennsylvania Bureau of Industrial Statistics* (hereafter PBIS), *Volume 17,* B4–B15. Mines not open or mines with questionable numbers, such as being open more than 365 days or illegible entries, were omitted, yielding an N of 1,668.

15. PBIS, *Volume 12,* 60.

16. *Reports of the Inspectors of Mines for the Anthracite Coal Regions of Pennsylvania for the Year 1883* (Harrisburg, PA: Lane S. Hart, 1884), 2.

17. PBIS, *Volume 10,* iii.

18. Michael Novak, *The Guns of Lattimer* (New Brunswick, NJ: Transaction, 1996), 17; Paul Shakel, *Remembering Lattimer* (Urbana: University of Illinois Press, 2018); and "The Lattimer Massacre of 1897," *Pennsylvania History* 69, no. 1 (Winter 2002).

19. US Strike Commission, *Report on the Chicago Strike of June–July, 1894* (Washington, DC: GPO, 1895), 440.

20. Powderly, "Army of the Discontented," 369–70.

21. INBLS, *Sixth Annual Report,* 223.

22. Carroll Wright, *Third Annual Report of the Commissioner of Labor, 1877: Strikes and Lockouts* (Washington, DC: GPO, 1888), 830, 906, 908.

23. Robert Bruce, *1877: Year of Violence* (Chicago: Ivan Dee, 1989), 10.

24. USBC, *Historical Statistics*, "Chapter H: Social Statistics," table H1168–1170, 70.

25. Paul Gilje and Peter Turchin, "Riots in the United States," Ohio State University Criminal Justice Research Center, accessed July 11, 2021, https://cjrc.osu.edu/research/interdisciplinary/hvd/united-states/riots.

26. Randolph Roth, *American Homicide* (Cambridge, MA: Harvard University Press, 2009), 15.

27. Ohio Bureau of Labor Statistics, *First Annual Report*, 339.

28. NYBLS, *Third Annual Report*, 167.

29. Powderly, "Army of the Discontented," 371.

30. Terence Powderly, *The Path I Trod; The Autobiography of Terence V. Powderly*, ed. Harry J. Carman, Henry David, and Paul N. Guthrie (New York: Columbia University Press, 1940), 27.

31. John Sherman, *Trusts: Speech of Hon. John Sherman, of Ohio, Delivered in the Senate of the United States* (Washington, DC, 1890), 15; James Jones, *Congressional Record*, February 23, 1887 (Washington, DC: GPO, 1887), 2111.

32. James Garfield, *The Future of the Republic: Speech at Hudson College, July 2, 1873* (Cleveland, OH: Nevins, 1873), 31.

33. James Madison, Alexander Hamilton, and John Jay, *The Federalist Papers*, ed. Isaac Kramnick (New York: Penguin, 1987), 124 (italics added).

34. Abraham Lincoln, "Speech at New Haven Connecticut, March 6, 1860," in *The Collected Works of Abraham Lincoln*, vol. 4, ed. Roy B. Basler (New Brunswick, NJ: Rutgers University Press, 1953), 24; Gabor Borritt, *Lincoln and the Economics of the American Dream* (Urbana: University of Illinois Press, 1994), ix.

35. World Bank, *Equity and Development* (New York: Oxford University Press, 2006), 2.

36. Charles Calhoun, *The Gilded Age* (New York: Rowman & Littlefield, 2007), 12.

37. "Anarchy in High Places," *Kansas Agitator* [Garnett, KS], November 26, 1897, 1.

CHAPTER ONE

The Grittiest Generation

Sheet music found in the University of Maine vocal popular sheet music collection, 7, https://digitalcommons.library.umaine.edu/cgi/viewcontent.cgi?article=2315&context=mmb-vp.

1. E. Benjamin Andrews, "The Panic of 1873," in *Great Epochs in American History: Described by Famous Writers from Columbus to Roosevelt, Vol. 9, The Reconstruction Period*, ed. Francis Whiting Halsey (New York: Funk and Wagnalls, 1912), 183; A Journalist, *History of the Terrible Financial Panic of 1873: Graphic and Authentic Account of the Event: Downfall of the Money Kings: Perils of the Stock Exchange: Pen and Ink Sketches of the Stricken Moguls of Wall St: Review of Past Financial Panics* (Western News, 1873).

2. A Journalist, *History of the Terrible Financial Panic*, 11.

3. A Journalist, 12.

4. This amount is adjusted for inflation. I am indebted to Louis Johnston for his help in reconfiguring this and other data.

5. A Journalist, *History of the Terrible Financial Panic*, 12.

6. George Edwin McNeill, *The Labor Movement: The Problem of To-day* (New York: Hazen, 1888), 590.

7. "Plucky Pedestrianism," *Omaha Daily Bee*, October 30, 1874, 4.

8. Signal Service of the US Army, "Daily Bulletin of Weather-Reports, Signal-Service United States Army, Taken at 7.35 a.m., 4.35, p.m., and 11 p.m., Washington Mean Time, with the Synopses, Probabilities, and Facts for the Month of October 1874" (Washington, DC: GPO, 1877).

9. "Plucky Pedestrianism," 4.

10. "Treasurer's Sale of Unseated Lands in Monroe County," *Jeffersonian* [Stroudsburg, PA], March 30, 1876, 3; "Real Estate Transfers," *Springfield [OH] Daily Republic*, April 6, 1888, 4; "Notice for Publication," *Dodge City [KS] Times*, December 20, 1888, 2; "Surprise Parties," *San Francisco Call*, February 23, 1896, 18; "Died," *Pittsburg Dispatch*, April 27, 1891, 5; "The Courts," *Daily Globe* [St. Paul, MN], September 5, 1883, 2; "Home News," *New Northwest* [Portland, OR], August 7, 1879, 3.

11. S. Merlino, "Italian Immigrants and Their Enslavement," *The Forum*, April 1893, 188.

12. Walter Wycoff, *A Day with a Tramp* (New York: Scribners, 1901), 3.

13. Arthur Cooper Wakely, *Omaha: The Gate City, and Douglas County, Nebraska*, vol. 2 (Chicago: S. J. Clarke, 1917), 813.

14. The *Weekly Caucasian* published articles like "Lo, the Poor N——," which stated, "The cares of state wear him out, freedom is a pestilence to him, liberty the gangway to his grave." *Weekly Caucasian* [Lexington, MO], October 11, 1873, 1.

15. "The Plutocrats Love the People," *Barbour County Index* [Medicine Lodge, KS], May 20, 1896, 2; "Fair Dues and a Change of Benefits," *Cigar Makers Official Journal*, August 15, 1910, 8. The reference is to a communication from May 1877.

16. Richard Croker, "Tammany Hall and the Democracy," *North American Review* 154, no. 423 (February 1892): 225–30.

17. Gerald Gamm and Robert D. Putnam, "The Growth of Voluntary Associations in America, 1840–1940," *Journal of Interdisciplinary History* 29, no. 4 (Spring 1999): 525, 540; John E. Tapia, *Circuit Chautauqua* (Jefferson, NC: McFarland, 1997), 21.

18. Jane Addams, "Social Settlements," in *National Conference Charities and Correction Twenty-Fourth Annual Session Held in Toronto, Ontario, July 7–14, 1897*, ed. Isabel C. Barrows (Boston: Ellis, 1898), 341–42.

19. William Jennings Bryan and Mary Baird Bryan, *The Memoirs of William Jennings Bryan* (Philadelphia: Winston, 1925), 288.

20. Katherine Buxbaum, "We Liked Chautauqua," in *Roundup: A Nebraska Reader*, ed. Virginia Faulkner (Lincoln: University of Nebraska Press, 1957), 303.

21. "Chautauqua Stars," *Everybody's Magazine* 33, no. 3 (September 1915): 323–34. For a discussion of the Midwestern theory, see Andrew Chamberlin Rieser, *The Chautauqua Moment: Protestants, Progressives, and the Culture of Modern America* (New York: Columbia University Press, 2003).

22. Gerald Carson, *Corn Flake Crusade* (New York: Rinehart, 1957).

23. US Elections Project, accessed November 22, 2017, http://www.electproject.org /home/voter-turnout/voter-turnout-data.

24. Edwin Percy Whipple, *Success and Its Conditions* (Boston: Houghton-Mifflin, 1880), 58.

25. W. E. B. Du Bois, *The Negro in Business* (Atlanta, GA: Atlanta University, 1899), 43.

26. "Another Rebel Massacre," *New York Tribune*, September 18, 1866, 1.

27. *Congressional Record*, March 21, 1890, 2488.

28. J. David Hacker, "A Census-Based Count of the Civil War Dead," *Civil War History* 57, no. 4 (December 2011): 307–48. Other estimates come from: Grady MacWhiney and Perry D. Jamieson, *Attack and Die: Civil War Military Tactics and the Southern Heritage* (Tuscaloosa: University of Alabama Press, 1982); Edward H. Bonekemper, *A Victor, Not a Butcher: Ulysses S. Grant's Overlooked Military Genius* (Washington, DC: Regnery, 2004); Mark E. Neely, *The Civil War and the Limits of Destruction* (Cambridge, MA: Harvard University Press, 2007).

29. MacWhiney and Jamieson, *Attack and Die*, 4.

30. Ella Lonn, *Desertion during the Civil War* (Lincoln: University of Nebraska Press, 1998), 134.

31. Lonn, 138. For a further discussion of Lonn's research, see Robert Fantina, *Desertion and the American Soldier, 1776–2006* (New York: Algora, 2006).

32. John Whiteclay Chambers and Fred Anderson, *The Oxford Companion to American Military History* (New York: Oxford University Press, 1999), 212. An army study suggests accepted desertion estimates may be extremely low. See Lt. Col. Leonard Lerwell, *The Personnel Replacement System in the United States Army* (Washington, DC: Department of the Army, 1954), 102–5.

33. Lonn, *Desertion during the Civil War*, 132.

34. Elizabeth Barr, "The Populist Uprising," in *A Standard History of Kansas and Kansans*, ed. William E. Connelley (New York: Lewis, 1918), 1115–95; Gerald Linderman, *Embattled Courage: The Experience of Combat in the American Civil War* (New York: Simon & Schuster, 1989). Linderman says: "It was with a combination of anger and envy that veterans regarded the financial and social success of such people" (285).

35. Carol Nackenoff, *The Fictional Republic: Horatio Alger and American Political Discourse* (New York: Oxford University Press, 1994), 488.

36. Ken Gonzalez-Day, *Lynching in the West* (Durham, NC: Duke University Press, 2006), 29.

37. James Weik Jr., MD, "The Sexual Criminal," *Medical Record* 47, no. 19 (May 11, 1895): 581–83.

38. "West and Southwest," *Chariton Courier* [Keytesville, MO], September 7, 1878, 1.

39. "Trio of Reds Swing Off" and "Others Will Swing," *Saint Paul [MN] Globe*, November 15, 1897, 1.

40. "Whipped for Keeping a Saloon," *The Sun* [New York City], July 25, 1894, 1.

41. J. H. Wood, "A Nation of Plutocrats," *Railroad Trainmen's Journal* 13, no. 148 (June 1896): 406.

42. David F. Trask, *The War with Spain in 1898* (New York: Free Press, 1981), 242; John Parker, *History of the Gatling Gun Detachment Fifth Army Corps, at Santiago* (Kansas City, MO: Hudson-Kimberly, 1898).

43. Julia Keller, *Mr. Gatling's Terrible Marvel: The Gun That Changed Everything and the Misunderstood Genius Who Invented It* (New York: Viking, 2008), 6.

44. "Trusts," *Hickman [KY] Courier*, January 12, 1900, 1; "Business Matters," *Wichita [KS] Eagle*, September 28, 1886, 1; "The Commercial World," *Arizona Republican* [Phoenix, AZ], July 30, 1903, 1; "Down to Business," *Bismarck [ND] Weekly Tribune*, September 14, 1894, 1; "The News," *Bismarck [D.T.] Weekly Tribune*, January 29, 1886, 1.

45. William McKinley, Second Inaugural Address, accessed July 21, 2020, https://www.presidency.ucsb.edu/documents/inaugural-address-44.

46. National Bureau of Economic Research, "US Business Cycle Expansions and Contractions," https://www.nber.org/research/data/us-business-cycle-expansions-and-contractions, accessed June 6, 2022. Joseph Davis, "An Improved Annual Chronology of U.S. Business Cycles since the 1790s," *Journal of Economic* History 66, no. 1 (March 2006): 103–21.

47. For US data, see Barry Siegel, *Money in Crisis: The Federal Reserve, the Economy, and Monetary Reform* (San Francisco: Pacific Institute for Public Policy Research, 1984), 31; Steven P. Reti, *Silver and Gold: The Political Economy of International Monetary Conferences, 1867–1892* (Westport, CT: Greenwood, 1998), 62; and John Harold Wood, *A History of Macroeconomic Policy in the United States* (New York: Routledge, 2009), 88. For European data, see Hans-Ulrich Wehler, *Deutsche Gesellschaftsgeschichte*, vol. 3 (München: DDR, 1995); and S. B. Saul, *The Myth of the Great Depression, 1873–1896* (London: Macmillan, 1969). For CPI data, see US Bureau of the Census (hereafter USBC), *Historical Statistics of the United States*, "Chapter E: Price and Price Indexes," table E135–166, 211.

48. Ohio Bureau of Labor Statistics (OHBLS), *First Annual Report*, 113.

49. Connecticut Bureau of Labor Statistics (CTBLS), *Tenth Annual Report*, 184.

50. William and James Sylvis, *The Life, Speeches, Labors, and Essays of William H. Sylvis* (Philadelphia: Claxton, Remsen, Haffelfinger, 1872), 399.

51. S. O. Daws and W. L. Garvin, *History of the National Farmers' Alliance and Cooperative Union of America* (Jacksboro, TX: J. H. Rogers, 1887), 94, 98.

52. Rose Elizabeth Cleveland, "Woman in the Home," *The Chautauquan* 7, no. 1 (October 1886):12.

53. Mary Lowe Dickinson, "Clerical Pursuits," *The Chautauquan* 7, no. 3 (December

1886): 136; Ida Tarbell, "Women in Journalism," *The Chautauquan* 7, no. 7 (April 1887): 393; Julia Ward Howe, "Women in the Professions, *The Chautauquan* 7, no. 8 (May 1887): 460–63.

54. Ann Crittenden, *The Price of Motherhood* (New York: Holt, 2001).

55. William Hosley, *Colt: The Making of an American Legend* (Amherst: University of Massachusetts Press, 1996); Morgen Witzel, *Management History* (New York: Routledge, 2009), 225.

56. Hosley, *Colt*, 76.

57. "Woman Items," *Woodhull and Claflin's Weekly*, August 12, 1871, https://www.victoria-woodhull.com/wc081200.htm.

58. Carroll Wright, *Working Women in Large Cities, Fourth Annual Report of the Commissioner of Labor* (Washington, DC: GPO, 1889), 62.

59. Edith Abbott, *Women in Industry: A Study in American Economic History* (New York: D. Appleton, 1909), 312.

60. Wright, *Working Women in Large Cities*, 62.

61. Massachusetts Bureau of Statistics of Labor, *Twentieth Annual Report*, 524–31.

62. Bureau of the Census, *Statistics of Women at Work* (Washington, DC: GPO, 1907), 10.

63. *Women at Work*, 163.

64. Helen Sumner, *Report on the Conditions of Women and Child Wage Earners in the United States* (Washington, DC: GPO, 1910); Kathryn Kish Sklar, "American Female Historians in Context, 1770–1930," *Feminist Studies* 3, no. 1–2 (Autumn 1975): 171–84; Frederick Olson, "Helen Laura Sumner Woodbury," in *Notable American Women*, vol. 3, ed. Edward T James, Janet W. James, and Paul Boyer (Cambridge, MA: Harvard University Press, 1971).

65. Nebraska State Board of Agriculture, *Annual Report of Agriculture for the Year 1887* (Lincoln, NE: State Journal, 1888), 192.

66. Ronald R. Kline, *Consumers in the Country: Technology and Social Change in Rural America* (Baltimore: Johns Hopkins University Press, 2000), 12.

67. Iowa Board of Control of State Institutions, *Bulletin of State Institutions*, vol. 1 (1899), 118.

68. Ohio State Board of Agriculture, *Annual Report*, vol. 54 (Columbus, OH: Heer, 1899), 645.

69. Barbara Handy-Marchello, *Women of the Northern Plains: Gender and Settlement on the Homestead Frontier, 1870–1930* (St. Paul: Minnesota Historical Society Press, 2007), 80.

70. Deborah Fink, *Agrarian Women: Wives and Mothers in Rural Nebraska, 1880–1940* (Chapel Hill: University of North Carolina Press, 1992); Dorothy Schwieder, "Iowa Farm Wives," in *Farmers, Bureaucrats, and Middlemen: Historical Perspectives in American Agriculture*, ed. Trudy Peterson (Washington, DC: Howard University Press, 1980); Mary Neth, *Preserving the Family Farm: Women, Community, and the Foundations*

of Agribusiness in the Midwest 1900–1940 (Baltimore: Johns Hopkins University Press, 1998).

71. Annie Diggs, "Women in the Alliance," *The Arena* 6, no. 30 (July 1892): 161–79.

72. Kenneth D. Rose, *American Women and the Repeal of Prohibition* (New York: New York University Press, 1996), 17.

73. Bryan and Bryan, *Memoirs*, 290.

74. George Lowell Austin, *The Life and Times of Wendell Phillips* (Boston: Lee and Shepard, 1888), 261.

75. Joseph R. Gusfield, "Social Structure and Moral Reform: A Study of the Woman's Christian Temperance Union," *American Journal of Sociology* 61, no. 3 (November 1955): 222; Joseph R. Gusfield, *Symbolic Crusade: Status Politics and the American Temperance Movement* (Champaign: University of Illinois Press, 1986); Ruth Bordin, *Frances Willard: A Biography* (Chapel Hill: University of North Carolina Press, 2000), 154.

76. Gusfield, "Social Structure," 226.

77. Frances Willard, *Let Something Good Be Said: Speeches and Writings of Frances E. Willard* (Champaign: University of Illinois Press, 2007), 197.

78. Gusfield, *Symbolic Crusade*, 76.

79. Frances Willard, *Glimpses of Fifty Years: The Autobiography of an American Woman* (Chicago: Women's Christian Temperance Union, 1889), 427, 471.

80. Recent research posits that the rejection of marriage by women like Willard was a factor in their activism. Julie Matthei, "The Sexual Division of Labor, Marriage and Sexuality in the Nineteenth Century," in *Homo Economics: Capitalism, Community, and Lesbian and Gay Life*, ed. Amy Gluckman and Betsy Reed (New York: Routledge, 1997); Victoria Brown, *The Education of Jane Addams* (Philadelphia: University of Pennsylvania Press, 2004), 361–62; Carroll Smith-Rosenberg, *Disorderly Conduct: Visions of Gender in Victorian America* (New York: Oxford University Press, 1985), 75; Leila J. Rupp, "Women's History in the New Millennium: Carroll Smith-Rosenberg's 'The Female World of Love and Ritual' after Twenty-Five Years," *Journal of Women's History* 12, no. 3 (Autumn 2000).

81. Willard, *Glimpses of Fifty Years*, 427.

82. Mary Lynn Bryan, Barbara Bair, Maree de Angury, and Jane Addams, *The Selected Papers of Jane Addams, Vol. 1, Preparing to Lead, 1860–81* (Chicago: University of Illinois Press, 2003), 144.

83. Daniel Brinton, *The American Race: A Linguistic Classification and Ethnographic Description of the Native Tribes of North and South America* (New York: Hodges, 1891), 39.

84. Josiah Strong, *Our Country* (New York: Baker & Taylor, 1885), 165.

85. "Speech of the Hon. Geo. H. Pendleton," *Evening Argus* [Rock Island, IL], September 21, 1867, 2.

86. "Calls It a Myth," *Wichita [KS] Daily Eagle*, October 19, 1892, 4. Lease later denied reports of portions of this interview, yet the details are too exact to have been manufactured.

87. W. E. B. Du Bois, *The Souls of Black Folk* (Chicago: A. C. McClurg, 1909), 13; W. E. B. Du Bois, *Black Reconstruction in America* (Piscataway, NJ: Transaction, 2012), 649.

88. Peter Roberts, *The Anthracite Coal Communities* (New York: Macmillan, 1904), 22.

89. Rachelle D. Henry, *Creating the Black Utopia of Buxton, Iowa* (Charleston, SC: History Press, 2019). The use of African Americans as strikebreakers is referenced in Iowa Bureau of Labor Statistics (hereafter IABLS), *Second Biennial Report*, 189.

90. Sara R. Massey, ed., *Black Cowboys of Texas* (College Station: Texas A&M University Press, 2000), xiii.

91. Ida B. Wells, "Lynch Law," in *The Reason Why the Colored American Is Not in the World's Columbian Exposition*, ed. Robert Rydell (Chicago: University of Illinois Press, 1999), 31.

92. Elliott M. Rudwick and August Meier, "Black Man in the 'White City': Negroes and the Columbian Exposition, 1893," *Phylon* 26, no. 4 (1965): 354–61.

93. Norm Bolotin and Christine Laing, *The World's Columbian Exposition: The Chicago World's Fair of 1893* (Urbana: University of Illinois Press, 2002); Curtis M. Hinsley, "The World as Marketplace: Commodification of the Exotic at the World's Columbian Exposition, Chicago, 1893," in *Exhibiting Cultures: The Poetics and Politics of Museum Display*, ed. Ivan Karp and Steven D. Lavine (Washington, DC: Smithsonian, 1991); James Gilbert, "A Contest of Cultures," *History Today* 42 (July 1992): 33–39.

94. A. H. Saxon, *P. T. Barnum: The Legend and the Man* (New York: Columbia University Press, 1989), 98–99.

95. William J. Schafer and Johannes Riedel, *The Art of Ragtime* (New York: Da Capo, 1977), 28; and Colorado Digital Sheet Music Collection, https://content.cu.edu/digitallibrary/sheetmusic.html.

96. Theodore Roosevelt, *The Winning of the West* (New York: Putnam, 1889), 7.

97. Frederick Jackson Turner, *The Significance of the Frontier in American History* (New York: Holt, 1920), 14.

98. Irvine Garland Penn, "The Progress of the Afro-American since Emancipation," in *The Reason Why the Colored American Is Not in the World's Columbian Exposition*, ed. Robert Rydell (Chicago: University of Illinois Press, 1999), 52.

99. Wells, *The Reason Why*, 7.

100. Indiana Bureau Statistics (INBLS), *Third Annual Report*, 138.

101. Immigration numbers come from USBC, *Historical Statistics*, "Chapter C: Migration," table C89–119, 106.

102. Frank Julian Warne, *The Slav Invasion and the Mine Workers: A Study in Immigration* (Philadelphia: Lippincott, 1904), 51.

103. John R. Commons, *Immigration and Its Economic Effects: Reports of the Industrial Commission on Immigration*, vol. 15 (Washington, DC: GPO, 1901), 295–96.

104. USBC, *Historical Statistics*, "Chapter C: Migration," table C120–137, 111.

105. Albert Clarke, *Reports of the Industrial Commission on Immigration* (Washington, DC: GPO, 1901), xc. Testimony on rates come from the companies.

106. John D. Hicks, *The Populist Revolt* (Minneapolis: University of Minnesota Press, 1931), 15.

107. Hicks, 15.

108. Hicks, 27.

109. Oscar Handlin, *The Uprooted* (Boston: Little, Brown, 1973), 55.

110. "Steerage Accommodations on the Cunard Steamship Line—1879," *Pall Mall Gazette* [London, UK], August 9, 1879, 9–12, https://www.ggarchives.com/Ocean Travel/Steerage/SteerageAccommodationsCunardLine-1879.html.

111. Robert Louis Stevenson, *The Amateur Immigrant* (Chicago: Stone and Kimball, 1895), 50–51.

112. Mary Antin, *The Promised Land* (Boston: Houghton-Mifflin, 1912), 173.

113. Henry Edward Rood, "A Pennsylvania Colliery Village," *The Century* 55, no. 5 (March 1898): 811, 814, 816.

114. Fred Stopsky, "Crime: The Neglected Areas of Multicultural Education," in *Proceedings of the National Association for Multicultural Education: Seventh Annual Name Conference,* ed. Carl A. Grant (Washington, DC: National Association for Multicultural Education, 1999), 449; Gusfield, *Symbolic Crusade,* 196.

115. IABLS, *Second Biennial Report,* 146.

116. California Bureau of Labor Statistics (CABLS), *Second Biennial Report,* 60.

117. Pennsylvania Bureau of Labor/Industrial Statistics (PBIS), *Volume 12,* 66; New York Bureau of Labor Statistics (NYBLS), *Third Annual Report,* 385.

118. *An Act to Execute Certain Treaty Stipulations Relating to Chinese, Papers Relating to the Foreign Relations of the United States* (Washington, DC: GPO, 1893), 110–13.

119. Richard Gray, *A History of American Literature* (Malden, MA: Blackwell, 2004), 246.

120. Elizabeth V. Burt, *The Progressive Era: Primary Documents on Events from 1890 to 1914* (Westport, CT: Greenwood, 2004), 24.

121. Dirk Hoerder, "Immigration and the Working Class: The Remigration Factor," *International Labor and Working-Class History* 21 (Spring 1982): 28–41; Matthew Simon, "The United States Balance of Payments," in *Trends in the American Economy in the Nineteenth Century,* ed. National Bureau of Economic Research (Princeton, NJ: Princeton University Press, 1960), 688–89.

122. Dean Strang, *Worse Than the Devil: Anarchists, Clarence Darrow, and Justice in a Time of Terror* (Madison: University of Wisconsin Press, 2013), 8.

123. Kerby Miller, *Ireland and Irish America: Culture, Class, and Transatlantic Migration* (Dublin, Ireland: Field Day, 2008), 332.

124. "Quaint Haunts of Cherished Freedom," *Omaha Daily Bee,* December 3, 1899, 28.

125. "Chief Narris' Address," *Kansas City Daily Journal,* September 14, 1896, 2.

126. A. E. Sheldon, "A Hero of the Nebraska Frontier," *Nebraska History and Record of the Pioneer Days* 1, no. 1 (1918): 5.

127. "Andrew Jackson Beard," Hall of Fame inventor profile, accessed December 10, 2017, https://www.youtube.com/watch?v=IO5AzG36MQI; Patricia Carter Sluby, *The Inventive Spirit of African Americans: Patented Ingenuity* (Westport, CT: Praeger, 2004).

128. Walter Wycoff, *A Day with a Tramp* (New York: Scribner, 1901), 45.

CHAPTER TWO
Transition Stages Are Always Harsh

Roger Welsch, "Sweet Nebraska Land," Folkways Records, no. FH53337, 1965.

1. Henry George Jr., *The Life of Henry George* (New York: Doubleday, 1900), 149.

2. George, 210.

3. Henry George, *Progress and Poverty: An Inquiry into the Cause of Industrial Depressions and of the Increase of Want with the Increase of Wealth* (New York: Appleton, 1886), 6, 3, 4, 475. The recent collected edition of George's work includes the 1880 edition. See also *The Annotated Works of Henry George: Progress and Poverty*, ed. Francis K. Peddle and William S. Peirce (Madison, NJ: Farleigh Dickinson University Press, 2017).

4. "Three Authors of Note," *Wichita [KS] Daily Eagle*, February 17, 1891, 3.

5. Jacob Riis, *The Making of an American* (New York: MacMillan, 1901), 423.

6. Riis, 271.

7. New York Bureau of Labor Statistics, *Second Annual* Report, 181.

8. *Report of the Tenement House Committee as Authorized by Chapter 479 of the Laws of 1894* (Albany, NY: James Lyon, 1895), 213, 14, 32.

9. Carol Nackenoff, *The Fictional Republic: Horatio Alger and American Political Discourse* (New York: Oxford University Press, 1994); Richard M. Huber, *The American Idea of Success* (New York: Pushcart, 1988); Horatio Alger, *Tom Turner's Legacy* (New York: A. L. Burt, 1902), 230.

10. Howard Zinn, *A People's History of the United States: 1492–Present* (New York: Routledge, 2013), 254.

11. Moses Yale Beach, *The Wealth and Biography of the Wealthy Citizens of the City of New York* (New York: New York Sun, 1845).

12. *The Tribune's List of All Persons in the United States Reporting to Be Worth a Million or More* (New York: Tribune, 1892).

13. Ohio Bureau of Labor Statistics, *Thirteenth Annual Report*, machinery: 76; whiskey: 56; agricultural implements: 85.

14. Massachusetts Bureau of Statistics of Labor, *Sixteenth Annual Report*, 181.

15. Indiana Bureau of Statistics, *Sixth Annual Report*, 368.

16. Walter Licht, *Working for the Railroad* (Princeton, NJ: Princeton University Press, 1987).

17. US Bureau of the Census (hereafter USBC), *Historical Statistics of the United States*, "Chapter Q: Transportation," table Q321–328, 731.

18. John Hicks, "The Political Career of Ignatius Donnelly," *Mississippi Valley Historical Review* 8, no. 1–2 (June–September 1921): 80–132; *Thomas vs. Cincinnati, N.O. & T.P.R. RR Co.*, *Interstate Commerce Reports*, vol. 4 (Rochester, NY: Lawyers Cooperative, 1895), 788–98.

19. Sharon Sessions Rugh, *Our Common Country* (Bloomington: University of Indiana Press, 2001), 137.

20. Finley Peter Dunne, *Mr. Dooley's Opinions* (Whitefish, MT: Kessinger, 2004), 189.

21. George K. Holmes, "The Concentration of Wealth," *Political Science Quarterly* 8, no. 4 (December 1893): 589–600.

22. William Scott, "Distribution of Wealth in the United States," *The Chautauquan* 19 (April 1894): 270.

23. Charles Spahr, *An Essay on the Present Distribution of Wealth in the United States* (New York: Crowell, 1896), 69; Henry Laurens Call, *The Concentration of Wealth* (Boston: Chandler, 1907), 7; Rufus Tucker, "The Distribution of Income Among Income Taxpayers in the United States, 1863–1935," *Quarterly Journal of Economics* 52, no. 4 (August 1938): 547–87; Thomas Piketty and Emmanuel Saez, "Income Inequality in the United States, 1913–1998," *Quarterly Journal of Economics* 118, no. 1 (February 2003): 1–39.

24. "The Marlborough-Vanderbilt Marriage," *Leslie's Weekly*, November 7, 1895, 303; "Kansas Is Not a Republican State," *Kansas Agitator* [Garnett, KS], October 25, 1895, 4; "Gowns of a Duchess," *Wood County Reporter* [Grand Rapids, WI], October 31, 1895, 2.

25. "Mrs. Stanford's Diamonds," *New York Times*, November 22, 1885, 6.

26. Andrew Carnegie, "Wealth," *North American Review*, 48, no. 391 (June 1889): 655.

27. William James Ghent, *Our Benevolent Feudalism* (New York: Macmillan, 1903), 29.

28. William Graham Sumner, *What Social Classes Owe to Each Other* (New York: Harpers, 1884), 54.

29. William Graham Sumner, *The Forgotten Man and Other Essays* (New Haven, CT: Yale University Press, 1919), 475.

30. S. C. T. Dodd, "Aggregated Capital," in *The Trust: Its Book*, ed. James H. Bridge (New York: Doubleday, 1902), 72.

31. Peter Roberts, *The Anthracite Coal Communities* (New York: Macmillan, 1904), 83, 85.

32. "Good Wholesome Starvation," *Morning Call* [San Francisco, CA], December 11, 1891, 4.

33. Carroll D. Wright, *Some Ethical Phases of the Labor Question* (Boston: American Unitarian Association, 1902), 141.

34. *Constitution of the General Assembly, District Assemblies, and Local Assemblies of the Order of the Knights of Labor in America* (Marblehead, MA: Statesman, 1883), 3.

35. Emily Lee Sherwood, "Carroll D. Wright, A.M. LL.D., Commissioner of Labor," *To-Day*, February 1896, 66.

36. Carroll D. Wright, "The Evolution of Wage Statistics," *Quarterly Journal of Economics* 6, no. 2 (January 1892): 151–89.

37. "Woman in the Field of Labor," *New York Times*, January 13, 1892, 3.

38. Carroll D. Wright, *The Industrial Evolution of the United States* (New York: Scribner, 1901), 17.

39. Carroll Wright, "Cheaper Living and the Rise of Wages," *The Forum*, October 1893, 221–28; Frederick Waite, *Prices and Wages: A Dissection of the Senate Finance Committee's Great Report as Interpreted by Its Statistician and the Hon. Carroll D. Wright*, presented to the National Statistical Association at the Columbia University, Washington, DC, November 13, 1894; "Official Statistical Liar" and dismissal, H. L. Bliss, *Plutocracy's Statistics* (Chicago: Kerr, 1909), 2, 3; James Leiby, *Carroll Wright and Labor Reform* (Cambridge, MA: Harvard University Press, 1960), 202.

40. Stanley Lebergott, *Manpower in Economic Growth* (New York: McGraw-Hill, 1964), 169.

41. Steven R. Kinsella, *900 Miles from Nowhere: Voices from the Homestead Frontier* (Minneapolis: Minnesota Historical Society Press, 2006), 54.

42. Susan Sessions Rugh, *Our Common Country: Family Farming, Culture, and Community in the Nineteenth-Century Midwest* (Bloomington: University of Indiana Press, 2001), xx; James Livingston, "Households to Markets," in *Pragmatism and the Political Economy of Cultural Revolution, 1850–1940*, ed. James Livingston (Chapel Hill: University of North Carolina Press, 1997); Bruce Laurie, "Household to Factory," in *Artisans into Workers: Labor in Nineteenth-Century America* (New York: Hill and Wang, 1989); Richard Schneirov, "Thoughts on Periodizing the Gilded Age: Capital Accumulation, Society, and Politics, 1873–1898," *Journal of the Gilded Age and Progressive Era* 5, no. 3 (July 2006): 189–224; Julie Husband and Jim O'Laughlin, *Daily Life in the Industrial United States, 1870–1900* (Westport, CT: Greenwood, 2004); Steven Hahn, *The Roots of Southern Populism* (New York: Oxford University Press, 2006). The transition to a "consumer society" is central to the works of Eric J. Hobsbawm, *Industry and Empire: From 1750 to the Present Day* (New York: Penguin, 1969); and Geoffrey Barraclough, *An Introduction to Contemporary History* (New York: Penguin, 1969).

43. George B. Emerson and Charles L. Flint, *Manual of Agriculture, for the School, the Farm, and the Fireside* (Boston: Swan, Brewer & Tileston, 1862), 1–2.

44. Lebergott, *Manpower*, 145.

45. Rugh, *Our Common Country*, 85.

46. Michael Katz, *In the Shadow of the Poorhouse: A Social History of Welfare in America* (New York: Basic, 1996), 9.

47. Brooks Blevins, *Hill Folks: A History of Arkansas Ozarkers and Their Image* (Chapel Hill: University of North Carolina Press, 2002), 65; Helen Sheumaker and Shirley Teresa Wajda, *Material Culture in America: Understanding Everyday Life* (New

York: ABC-CLIO, 2008); Lewis Eldon Atherton, *The Southern Country Store, 1800–1860* (Westport, CT: Greenwood, 1968); Lewis Eldon Atherton, *Pioneer Merchant in Mid-America* (Columbia: University of Missouri Press, 1936); Gerald Carson, *The Old Country Store* (New York: Oxford University Press, 1954); Stanley J. Shapiro and Alton F. Doody, *Readings in the History of American Marketing: Settlement to Civil War* (New York: R. D. Irwin, 1968).

48. Rugh, *Our Common Country*, 24.

49. Sam Bass Warner, *The Private City: Philadelphia in Three Periods of Its Growth* (Philadelphia: University of Pennsylvania Press, 1987), 58.

50. Lebergott, *Manpower*, 6–7, 116.

51. James Livingston finds the roots of the consumer culture in the years preceding the Civil War; Jackson Lears finds the beginning around 1880; Richard Schneirov dates it to 1871.

52. Edward Bellamy, *Looking Backward: 2000–1887* (New York: Random House, 1917), 248.

53. Katz, *In the Shadow*, 4.

54. Louis Dembitz Brandeis, *Business—A Profession* (Boston: Small, Maynard, 1914), 65.

55. Sally Ann McMurry, *Families and Farmhouses in Nineteenth-Century America: Vernacular Design and Social Change* (New York: Oxford University Press, 1988).

56. Carl Robert Keyes, "Early American Advertising: Marketing and Consumer Culture in Eighteenth-Century Philadelphia" (PhD diss., Johns Hopkins University, 2008).

57. "In Printer's Ink the Secret," *New York Times*, October 14, 1894, 21.

58. Pamela Walker Laird, *Advertising Progress: American Business and the Rise of Consumer Marketing* (Baltimore: Johns Hopkins University Press, 1998), 49; Jackson Lears, *Fables of Abundance: A Cultural History of Advertising in America* (New York: Basic, 1994).

59. "In Printer's Ink the Secret," October 14, 1894.

60. Lears, *Fables of Abundance*, 10.

61. Rugh, *Our Common Country*, 162.

62. "Cash Purchases," *Hardware*, August 10, 1897, 27.

63. Theodore Dreiser, *Sister Carrie* (New York: Bantam, 1958), 17.

64. Lori Merish, *Sentimental Materialism* (Durham, NC: Duke University Press, 2000), 1; Gillian Brown, *Domestic Individualism: Imagining Self in Nineteenth-Century America* (Berkeley: University of California Press, 1990).

65. Gerald J. Baldasty, *The Commercialization of News in the Nineteenth Century* (Madison: University of Wisconsin Press, 1992), 117.

66. "The Woman Who Pilfers," *New York Times*, May 31, 1878, 3.

67. Elaine Abelson, *When Ladies Go A-Thieving: Middle-Class Shoplifters in the Victorian Department Store* (New York: Oxford University Press, 1992), 11; Patricia O'Brien, "The Kleptomania Diagnosis: Bourgeois Women and Theft in Late Nineteenth-Century France," *Journal of Social History* 17, no. 1 (Autumn 1983): 65–77.

68. American Antiquarian, "Trade Cards," accessed August 4, 2021, http://www
.americanantiquarian.org/Exhibitions/Food/tradecards.htm.

69. Margaret Walsh, "Women's Place on the American Frontier," *Journal of American Studies* 29, no. 2 (August 1995): 244; Barbara Handy-Marchello, *Women of the Northern Plains: Gender and Settlement on the Homestead Frontier, 1870–1930* (St. Paul: Minnesota Historical Society Press, 2007), 29.

70. Rugh, *Our Common Country*, 146. Sally Ann McMurry also writes, "The prosperity of the farm depends largely on the proper performance of the duties of the wife" (*Families and Farmhouses*, 59).

71. *Journal of Proceedings of the Eleventh Session of the National Grange of the Patrons of Husbandry* (Louisville, KY: Morton, 1878), 14.

72. Hahn, *Roots of Southern Populism*.

73. USBC, *Historical Statistics*, "Chapter K: Agriculture," 461.

74. Ebbie Julian Watson, *Handbook of South Carolina* (Columbia, SC: State Printer, 1908), 243.

75. David B. Sicilia, "Industrialization and the Rise of Corporations, 1860–1900," in *Companion to 19th-Century America*, ed. William L. Barney (Malden, MA: Wiley-Blackwell, 2006), 142.

76. Stephan Thernstrom and Peter R. Knights, "Men in Motion: Some Data and Speculations about Urban Population Mobility in Nineteenth-Century America," *Journal of Interdisciplinary History* 1, no. 1 (Autumn 1970): 8–9. As Richard Hofstadter writes, farmers had a "tremendous passion for moving" (*The Age of Reform* [New York: Vintage, 1955], 42).

77. Michael P. Conzen, "Local Migration Systems in Nineteenth-Century Iowa," *Geographical Review* 64, no. 3 (July 1974): 344, 346.

78. National Park Service, "Homesteading by the Numbers," accessed June 22, 2020, https://www.nps.gov/home/learn/historyculture/bynumbers.htm.

79. Elizabeth Watkins Jorgensen and Henry Irvin Jorgensen, *Thorstein Veblen: Victorian Firebrand* (Armonk, NY: Sharpe, 1999), 18; John P. Diggins, *Thorstein Veblen: Theorist of the Leisure Class* (Princeton, NJ: Princeton University Press, 1978); Douglas Fitzgerald Dowd, *Thorstein Veblen* (New Brunswick, NJ: Transaction, 2000); Joseph Dorfman, *Thorstein Veblen and His America* (New York: Viking, 1934); Rick Tilman, *The Intellectual Legacy of Thorstein Veblen: Unresolved Issues* (Westport, CT: Greenwood, 1996).

80. Jorgensen and Jorgensen, *Thorstein Veblen*, 18.

81. Thorstein Veblen, *A Veblen Treasury*, ed. Rick Tillman (New York: Sharpe, 1993), xiii.

82. E. Ray Canterbery, *A Brief History of Economics: Artful Approaches to the Dismal Science* (River Edge, NJ: World Scientific, 2002), 170. John Kenneth Galbraith states there is no truth to this story. See Galbraith, *Economics in Perspective: A Critical History* (New York, Houghton Mifflin, 1988), 171.

83. Jorgensen and Jorgensen, *Thorstein Veblen*, 3.

84. C. M. A. Clark, "Veblen, Thorstein Bunde," in *Encyclopedia of Political Economy*, vol. 2, ed. P. A. O'Hara (London: Routledge, 1999), 1223.

85. Thorstein Veblen, *Theory of the Leisure Class* (New York: Macmillan, 1899), 73.

86. "Kansas Is Not a Republican State," *Kansas Agitator*, October 25, 1895, 4.

87. Connecticut Bureau of Labor Statistics, *Third Annual* Report, 344.

88. Veblen, *Theory of the Leisure Class*, 301.

89. Thorstein Veblen, *The Theory of Business Enterprise* (New York: Scribners, 1919), 2, 5.

90. "Watches Become Crazy," *Daily Herald* [Brownsville, TX], June 12, 1893, 1.

91. Jack Beatty, *Age of Betrayal: The Triumph of Money in America, 1865–1900* (New York: Vintage, 2007), 4.

92. Veblen, *Theory of Business Enterprise*, 123.

93. Veblen, 11.

94. Massachusetts Bureau of Statistics of Labor, *Sixteenth Annual Report of the Bureau of Statistics of Labor* (Boston: Wright & Potter, 1885), 164.

95. Henry David Thoreau wrote: "There are so many keen and subtle masters that enslave both North and South. It is hard to have a Southern overseer; it is worse to have a Northern one; but worst of all is when you are a slave-driver to yourself" (*Walden and Other Writings* [New York: Bantam, 2004], 165).

96. Morgan Witzel, *Management History* (New York: Routledge, 2009), 63.

97. Mark Enrique Van Rhyn, "Beyond the Battlefield: Post-War Careers of Middle-Rank Civil War Generals," January 1, 2003, ETD Collection for the University of Nebraska–Lincoln, paper no. AAI3092604.

98. Marc Bloch, *Feudal Society*, vol. 2 (New York: Routledge, 1965), 164.

99. Pennsylvania Bureau of Labor/Industrial Statistics, *Volume 12*, v.

100. Charles B. Spahr, "America's Working People," *Outlook* 58, no. 1 (September 2, 1899): 69–75.

101. US House of Representatives Committee on Banking and Currency, *Money Trust Investigation: Investigation of Financial and Monetary Conditions in the United States* (Washington, DC: GPO, 1912), 1050.

102. Andrew Carnegie, *Autobiography of Andrew Carnegie* (New York: Houghton-Mifflin, 1920), 142.

103. Ron Chernow, *The House of Morgan: An American Banking Dynasty and the Rise of Modern Finance* (New York: Grove-Atlantic, 2010), 92.

104. Chernow, *House of Morgan*, 54–60.

105. Ray Ginger, *Altgeld's America* (Chicago: Quadrangle, 1958), 188.

106. *Mr. Rockefeller's Ledger: Lessons for Young Men from Its Items*, Address Delivered at a Social Gathering of the Young Men's Bible Class of the Fifth Avenue Baptist Church, Saturday Evening, March 27, 1897, issued by the class.

107. The earliest use appears in "In Favor Of," *Weekly Democratic Statesman* [Austin, TX], March 15, 1883, 5.

108. Ron Chernow, *Titan: The Life of John D. Rockefeller* (New York: Vintage, 1999), xx.

109. Ida Tarbell, *The History of the Standard Oil Company*, vol. 1 (New York: McClure, 1901), 136.

110. Veblen, *Theory of Business Enterprise*, 30.

111. U. H. Painter, US Congress, *Interstate Commerce: Debate in the Second Session of Forty-Ninth Congress on the Bill to Establish a Board of Commissioners on Interstate Commerce, and to Regulate such Commerce, etc.* (Washington, DC: GPO, 1887), 115.

112. J. Laurence Laughlin, "Gold and Prices, 1890–1907," *Journal of Political Economy* 17, no. 5 (May 1909): 257–71.

113. USBC, *Historical Statistics*, "Chapter P: Manufacturing," table P194–204, 687.

114. Naomi R. Lamoreaux, "Entrepreneurship, Business Organization, and Economic Concentration," in *The Cambridge Economic History of the United States*, ed. Stanley L. Engerman and Robert E. Gallman (New York: Cambridge University Press, 1997), 424.

115. See *State ex rel. v. Standard Oil Company* (49 O.S., 137). See also Albert Martin Kales, *Cases on Contracts and Combinations in Restraint of Trade*, vol. 2 (Chicago: Callahan, 1916), 678; and Augustus Owsley Stanley, *Violations of Antitrust Act of 1890: Hearings Before the Committee on Rules* (Washington, DC: GPO, 1911), 72.

116. See Edward N. Costikyan, "Politics in New York City: A Memoir of the Post-War Years," *New York History* 74, no. 4 (1993): 414–34; Adonica Y. Lui, "The Machine and Social Policies: Tammany Hall and the Politics of Public Outdoor Relief, New York City, 1874–1898," *Studies in American Political Development* 9, no. 2 (Fall 1995): 386–403.

117. Jane Addams, "The Morals of Municipal Corruption," *The Nation* 66, no. 1712 (April 11, 1898): 297–98.

118. Hamilton Holt, "The Life Story of a Lithuanian," in *The Life Stories of Undistinguished Americans as Told by Themselves*, ed. Hamilton Holt (New York: Pott, 1908), 28.

119. Joseph D. Reid Jr. and Michael Kurth, "The Rise and Fall of Urban Political Patronage Machines," in *Strategic Factors in Nineteenth Century American Economic History*, ed. Robert William Fogel, Claudia Dale Goldin, and Hugh Rockoff (Chicago: University of Chicago Press, 1992), 427.

120. Richard Croker, "Tammany Hall and the Democracy," *North American Review* 154, no. 423 (February 1892): 226.

121. Euphemia Blake, *History of the Tammany Society; Or, Columbian Order from Its Organization to the Present Time* (New York: Souvenir, 1901), 161.

122. Blake, 182.

123. Solon Buck, *The Granger Movement* (Cambridge, MA: Harvard University Press, 1913), 80.

124. Jeffry A. Frieden, "Monetary Populism in Nineteenth-Century America: An Open Economy Interpretation," *Journal of Economic History* 57, no. 2 (June 1997): 367–95.

125. Fred Wayne Catlett, "The Millionaire in Politics," *Harvard Advocate* 67, no. 10 (June 29, 1904): 134–36.

126. Richard Welch, *The Presidencies of Grover Cleveland* (Lawrence: University of Kansas Press, 1980), 14.

127. Allan Nevins, *Grover Cleveland: A Study in Courage* (New York: Dodd and Mead, 1932), 75.

128. National Democratic Committee, *Campaign Text Book of the National Democratic Party 1896* (Chicago: National Democratic Committee, 1896), 10.

129. Hugh Rockoff, "The 'Wizard of Oz' as a Monetary Allegory," *Journal of Political Economy* 98, no. 4 (August 1990): 751.

130. "Plays and Players," *The Herald* [Los Angeles, CA], July 5, 1896, 14.

131. Helena Maguire, "'Rag-Time' Familiarly Considered," *Elliott's Magazine* 30–31, no. 3 (October 1899): 168.

132. Herbert F. Hershey, "The 'Coon Song' Fad," *The Conservative* 1, no. 41 (April 20, 1899): 11.

133. "Thrilling Train Robberies Are Manufactured to Your Order," *Washington [DC] Times*, May 29, 1904, 26.

134. Noel Burch, *Life to Those Shadows* (Berkeley: University of California Press, 1990), 176; Kristin Thompson and David Bordwell, "Linearity, Materialism, and the Study of Early American Cinema," *Wide Angle* 5, no. 3 (1983): 4–15.

135. Henry Adams, *The Education of Henry Adams* (Boston: Massachusetts Historical Society, 1918), 457.

136. Charles Francis Adams and Henry Adams, *A Chapter of Erie and Other Essays* (Boston: Osgood, 1871), 87.

137. Call, *Concentration of Wealth*, 9.

CHAPTER THREE
Dark Corners

Dahlhart and others recorded this song many times. These lyrics are from Victor 21331. George Korson recorded the song as sung by a Pittsburgh woman in *Pennsylvania Songs and Legends* (Philadelphia: University of Pennsylvania, 1946), 382–83. Dwight Yokum recorded a similar lament but with different lyrics in a song titled "Miner's Prayer."

1. "Dying of Starvation," *New York Times*, January 1, 1883, 5.

2. Efforts to find information on her brother turned up nothing. One sign of advanced starvation is cognitive dissonance. An 1872 article noted, "The persistent conviction of the death of a friend or relative is a common delusion." See William Aitkin, "The Delirium of Inanition," *The Science and Practice of Medicine*, vol. 2 (Philadelphia: Lindsay & Blackiston, 1872), 892.

3. New York Bureau of Labor Statistics (hereafter NYBLS), *Third Annual Report*, 165.

4. New York State Department of Labor, *State Standard Building Code for Places*

of Public Assembly, sec. 36.2.2, par. 3, accessed March 7, 2017, https://labor.ny.gov/work erprotection/safetyhealth/sh36.shtm#36.3 (webpage no longer available); Paul Delaney, *Sandhogs: A History of the Tunnel Workers of New York* (New York: Longfield, 1983), 3.

5. "The East River Bridge," *New York Times*, June 19, 1870 8.

6. Thomas Oliver, "Caisson Disease or Compressed Air Illness," *The Lancet*, February 11, 1899, 356.

7. "The Grecian Bend," *The Ladies' Cabinet of Fashion, Music & Romance*, vol. 33 (London: George Vickers, 1868), 110.

8. David McCullough, *The Great Bridge: The Epic Story of the Building of the Brooklyn Bridge* (New York: Simon & Schuster, 1972).

9. "Dying of Starvation," 5.

10. Julia Bess Frank, "Body-Snatching: A Grave Medical Problem," *Yale Journal of Biology and Medicine* 49 (September 1976): 399–410; Kenneth C. Nystrom, *The Bioarchaeology of Dissection and Autopsy in the United States* (New York: Springer, 2017).

11. William James, *On Some of Life's Ideals* (New York: Holt, 1899): "no dark corners," 55; "take my chances," 56; "fields of heroism," 60; "clanging fights," 60.

12. W. P. Butler, "Caisson Disease During the Construction of the Eads and Brooklyn Bridges: A Review," *Undersea and Hyperbaric Medicine* 31, no. 4 (2004): 455.

13. Anthracite Coal Strike Commission, *Report to the President on the Anthracite Coal Strike of May–October 1902* (Washington, DC: GPO, 1903) (hereafter *1902 Anthracite Strike Report*), 29.

14. US Bureau of Labor Statistics (USBLS), "Injuries, Illnesses, and Fatalities in the Coal Mining Industry," accessed March 7, 2021, https://www.bls.gov/iif/oshwc /osh/os/osar0012.htm.

15. Peter Roberts, *The Anthracite Coal Communities* (New York: Macmillan, 1904), 65, 271.

16. Roberts, 271, 267.

17. Jay Hambidge, "An Artist's Impression of the Colliery Region," *The Century* 55, no. 5 (March 1898): 822.

18. Richard Rothwell, ed., "Fatal Accidents in Coal Mines," in *The Mineral Industry*, vol. 6 (New York: Scientific, 1898), 752.

19. *1902 Anthracite Strike Report*, 28; Gerald Grob, *The Deadly Truth: A History of Disease in America* (Cambridge, MA: Harvard University Press, 2002).

20. Mark Aldrich, *Death Rode the Rails: American Railroad Accidents and Safety, 1828–1965* (Baltimore: Johns Hopkins University Press, 2008), 326. Aldrich explains that railroad injuries "cannot be compared to those from any other industry" because of differences in the definition of a "reportable injury." See also John Williams-Searle, "Death Rode the Rails: American Railroad Safety 1828–1965," *Annals of Iowa* 66, no. 3 (Summer 2007): 333–35.

21. Interstate Commerce Commission, *Fourth Annual Report, December 1, 1890* (Washington, DC: GPO, 1891), 60.

22. New Jersey Bureau of Statistics of Labor (hereafter NJBLS), *Eleventh Annual Report*, 30.

23. "Slaughter of Railroad Employees Stopped," *Railroad Trainmen's Journal* 13, no. 148 (June 1896): 423–26.

24. "Train Accidents in 1890," *Railroad Gazette*, February 13, 1891, 116.

25. "Slaughter of Railroad Employees," 423.

26. US Senate, *Automatic Couplers and Power-Brakes, Hearings Before the Committee on Interstate Commerce, United States Senate* (Washington, DC: GPO, 1890), 22, J. David Hacker, "A Census-Based Count of the Civil War Dead," *Civil War History* 57, no. 4 (December 2011): 307–48.

27. NJBLS, *Eleventh Annual Report*, 68.

28. "Recent Casualties," *Railway Age Monthly and Railway Service Magazine* 3, no. 9 (September 1882): 603. This was a monthly feature in this publication that often ran several pages.

29. US Senate, *Automatic Couplers and Power-Brakes*, 19.

30. US Interstate Commerce Commission (hereafter ICC), *Second Annual Report on the Statistics of Railways in the United States* (Washington, DC: GPO, 1890), 36; ICC, *Third Annual Report on the Statistics of Railways in the United States* (Washington, DC: GPO, 1891), 75; ICC, *Fourth Annual Report on the Statistics of Railways in the United States* (Washington, DC: GPO, 1892), 92.

31. "The Massachusetts Car-Coupling Examination," *American Railroad Journal* 58, no. 3 (June 1884): 202.

32. US Senate, *Automatic Couplers and Power-Brakes*, 19.

33. Hamlin Garland, "Homestead and Its Perilous Trades," *McClure's Magazine* 3, no. 1 (June 1894): 3–20.

34. L. W., "Homestead as Seen by One of Its Workmen," *McClure's Magazine* 3, no. 4 (July 1894): 163–69.

35. "Cremated in Metal," *Pittsburg Dispatch*, August 31, 1889, 1.

36. Robert Watchorn, "What Occupations Should be Regarded as Dangerous to Life and Limb or to Health?," in *Fifth Annual Report of the Chief Factory Inspector for the Commonwealth of Pennsylvania* (Harrisburg, PA: Busch, 1895), 454.

37. US Department of Labor, *Report on Conditions of Employment in the Iron and Steel Industry in the United States*, vol. 4 (Washington, DC: GPO, 1913), 11.

38. Factory Inspector of Illinois, *Annual Report: 1895–1896* (Springfield, IL: Phillips Brothers, 1897), 36.

39. "A Courier's Terrible Story," *New York Times*, June 12, 1882, 1; "Starvation in Iowa," *New York Times*, November 22, 1873, 10; "Starving Texans," *New York Times*, April 3, 1887, 3; Walsh County "In Danger of Starvation," *New York Times*, January 13, 1889, 1; "People Who Are Starving," *New York Times*, January 27, 1889, 16; "Starving in Oklahoma," *New York Times*, December 16, 1890, 3; "Illinois Miners in Want," *New York Times*, May 30, 1894 ("Dandelions" is the subhead); "Starving in Hocking Valley," *New*

York Times, February 2, 1895, 9. Mysteriously, Michael K. Rosenow does not reference starvation in *Death and Dying in the Working Class, 1865–1920* (Urbana: University of Illinois Press, 2015).

40. Stephen Crane, "Nebraska's Bitter Fight for Life," *Birmingham [AL] Age-Herald*, February 24, 1895, 12.

41. Carlos C. Closson, "The Unemployed in American Cities," *Quarterly Journal of Economics* 8, no. 2 (January 1894): 178.

42. Closson, 194.

43. "Appealed for Aid Only When Hunger Lured Death On," *San Francisco Call*, December 19, 1898, 1.

44. "Talmage's Sermon," *Iola Register*, October 2, 1896.

45. Anup Kumar Srivastava and Manisha Tiwary, *Right to Food* (New Delhi, India: Human Rights Law Network, 2009), 409.

46. Douglas L. Anderton and Susan Hautaniemi Leonard, "Grammars of Death: An Analysis of Nineteenth-Century Literal Causes of Death from the Age of Miasmas to Germ Theory," *Social Science History* 28, no. 1 (Spring 2004): 111–43; David Hacker, "Decennial Life Tables for the White Population of the United States, 1790–1900," *Historical Methods* 43, no. 2 (April 2010): 45–79.

47. Frederick A. P. Barnard and Arnold Guyot, eds., *Johnson's Universal Cyclopaedia*, vol. 5 (New York: A. J. Johnson, 1890), 768; Massachusetts Legislature, *Twenty-Second Report Relating to the Reporting of Births, Marriages, and Deaths in the Commonwealth for the Year Ending December 31, 1863* (Boston: Wright & Potter, 1863), ciii; Michigan Secretary of State, *Tenth Annual Report Relating to the Report of Births, Marriages and Deaths for the Year 1876* (Lansing, MI: W. S. George, 1881), 178; A. M. Linn, "Acute Inanition," *Homeopathic Journal of Obstetrics, Gynecology, and Pedology* 20, no. 4 (July 1898): 321.

48. "Twelve Things You Probably Didn't Know About John Shaw Billings," *NLM in Focus*, April 12, 2017, https://infocus.nlm.nih.gov/2017/0/12/twelve-things-you -probably-didn't-know-about-john-shaw-billings/.

49. NJBLS, *Tenth Annual Report*, 206.

50. NYBLS, *Second Annual Report*, 136.

51. John S. Billings, *Report on the Mortality and Vital Statistics of the United States as Returned at the Tenth Census, Part 2* (Washington, DC: GPO, 1886), 44, 46; John S. Billings, *Report on the Vital and Social Statistics of the United States at the Eleventh Census of the United States, Part 3: Death Statistics* (Washington, DC: GPO, 1894), 16; US Census Office, *Twelfth Census of the United States, Census Reports, Vol. 4: Vital Statistics, Part 2: Statistics of Deaths* (Washington, DC: US Census Office, 1902), 116, 118. Deaths were divided by population to compute the rate per 100,000. Population numbers appear on page 3 of the 1890 report and page 2 of the 1900 report.

52. "World Health Rankings," accessed September 22, 2021, https://www.worldlife expectancy.com/cause-of-death/malnutrition/by-country/.

53. Illinois State Board of Health, *Seventh Annual Report* (Springfield, IL: H. W.

Rokker, 1885), 153, 174, 195, 216, 244, 258, 279, 300; Illinois State Board of Health, *Ninth Annual Report* (Springfield, IL: Springfield Printing, 1889), 200.

54. For health reports, see Pennsylvania State Board of Health, *First Annual Report* (Harrisburg, PA: Edwin Meyers, 1886), 163; and City of New York, *Annual Report of the Health Department* (New York: Martin B. Brown, 1891), 128. For population statistics, see *Encyclopaedia Britannica*, 9th ed., vol. 18 (Edinburgh: Adam & Charles Black, 1885), 738; and State of New York, *1790–2000 NYC Historical and Foreign Born Population*, accessed March 7, 2017, https://www.nyc.gov/assets/planning/download/pdf/data-maps/nyc-population/historical-population/1790–2000_nyc_total_foreign_birth.pdf.

55. World Health Organization, "Children: Reducing Mortality," October 31, 2017, http://www.who.int/en/news-room/fact-sheets/detail/children-reducing-mortality.

56. "Life and Death Records," *New York Times*, January 1, 1883, 8.

57. Kenneth D. Kochanek, Sherry L. Murphy, Jiaquan Xu, and Betzaida Tejada-Vera, "Deaths: Final Data for 2014," *National Vital Statistics Reports* 65, no. 4 (June 30, 2016).

58. Samuel Preston and Michael Haines, *Fatal Years: Child Mortality in Late Nineteenth-Century America* (Princeton, NJ: Princeton University Press, 1991), 43, 122, 126, 103.

59. Preston and Haines, 60, 59.

60. Robert Fogel, *The Escape from Hunger and Premature Death, 1700–2100: Europe, America, and The Third World* (New York: Cambridge University Press, 2004), 19.

61. Dora Costa and Richard Steckel, "Long-Term Trends in Health, Welfare, and Economic Growth," in *Health and Welfare during Industrialization*, ed. Richard Steckel and Roderick Floud (Chicago: University of Chicago Press, 1997), 67.

62. Charles Wingate, "The Tenement House Problem in the United States," *Annual Reports for 1886, Made to the General Assembly of the State of Ohio, Part 2* (Columbus, OH: Westbote, 1886), 1548.

63. NYBLS, *Second Annual Report*, 149.

64. "Nebraska Calling for Help," *New York Times*, December 17, 1874, 2.

65. Alexandra M. Wagner, "Grasshoppered: America's Response to the 1874 Rocky Mountain Locust Invasion," *Nebraska History* 89 (2008): 154–67.

66. *Appleton's Cyclopaedia of American Biography: Lodge-Pickens* (New York: D. Appleton, 1888), 584; Bernarr Cresap, *Appomattox Commander: Story of General E. O. C. Ord* (San Diego, CA: A. S. Barnes, 1981).

67. Letter, Maj. Nathan Dudley, November 6, 1874, *Reports and Recommendations of Generals Pope and Ord Relative to the Ravages of Grasshoppers, 43rd Congress, 2nd Session, 1874–75, November 14, 1874* (Washington, DC: GPO, 1875), 8 (hereafter Grasshopper Letters).

68. "The Nebraska Sufferers," *Fremont [OH] Weekly Journal*, October 30, 1874, 1.

69. Philip Sheridan, Letter to the Secretary of War, Grasshopper Letters, xliv, xli.

See also Michael L. Tate, *The Frontier Army in the Settlement of the West* (Norman: University of Oklahoma Press, 1999); and Annette Atkins, *Harvest of Grief* (St. Paul: Minnesota Historical Society, 1984).

70. Charles V. Riley, *Seventh Annual Report on the Noxious, Beneficial, and Other Insects of the State of Missouri* (Jefferson City, MO: P. Egan & Carter, 1875), 150.

71. "Ten thousand persons in Nebraska and twenty thousand in Kansas must be provided for until spring, or they will die of cold and hunger" ("Destitution in Kansas and Nebraska," *American Agriculturist*, January 1875, 5). See also Jeffrey Lockwood, *Locust: The Devastating Rise and Mysterious Disappearance of the Insect That Shaped the American Frontier* (New York: Basic, 2004), 84.

72. John Hill Brinton, *Personal Memoirs of John H. Brinton: Civil War Surgeon, 1861–1865* (Carbondale: Southern Illinois University Press, 1996), 290; Lacy K. Ford, *A Companion to the Civil War and Reconstruction* (Malden, MA: Blackwell, 2005); US War Department, *The War of the Rebellion: A Compilation of the Official Records of the Union and Confederate Armies, Series 1, Volume 37, Part 2: Correspondence* (Washington, DC: GPO, 1891), 301.

73. Thomas W. Chinn, H. Mark Lai, and Philip P. Choy, *A History of the Chinese in California: A Syllabus* (San Francisco: Chinese Historical Society of America, 1969).

74. Henry Demarest Lloyd, *A Strike of Millionaires Against Miners, or the Story of Spring Valley* (Chicago: Belford-Clarke, 1890), 172.

75. Illinois Bureau of Labor Statistics (hereafter ILBLS), *Eighth Biennial Report*, 477.

76. California Bureau of Labor Statistics (hereafter CABLS), *Third Biennial Report*, 80.

77. "Died for His Children," *Evening Bulletin* [Maysville, KY], April 16, 1890, 1.

78. "Kansas Democracy," *Kansas Agitator* [Garnett, KS], August 4, 1891, 1.

79. Emile Durkheim, *Suicide: A Study in Sociology* (New York: Routledge and Kegan Paul, 1952).

80. Davis R. Dewey, "Statistics of Suicides in New England," *Publications of the American Statistical Association*, vol. 3 (Boston: Schofield, 1893), 168.

81. Florence Kelley and Alzina Stevens, "Wage-Earning Children," *Hull House Maps and Papers* (Chicago: University of Illinois Press, 2007), 86, 74.

82. Massachusetts Bureau of Statistics of Labor, *Sixth Annual Report*, 301, 445, 446.

83. Charles B. Spahr, *An Essay on the Present Distribution of Wealth in the United States* (New York: Crowell, 1896), 103, 106.

84. Lincoln Steffens, "Rhode Island: A State For Sale," *McClure's Magazine* 24, no. 4 (February 1905): 337–53.

85. US Senate Committee on Finance, *Wholesale Prices, Wages and Transportation* (Washington, DC: GPO, 1893) (hereafter Aldrich Report), 177.

86. Joseph Weeks, *Report on the Statistics of Wages in Manufacturing Industries* (Washington, DC: GPO, 1886). Weeks's tables rely on data supplied by employers (xvi), but his data are not included because they do not cover all of the 1880s.

87. Aldrich Report, 11.

88. H. M. Douty, "A Century of Wage Statistics: BLS' Contribution," *Monthly Labor Review*, November 1984, 18.

89. Gary M. Walton and Hugh Rockoff, *History of the American Economy* (Boston: Thomsen Learning, 2002), 392.

90. Clarence Long, *Wages and Earnings in the United States: 1860–1890* (Princeton, NJ: Princeton University Press, 1960), 94.

91. Robert Margo, *The Labor Force in the Late Nineteenth Century* (Cambridge, MA: National Bureau of Economic Research, 1992), 11, 15.

92. Aldrich Report, 20.

93. Frederick Waite, *Prices and Wages: A Dissection of the Senate Finance Committee's Great Report as Interpreted by Its Statistician and the Hon. Carroll D. Wright*, presented to the National Statistical Association at the Columbia University, Washington, DC, November 13, 1894, 29.

94. Charles B. Spahr, *An Essay on the Present Distribution of Wealth in the United States* (New York: Crowell, 1896), 103, 106.

95. Spahr, 103, 106–7.

96. Wesley Clair Mitchell, *Gold, Prices, and Wages Under the Greenback Standard* (Berkeley: University of California Press, 1908), 169.

97. Stanley Lebergott, *Manpower in Economic Growth* (New York: McGraw-Hill, 1964), 289.

98. Mary Furner and Barry Supple, *The State and Economic Knowledge: The American and British Experiences* (New York: Cambridge University Press, 2002), 254.

99. Colorado Bureau of Labor Statistics (COBLS), *Third Biennial Report*, 7; Iowa Bureau of Labor Statistics (hereafter IABLS), *Third Biennial Report*, 8.

100. IABLS, *Third Biennial Report*, 8.

101. Ohio Bureau of Labor Statistics (hereafter OHBLS), *First Annual Report*, 9.

102. OHBLS, *Fourteenth Annual Report*, 5.

103. Carroll Wright, *Fifth Annual Report of the Commissioner of Labor, 1889: Railroad Labor* (Washington, DC: GPO, 1890), 76.

104. OHBLS, *Eleventh Annual Report*, 7.

105. CABLS, *Second Biennial Report*, 607.

106. OHBLS, *Thirteenth Annual Report*, 5.

107. US House of Representatives, Frick Testimony, "Investigation of the Employment of Pinkerton Detectives in Connection with the Labor Troubles at Homestead, PA," *Report 2447, 52d Congress, 2nd Session, 1892–93, Congressional Edition, Vol. 3142, Issue 1* (Washington, DC: GPO, 1893), 4.

108. Pennsylvania Bureau of Labor/Industrial Statistics (hereafter PBIS), *Volume 12*, 4.

109. PBIS, *Volume 12*, 5.

110. PBIS, *Volume 12*, 3.

111. *Investigation of Labor Troubles in the Anthracite Region of Pennsylvania, 1887–1888* (Washington, DC: GPO, 1889) (hereafter 1888 Anthracite Report), vii.

112. OHBLS, *Eleventh Annual Report*, 10.

113. NJBLS, *Seventh Annual Report*, 243.

114. Wright, *Fifth Annual Report*, 82; 1888 Anthracite Report, lxiv; Carroll D. Wright, *Eighteenth Annual Report of the Commissioner of Labor* (Washington, DC: GPO, 1903), 41–46.

115. Wright, *Eighteenth Annual Report*; Massachusetts Dept. of Labor and Industries, Division of Statistics (Boston: Wright and Potter, 1887), 294.

116. ILBLS, *Sixth Biennial Report*, lx.

117. Spahr, *Essay on Present Distribution*, 95.

118. In 1883 there were only ten state bureaus of labor statistics; by 1887, twenty. See New York Department of Labor, *Report on the Growth of Industry in New York* (Albany, NY: Argus, 1904); Connecticut Bureau of Labor Statistics, *Eighteenth Annual Report*; Missouri Bureau of Labor Statistics, *Sixteenth Annual Report*, *Seventh Annual Report*, and *Fourteenth Annual Report*; IABLS, *Third Biennial Report* and *Fourth Biennial Report*; NYBLS, *Tenth Annual Report*; PBIS, *Volume 21*; Minnesota Bureau of Labor Statistics, *Second Biennial Report*; COBLS, *Third Biennial Report*; OHBLS, *Thirteenth Annual Report*; Wisconsin Bureau of Labor Statistics, *Fifth Biennial Report*.

119. OHBLS, *Fifteenth Annual* Report, 169.

120. OHBLS, *Fourteenth Annual Report*, 112; ILBLS, *Sixth Biennial Report*, lx; West Virginia Department of Labor, *Report of the Commissioner of Labor, 1893–1894* (Charleston, WV: Donnally, 1894), 76.

121. Carroll Wright, *Report on Manufacturing Industries in the United States at the Eleventh Census: Textiles* (Washington, DC: GPO, 1894), 173.

122. Wright, *Fifth Annual Report*, 101, and tables following; "Railroad Employees and Their Pay," *Brotherhood of Locomotive Firemen and Enginemen's Magazine* 14, no. 7 (July 1890): 628.

123. *1902 Anthracite Strike Report*, 196.

124. G. O. Virtue, "The Anthracite Mine Laborers," *Bulletin of the Department of Labor* 2, no. 13 (November 1897): 762.

125. John Mitchell, *Organized Labor: Its Problems, Purposes, and Ideals* (Philadelphia: Dunlap, 1903), 360.

126. Perry K. Blatz, *Democratic Miners: Work and Labor Relations in the Anthracite Coal Industry, 1875–1925* (Albany: State University Of New York Press, 1994), 9.

127. PBIS, *Volume 17*, 2.

128. Douglas Hoover, *Women in Nineteenth-Century Pullman* (Master's thesis, University of Arizona, 1988).

129. Weeks, *Report on the Statistics of Wages*, xii.

130. NJBLS, *Tenth Annual Report*, 187.

131. OHBLS, *First Annual Report*, 144.

132. NJBLS, *Tenth Annual Report*, 203.

133. NYBLS, *Second Annual Report*, 149–50.

134. "The Iron Clad Oath," *The Electrician*, May 7, 1886, 507.

135. NYBLS, 587; IABLS, *Third Biennial Report*, 171.

136. Wright, *Eighteenth Annual Report*, 61.

137. Josiah Strong, *Our Country* (New York: Baker & Taylor, 1885), 106.

138. NYBLS, *Third Annual Report*, 366.

139. NYBLS, 521; NJBLS, *Tenth Annual Report*, 20–21.

CHAPTER FOUR
A Threat of Endlessness

Roger Welsch, "Sweet Nebraska Land," Folkways Records, no. FH53337, 1965.

1. Jay Hambidge, "An Artist's Impression of the Colliery Region," *The Century* 55, no. 5 (March 1898): 822–28.

2. Hambidge, 826.

3. "Condition of Society in the Coal Regions," *Cambria Freeman* [Ebensburg, PA], July 6, 1877, 1.

4. Stephen Crane, "In the Depths of a Coal Mine," *McClure's Magazine* 3, no. 3 (August 1894): 203.

5. Michael Burgan, *Breaker Boys: How a Photograph Helped End Child Labor* (Mankato, MN: Capstone, 2011).

6. Illinois Bureau of Labor Statistics, *First Biennial Report*, 449.

7. Crane, "In the Depths," 203.

8. Anthracite Coal Strike Commission, *Report to the President on the Anthracite Coal Strike of May–October 1902* (Washington, DC: GPO, 1903) (hereafter *1902 Anthracite Strike Report*), 3.

9. Alan Derickson, *Black Lung: Anatomy of a Public Health Disaster* (Ithaca, NY: Cornell University Press, 1998), xii.

10. Andrew Roy, *A History of the Coal Miners of the United States* (Columbus, OH: Traubman, 1907), 442.

11. Ohio Bureau of Labor Statistics, *Third Annual Report*, 104–5.

12. *Annual Report of the Secretary of Internal Affairs of the Commonwealth of Pennsylvania, Vol. 12: 1884, Part 3: Industrial Statistics* (Harrisburg, PA: Hart, 1885), 60, 54.

13. Chicago, Milwaukee, and St. Paul Railway Company, pltf. in err., v. Duane O. Ross, *Cases Argued and Decided in the Supreme Court of the United States in October Term 1883, 1884, Book 28* (Rochester, NY: Lawyers Co-Operative, 1886), 789.

14. Peter Roberts, *The Anthracite Coal Communities* (New York: Macmillan, 1904), 78–79.

15. *1902 Anthracite Strike Report*, 26

16. Roberts, *Anthracite Coal Communities*, 132.

17. Leifer Magnusson, *Company Housing in the United States*, US Bureau of Labor Statistics Bulletin No. 263 (Washington, DC: GPO, 1920), 102.

18. Francis Nichols, "Children of the Coal Shadow," *McClure's Magazine* 20, no. 4 (February 1903): 435–44.

19. Henry Edward Rood, "A Pennsylvania Colliery Village," *The Century* 55, no. 5 (March 1898): 809.

20. "Down in the Coal Mines," *Abbeville [SC] Press and Banner*, March 1, 1876, 1.

21. Merle Travis, "Dark as a Dungeon," lyrics recorded by Merle Travis on August 8, 1946, Hollywood, CA, originally released as Capitol Records, no. 48001.

22. Roberts, *Anthracite Coal Communities*, 7.

23. Nichols, "Children of the Coal Shadow," 444.

24. *1902 Anthracite Strike Report*, 175.

25. *1902 Anthracite Strike Report*, 185.

26. Roberts, *Anthracite Coal Communities*, 15.

27. Roy, *History of the Coal Miners*, 275.

28. John Mitchell, *Organized Labor: Its Problems, Purposes, and Ideals* (Philadelphia: Dunlap, 1903), 359.

29. G. O. Virtue, "The Anthracite Mine Laborers," *Bulletin of the Department of Labor* 2, no. 13 (November 1897): 760.

30. Insurance Commissioner of the State of Pennsylvania, *Twelfth Annual Report, Part 2: Life and Accident Insurance* (Harrisburg, PA: Lane S. Hart, 1885), 43.

31. "Condition of Society in the Coal Regions," *Cambria Freeman*, July 6, 1877, 1.

32. Hambidge, "An Artist's Impression," 827.

33. Hambidge, 824–25.

34. Mary Harris Jones, *Autobiography of Mother Jones* (Chicago: Kerr, 1925), 113.

35. Willa Cather, *My Ántonia* (Boston: Houghton Mifflin, 1918), 75.

36. For Bierstadt see Peter Hassrick, *Albert Bierstadt: Witness to a Changing West* (Norman: University of Oklahoma Press, 2008).

37. Trina Williams, "The Homestead Act: A Major Asset-Building Policy in American History," Center for Social Development Working Paper 00-9 (Washington, DC: GPO, 2000), 5.

38. Williams, 6.

39. Williams, 12.

40. Clinton Cox, *The Forgotten Heroes: The Story of the Buffalo Soldiers* (St. Louis, MO: San Val, 1996).

41. Frank N. Schubert, *Voices of the Buffalo Soldier* (Albuquerque: University of New Mexico Press, 2009), 178.

42. Peter Mancall and Benjamin Heber Johnson, eds., *Making of the American West: People and Perspectives* (Santa Barbara, CA: ABC Clio, 2007), 148.

43. US Bureau of the Census, *Historical Statistics of the United States*, "Chapter A: Population," table A161–171, 21.

44. Susan Sessions Rugh, *Our Common Country: Family Farming, Culture, and Community in the Nineteenth-Century Midwest* (Bloomington: Indiana University Press, 2001).

45. Jeffrey G. Williamson, *Late Nineteenth-Century American Development: A General Equilibrium History* (New York: Cambridge University Press, 2008), 157; Aaron Morton Sakolski, *The Great American Land Bubble: The Amazing Story of Land-Grabbing, Speculations, and Booms from Colonial Days to the Present Time* (New York: Harper, 1932); Paul Wallace Gates, "The Homestead Law in an Incongruous Land System," *American Historical Review* 41, no. 4 (July 1936): 652–81. Aaron Sakolski trained under Carroll Wright.

46. Figures courtesy of Homestead National Monument, Beatrice, Nebraska, accessed June 12, 2020, http://www.nps.gov/home/historyculture/statenumbers.htm.

47. Joseph Frazier Wall and Bea Wall, *Grinnell College in the Nineteenth Century: From Salvation to Service* (Ames: Iowa State University Press, 1997), 6.

48. Willa Cather, *O Pioneers!* (Boston: Houghton-Mifflin, 1913), 15.

49. Hamlin Garland, *Main-Travelled Roads* (New York: Harper, 1899), 143.

50. Arthur F. Bentley, *The Condition of the Western Farmer as Illustrated by the History of One Nebraska Township* (Baltimore: Johns Hopkins University Press, 1893), 28.

51. Cass Grove Barns, *The Sod House* (Lincoln, NE: Bison Books, 1970), 58.

52. Steven R. Kinsella, *900 Miles from Nowhere: Voices from the Homestead Frontier* (Minneapolis: Minnesota Historical Society Press, 2006), 59.

53. Smithsonian Institution, "Life in a Sod House," accessed March 10, 2020, https://historyexplorer.si.edu/resource/life-sod-house-homepage.

54. "Curious Crime of a Nebraska Man," *Evening Star* [Washington, DC], May 9, 1888, 1.

55. Richard Edwards, "Why Homesteading Data Are so Poor," *Great Plains Quarterly* 28 (Summer 2008): 181–90; US Senate, *Report of the Public Lands Commission, 1905, Senate Document 189* (Washington, DC: GPO, 1905). For more on the Chrismans, see "Female Homesteaders," accessed April 14, 2020, http://www.nebraskastudies.org/en/1850-1874/who-were-the-settlers-who-was-daniel-freeman/female-homesteaders/.

56. Richard White, *"It's Your Misfortune and None of My Own": A New History of the American West* (Norman: University of Oklahoma Press, 1991), 228.

57. Barb Ogg, "Wolf Spiders in Nebraska," accessed January 5, 2020, http://lancaster.unl.edu/pest/resources/wolfspider.shtml.

58. "Habits of the Locust at Night," *First Annual Report of the United States Entomological Commission* (Washington, DC: GPO, 1878), appendix 17, 209.

59. Oliver Kelley, "Minnesota," in *Report of the Commissioner of Agriculture for the Year 1863* (Washington, DC: GPO, 1863), 36.

60. Barbara Handy-Marchello, *Women of the Northern Plains: Gender and Settlement on the Homestead* (St. Paul: Minnesota Historical Society Press, 2005), 27.

61. Ora A. Clement, "The Blizzard of 1888," in *Roundup: A Nebraska Reader*, ed. Virginia Faulkner (Lincoln: University of Nebraska Press, 1957), 263–69.

62. "The Blizzard," *New York Times*, January 14, 1888, 4.

63. Handy-Marchello, *Women of the Northern Plains*, 30.

64. "The Doctor" and "The Doctor's Wife," in *Roundup: A Nebraska Reader*, ed. Virginia Faulkner (Lincoln: University of Nebraska Press, 1957), 11–18.

65. Eric Monkkonen, *Police in Urban America, 1860–1920* (New York: Cambridge University Press, 1981), 88–89.

66. J. V. N. Yates, "Report on the Subject of Pauperism," *Journal of the Assembly, State of New York, 1824* (Albany: Leake & Croswell, 1824), 386–99 (italics added).

67. Mathew Carey, *Miscellaneous Essays* (Philadelphia: Carey and Hart, 1830), 154–56, 157–58, 163, 166 (italics in the originals).

68. Michigan State Board of Corrections and Charities, *Third Biennial Report of the Board of State Commissioners for the General Supervision of Charitable, Penal, Pauper and Reformatory Institutions* (Lansing, MI: W. S. George, 1876) (hereafter *Third Michigan Report*), 15–16.

69. *Third Michigan Report*, 16, 17.

70. *Third Michigan Report*, 11.

71. *Third Michigan Report*, 195, 196.

72. Wisconsin State Board of Charities and Reform (hereafter WSBCR), *Report Volume 9, Part 1879* (Madison, WI: David Atwood, 1880), 24.

73. Guy Ashton Brown, *The Compiled Statutes of the State of Nebraska, 1881* (Omaha, NE: Gibson, Miller & Richardson, 1887), 545.

74. Elijah Middlebrook Haines, *A Compilation of the Laws of Illinois, Relating to Township Organization and Management of County Affairs* (Chicago: Legal Advisor, 1883), 320–21.

75. New York State Department of Social Services, *Annual Report of the State Board of Charities for the Year 1891* (Albany, NY: James R. Lyon, 1891), 59; New York State Board of Charities (hereafter NYSBC), *Eleventh Annual Report* (Albany, NY: Jerome Permenter, 1878), 289.

76. WSBCR, *Volume 9*: "siding," 42; "inhuman," 40.

77. New York Department of Social Welfare, *Thirteenth Annual Report of the State Board of Charities* (Albany, NY: Weed, Parsons, 1880), 188–92.

78. "Patients Almost Starved," *New York Times*, January 27, 1886, 2.

79. WSBCR, *Fourth Biennial Report*, 91–94.

80. NYSBC, *Annual Report for the Year 1893* (Albany, NY: James Lyon, 1894); for "stomach": 488.

81. Mrs. Charles Russell Lowell, "The Economic and Moral Effects of Public Outdoor Relief," *Proceedings of the National Conference of Charities and Correction, May 14–21, 1890* (Boston: George Ellis, 1890), 81.

82. Joan Waugh, *Unsentimental Reformer: The Life of Josephine Shaw Lowell* (Cambridge, MA: Harvard University Press: 1997), 104; Katherine Kish Sklar, *Florence Kelley*

and the Nation's Work: The Rise of Women's Political Culture (New Haven, CT: Yale University Press, 1992), 149.

83. Lowell, "Economic and Moral Effects," 82.

84. NYSBC, *Seventeenth Annual Report* (Albany, NY: Weed, Parsons, 1884), 160.

85. Michael Katz, *In the Shadow of the Poorhouse* (New York: Basic, 1996), 39.

86. John Middlemist Herrick and Paul H. Stuart, *Encyclopedia of Social Welfare History in North America* (Thousand Oaks, CA: Sage, 2005), 276.

87. Amos Griswold Warner, George Elliott Howard, and Mary Roberts Coolidge, *American Charities* (New York: Thomas Crowell, 1894), 217.

88. Stephen Humphreys Villiers Gurteen, *A Handbook of Charity Organization* (Buffalo, NY: Self-published, 1882), 123.

89. Charity Organization Society of the City of New York, *Hand-book for Friendly Visitors among the Poor* (New York: Putnam, 1883), 1 (italics added).

90. Charles Loring Brace, *The Life of Charles Loring Brace: Chiefly Told in His Own Letters*, vol. 3., ed. "By His Daughter" (New York: Scribners, 1894), 171–74.

91. Cather, *My Ántonia*, 304.

CHAPTER FIVE

To Advance Agriculture

Caroline Arabella Hall, "The Hand that Holds the Bread," *Songs for the Grange* (Philadelphia: Wagenseller, 1874).

1. Rhoda R. Gilman and Patricia Smith, "Oliver Hudson Kelley, Minnesota Pioneer, 1849–1868," *Minnesota History* 40, no. 7 (Fall 1967): 330–38.

2. William D. Barns, "Oliver Hudson Kelley and the Genesis of the Grange: A Reappraisal," *Agricultural History* 41, no. 3 (July 1967): 229–42; Thomas A. Woods, *Knights of the Plow: Oliver H. Kelley and the Origins of the Grange in Republican Ideology* (Ames: Iowa State University Press, 1991); Dennis Sven Nordin, *Rich Harvest: A History of the Grange, 1867–1900* (Oxford: University Press of Mississippi, 1974).

3. Kelley farm exhibit, Minnesota Historical Society Museum, Elk River, Minnesota.

4. Woods, *Knights of the Plow*, 41.

5. Woods, 38.

6. Oliver Hudson Kelley, *Origin and Progress of the Order of the Patrons of Husbandry in the United States* (Philadelphia: Wagenseller, 1875), 15.

7. "The Schoolmaster," *National Teacher* 2, no. 8 (August 1872): 262, 261, 263.

8. "The School Master," 263.

9. When Rowena meets Ivanhoe he mentions the "mean precincts of a country grange," to which she replies, "Sir Knight the grange which you contemn hath been my shelter from infancy; and, trust me, when I leave it—should that day ever arrive—it shall be with one who has not learnt to despise the dwelling and manners in which I have been brought up." Sir Walter Scott, *Ivanhoe* (Paris: Baudry, 1835), 199.

10. Kelley, *Origin and Progress*, 17.

11. Charles Postel, *Equality: An American Dilemma, 1866–1896* (New York: Farrar, Straus & Giroux, 2019), 42.

12. Kelley, *Origin and Progress*, 19.

13. Kelley, 423.

14. Caroline Arabella Hall, *Songs for the Grange* (Philadelphia: Wagenseller, 1874), 4, 16–17.

15. Donald Marti, "Sisters of the Grange: Rural Feminism in the Late Nineteenth Century," *Agricultural History* 58, no. 3 (July 1984): 249.

16. Marti, 248.

17. Marti, 253.

18. Marti, 254.

19. Woods, *Knights of the Plow*, 47.

20. Woods, 47.

21. W. S. Harwood, "Secret Societies in America," *North American Review* 164, no. 5 (May 1897): 623.

22. Mark Smith, *Listening to Nineteenth-Century America* (Chapel Hill: University of North Carolina Press, 2001).

23. "Patrons of Husbandry," *Rocky Mountain Husbandman* [Diamond City, MT], April 6, 1876, 6.

24. "Notes and Opinion," *Chicago Daily Tribune*, June 24, 1873, 4.

25. Ignatius Donnelly, *Donnelliana* (Chicago: Schulte, 1892), 131.

26. Daniel J. Boorstin, *The Americans: The National Experience* (New York: Random House, 1965), 308, 312.

27. Bennett Valley Grape Growers, "History," accessed January 17, 2022, https://bvgg.org/history.

28. Masonic Museum, "Patrons of Husbandry," accessed September 22, 2020, http://www.phoenixmasonry.org/masonicmuseum/fraternalism/grange.htm.

29. "Patrons of Husbandry," *Rocky Mountain Husbandman*, April 6, 1876, 6.

30. "National News," *Rocky Mountain Husbandman*, December 9, 1875, 6.

31. "Patrons of Husbandry," *Vermont Farmer* [Newport, VT], December 3, 1875, 3. This section as titled here and earlier often posted news sent by Hall and Kelley.

32. "From Tennessee," *Patron of Husbandry* [Columbus, MS], July 31, 1880, 4.

33. Postel, *Equality*; Garry Wills, *Lincoln at Gettysburg* (New York: Simon & Schuster, 1992).

34. Theodore Saloutos, "The Grange in the South, 1870–1877," *Journal of Southern History* 19, no. 4 (November 1953): 477.

35. Kelley, *Origin and Progress*, 86.

36. Kelley, 92.

37. Woods, *Knights of the Plow*, 191.

38. Kelley, *Origin and Progress*, 117.

39. Kelley, 97.

40. Kelley, 202.

41. "Oje Town," *Red Cloud [NE] Chief*, March 12, 1874, 2.

42. Hamlin Garland, *A Son of the Middle Border* (New York: Macmillan, 1917), 165–66.

43. "Communicated," *Red Cloud Chief*, January 11, 1877, 2.

44. Kelley, *Origin and Progress*, 361.

45. *The Connecticut Granges* (New Haven: Industrial, 1900), xii.

46. *Proceedings of the Seventh Session of the National Grange of the Patrons of Husbandry* (New York: S. W. Green, 1874), 80.

47. Charles Person, "The Outcome of the Granger Movement," *Popular Science Monthly* 32 (January 1888): 369.

48. Person, 378.

49. Saloutos, "Grange in the South."

50. "Grange Store" and "New Goods," *Red Cloud Chief*, December 16, 1874, 4, and January 20, 1875, 3, respectively.

51. *Proceedings of the Seventh Session*, 22.

52. *Proceedings of the Eighth Session of the National Grange of the Patrons of Husbandry* (Claremont, NH: Claremont Manufacturing, 1875), 33, 6.

53. "Grangers Secede," *Nebraska Advertiser* [Brownville, NE], July 23, 1874, 2.

54. *Proceedings of the Seventh Session*, 12.

55. *Proceedings of the Seventh Session*, 32.

56. *Proceedings of the Seventh Session*, 58–59; and Thomas Clark Atkeson, *Semi-Centennial History of the Patrons of Husbandry* (New York: Judd, 1924), 71. Introduced in 1874, these principles were reinforced in later meetings.

57. *Proceedings of the Ninth Session of the National Grange of the Patrons of Husbandry* (Louisville, KY: Morton, 1875), 177.

58. *Proceedings of the Thirteenth Session of the National Grange of the Patrons of Husbandry* (Philadelphia: Wagenseller, 1879), 7.

59. Kelley, *Origin and Progress*, 256.

60. Woods, *Knights of the Plow*, 192.

61. Woods, 187.

62. Hall, *Songs for the Grange*, 101, 81.

63. Woods, *Knights of the Plow*, 202.

64. *Journal of the Proceedings of the Eleventh Session of the National Grange of the Patrons of Husbandry* (Louisville, KY: John Morton: 1878), 136.

65. *Proceedings of the Twelfth Session of the National Grange of the Patrons of Husbandry* (Philadelphia: Wagenseller, 1878), 37.

66. The slight continues. A National Grange Facebook post on the December 4, 2021, anniversary of the founding says, "Oliver Kelley and six men founded the Order of the Patrons of Husbandry." See https://www.facebook.com/photo.php?fbid=26

9087981910350&set=a.2219117366627975&type=3&theater, accessed December 23, 2021.

67. Annie Diggs, "The Women in the Alliance," *The Arena* 6, no. 30 (July 1892): 161–79.

68. Atkeson, *Semi-Centennial History*, 350.

69. Person, "Outcome," 369.

70. Sharon Sessions Rugh, *Our Common Country* (Bloomington: Indiana University Press, 2001), 143.

71. "What Will the Grangers Do?," *Red Cloud Chief*, July 18, 1874, 4.

72. Solon Buck, *The Agrarian Crusade* (New Haven, CT: Yale University Press, 1920), 34.

73. "Platform of Principles Adopted by the State Grange of Kansas," *Weekly Kansas Chief* [Troy, KS], August 7, 1873, 2.

74. *The Constitution of the State of Illinois as Adopted in Convention*, May 18, 1870 (Chicago: Western News, 1870), 36. For a detailed discussion, see Mark T. Kanazawa and Roger G. Noll, "The Origins of State Railroad Regulation: The Illinois Constitution of 1870," in *The Regulated Economy: A Historical Approach to Political Economy*, ed. Claudia Goldin and Gary D. Libecap (Chicago: University of Chicago Press, 1994), 13–54; and George H. Miller, *Railroads and the Granger Laws* (Madison: University of Wisconsin Press, 1971).

75. Buck, *Agrarian Crusade*, 59.

76. Munn v. Illinois, 94 U.S. 113.

77. US Bureau of the Census (hereafter USBC), *Historical Statistics of the United States*, "Chapter K: Agriculture," corn and wheat: table K502–516, 512; cotton: table K550–553, 517; potatoes: table K532–537, 515.

78. USBC, table K1–16, 457.

79. Yields appear in the tables cited in the previous notes. Regarding rainfalls, see Cary Mock, "Rainfall in the Garden of the United States Great Plains, 1870–1899," *Climatic Change* 44 (2000): 173–95.

80. "The Grange Lecturer," *Farmer and Mechanic* [Raleigh, NC], November 8, 1877, 3.

81. "Value of the Grange to Farmers," *Rocky Mountain Husbandman* [Diamond City, MT], June 1, 1876, 6.

82. Woods, *Knights of the Plow*, xx.

83. *Journal of Proceedings of the Thirty-First Session of the National Grange of the Patrons of Husbandry* (Mechanicsburg, PA: Farmer's Press, 1897).

CHAPTER SIX

To Win Fair Treatment for the Living

George Korson, *Songs and Ballads of the Anthracite Miners* (Library of Congress, AFS L16, Washington, DC, 1976), 3.

1. Pennsylvania Senate, *Report of the Judiciary Committee, General, in Relation to the Anthracite Coal Difficulties* (Harrisburg, PA: Singerly, 1871) (hereafter 1871 Anthracite Hearings), 182. I am indebted to Anthony F. C. Wallace's views of Siney's three "identities." See Wallace, *St. Clair: A Nineteenth-Century Coal Town's Experience with a Disaster-Prone Industry* (Ithaca, NY: Cornell University Press, 1988); also Edward Pinkowski, *John Siney, The Miners' Martyr* (Philadelphia: Sunshine, 1963); and Charles Edward Killeen, *John Siney: The Pioneer in American Industrial Unionism and Industrial Government* (Madison: University of Wisconsin, 1975). For more on Siney, particularly his involvement with bituminous coal miners and events like the Clearfield strike, see Andrew Arnold, *Fueling the Gilded Age: Railroads, Miners, and Disorder in Pennsylvania Coal Country* (New York: New York University Press, 2014). Arnold's interindustrial focus on bituminous miners contrasts with this book's focus on the anthracite regions.

2. Andrew Roy, *A History of the Coal Miners of the United States* (Columbus, OH: J. L. Trauger, 1907), 228.

3. Pennsylvania Bureau of Labor/Industrial Statistics, *First Annual Report*, 532.

4. US Bureau of Labor, *Annual Report of the Commissioner of Labor*, vol. 2 (Washington, DC: GPO, 1887), 1130.

5. *Commonwealth vs. John Hunt & Others*, 4 Met. 111, 45 Mass. 111, March 1842, accessed October 21, 2019, http://masscases.com/cases/sjc/45/45mass111.html.

6. John R. Commons, David Joseph Saposs, Helen Laura Sumner, John B. Andrews, Selig Perlman, and Henry Elmer Hoagland, *History of Labour in the United States*, vol. 2 (New York: Macmillan, 1918), 47.

7. William H. Sylvis and James C. Sylvis, *The Life, Speeches, Labors, and Essays of William H. Sylvis* (Philadelphia: Claxton, Remsen, Haffelfinger, 1872), 65.

8. Sylvis and Sylvis, 233.

9. Carroll Wright, *The First Annual Report of the Commissioner of Labor: Industrial Depressions* (Washington, DC: GPO, 1886), 81–85; "A Patent Case of General Interest," *Scientific American*, July 17, 1880, 33.

10. Massachusetts Bureau of Statistics of Labor (hereafter MABLS), *Sixteenth Annual Report*, 183.

11. Wright, *First Annual Report*, 81.

12. Wright, 80.

13. George Edwin McNeill, *The Labor Movement: The Problem of To-day* (New York: Hazen, 1888), 133.

14. David Montgomery, "William H. Sylvis and the Search for Working Class Citizenship," in *Labor Leaders in America*, ed. Melvyn Dubofsky and Warren R. Van Tine (Urbana: University of Illinois Press, 1987), 14.

15. "Workingmen's Platform," *Evening Argus* [Rock Island, IL], September 1, 1866, 2.

16. Sylvis and Sylvis, *Life, Speeches, Labors*, 84.

17. "The National Labor Congress," *New York Herald*, September 22, 1868, 4.

18. Sylvis and Sylvia, *Life, Speeches, Labors*, 68.

19. "The National Labor Congress," *New York Herald*, September 26, 1868, 8.

20. "The National Labor Congress," September 26, 1868.

21. Carole Turbin, *Working Women of Collar City: Gender, Class, and Community in Troy, 1864–1886* (Urbana: University of Illinois Press, 1992), 113, 143–44; Gina Sigillito, *The Daughters of Maeve: 50 Irish Women Who Changed the World* (New York: Citadel, 2007), 52–55. Mullaney's name is spelled Mullany in some sources. Her death certificate, mother's will, and court records use "Mullaney." Census records, directory listings, church records, cemetery records, and most of the obituaries omit the "e." See US Department of the Interior, National Park Service, National Historic Landmark Nomination—Kate Mullany House, September 4, 1997, https://www.katemullanynhs.org/landmark-nomination.

22. "The National Labor Congress," *New York Herald*, September 27, 1868, 5.

23. Montgomery, "William H. Sylvis and the Search for Working Class Citizenship," 24.

24. "Condition of Society in the Coal Regions," *Cambria Freeman* [Ebensburg, PA], July 6, 1877, 1.

25. G. O. Virtue, "The Anthracite Mine Laborers," *Bulletin of the Department of Labor* 2, no. 13 (November 1897): 732.

26. 1871 Anthracite Hearings, 20; MABLS, *Twelfth Annual Report*, 21–44.

27. 1871 Anthracite Hearings, 197, 200–201.

28. 1871 Anthracite Hearings, 197.

29. For "Hatton," see Sandra Campbell, "For 110, the 'Fine' Avondale Mine Was a Disaster," *Mine Safety & Health*, January–February 1980, 20; J. Stewart Richards, *Death in the Mines: Disasters and Rescues in the Anthracite Coal Fields of Pennsylvania* (Charleston, SC: History Press, 2007). For "impossible" see "The Mining Holocaust," *Evening Telegraph* [Philadelphia, PA], September 8, 1869, Fifth Edition, 1.

30. Philip S. Klein and Ari Hoogenboom, *A History of Pennsylvania* (Englewood Cliffs, NJ: McGraw Hill, 1973), 323.

31. Terence Powderly, *The Path I Trod; The Autobiography of Terence V. Powderly*, ed. Harry J. Carman, Henry David, and Paul N. Guthrie (New York: Columbia University Press, 1940), 24; Richard Oestreicher, "Terence Powderly, the Knights of Labor and Artisanal Republicanism," in *Labor Leaders in America*, ed. Melvyn Dubofsky, and Warren R. Van Tine (Urbana: University of Illinois Press, 1987), 30–62.

32. "Special Notices," *Charleston [SC] Daily News*, September 18, 1869, 1.

33. *Memphis [TN] Daily Appeal*, September 15, 1869, 2.

34. "Governor's Message," *Bedford [PA] Gazette*, January 13, 1870, 1.

35. Pennsylvania General Assembly, *Journal of the Senate of the Commonwealth of Pennsylvania for the Session Begun at Harrisburg on the Third Day of January, 1871* (Harrisburg: PA: B. Singerly, 1871), 529.

36. Figure based on total anthracite mine workers from 1876 to 1900. The actual total is 3,596, but this is probably a bit high since it includes all anthracite workers. Figures

from US Bureau of the Census, *Historical Statistics of the United States: Colonial Times to 1970*, Chapter M: Minerals, (Washington, DC: GPO, 1975), 593.

37. Anthracite Coal Strike Commission, *Report to the President of the Anthracite Coal Strike of May–October 1902* (Washington, DC: GPO, 1903), 29; Albert Fay, *Coal Mine Fatalities in the United States, 1870–1914* (Washington, DC: Bureau of Mines, 1914), 24.

38. Marvin W. Schlegel, *Ruler of the Reading: The Life of Franklin B. Gowen, 1836–1889* (Harrisburg: Archives Publishing of Pennsylvania, 1947), 273.

39. 1871 Anthracite Hearings, 81.

40. 1871 Anthracite Hearings, 224.

41. Marvin W. Schlegel, "America's First Cartel," *Pennsylvania History* 13, no. 1 (January 1946): 1–16.

42. 1871 Anthracite Hearings, 204, 147.

43. 1871 Anthracite Hearings: "you nor any other," 107; "hoarded," 243; "minds," 232.

44. 1871 Anthracite Hearings, 97.

45. 1871 Anthracite Hearings, 197.

46. 1871 Anthracite Hearings, 4. The final words come from William Thomas Thornton, *On Labour, Its Wrongful Claims and Rightful Dues, Its Actual Present and Possible Future* (Macmillan: London, 1870), 248.

47. PABLS, *First Annual Report*, 533–37.

48. Carroll Wright, *Third Annual Report of the Commissioner of Labor, 1887: Strikes and Lockouts* (Washington, DC: GPO, 1887), 1091.

49. "Northern Miners on the Rampage," *Nashville [TN] Union and American*, October 28, 1874, 1.

50. Wallace, *St. Clair*, 427.

51. James Patrick Shalloo, *Private Police: With Special Reference to Pennsylvania* (Philadelphia: American Academy of Political and Social Science, 1933), 61.

52. Spencer Sadler, *Pennsylvania's Coal and Iron Police* (Chicago: Arcadia, 2009), 8.

53. Allan Pinkerton, *Strikers, Communists, Tramps, and Detectives* (New York: Carleton, 1878), xii.

54. "Pinkerton's Preventive Patrol," *Locomotive Fireman's Magazine*, October 1888, 726.

55. Albert Burgoyne states: "The chiefs could control, on a day's notice, a force of 2,000 drilled men, and this could be expanded by drawing on the reserves registered on the books of the agency for service on demand, to 30,000, if necessary—more men than are enrolled in the standing army of the United States." See Burgoyne, *Homestead: A Complete History of the Struggle of July, 1892, Between the Carnegie Steel Company, Limited, and the Amalgamated Association of Iron and Steel Workers* (Pittsburgh, PA: Rawsthorne, 1893), 43.

56. "Provoked by Carnegie," *New York Times*, July 7, 1892.

57. US Department of State, *United States Statutes at Large: 1891–1893* (Washington, DC: GPO, 1893), 591.

58. Allan Pinkerton to George Bangs, May 18, 1873, Pinkerton MS, box 47, folder 7, Library of Congress, Washington, DC.

59. Allan Pinkerton and Benjamin Franklin to F. B. Gowen, November 13, 1874, Reading Company File Related to the Pinkerton Detective Agency, Hagley Digital Archives, accessed February 22, 2020, https://digital.hagley.org.

60. "End of the Long Strike," *Chicago Tribune*, June 16, 1875, 4.

61. MABLS, *Twelfth Annual Report*, 21.

62. "Deferred Articles," *The Jeffersonian* [Stroudsburg, PA], August 31, 1854, 1.

63. Kevin Kenny, "Nativism, Labor, and Slavery: The Political Odyssey of Benjamin Bannan, 1850–1860," *Pennsylvania Magazine of History and Biography* 118, no. 4 (October 1994): 326–51.

64. *Columbia Democrat and Star of the North* [Bloomsburg, PA], May 30, 1866, 2.

65. Kenny, "Nativism, Labor, and Slavery," 332.

66. "Condition of Society," *Cambria Freeman*, 1.

67. Grace Palladino, *Another Civil War: Labor, Capital, and the State in the Anthracite Regions of Pennsylvania, 1840–1868* (New York: Fordham University Press, 2006), 13.

68. "Condition of Society," *Cambria Freeman*, 1.

69. "Political Notes," *Portland [ME] Daily Press*, July 22, 1871, 2.

70. Wilkes University Election Statistics Project, accessed March 7, 2018, https://staffweb.wilkes.edu/harold.cox/index.html. Anthony Wallace shows the Irish population grew to 27 percent by 1880.

71. Anne Flaherty, "The 'Molly Kings' and Greenback Labor Reform," in *From John Kehoe's Cell*, accessed February 22, 2020, http://mythofmollymaguires.blogspot.com/p/the-molly-kings-and-greenback-labor_29.html.

72. This is referenced in numerous places but the best explanation of it comes from Kevin Kenny, *Making Sense of the Molly Maguires* (New York: Oxford University Press, 1998), 236.

73. 1871 Anthracite Hearings, 19.

74. 1871 Anthracite Hearings, 32.

75. Allan Pinkerton and Benjamin Franklin to F. B. Gowen, October 29, 1873, Reading Company File Related to the Pinkerton Detective Agency, Hagley Digital Archives, , accessed February 22, 2020, https://digital.hagley.org. The spelling of McParlan/McParland continues to cause problems because in truth both are correct: he added the extra letter in middle age. At the time of the Molly Maguire trials he was using McParlan, so this spelling is used to avoid source confusion.

76. "Molly Maguire Assassins," *Daily State Journal* [Alexandria, VA], August 14, 1872, 1. The same story was circulated to several other papers such as "Molly Maguire Assassins," *Daily Dispatch* [Richmond, VA], August 15, 1872, 1.

77. "Ireland," *Somerset [PA] Herald and Farmers' and Mechanics' Register*, October 13, 1846, 2. The article quotes an Irish publication, *The Clare Journal*.

78. "A New Secret Order," *Glasgow [MO] Weekly Times*, October 8, 1857, 2.

79. "Outrages in the North," *Nashville [TN] Union and American*, March 17, 1871, 2.

80. "Molly Maguires," *Evening Telegraph* [Philadelphia], December 15, 1868, 5th ed., 1; "The 'Molly Maguires,'" *Memphis Daily Appeal*, December 22, 1868, 1.

81. "Crime," *Chicago Daily Tribune*, November 26, 1873, 8.

82. William Gannaway Brownlow, *Americanism Contrasted with Foreignism, Romanism and Bogus Democracy in the Light of Reason, History and Scripture; In which Certain Demagogues in Tennessee, and Elsewhere Are Shown Up in Their True Colors* (Nashville, TN: Self-published, 1856), 110.

83. Pinkerton and Franklin to Gowen, November 13, 1874.

84. The "rat" was Jimmy Kerrigan. See Kenny, *Making Sense*, 30.

85. *The Commonwealth vs. John Kehoe et al.* (Pottsville, PA: Miners Journal Book and Job Rooms, 1876), 177.

86. Kenny, *Making Sense*, 201.

87. "Condition of Society," *Cambria Freeman*, 1.

88. USBLS, *Chapter V: Business Enterprise*, table V20–30, 741–55.

89. "King of Frauds," *Charleston [SC] Daily News*, September 11, 1872, 1.

90. "The Icemen's Strike," *National Republican* [Washington, DC], January 4, 1877, 1.

91. John Burroughs, "Our River," *Scribner's Monthly* 20, no. 4 (August 1880): 481–93.

92. Tom Lewis, *The Hudson: A History* (Harrisonburg, VA: Donnelly, 2006), 244.

93. "The Reduction of the Army and the Establishment of a Militia," *Anderson [Court House, SC] Intelligencer*, August 23, 1877, 1.

94. Commonwealth of Pennsylvania, *Report of the Committee Appointed to Investigate the Railroad Riots in July, 1877* (Harrisburg, PA: Hart, 1878) (hereafter Pennsylvania Riot Committee Report), 682, 551, 560, 591.

95. *The Biographical Encyclopaedia of Pennsylvania* (Philadelphia: Galaxy, 1874), 536; Robert Bruce, *1877: Year of Violence* (Chicago: Ivan Dee, 1989), 59–65.

96. Pennsylvania Riot Committee Report, 22.

97. Pennsylvania Riot Committee Report, 671.

98. "A Detective's Views," *Juniata Sentinel and Republican* [Mifflintown, PA], July 25, 1877, 2.

99. Pennsylvania Riot Committee Report, 684.

100. Michael Caplinger and John Bond, The Baltimore and Ohio Railroad Martinsburg Shops, National Park Service, National Historic Landmark Nomination, form 10-900, October 2003.

101. Miller Center, Presidential Speeches: Rutherford B. Hayes, July 18, 1877, "Message Regarding Railroad Strike," University of Virginia, https://millercenter.org/the-presidency/presidential-speeches/july-18-1877-message-regarding-railroad-strike.

102. "The Use of the Regular Army as a Police Unconstitutional," *The Sun* [New York, NY], August 4, 1877, 2.

103. Scott Reynolds Nelson, *Iron Confederacies: Southern Railways, Klan Violence, and Reconstruction* (Chapel Hill: University of North Carolina Press, 1999), 74.

104. Thomas Scott, "The Recent Strikes," *North American Review* 125, no. 258 (September–October 1877): 356, 361.

105. Michael A. Bellesiles, *1877: America's Year of Living Violently* (New York: New Press, 2010).

106. Pennsylvania Riot Committee Report, 135.

107. Scott, "The Recent Strikes," 357.

108. Pennsylvania Riot Committee Report, 18.

109. Pennsylvania Riot Committee Report, 763, 93.

110. Pennsylvania Riot Committee Report, 789.

111. "The Strikers' Camp," *New Orleans [LA] Daily Democrat*, July 28, 1877, 1.

112. Pennsylvania Riot Committee Report, 22.

113. "The Strikers' Camp," July 28, 1877.

114. Pennsylvania Riot Committee Report, 31, 38.

115. "Strikes and Lockouts Prior to 1881" in Carroll Wright, *Third Annual Report of the Commissioner of Labor, 1887: Strikes and Lockouts* (Washington, DC: GPO, 1888), 1067–79.

116. David Stowell, *The Great Strikes of 1877* (Champaign: University of Illinois Press, 2008); David Stowell, *Streets, Railroads, and the Great Strike of 1877* (Chicago: University of Chicago Press, 1999). See also Eric Foner, *Reconstruction: America's Unfinished Revolution, 1863–1877* (New York: HarperCollins, 2002); Clayton David Laurie and Ronald H. Cole, *The Role of Federal Military Forces in Domestic Disorders, 1877–1945* (Washington, DC: US Army, 1997); and Philip S. Foner, *The Great Labor Uprising of 1877* (New York: Pathfinder, 2002).

117. Karl Marx, *The Letters of Karl Marx*, ed. Saul Kussiel Padover (Englewood Cliffs, NJ: Prentice-Hall, 1979), 318.

118. "Women on a Strike," *National Republican* [Washington, DC], August 16, 1877, 1.

119. "Current Opinion," *Chicago [IL] Daily Tribune*, September 17, 1877, 6.

120. J. R. Kendrick, *The Carpet Industry of Philadelphia, Annual Report of the Secretary of Internal Affairs of the Commonwealth of Pennsylvania, Vol. 18, Part 3, Industrial Statistics* (Harrisburg, PA: E. K. Meyers, 1890): Murkland weaver, 16; wages for 1880, 32.

121. Palladino, *Another Civil War*, 13.

122. Joseph A. Dacus, *Annals of the Great Strikes in the United States* (Chicago: L. T. Palmer, 1877), 5.

123. Ohio Bureau of Labor Statistics (OHBLS), *First Annual Report*, 289.

124. Barbara Freese, *Coal: A Human History* (New York: Basic, 2003), 134.

125. "New and Other Notings," *Cambria Freeman* [Ebensburg, PA], July 27, 1877, 2.

126. Schlegel, *Ruler of the Reading*, 269.

127. "State Items," *Juniata Sentinel and Republican* [Mifflintown, PA], April 28, 1880, 2.

128. Frank Julian Warne, "The Union Movement Among Coal Mining Workers," *Bulletin of the Bureau of Labor* 51 (Washington, DC: GPO, 1904), 381.

129. Kenny, *Making Sense*, 286.

CHAPTER SEVEN
From Some Lofty Height of Vision

National Greenback Campaign Songs, as sung by the Des Moines Greenback Glee Club (Des Moines: Mills, 1878).

1. John Hicks, "The Political Career of Ignatius Donnelly," *Mississippi Valley Historical Review* 8, no. 1–2 (June–September 1921): "erratic," 104; "impractical," 94; "a political nuisance," 87; "a parliamentarian of extraordinary skill and a born politician," 83.

2. Barton Shaw, *The Wool-Hat Boys* (Baton Rouge: Louisiana State University Press, 1984), 167.

3. Ad for W. R. Warner & Co., *Charleston [SC] Daily News*, May 21, 1872, 3.

4. Alexander Campbell, *The True Greenback: Or, The Way to Pay the National Debt Without Taxes, and Emancipate Labor* (Chicago: Republican Book and Job Office, 1868), 7.

5. Frederick Emory Haynes, *Third Party Movements Since the Civil War, with a Special Reference to Iowa* (Iowa City, IA: The State Historical Society of Iowa, 1916), 108.

6. Ohio numbers and quote: Ohio State Grange of Patrons of Husbandry, *Journal of Proceedings of the Third Annual Session* (Sandusky, OH: Register Steam, 1876), 10, 17; for Indiana numbers, see Logan Esarey, *A History of Indiana from 1850 to the Present* (Indianapolis: Bowen, 1918), 854.

7. "Speech of the Hon. Geo. H. Pendleton," *Evening Argus* [Rock Island, IL], September 21, 1867, 2.

8. "Paper Money," *Chicago Daily Tribune*, November 14, 1873, 3.

9. "Campbellism," *Ottawa [IL] Free Trader*, December 27, 1873, 4.

10. "Political," *Chicago Daily Tribune*, June 13, 1874, 12.

11. "Reform," *Indiana Farmer* 9, no. 23 (June 13, 1874), 1.

12. "Political," *Chicago Daily Tribune*, March 12, 1875, 2.

13. "West and South," *Jasper [IN] Weekly Courier*, September 10, 1875, 2.

14. "Political," March 12, 1875, 2.

15. "Greenback Enthusiasts," *Chicago Daily Tribune*, March 13, 1875, 9.

16. "The Wonderful Growth of the Independent Party," *Anti-Monopolist* [Saint Paul, MN], October 5, 1876, 1. This was Donnelly's paper.

17. "The Indianapolis Riot," *Chicago Daily Tribune*, May 5, 1876, 2.

18. "The Independent Greenbackers," *Anti-Monopolist* [St. Paul, MN], May 25, 1876, 2. Although biased, Donnelly's notes of the Indianapolis convention are probably the best guide.

19. "The Independent Greenbackers," 7.

20. Matthew Hild, *Greenbackers, Knights of Labor, and Populists: Farmer-Labor*

Insurgency in the Late-Nineteenth-Century South (Athens, GA: University of Georgia Press, 2007), 26.

21. "The Lincoln and Johnson Parties," *Highland Weekly News* [Hillsborough, OH], October 4, 1866, 1.

22. Frank Klement, "'Brick' Pomeroy and the Democratic Processes: A Study in Civil War Politics," paper presented to the 92nd annual meeting of the Wisconsin Academy of Sciences, Arts and Letters, 1961, 159–69.

23. "Brick Pomeroy's Campaign Smoking Tobacco," Library of Congress, accessed May 14, 2021, https://www.loc.gov/resource/cph.3b37054/.

24. Ignatius Donnelly, *Donnelliana* (Chicago: Donohue & Henneberry, 1892), pt. 6.

25. "What Will They Do Now?" *Grange Advance* [Red Wing, MN], May 24, 1876, 4.

26. All quotes in this paragraph are from "Startling Facts," *Emporia [KS] News*, November 1, 1878, 2.

27. "Startling Facts," November 1, 1878.

28. "The Natural Affiliation of the Greenbackers," *Sacramento Daily Record-Union*, September 11, 1880, 5.

29. *Report of the Judge Advocate General on "The Order of American Knights" Alias "The Sons of Liberty": A Western Conspiracy in Aid of the Southern Rebellion* (Washington, DC: Chronicle, 1864), 5.

30. Dewees is usually cited as Hughes's nephew, but the two were definitely partners in a Pottsville law firm, meaning he was authoring a book that was lauding the achievements of his partner. The timing of the book also fits with Hughes's switch to the Greenback Party.

31. Francis Wade Hughes, *Commonwealth Versus Patrick Hester, Patrick Tully, and Peter McHugh: Tried and Convicted of the Murder of Alexander W. Rhea* (Philadelphia: G. V. Town, 1877), 112.

32. "A Sample Laborer," *Clearfield [PA] Republican*, July 31, 1878, 2.

33. Editorial in *Sunbury [PA] American*, September 17, 1875, 2.

34. Francis Percival Dewees, *The Molly Maguires: The Origin, Growth, and Character of the Organization* (New York: Burt Franklin, 1877), 33.

35. Anne Flaherty, "The 'Molly Maguires' and the National Labor Union," *From John Kehoe's Cell*, accessed June 22, 2022, https://mythofmollymaguires.blogspot.com/p/v-behaviorurldefaultvmlo.html.

36. John D. French, "'Reaping the Whirlwind': The Origins of the Allegheny County Greenback-Labor Party in 1877," *Western Pennsylvania Historical Magazine* 64, no. 2 (April 1981): 113.

37. "Greenbackers," *Daily Globe* [St. Paul, MN], February 23, 1878, 1.

38. "Connecticut Third Party," *New York Tribune*, August 15, 1878, 1.

39. This and the next quotes are taken from Articles 6 and 7. See Ellis Baker Usher, *The Greenback Movement of 1875–1884 and Wisconsin's Part in It* (Milwaukee, WI: Melsenheimer, 1911), 80.

40. See Article 10 in Usher, *Greenback Movement*, 80.

41. "Greenbackers," *New York Herald*, August 15, 1878, 4.

42. William H. Sylvis and James C. Sylvis, *The Life, Speeches, Labors, and Essays of William H. Sylvis* (Philadelphia: Claxton, Remsen, Haffelfinger, 1872), 146.

43. "Greenbackers," *Daily Globe*, 1.

44. Usher, *Greenback Movement*, 79.

45. See "Hooten," https://www.findagrave.com/memorial/23288238/marsena -mcgavran-hooton, accessed May 12, 2018. For "them steers" story, see Samuel Leavitt, *Our Money Wars: The Example and Warning of American Finance* (Boston: Arena, 1896), 197–200.

46. For the 1878 New York platform, see "New York Nationals," *Chicago Daily Tribune*, July 25, 1878, 1; for the 1878 Connecticut platform: "Connecticut Third Party," *New York Tribune*, August 15, 1878, 1; for the 1878 national platform: "Greenbackers," *Daily Globe* [St. Paul, MN], February 23, 1878. The 1880 platform is from Usher, *Greenback Movement*, 79–80.

47. "Workingmen's Platform," *Evening Argus* [Rock Island, IL], September 1, 1866, 2. A slightly different version appeared in "National Labor Congress," *Western Sentinel* [Winston-Salem, NC] September 7, 1866, 1; it substituted "has" for "having" and "crushed" for "averted." The differences in the text probably come from reporters' transcriptions.

48. John R. Commons, David Joseph Saposs, Helen Laura Sumner, John B. Andrews, Selig Perlman, and Henry Elmer Hoagland, *History of Labour in the United States*, vol. 2 (New York: Macmillan, 1918), 245–48.

49. "The Greeenbackers," *Red Cloud [NE] Chief*, September 12, 1878, 4; and Pomeroy "Look Out for Fun," February 10, 1876, 4.

50. *Red Cloud [NE] Chief*, September 4, 1879, 1; and "The Washington Letter," July 31, 1879, 1.

51. "Local Matters," *Red Cloud [NE] Chief*, October 14, 1880, 4.

52. "Local Matters," *Red Cloud [NE] Chief*, October 23, 1879, 4.

53. Dewees, *Molly Maguires*, 175; Anne Flaherty, "The 'Molly Kings' and Greenback Labor Reform," in *From John Kehoe's Cell*, accessed June 21, 2020, https://mythofmolly maguires.blogspot.com/p/the-molly-kings-and-greenback-labor_29.html.

54. Paul Kleppner, *The Third Electoral System, 1853–1892: Parties, Voters, and Political Cultures* (Chapel Hill: University of North Carolina Press, 1979), 271–73.

55. Ralph R. Ricker, *The Greenback Labor Party in Pennsylvania* (Bellefonte, PA: Pennsylvania Heritage, 1966), 63.

56. Craig Phelan, *Grand Master Workman: Terence Powderly and the Knights of Labor* (Westport, CT: Greenwood, 2000), 64–65.

57. Mark Lause, *The Civil War's Last Campaign: James B. Weaver, the Greenback-Labor Party & the Politics of Race & Section* (Lanham, MD: University Press of America, 2001).

58. Haynes, *Third Party Movements*, 139.

59. "Workingmen's Platform," *Evening Argus*, 2.

60. Haynes, *Third Party Movements*, 222.

61. Haynes, 426.

62. Usher, *Greenback Movement*, 5.

63. J. C. Bancroft Davis, *United States Reports, Vol. 109, Cases Adjudged in the Supreme Court at October Term 1883* (New York: Banks & Brothers, 1884), 14.

CHAPTER EIGHT
In All Things Essential

Farmers' Alliance Songs of the 1890s, Nebraska Folk Lore Pamphlet no. 18, Nebraska Federal Writers Project, December 1938; Douglas A. Bakken, "Luna E. Kellie and the Farmers' Alliance," *Nebraska History* 50 (1969): 184–205.

1. Annie Diggs, "The Farmers' Alliance and Some of Its Leaders," *The Arena* 5, no. 29 (April 1892): 600.

2. Charles W. Macune Jr., "The Wellsprings of a Populist: Dr. C. W. Macune Before 1886," *Southwestern Historical Quarterly* 90, no. 2 (October 1986): 150, 151.

3. US Bureau of the Census (hereafter USBC), *Historical Statistics of the United States*, "Chapter K: Agriculture," table K550–563, 518.

4. Elizabeth Barr, "The Populist Uprising," in *A Standard History of Kansas and Kansans*, ed. William E. Connelley (New York: Lewis, 1918), 1144.

5. John D. Hicks, *The Populist Revolt* (Minneapolis: University of Minnesota Press, 1931), 30; Neal R. Peirce, *The Great Plains States of America* (New York: Norton, 1973), 44.

6. Everett Dick, "The Great Nebraska Drouth of 1894: The Exodus," *Arizona and the West* 15, no. 4 (Winter 1973): 333–44.

7. USBC, *Historical Statistics*, "Chapter F: National Income & Wealth," table 250–261, 240.

8. Robert A. McGuire, "Economic Causes of Late-Nineteenth Century Agrarian Unrest: New Evidence," *Journal of Economic History* 41, no. 4 (December 1981): 835–52.

9. Douglass North, *Growth and Welfare in the American Past: A New Economic History* (Englewood Cliffs, NJ: Prentice- Hall, 1974); Robert Higgs, "Railroad Rates and the Populist Uprising," *Agricultural History* 44 (1970): 291–97; Anne Mayhew, "A Reappraisal of the Causes of Farm Protest in the United States, 1870–1900," *Journal of Economic* History 32, no. 2 (June 1972): 464–75; James Stewart, "The Economics of American Farm Unrest, 1865–1900," EH.Net Encyclopedia, February 10, 2008, http://eh.net/encyclopedia/the-economics-of-american-farm-unrest-1865-1900/.

10. Kansas State Board of Agriculture, *Report for the Month Ending July 31, 1890* (Topeka, KS: Baker, 1890).

11. Walter Wycoff, *A Day with a Tramp* (New York: Scribner, 1901), 61.

12. "The Farmers and the Railroads," *Red Cloud [NE] Chief*, January 26, 1882, 2.

13. Solon Buck, *The Agrarian Crusade* (New Haven, CT: Yale University Press, 1920), 111–12.

14. Nelson A. Dunning, ed., *Farmers' Alliance History and Agricultural Digest* (Washington, DC: Alliance, 1891), 20.

15. *History of Texas* (Chicago: Lewis, 1895), 452.

16. Lawrence Goodwyn, *The Populist Moment* (New York: Oxford University Press, 1978), 26; William Holmes, *American Populism* (Lexington, MA: Heath, 1994), 27.

17. Dunning, *Farmers' Alliance*, 294.

18. Roscoe C. Martin, "The Greenback Party in Texas," *Southwestern Historical Quarterly* 30, no. 3 (January 1927): 161–77; Matthew Hild, *Greenbackers, Knights of Labor, and Populists: Farmer-Labor Insurgency in the Late-Nineteenth-Century South* (Athens: University of Georgia Press, 2007).

19. Goodwyn, *Populist Moment*, 39.

20. Goodwyn, 43.

21. Donna Barnes, "Rebel Farmers," in *The Texas Left*, ed. David O'Donald Cullen & Kyle Wilkison (College Station, TX: Texas A&M, 2010), 41–52.

22. The Cleburne Demands can be found in Dunning, *Farmers' Alliance*, 41–43.

23. Robert McMath, *American Populism, A Social History* (New York: Hill & Wang, 1992), 80.

24. Ellis Usher, *The Greenback Movement of 1875–1884 and Wisconsin's Part in It,* (Milwaukee: Meisinheimer, 1911), 79–80.

25. McMath, *American Populism*, 68.

26. Kirk Porter, *National Party Platforms* (New York: Macmillan, 1924), 103.

27. William D. P. Bliss, *The Encyclopedia of Social Reforms* (New York: Funk & Wagnalls, 1897), 674.

28. Dunning, *Farmers' Alliance*, 40.

29. "A Texas Tragedy," *Indianapolis [IN] Journal*, December 26, 1883, 1.

30. Hicks, *Populist Revolt*, 105.

31. "Editorial Notes," *Iola [KS] Register*, December 12, 1890, 1.

32. Samuel Proctor, "The National Farmers' Alliance Convention of 1890 and Its 'Ocala Demands,'" *Florida Historical Quarterly* 28, no. 3 (January 1950): 170.

33. On the number of members, see Edward Ayers, *The Promise of the New South* (New York: Oxford University Press, 2007), 225; on Confederates, see USBC, *Report of the Population at the Eleventh Census*, vol. 2 (Washington, DC: GPO, 1897), clxxiv.

34. New York claims to have founded the Northern Alliance in 1877, a date challenged by Kansas, which claims it founded an alliance in 1874. Alliance historian John Hicks states: "The first really effective Northern Alliance organization was founded by Chicago editor Milton George." Hicks, *Populist Revolt*, 98.

35. Milton George, *The Western Rural Yearbook* (Chicago: Milton George, 1886), 134; Roy V. Scott, "Milton George and the Farmers' Alliance Movement," *Mississippi Valley Historical Review* 45, no. 1 (June 1958): 90–109.

36. George, *Western Rural Yearbook*, 137.

37. *Red Cloud [NE] Chief*, April 21, 1881, 1.

38. USBC, *Historical Statistics*, "Chapter R: Communications," table R244–257, 810; *The Men Who Advertise* (New York: Rowell, 1870), Iowa R648–53, Kansas R653–55, Nebraska R685–87; *American Newspaper Directory* (New York: Rowell, 1893): Iowa R897–904, Kansas R904–9, Nebraska R940–44, Lincoln and Topeka R942, 948, Columbus: R943, Salina R908.

39. USBC, *Historical Statistics*, "Chapter R: Communications," table R56–70, 788.

40. "Stillwater Home," *Red Cloud [NE] Chief*, June 8, 1882, 1.

41. "Pleasant Hill," *Red Cloud [NE] Chief*, February 8, 1884, 1.

42. *Wabash, St. Louis & Pacific Railway Company v. Illinois*, 118 U.S. 557 (1886).

43. "The Week," *The Nation*, October 28, 1886, 339.

44. Proctor, "National Farmers' Alliance Convention," 163.

45. Ayers, *Promise*, 220.

46. American Economic Association, *Handbook of the American Economic Association* (New York: Macmillan, 1897), 196.

47. William Peffer, *The Farmer's Side: His Troubles and Their Remedy* (New York: Appleton, 1891), 158.

48. Barr, "Populist Uprising," 1137.

49. Diggs, *The Story of Jerry Simpson* (Wichita, KS: Jane Simpson, 1908), 61.

50. Barr, "Populist Uprising," 1165.

51. Diggs, *Story of Jerry Simpson*, 84.

52. *Red Cloud [NE] Chief*, April 21, 1881, 1.

53. Buck, *Agrarian Crusade*, 120.

54. Ignatius Donnelly, *Donnelliana* (Chicago: Schulte, 1892), 193.

55. "Agriculture," *Wessington Springs [SD] Herald*, June 4, 1886, 1.

56. Hicks, *Populist Revolt*, 178.

57. Congressional Record (hereafter CR), March 31, 1890, 2868–69.

58. Diggs, *Story of Jerry Simpson*, 108.

59. Diggs, 48.

60. Diggs, 48, 54.

61. Hamlin Garland, "The Alliance Wedge in Congress," *The Arena* 5, no. 15 (December 1891): 453.

62. Diggs, *Story of Jerry Simpson*, 56.

63. Hicks, *Populist Revolt*, 271.

64. Hicks, 270.

65. Dunning, *Farmers' Alliance*, 136; Dennis Nordin, "A Revisionist Interpretation of the Patrons of Husbandry, 1867–1900," *Historian* 32, no. 4 (August 1970): 630–43.

66. Theodore Mitchell, *Political Education in the Southern Farmers' Alliance: 1887–1900* (Madison: University of Wisconsin Press, 1987), 57.

67. Annie Diggs, "Women in the Alliance," *The Arena* 6, no. 30 (July 1892): 166.

68. Louise Scoggins Self, *Agrarian Chautauqua: The Lecture System of the Southern Farmers' Alliance Movement* (PhD diss., University of Wisconsin, 1981), xiv.

69. William Hope Harvey, *Coin's Financial School* (Chicago: Coin, 1894), 176.

70. Patrick M. Garry, *Scrambling for Protection: The New Media and the First Amendment* (Pittsburgh, PA: University of Pittsburgh Press, 1994), 130.

71. Charles Postel, *The Populist Vision* (New York: Oxford University Press, 2009), 69.

72. Norman Pollak, *The Populist Response to Industrial America* (Cambridge, MA: Harvard University Press, 1962), 46.

73. W. Scott Morgan, *History of the Wheel and Alliance and the Impending Revolution*, vol. 3 (Fort Scott, KS: J. M. Rice, 1889), 776 (italics in the original).

74. "Alliance Talks," *Cherokee Scout* [Murphy, NC], November 10, 1891, 2.

75. See Goodwyn, *The Populist Moment*, chap. 2.

76. Mitchell, *Political Education*, 96–100.

77. Robert McGrath, *American Populism: A Social History, 1877–1898* (New York: Hill and Wang, 1992).

78. "Farmers' Alliance," *Fort Worth [TX] Weekly Gazette*, August 19, 1887, 1.

79. Bruce Baker, "The Farmer's Alliance Store in Siler City, North Carolina, 1888–1899," unpublished paper, accessed February 19, 2018, http://bruceebaker.com/BakerBE-FarmersAllianceStore1999.pdf, site discontinued.

80. Hicks, *Populist Revolt*, 139.

81. Edward W. Bemis, "Cooperation in New England" in *History of Coöperation in the United States*, vol. 6, ed. Richard Ely (Baltimore: Johns Hopkins University Press, 1888), 129.

82. Stewart, "Economics of American Farm Unrest," 11.

83. MaryJo Wagner, "Women in the Farmer's Alliance," paper presented at the annual meeting of the Organization of American Historians, Washington, DC, March 22–25, 1990.

84. Nancy F. Cott, *Root of Bitterness: Documents of the Social History of American Women* (Lebanon, NH: Northeastern University Press, 1996), 415.

85. Richard Schiller, *Queen of Populists: The Story of Mary Elizabeth Lease* (New York: Crowell, 1970), 100.

86. Dunning, *Farmers' Alliance*, 309.

87. Dunning, 310.

88. "Alliance Platform," *Red Cloud [NE] Chief*, February 6, 1891, 3.

89. Dunning, *Farmers' Alliance*, 35.

90. Dunning, 309.

91. Floyd J. Miller, "Black Protest and White Leadership: A Note on the Colored Farmers' Alliance," *Phylon* 33, no. 2 (2nd Quarter 1972): 169–74.

92. Dunning, *Farmers' Alliance*, 289.

93. Miller, "Black Protest," 172.

94. Dunning, *Farmers' Alliance*, 289.

95. Dunning, 292.

96. William F. Holmes, "The Arkansas Cotton Pickers Strike of 1891 and the Demise

of the Colored Farmers' Alliance," *Arkansas Historical Quarterly* 32, no. 2 (Summer 1973): 107–19.

97. Judith Freeman Clark, *The Gilded Age* (New York: Infobase, 2006), 137.

98. This speech appears in several anthologies, none of which provide a source. Citations usually refer to Elizabeth Barr, "The Populist Uprising," in *A Standard History of Kansas and Kansans*, ed. William E. Connelly (New York: Lewis, 1918), 1167; Peter Argersinger, *The Limits of Agrarian Radicalism* (Lawrence: University Press of Kansas, 1995), 53. The case is made more interesting by the appearance in the *Wichita Eagle* (Lease's hometown) of an anonymous author stating, "Wall Street does not own the people of this country, yet it directly and indirectly controls a large minority of them" ("And Still a Little More of It," January 22, 1890, 4).

99. Connie Lester, *Up from the Mudsills of Hell* (Athens: University of Georgia Press, 2006), 106.

100. Susan Klopfer, *Who Killed Emmitt Till?* (Mount Pleasant, IA: Lulu, 2010), 251.

101. Donna Barnes, *Farmers in Rebellion* (Austin: University of Texas Press, 1984).

102. "Keep It Before the People," *Saline County [KS] Journal*, May 7, 1891, 1.

103. "Two Kinds of Alliances," *Thomas County Cat* [Colby, KS], January 29, 1891, 1.

104. "Opposed to It," *Fort Worth [TX] Gazette*, April 24, 1891, 1.

105. "Keep It Before the People," May 7, 1891.

106. "Editorial Notes," *Iola [KS] Register*, January 30, 1891, 1.

107. Terence Powderly, *Thirty Years of Labor, 1859–1889* (Columbus, OH: Excelsior, 1889), 342.

108. Craig Phelan, *Grand Master Workman: Terence Powderly and the Knights of Labor* (Westport, CT: Greenwood, 2000), 249.

109. Phelan, 250.

110. Goodwyn, *Populist Moment*, 33.

111. Elizabeth Sanders, *Roots of Reform: Farmers, Workers, and the American State, 1877–1917* (Chicago: University of Chicago Press, 1991), 1.

CHAPTER NINE

To Help and Assist All Employed and Unemployed

Clark Halker, *For Democracy, Workers, and God: Labor Song-Poems and Labor Protest, 1865–95* (Urbana: University of Illinois Press, 1991), 35–36.

1. Kim Voss, *The Making of American Exceptionalism: The Knights of Labor* (Ithaca, NY: Cornell University Press, 1993); Herbert Gutman, "Protestantism and the American Labor Movement: The Christian Spirit in the Gilded Age," *American Historical Review* 72, no. 1 (October 1966): 74–101; William Birdsall, "The Problem of Structure in the Knights of Labor," *Industrial and Labor Relations Review* 6, no. 4 (July 1953): 532–46; Robert Weir, *Beyond Labor's Veil: The Culture of the Knights of Labor* (University Park: Pennsylvania State University Press, 1996).

2. "Our Grand Master Workman," *Journal of United Labor* 1, no. 1 (May 15, 1880): 2; "Labor Party Dissensions," *New York Herald*, July 31, 1879, 3.

3. Samuel Gompers, *The Samuel Gompers Papers: The Early Years of the American Federation of Labor, 1887–1890*, vol. 2, ed. Stuart Kaufman (Champaign: University of Illinois Press, 1987), 339; Norman Ware, *The Labor Movement in the United States* (New York: Vintage, 1964), xvi; Harry J. Carman, "Terence Powderly: A Reappraisal," *Journal of Economic History* 1, no. 1 (May 1941): 84.

4. Terence Powderly, *The Path I Trod: The Autobiography of Terence V. Powderly*, ed. Harry J. Carman, Henry David, and Paul N. Guthrie (New York: Columbia University Press, 1940), 45.

5. *Knights of Labor Illustrated: "Adelphon Kruptos"* (Chicago: Ezra Cook, 1886), 50.

6. Carroll D. Wright, "An Historical Sketch of the Knights of Labor," *Quarterly Journal of Economics* 1, no. 1 (January 1887): 139.

7. Franz Boas and George Hunt, *The Social Organization and the Secret Societies of the Kwakiutl Indians* (Washington, DC: GPO, 1897), 396, 663.

8. Gregory S. Kealey, *Workers and Canadian History* (Montreal, CA: McGill-Queens University Press, 1995), 238. Weir attributes this to Terence Powderly's brother, "Big John" Powderly, whose nickname came from his linebacker's physique. See Weir, *Beyond Labor's Veil*, 65.

9. Weir, *Beyond Labor's Veil*, 65.

10. Symmes M. Jelley, *The Voice of Labor* (Philadelphia: H. J. Smith, 1888), 195.

11. *Knights of Labor Illustrated*, 24.

12. *Knights of Labor Illustrated*, 42.

13. "Federation of Organized Trades and Labor Unions," *Journal of United Labor* 2, no. 7–8 (November–December 1881): 168.

14. *Knights of Labor Illustrated*, 6.

15. "Greenbackers," *Daily Globe* [St. Paul, MN], February 23, 1878, 1.

16. Terence Powderly, *Constitution of the General Assembly, District Assemblies, and Local Assemblies of the Order of the Knights of Labor in America* (Marblehead, MA: Statesman, 1883), 3, 4.

17. Powderly, *Path I Trod*, 5.

18. Terence Powderly, *Thirty Years of Labor, 1859–1889* (Columbus, OH: Excelsior, 1889), 622.

19. Leon Fink, *Workingmen's Democracy: the Knights of Labor and American Politics*, (Champaign: University of Illinois Press, 1985), 12.

20. Iowa Bureau of Labor Statistics (hereafter IABLS), *Second Biennial Report*, 2.

21. Powderly, *Thirty Years*, 496.

22. Paul Starr, *The Creation of the Media: Political Origins of Modern Communications* (New York: Basic, 2004), 14.

23. Alfred Marshall, *Principles of Economics*, vol. 1 (London: Macmillan, 1891), 734.

24. Simon Newton Dexter North, *History and Present Condition of the Periodical Press of the United States* (Washington, DC: GPO, 1884), 107.

25. Starr, *Creation of the Media*, 184.

26. US Senate, "Testimony of A.P. Swineford," *Testimony Taken by the Committee on Post Offices and Post Roads, In Reference to Postal Telegraph*, 48th Congress, First Session, Report 577, Part 2 (Washington, DC: GPO, 1884) (hereafter Post Office Hearings), 281–82.

27. "Testimony of Lloyd Breezee," Post Office Hearings, 284.

28. "Testimony of William Henry Smith," Post Office Hearings, 292–93.

29. US Senate, *Report to Accompany the Bill S. 2022, the Committee on Post Offices and Post Roads*, 48th Congress, First Session, Report 577, Part 2 (Washington, DC: GPO, 1884), 19.

30. Fink, *Workingmen's Democracy*, 11.

31. Wisconsin Bureau of Labor and Industrial Statistics, *Twelfth Biennial Report*, 28.

32. Susan Levine, "Labor's True Woman: Domesticity and Equal Rights in the Knights of Labor," *Journal of American History* 70, no. 2 (September 1983): 323–39.

33. "Correspondence," *Union Pacific Employees' Magazine* 4, no. 5 (June 1889): 160.

34. *Report of the International Council of Women* (Washington, DC: Rufus H. Darby, 1888), 155.

35. Anne Nathan Meyer, *Woman's Work in America* (New York: Holt, 1891), 299.

36. "Mrs. Barry's Mission," *Indianapolis [IN] Journal*, August 17, 1887, 3.

37. "Wild Talk to Bryanites," *The Sun*, October 31, 1896, 5.

38. Dorothy Richardson, *The Long Day: The Story of a New York Working Girl as Told by Herself* (New York: Century, 1905); Helen Campbell, *Prisoners of Poverty: Women Wage-Workers, Their Trades and Their Lives* (Boston: Little Brown, 1900).

39. Melissa MacKinnon, "'A Deadly Menace to All Womankind': Seduction and Protective Legislation in America, 1850–1923 (PhD diss., Syracuse University, 2021).

40. Like data on corporal punishment, the lack of documentation makes research about industrial workplace harassment difficult. Useful sources for this section are: Catherine MacKinnon, *Sexual Harassment of Working Women* (New Haven: Yale University Press, 1979); Constance Backhouse and Leah Cohen, *The Secret Oppression: Sexual Harassment of Working Women* (Toronto: Macmillan of Canada, 1978); and Rosemarie Skaine, *Power and Gender: Issues in Sexual Dominance and Harassment* (Jefferson, NC: McFarland, 1996), esp. chap. 2, "The History of Sexual Harassment in America."

41. Skaine, *Power and Gender*, 33.

42. Leonora Barry, *Tenth Annual Report of the Bureau of Statistics of Labor and Industries of New Jersey* (Somerville, NJ: State Printer, 1888), 202–4.

43. "Their True Inwardness," *Flaming Sword* 3, no. 25 (June 18, 1892): 10.

44. Leonora Barry, "Report of the General Investigator," in *General Assembly of the Knights of Labor of America, Eleventh Regular Session Held at Minneapolis, Minnesota, October 4–19, 1887* (Knights General Assembly, 1887), 1581–88.

45. Carroll D. Wright, *The First Annual Report of the Commissioner of Labor: Industrial Depressions* (Washington, DC: GPO, 1885), 66.

46. US Bureau of the Census, *Historical Statistics of the United States*, "Chapter V: Business Enterprise," table V20–30, 741–745; "Chapter X: Banking," table X 751–755, 1038.

47. Wright, *First Annual Report*, 11.

48. Theresa Ann Case, *The Great Southwest Railroad Strike and Free Labor* (College Station: Texas A&M University Press, 2010), 147; Donald L. Kemmerer and Edward D. Wickersham, "Reasons for the Growth of the Knights of Labor in 1885–1886," *ILR Review* 3, no. 2 (January 1950): 213–20.

49. Case, *Great Southwest Railroad Strike*, 147.

50. "The Labor Situation," *Princeton Review* 1, no. 3 (January 1886): 434.

51. Powderly, *Thirty Years*, 497.

52. Van Wyck Brooks, *The Flowering of New England* (New York: Dutton, 1955).

53. William R. Stead, *If Christ Came to Chicago* (Chicago: Laird & Lee, 1897), 90.

54. City of Chicago, *Report of the General Superintendent of Police to the City Council for the Fiscal Year Ending December 31st, 1877* (Chicago: Clark & Edwards, 1877), 23–24.

55. Citizens' Association of Chicago, *Annual Report, Chicago 1886* (Chicago: City of Chicago, 1886), 35, 33.

56. James Green, *Death in the Haymarket* (New York: Random House, 2006), 76.

57. Library of Congress, https://www.loc.gov/resource/rbpe.33700400/.

58. Ray Ginger, *Altgeld's America* (Chicago: Quadrangle, 1958), 48.

59. Ginger, 52.

60. Florence Kelley, "I Go to Work," *The Survey* 67 (June 1, 1927), 274.

61. Joe Howard Jr., "How They Died," *St. Paul [MN] Daily Globe*, November 12, 1887, 1; "Death by Rope," *Evening Star* [Washington, DC], June 21, 1877, 1. The Espy file shows there were four hangings in Illinois in 1886, with only the Haymarket executions a sorrier disaster.

62. Ginger, *Altgeld's America*, 84.

63. Richard Junger, *Becoming the Second City: Chicago's Mass News Media, 1833–1889* (Champaign: University of Illinois Press, 2010), 120.

64. "Demons of Hell," *Wichita [KS] Daily Eagle*, May 5, 1886, 1.

65. Powderly, *Thirty Years*, 543.

66. Missouri Bureau of Labor Statistics and Inspection, *The Official History of the Great Strike of 1886 on the Southwest Railway System* (Jefferson City, MO: Tribune, 1886) (hereafter Missouri SW Strike), 5.

67. US House of Representatives, *Investigation of Labor Troubles in Missouri, Arkansas, Kansas, Texas, and Illinois, Part 2, 49th Congress, Second Session, Report No. 4174* (Washington, DC: GPO, 1887) (hereafter Congress SW2), 206.

68. Texas State Historical Association, "Martin Irons," accessed October 5, 2022, https://tshaonline.org/handbook/online/articles/fir07.

69. Congress SW2, 450.

70. Murat Halstead and J. Frank Beale, *Life of Jay Gould: How He Made His Millions* (New York: Edgewood, 1892), 202; Maury Klein, *The Life and Legend of Jay Gould* (Baltimore: Johns Hopkins University Press, 1997).

71. Halstead and Beale, *Life of Jay Gould*, 171.

72. Missouri SW Strike, 117.

73. "The Great Railway Strike," *Indianapolis [IN] Journal*, March 10, 1886, 1.

74. Congress SW II, 437 (italics added).

75. Missouri SW Strike, 19.

76. US House of Representatives, *Investigation of Labor Troubles in Missouri, Arkansas, Kansas, Texas, and Illinois, Part One, 49th Congress, Second Session, Report No. 4174* (Washington, DC: GPO, 1887) (hereafter Congress SW1), xiv.

77. Congress SW2, 241.

78. "The Aristocratic Workingman," *Labor Herald* [Richmond, VA], April 17, 1886, 1.

79. "The Labor Troubles," *Salt Lake [UT] Herald*, March 10, 1886, 1.

80. Congress SW2, 179.

81. "The Aristocratic Workingman," April 17, 1886.

82. F. Ray Marshall, *Labor in the South* (Cambridge, MA: Harvard University Press, 1967), 22.

83. Susan Millar Williams and Stephen G. Hoffius, *Upheaval in Charleston: Earthquake and Murder on the Eve of Jim Crow* (Athens: University of Georgia Press, 2012), 87.

84. John H. Bracey, August Meier, and Elliott M. Rudwick, *Black Workers and Organized Labor* (Belmont, CA: Wadsworth, 1971), 15.

85. "Opposing the Knights of Labor," *Evening Star* [Washington, DC], December 18, 1886, 6.

86. Walter Allen, *Governor Chamberlain's Administration in South Carolina: A Chapter of Reconstruction in the Southern States* (New York: Putnam, 1888), 319; Stephen Budiansky, *The Bloody Shirt: Terror after the Civil War* (New York: Penguin, 2008).

87. "The Aristocratic Workingman," April 17, 1886.

88. US Patent Office, *Annual Report of the Commissioner of Patents for the Year 1892* (Washington, DC: GPO, 1893), 117; Peter J. Rachleff, *Black Labor in Richmond, 1865–1890* (Champaign: University of Illinois Press, 1989), 171–79.

89. Craig Phelan, *Grand Master Workman: Terence Powderly and the Knights of Labor* (Westport, CT: Greenwood, 2000), 153.

90. "Session of Knights," *Stark County [OH] Democrat*, October 7, 1886: "Baltimore district representatives are congratulating themselves that they had their way at the St. Charles in inducing the proprietor by threats of withdrawal to entertain Joseph Ward, one of their colored delegates" (1).

91. *Frank Leslie's Illustrated Newspaper*, October 16, 1886.

92. Knights of Labor, *Record of the Proceedings of the Tenth General Assembly, Held at Richmond, Va, October 4–20, 1886*, vol. 4 (Knights General Assembly, 1886), 7–8, 12. Mathew Hild uses a reproduction of the scene as the cover for his *Greenbackers, Knights of Labor, and Populists: Farmer-Labor Insurgency in the Late-Nineteenth-Century South* (Athens: University of Georgia Press, 2007).

93. Powderly, *Thirty Years*, 657–59.

94. Congress SWI, xxiv, xxviii.

95. Phelan, *Grand Master Workman*, 252, 254.

96. "A Monument to Martin Irons," *International Woodworker* 17, no. 10 (October 1907): 13.

97. Pennsylvania Bureau of Labor Statistics (hereafter PBIS), *Volume 15*, 36G.

98. James Howard Bridge, *The Inside History of the Carnegie Steel Company: A Romance of Millions* (New York: Aldine, 1903), 190.

99. Robert Weir, *Knights Unhorsed: Internal Conflict in a Gilded Age Social Movement* (Detroit: Wayne State University Press, 2000), 15; Phelan, *Grand Master Workman*, 172.

100. New York Bureau of Labor Statistics, *Fifth Annual Report*, 258.

101. Connecticut Bureau of Labor Statistics (hereafter CTBLS), *Third Annual Report*, 15.

102. California Bureau of Labor Statistics, *Third Biennial Report*, 166.

103. Richard Oestricher, *Solidarity and Fragmentation: Working People and Class Consciousness in Detroit, 1875–1900* (Urbana: University of Illinois Press, 1986).

104. PBIS, *Volume 15*, 39G.

105. IABLS, *Third Biennial Report*, 2.

106. State of Michigan, *Fifth Annual Report of Factory Inspection, 1897* (Lansing, MI: Robert Smith, 1898), 23; Wisconsin Bureau of Labor and Industrial Statistics, *Ninth Biennial Report, 1898–99* (Madison, WI: Democrat, 1901), 252.

107. CTBLS, *First Annual Report*, 35.

CHAPTER TEN

The Reinvention of America

Farmers Alliance Songs of the 1890s, Nebraska Folk Lore Pamphlet No. 18, Nebraska Federal Writers Project, December 1938.

1. John Henninger Reagan, *Memoirs, with Special Reference to Secession and the Civil War* (New York: Neale, 1906), 311.

2. Ben H. Procter, *Not Without Honor: The Life of John H. Reagan* (Austin: University of Texas Press, 1962), 209.

3. "Hon. John H. Reagan," *Austin [TX] Weekly Statesman*, February 3, 1887 (hereafter Reagan 1887 Speech).

4. Reagan, *Memoirs*, 243.

5. Elizabeth Sanders, *Roots of Reform: Farmers, Workers, and the American State, 1877–1917* (Chicago: University of Chicago Press, 1991), 182.

6. "Railroad Legislation," *Lake Charles [LA] Echo*, August 12, 1882, 2.

7. *Proceedings Twelfth Session of the National Grange of the Patrons of Husbandry* (Philadelphia: Wagenseller, 1878), 135.

8. "The Farm," *Midland Journal* [Rising Sun, MD], June 24, 1887, 1. An alternate appraisal comes from Solon Buck: "No student of national legislation would be willing to accept the claim of many members of the order that it was chiefly instrumental in securing the passage of the interstate commerce act" (Buck, *The Granger Movement* [Cambridge, MA: Harvard University Press, 1913], 122).

9. Wisconsin grain dealer Robert Elliott, US Congress, "Debate of Interstate Commerce in the House of Representatives," *Interstate Commerce Debate of the 48th Congress*, Second Session (Washington, DC: GPO, 1884) (hereafter House ICA Debate 1884), 312.

10. William L. Burton, "Wisconsin's First Railroad Commission: A Case Study in Apostasy," *Wisconsin Magazine of History* 45, no. 3 (Spring, 1962), 190–98.

11. House ICA Debate 1884, 284. The states were Arkansas, Illinois, Missouri, Nebraska, Pennsylvania, Texas, and Georgia.

12. Richard Franklin Bensel, *The Political Economy of American Industrialization, 1877–1900* (New York: Cambridge University Press, 2000), 120.

13. Thomas K. McCraw, *Prophets of Regulation* (Cambridge, MA: Harvard University Press, 1984), 56–59.

14. Charles Francis and Henry Adams, *A Chapter of Erie and Other Essays* (Boston: Osgood, 1871), 1.

15. Reagan 1887 Speech.

16. Richard White, *Railroaded: The Transcontinentals and the Making of Modern America* (New York: Norton, 2011), 161.

17. Thomas W. Gilligan, William J. Marshall, and Barry R. Weingast, "Regulation and the Theory of Legislative Choice: The Interstate Commerce Act of 1887," *Journal of Law & Economics* 32, no. 1 (April 1989): 35–61; Keith T. Poole and Howard Rosenthal, "The Enduring Nineteenth-Century Battle for Economic Regulation: The Interstate Commerce Act Revisited," *Journal of Law and Economics* 36, no. 2 (October 1993): 837–60.

18. House ICA Debate 1884, 397.

19. House ICA Debate 1884, 312.

20. J. M. H. Frederick, *National Party Platforms* (Akron, OH: Frederick, 1896), 55.

21. House ICA Debate 1884, 329. The Brumm vote is key in suggesting the alternate explanation for the ICA vote as centered on race. Poole and Rosenthal suggest

the South's strong support was economic, but equally crucial were opposing votes from those in the north like Brumm, who might have been inclined to support it but were put off by the addition of the "separate but equal" clause.

22. House ICA Debate 1884, 333.

23. House ICA Debate 1884, 463, 397.

24. US Congress, "Debate of Interstate Commerce in the Senate of the United States," *Interstate Commerce Debate of the 48th Congress* (Washington, DC: GPO, 1884) (hereafter Senate ICA Debate), 2.

25. Senate ICA Debate, 159.

26. "Senator Van Wyck of Nebraska," *Grange Visitor* [Schoolcraft, MI], August 1, 1884, 5.

27. Senate ICA Debate, 159.

28. Senate ICA Debate, 1.

29. US Senate, *Report of the Senate Select Committee on Interstate Commerce* (Washington, DC: GPO, 1886), 1340.

30. US Senate, *Report of the Select Committee on Interstate Commerce,* summary report (Washington, DC: GPO, 1886), 7, 42.

31. Sanders, *Roots of Reform,* 191.

32. Transcript of Interstate Commerce Act (1887), accessed August 4, 2020, https://www.ourdocuments.gov/doc.php?flash=false&doc=49&page=transcript.

33. Gabriel Kolko, *The Triumph of Conservatism* (New York: Free Press, 1963), 3.

34. Gabriel Kolko, *Railroads and Regulation 1877–1916* (Princeton, NJ: Princeton University Press, 1965), 238.

35. Robert L. Bradley Jr. and Roger Donway, "Reconsidering Gabriel Kolko: A Half-Century Perspective," *Independent Review* 17, no. 4 (Spring 2013): 561–75; Robert W. Harbeson, "Railroads and Regulation, 1877–1916: Conspiracy or Public Interest?" *Journal of Economic History* 27, no. 2 (June 1967): 230–42.

36. "Cullom on the Interstate," *Butte [MT] Semi-Weekly Miner*, March 26, 1887, 1. This explains in part why libertarians have become the strongest supporters of the Kolko thesis.

37. The Hatch Act of 1887 [As Amended through Public Law 107-293, November 13, 2002], https://www.govinfo.gov/content/pkg/COMPS-10292/pdf/COMPS-10292.pdf,accessed July 8, 2021.

38. Coy F. Cross II and Coy F. Cross, *Justin Smith Morrill: Father of the Land-Grant Colleges* (East Lansing: Michigan State University Press, 1999), 13; US Senate, "Justin Morrill," accessed January 22, 2021 https://www.senate.gov/artandhistory/history/minute/Justin_S_Morrill.htm.

39. Justin Morrill, "Speech on the Bill Granting Lands for Agricultural Colleges," *Congressional Globe*, April 20, 1858, 1694.

40. Morrill, 1696.

41. US Senate, "An Act Donating Public Lands to the Several States and Territories which May Provide Colleges for the Benefit of Agriculture and the Mechanic Arts," 37th Congress, Sess. 2, Chap. 130, 1862, *United States Statutes at Large*, vol. 12 (Boston: Little, Brown, 1863), 504.

42. Alfred True, *A History of Agricultural Experimentation and Research in the United States 1807–1925: Including a History of the United States Department of Agriculture* (Washington, DC: GPO, 1937), 126.

43. Joseph Cannon Bailey, *Seaman Knapp: Schoolmaster of American Agriculture* (New York: Arno, 1971).

44. Quoted in Eugene Brooks, "Seaman A. Knapp," *Agricultural and Rural Life Day: Materials for Its Observance*, United States Bureau of Education Bulletin No. 43, Whole No. 553 (Washington, DC: GPO, 1913), 26. Knapp ranks second after George Washington in that volume's list of "Men Influential in Improving Agriculture."

45. *Progressive Farmer* [Winston, NC], February 10, 1886, 4. *Progressive Farmer* is the paper founded by Alliance leader Leonidas Polk. The distinction between "systematic" and "scientific" farming is discussed by Alan Marcus, *Agricultural Science and the Quest for Legitimacy* (Ames: Iowa State University Press, 1986); and Roger Williams, *Origins of Federal Support for Higher Education: George W. Atherton and the Land Grant College Movement* (University Park: Pennsylvania State University Press, 1991).

46. True, *History of Agricultural Experimentation*, 120.

47. True, 127.

48. Williams, *Origins of Federal Support*.

49. *Journal of Proceedings of the Twenty-First Annual Session of the National Grange of the Patrons on Husbandry* (Lansing, MI: Thorp & Godfrey, 1887), 176.

50. "Farmers and Knights," *Saint Paul [MN] Daily Globe*, February 4, 1887, 8.

51. True, *History of Agricultural Experimentation*, 129.

52. True, 38. For information on staff and income, see 137–38.

53. Charles E. Rosenberg, *No Other Gods: On Science and American Social Thought* (Baltimore: Johns Hopkins University Press, 1997), 148.

54. True, *History of Agricultural Experimentation*, 130.

55. Williams, *Origins of Federal Support*, 89.

56. Association of American Agricultural Colleges and Experiment Stations, *Proceedings of the Fourth Annual Convention* (Washington, DC: GPO, 1891), 20.

57. Association of American Agricultural Colleges and Experiment Stations, 20–21.

58. US House of Representatives, *Congressional Record, Fifty-First Congress, First Session*, vol. 21 (Washington, DC: GPO, 1890) (hereafter House Second Morrill Debate), 8835.

59. House Second Morrill Debate, 8836.

60. House Second Morrill Debate, 8836.

61. House Second Morrill Debate, 8836.

62. House Second Morrill Debate, 8837.

63. House Second Morrill Debate, 8834.

64. US Congress, Act of August 30, 1890, Chap. 841, 26 Stat. 417, 7 U.S.C. 322 et seq., 51st Congress, accessed April 22, 2021, https://www.govinfo.gov/content/pkg/COMPS-10284/pdf/COMPS-10284.pdf.

65. Lee Craig, "'Raising Among Themselves': Black Educational Advancement and the Morrill Act of 1890," *Agriculture and Human Values* 9, no. 1 (Winter 1992): 31–37.

66. The State of Ohio, *General and Local Acts Passed and Joint Resolutions Adopted at the Sixty-Ninth General Assembly*, vol. 86 (Columbus, OH: Westbote, 1891), 521.

67. Cynthia L. Jackson and Eleanor F. Nunn, *Historically Black Colleges and Universities: A Reference Handbook* (Santa Barbara, CA: ABC-CLIO, 2003).

68. *Congressional Record* (hereafter CR), June 10, 1897, 1643.

69. George Hoar, *Autobiography of Seventy Years*, vol. 2 (New York: Scribners, 1903), 23.

70. Hoar, 21.

71. CR, March 13, 1890, 2200, 2202.

72. CR, March 21, 1890, 2456.

73. Albert H. Walker, *History of the Sherman Law* (New York: Equity Press, 1910), 3–4.

74. CR, February 27, 1890, 1765–72.

75. CR, 1765–72.

76. John Sherman, *Trusts: Speech of Hon. John Sherman, of Ohio, Delivered in the Senate of the United States* (Washington, DC: GPO, 1890), 15.

77. CR, March 25, 1890, 2611.

78. CR, 2610.

79. CR, 2610.

80. CR, 2655.

81. CR, 2649.

82. Winfield Scott Kerr, *John Sherman: His Life and Public Services*, vol. 2 (Boston: Sherman, French, 1908), 203.

83. CR, March 21, 1890, 2463.

84. CR, March 24, 1890, 2562.

85. CR, March 25, 1890, 2644.

86. CR, March 24, 1890, 2561.

87. Hoar, *Autobiography*, 364. Martin Sklar argues the bill ought to be called the Edmunds Antitrust Bill since the Vermonter chaired the Judicial Committee, but Hoar better deserves the honor. See Sklar, *The Corporate Reconstruction of American Capitalism, 1890–1916* (New York: Cambridge University Press, 1988), 116.

88. Sherman, *John Sherman's Recollections*, 834–35.

89. William Letwin, *Law and Economic Policy in America: The Evolution of the Sherman Antitrust Act* (Chicago: University of Chicago Press, 1965), 3.

90. Richard Snow, "Lorenzo Coffin," *American Heritage* 30, no. 6 (October–November 1979).

91. L. M. Coffin, "Safety Appliances on the Railroads," *Annals of Iowa* 5, no. 8 (January 1903): 561.

92. Bureau of Statistics of Labor and Industry of New Jersey (hereafter NJBLS), *Eleventh Annual Report of the Bureau of Statistics of Labor and Industries of New Jersey for the Year Ending in October 31st, 1888* (Trenton, NJ: John L. Murphy, 1889), 32.

93. NJBLS, 22.

94. James Morgan, *The Life Work of Edward Moseley in the Service of Humanity* (New York: Macmillan, 1913), 60; H. H. Westinghouse, "Recent Improvements in Air Brakes," *Locomotive Engineers Monthly Journal* 24, no. 12 (December 1890): 947–52.

95. Coffin, "Safety Appliances," 565.

96. Coffin, 571.

97. Coffin, 576.

98. Coffin, 579.

99. "Slaughter of Railroad Employees Stopped," *Railroad Trainmen's Journal* 13, no. 148 (June 1896): 423–26.

100. For 1891 statistics, see US Interstate Commerce Commission (ICC), *Fourth Annual Report on the Statistics of Railways in the United States* (Washington, DC: GPO, 1892), 92. For 1898 statistics: ICC, *Tenth Annual Report on the Statistics of Railways in the United States* (Washington, DC: GPO, 1898), 86.

101. Lawrence Goodwyn, *The Populist Moment* (New York: Oxford University Press, 1978), 56.

CHAPTER ELEVEN
Widening the Gates of Opportunity

Roger Welsch, "Sweet Nebraska Land," Folkways Records, no. FH 5337, 1965.

1. Milton Meltzer, *Willa Cather: A Biography* (Minneapolis, MN: Twenty-First Century, 2008), 21.

2. Julie Abraham, *Are Girls Necessary?: Lesbian Writing and Modern Histories* (Minneapolis: University of Minnesota Press, 2008); Marilee Lindemann, *Willa Cather, Queering America* (New York: Columbia University Press, 1999).

3. Granville Hicks, "The Case against Willa Cather," *English Journal* 22, no. 9 (November 1933): 708.

4. Lindemann, *Willa Cather*, 16.

5. Susan Sessions Rugh, *Our Common Country: Family Farming, Culture, and Community in the Nineteenth-Century Midwest* (Bloomington: Indiana University Press, 2001).

6. Willa Cather, *O Pioneers!* (Boston: Houghton Mifflin, 1913), 98.

7. Cather, 56.

8. Lewis Wolfanger, *Soil Survey of Webster County, Nebraska* 44, series 1923 (Washington, DC: GPO, 1923), 1508; for weather data: 1510.

9. Cather, *O Pioneers!*, 170–71.

10. Herbert Osborn, *The Hessian Fly in the United States* (Washington, DC: GPO, 1899), 7–8.

11. US Congress, House Committee on Agriculture, *Hearings before the Committee on Agriculture, of the Hon. Secretary of Agriculture and Chiefs of Bureaus and Divisions of the Department of Agriculture on the Estimates of Appropriations for the Department* (Washington, DC: GPO, 1906), 360–61.

12. Alan L. Olmstead and Paul W. Rhode, *Creating Abundance: Biological Innovation and American Agricultural Development* (New York: Cambridge University Press, 2008), 53.

13. Olmstead and Rhode, 61.

14. Olmstead and Rhode, 61.

15. US Bureau of the Census (hereafter USBC), *Historical Statistics of the United States,* "Chapter K: Agriculture," table K 1–16, 457. The total figure quoted uses the lower value per farm.

16. *Guide to the Records of the Carnegie Steel Company, 1853–1912 (bulk 1869–1890),* accessed August 4, 2020, https://historicpittsburgh.org/islandora/object/pitt%3A US-QQS-MSS315/viewer.

17. Alfred True, *A History of Agricultural Experimentation and Research in the United States 1607–1925: Including a History of the United States Department of Agriculture* (Washington, DC: GPO, 1937), 41.

18. For "fly" see "Wheat in Indiana," *Indianapolis [IN] Journal,* August 6, 1900, 8; for "map" see "Climate Variations," *Mitchell [SD] Capital,* January 19, 1900, 10; for "Oklahoma," see "From the Experiment Station," *Wichita [KS] Daily Eagle,* September 19, 1900, 2.

19. *Report of the Industrial Commission on Agriculture and Agricultural Labor,* vol. 10 (Washington: GPO, 1901), clxix.

20. Alfred True and V. A. Clark, *The Agricultural Experiment Stations of the United States* (Washington, DC: GPO, 1900), 297. This volume, prepared for the Paris Exposition, reflects True's assessment of the stations' roles at the end of the Long Depression.

21. US Census Office (hereafter USCO), *Reports on the Statistics of Agriculture in the United States* (Washington: GPO, 1895), 22; US Bureau of Agriculture, Labor, and Industry, Department of Publicity, *Montana* (Helena, MT: Independent, 1909), 19.

22. USCO, *Reports on the Statistics of Agriculture,* 303.

23. New York State Department of Agriculture, *Twenty-Fifth Annual Report of the Department of Agriculture for the Year Ending September 30, 1917* (Albany, NY: J. B. Lyons, 1918), 710.

24. True and Clark, *Agricultural Experiment Stations,* 434. A more recent work on the stations is Ray Vernon Scott, *The Reluctant Farmer: The Rise of Agricultural Extension to 1914* (Champaign: University of Illinois Press, 1971).

25. The 20.5 bushels per acre was recorded in Michigan in 1898. United States

Department of Agriculture, *Wheat Acreage and Production by States, 1866–1943, Statistical Bulletin 158* (Washington, DC: GPO, 1955).

26. USBC, *Historical Statistics*, "Chapter K: Agriculture," 482.

27. Cather, *O Pioneers!*, 309.

28. A. C. True, *Experiment Station Record*, vol. 13 (Washington, DC: GPO, 1902), 103.

29. John Eaton, *Report of the Commissioner of Education for the Year 1874* (Washington, DC: GPO, 1874), lxxiv.

30. USBC, *Historical Statistics*, "Chapter H: Education": for degrees, table H751–765, 385; for doctorates, table H766–787, 388; for faculty, table H689–699, 383.

31. Allan Nevins, *The State Universities and Democracy* (Urbana: University of Illinois Press 1962), vi.

32. Stanley Lebergott, *Manpower in Economic Growth* (New York: McGraw-Hill, 1964), 224.

33. Scott Key, "Economics or Education: The Establishment of American Land-Grant Universities," *Journal of Higher Education* 67, no. 2 (March–April 1996): 216.

34. Bowdoin College, *Report for the Academic Year 1903–1904* (Brunswick, ME: Journal, 1904), 20.

35. Boston Public Schools, *Report of the Director of Physical Training* (Boston: Rockwell & Churchill, 1894), 19.

36. USCO, *Report on the Manufacturing Industries in the United States at the Eleventh Census: 1890, Part 1* (Washington, DC: GPO, 1895), 20.

37. W. E. B. Du Bois, *The Negro in Business* (Atlanta, GA: Atlanta University, 1899), 46.

38. Lee Craig, "'Raising Among Themselves': Black Educational Advancement and the Morrill Act of 1890," *Agriculture and Human Values* 9, no. 1 (Winter 1992): 34.

39. Worthington C. Ford et al., eds., "An Ordinance for the Government of the Territory of the United States Northwest of the River Ohio," *Journals of the Continental Congress, 1774–1789*, vol. 28 (Washington, DC: Library of Congress, 1904–37), 378.

40. Thomas Jefferson to Richard Price, Paris, January 8, 1789, US National Archives, "Founders Online," https://founders.archives.gov/documents/Jefferson/01-14-02-0196#:~:text=I%20concur%20with%20you%20strictly,to%20reason%20on%20this%20subject.

41. Fletcher Swift, *A History of Permanent Public School Funds in the United States, 1795–1905* (New York: Henry Holt, 1911), 199.

42. USBC, *Historical Statistics*, "Chapter H: Social Statistics," table H412–432, 368–69.

43. Lebergott, *Manpower*, 510; USBC, *Historical Statistics*, Chapter H: Social Statistics, table H520–530, 376.

44. Jared Warner Mills, *Mills' Annotated Statutes of the State of Colorado* (Chicago: E. B. Myers, 1891), 93.

45. Swift, *History,* appendix A.

46. Claudia Dale Goldin and Lawrence F. Katz, *The Race between Education and Technology* (Cambridge, MA: Harvard University Press, 2008), 181.

47. USBC, *Historical Statistics,* "Chapter H: Social Statistics," table H598–601, 379.

48. Marie Dugard, "The Coeducation of the Sexes in the United States," in *Report of the Federal Security Agency: Office of Education,* vol. 2 (Washington, DC: GPO, 1902), 1269, 1270.

49. Of the more than two hundred variables listed in a late nineteenth-century database compiled for this book, school enrollment showed the strongest relationship to patent registrations. A regression of those variables generated an adjusted R square of .799.

50. Percentages are calculated using the GDP table supplied by Louis Johnston, rebased to 1914 dollars.

51. Story Ladd, "Patents in Relationship to Manufactures," *Census Bulletin No. 242, August 10, 1902* (Washington, DC: GPO, 1902), 17.

52. Mark W. Van Wienen, "Men (and Women) of Iron: Labor, Power, and the Railroad in Willa Cather's Novels," *Modern Fiction Studies* 62, no. 2 (Summer 2016): 236–71; Mark A. R. Facknitz, "Changing Trains: Metaphors of Transfer in Willa Cather," *Cather Studies 9: Willa Cather and Modern Culture,* accessed March 5, 2020, https:// cather.unl.edu/scholarship/catherstudies/9/cs009.facknitz.

53. Willa Cather, *The Song of the Lark* (Boston: Houghton Mifflin, 1915), 81.

54. Alfred Chandler, *The Visible Hand* (Cambridge, MA: Harvard University Press, 1977), 145.

55. J. Bradford DeLong, "Trade Policy and America's Standard of Living: A Historical Perspective," in *Imports, Exports, and the American Worker,* ed. Susan Collins (Washington, DC: Brookings Institution, 1998), 380.

56. Fred A. Shannon, "Comment on the Railroad Land Grant Legend in American History Texts," in *The Public Lands,* ed. Vernon Carstensen (Madison: University of Wisconsin Press, 1963), 159.

57. Lloyd J. Mercer, *Railroads and Land Grant Policy* (Washington, DC: Beard Books: 2002).

58. W. H. Armstrong, *Annual Report of the Commissioner of Railroads for the Year Ending June 30, 1883* (Washington, DC: GPO, 1883), 24.

59. Commissioner of Railroads, *Annual Report to the Secretary of the Interior for the Fiscal Year Ended June 30, 1901* (Washington, DC: GPO, 1902).

60. Richard White, *Railroaded: The Transcontinentals and the Making of Modern America* (New York: Norton, 2011).

61. Henry George, *Our Land and Land Policy, National and State* (San Francisco: White & Bauer, 1871), 9.

62. Richard Welch, *The Presidencies of Grover Cleveland* (Lawrence: University of Kansas Press, 1980), 14.

63. Arthur F Bentley, *The Condition of the Western Farmer as Illustrated by the History of One Nebraska Township* (Baltimore: Johns Hopkins University Press, 1893), 69.

64. James Stewart, "Cooperation, Collective Action, and Farm Interest Group Membership," unpublished paper (2006), accessed March 11, 2011, at mauricio.econ.ubc.ca/pdfs/stewart.pdf, site no longer available.

65. Charles A. Beard and Mary R. Beard, *The Rise of American Civilization* (New York: Macmillan, 1943), 341.

66. Bruce A. Blonigen and Anca Cristea, "The Effects of the Interstate Commerce Act on Transport Costs: Evidence from Wheat Prices," *Review of Industrial Organization* 43, no. 1–2 (August 2013): 41–62.

67. ICC, *Interstate Commerce Reports* 4 (Rochester, NY: Lawyers Cooperative, 1895), 600, 885; ICC, *Fourteenth Annual Report of the Interstate Commerce Commission* (Washington, DC: GPO, 1901), 70, 600.

68. "Memorial Planned for Safety Pioneer," *Santa Fe Magazine* 19, no. 2 (January 1925), 51–53.

69. Mercer, 148.

70. Willa Sibert Cather, "Nebraska: The End of the First Cycle," *The Nation* 117, no. 3035 (September 5, 1923): 236. Alexander Field states: "The almost complete neglect of the telegraph by economic historians in the last three decades may not be warranted" (quoted in Ronnie Phillips, "Digital Technology and Institutional Change from the Gilded Age to Modern Times: The Impact of the Telegraph and the Internet," *Journal of Economic Issues* 34, no. 2 [June 2000]: 270).

71. US Senate Committee on Post Offices and Post Roads, *Report to Accompany the Bill S. 2022*, 48th Congress, First Sess., Report 577, Part 2 (Washington, DC: GPO, 1884), 16.

72. US Post Office (hereafter USPO), *An Argument in Support of the Limited Post and Telegraph* (Washington, DC: GPO, 1890), 48.

73. USPO, 223.

74. USPO, 51.

75. USPO, 214.

76. Murat Halstead and J. Frank Beale, *Life of Jay Gould: How He Made His Millions* (New York: Edgewood, 1892), 178.

77. E.I. Lewis, "The Telephone Mail," *Telephony* 7, no. 1 (January 1904): 71.

78. "Telephone Notice," *Red Cloud [NE] Chief*, July 14, 1899, 1.

79. Ronald Kline, *Consumers in the Country: Technology and Social Change in Rural America* (Baltimore: Johns Hopkins University Press, 2000), 31.

80. Milton Mueller, *Universal Service: Competition, Interconnection, and Monopoly in the Making of the American Telephone System* (Boston: MIT Press, 1997), 68.

81. Claude S. Fischer, *America Calling: A Social History of the Telephone to 1940* (Berkeley: University of California Press, 1994), 94.

82. "Once It Was a Toy, Now a Necessity," *American Telephone Journal*, December 19, 1903, 412.

83. Fischer, *America Calling*, 99.

84. Helen Sumner, *Report on the Conditions of Women and Child Wage Earners in the United States* (Washington, DC: GPO, 1910), 234.

85. Ann Crittenden, *The Price of Motherhood* (New York: Holt, 2001).

86. Joan Hoff, *Law, Gender and Injustice: A Legal History of U.S. Women* (New York: New York University Press, 1991), 128; B. Zorina Khan, *The Democratization of Invention: Patents and Copyrights in American Economic Development, 1790–1920* (New York: Cambridge University Press, 2005); Evan Roberts, "Women's Rights and Women's Labor: Married Women's Property Laws and Labor Force Participation, 1860–1900," paper presented at the Economic History Association annual meeting, Pittsburgh, Pennsylvania, September 2006, 14–16.

87. George James Bayles, Sallie Elizabeth Joy White, and William Herbert Carruth, *American Women's Legal Status* (New York: Collier, 1905), 219.

88. Khan, *Democratization of Invention*, 181.

89. For more on Lamar, see Edward Mayes, *Lucius Q. C. Lamar: His Life, Times, and Speeches, 1825–1893* (Nashville, TN: Methodist Episcopal Church, 1896), 483. Lamar's reputation has served as an interesting barometer of American race relations. In the 1930s Wirt Cate wrote a laudatory biography of Lamar portraying him as a moderate. See Wirt Armistead Cate, *Lucius Q. C. Lamar, Secession and Reunion* (Chapel Hill: University of North Carolina Press, 1935). John F. Kennedy portrayed him in *Profiles in Courage* (New York: Harper, 1956). In 1973 James Murphy recast Lamar as a "pragmatic patriot" in *L.Q.C. Lamar: Pragmatic Patriot* (Baton Rouge: Louisiana State University Press, 1973). Michael Gattis views him as an opportunist; see "L.Q.C. Lamar and the New South," paper presented at Midwest Political Science Association 67th Annual National Conference, Chicago, April 2, 2009. For Lamar's quote about authorship, see James Leiby, *Carroll Wright and Labor Reform* (Cambridge, MA: Harvard University Press, 1960), 107.

90. W. E. B. Du Bois, *The Negro in Business* (Atlanta, GA: Atlanta University, 1899), 5.

91. Du Bois, 19.

92. Du Bois, 24.

93. Du Bois, 25.

94. Carroll D. Wright, "The Condition of the Negro in Various Cities," *Bulletin of the Department of Labor, Volume 2, 1897* (Washington, DC: GPO, 1897), 257–371. I have attempted to maintain consistency with the table headings by following US Census categories wherever possible. In categories listed as railroad, lumber, and iron workers, occupations such as oiler or engine wiper were merged into one occupation for two reasons: occupations in the lumber category tended to be enumerator-created; and, because the railroads and iron factories were two main sources of Black industrial employment, it is more revealing to record their general status in these industries rather than break them down into categories. A difficult decision came in how to properly categorize railroad porters, an important occupation for African Americans. To maintain consistency,

these porters are included in the railroad category. Those entries for which data was missing, for example, a listed wage with no hours, or for which the occupation was not determined are listed as unclassified. Unemployment is a specific entry in the tables. By providing a picture of African American employment during the Long Depression, these data are intended to be suggestive for further research on this important topic.

95. Mark DeWolfe Howe, *The Pollack-Holmes Letters*, vol. 1 (New York: Cambridge University Press, 2015), 163.

96. US Attorney General, *Annual Report for the Year 1893* (Washington, DC: GPO, 1894), xvii.

97. David Millon, "The Sherman Act and the Balance of Power," 61 S. Cal. L. Rev. 1219 (1988), 1291; Barack Orback, "How Antitrust Lost Its Goal," *Fordham Law Review* 81, no. 5 (December 2013): 2274; E. Thomas Sullivan, ed., *The Political Economy of the Sherman Act* (New York: Oxford, 1991).

98. Almont Lindsey, *The Pullman Strike* (Chicago: University of Chicago Press, 1942), 159.

99. Walter Blackburn Harte, "A Review of the Chicago Strike of '94," *The* Arena 10, no. 55 (June 1894): 497–532.

100. *United States v. E. C. Knight Co.*, 156 U.S. 1 (1895), 156 (hereafter Sugar Trust Decision), 17.

101. Sugar Trust Decision, 10–11.

102. Sugar Trust Decision, 43.

103. David Marchese, "Thomas Piketty Thinks America Is Primed for Wealth Redistribution," *New York Times Magazine*, April 1, 2022, https://www.nytimes.com/interactive/2022/04/03/magazine/thomas-piketty-interview.html?searchResultPosition=1.

104. Geoffrey Ward, *Before the Trumpet, Young Franklin Roosevelt, 1882–1905* (New York: Harpers, 1985), 230.

CHAPTER TWELVE
How Much You Can Buy

Railroad Man's Magazine 22 (November 1913): 446–47. It is common in folk song transmission for words to change. In some versions "Alley" appears as "Allen" and "Hinton" as "Hampton." Sewell was formerly a town on the New River FFV route.

1. Norm Cohen, *Long Steel Rail: The Railroad in American Folksong*, 2nd ed. (Champaign: University of Illinois Press, 2000), 188; Ron Lane, "Folksongs of the C&O," unpublished manuscript. Somehow #134 was transposed to #143 in several versions of the song. Some versions also refer to Engine No. 4, which is the number of the FFV route, not the engine number. The valleys of Appalachia exhibit wide variations in the weather, so we must approach these weather reports with caution. See US War Department, *Monthly Weather Review, 1890* (Washington, DC: GPO, 1891), 261. The tracks in that

area had suffered the previous spring from "an unusually open and wet winter" that contributed to "more landslides . . . in the Huntington Division [where Alley's route ran] than had been known for years before." See Chesapeake and Ohio Railway Directors, *Annual Report to the Stockholders for the Fiscal Year 1890* (New York: Wheeler, 1890) (hereafter 1890 C&O Annual Report), 11–12.

2. "Fortunes in the South," *The Sun* [New York, NY], October 26, 1890, 13.

3. W. E. Dressler, "Railroadin'," *Hinton [WV] News*, January 7, 1979.

4. There were two ways to create a whistle "signature," either by manipulating the steam using long and short bursts in a specific pattern or by purchasing a unique whistle.

5. Mark Twain, *Life on the Mississippi* (Boston: Osgood, 1883), 105.

6. Michael Reynolds, *Locomotive Engine Driving: A Practical Manual for Engineers* (London: Crosby, 1888), 143. Although published in the United Kingdom, advertisements for this book appeared in publications like the Brotherhood of Locomotive Engineers monthly magazine.

7. Marshall Kirkman, *The Science of Railways: Operation of Trains* (Chicago: World Railway, 1894), 66.

8. Thomas Dixon, "The Story of the FFV," *Chesapeake and Ohio Historical Newsletter* 2, no. 5 (May 1970): 6. Vestibules enabled passengers to move from car to car out of the weather.

9. Charles E. Fisher, "The Famous Color Trains of America," *Railroad and Locomotive History Society* Bulletin No. 4 (1923), 27.

10. Jim Cox, *Rails Across Dixie: A History of Passenger Trains in the American South* (Jefferson, NC: McFarland, 2011), 80.

11. Thomas Dixon, "The Wrecks of the FFV," *Chesapeake and Ohio Historical Newsletter* 2, no. 5 (May 1970): 12.

12. *Railway World*, March 15, 1890, 247.

13. "Railroad Wrecks," *Wichita [KS] Daily Eagle*, October 23, 1890, 1; *Appleton's Annual Cyclopedia and Register of Important Events for the Year 1890*, vols. 15 and 30 (New York: Appleton, 1891), 256.

14. "Mr. Huntington's Career," *New York Times*, August 15, 1900, 1. For another view of Huntington, see Richard White, *Railroaded: The Transcontinentals and the Making of Modern America* (New York: Norton, 2011), especially 95–96.

15. Scott Reynolds Nelson, *Steel Drivin' Man: John Henry: The Untold Story of an American Legend* (New York: Oxford University Press, 2006).

16. David R. Berman, *Politics, Labor, and the War on Big Business: The Path of Reform in Arizona* (Boulder: University Press of Colorado, 2012), 26. Primary sources show little confirmation of this fear.

17. The reference to a vestibule train has led some to say FFV stood for "Fast Flying Vestibule." Among those making this mistake is John Harrington Cox, in his *Folk-Songs of the South* (Cambridge, MA: Harvard University Press, 1925), 221–30. Contemporaneous newspaper reports put the time of the wreck at 4:45 a.m. According to the October

22 timetable, the FFV was supposed to arrive in Hinton at 3:55 a.m., then was due at Ronceverte at 5:07 a.m. and at White Sulphur Springs at 5:30 a.m. Given that the wreck occurred near Hinton, this timing means that the train could have been as much as 30 to 45 minutes behind schedule. *Staunton [WV] Spectator*, October 22, 1890, 1.

18. A. P. Carter was notorious for collecting tunes and then putting his name on them. Folklorists have collected over seventy variants of the ballad of George Alley, with the author of the song as veiled in folklore as in the lyrics. Norm Cohen thinks it may have been a fellow engineer rather than the engine wiper, who is usually cited. See Cohen, *Long Steel Rail*, 189. Cohen cites two versions that include the chorus, one of which is by Charles Lewis Stine. Cohen also includes a text of a version by Bailey Briscoe. A recorded version that includes a chorus is by Bradley Kincaid, but his words change the meaning: "There's many a man been killed [not murdered] on [not by] the railroad." Several versions collected around 1916 appear in Cox, *Folk-Songs of the South*. The chorus appears in all the versions Cox lists, including one traced to Alley's sister. One plausible explanation for the song is that the wreck occurred during the campaign to pass the Safety Appliance Act. The 1913 text appears in Cohen, *Long Steel Rail*, 195. George Alley's sister confirmed this had been in oral tradition for some time.

19. Lane, "Folksongs of the C&O."

20. Cohen, *Long Steel Rail*, 14.

21. Thomas Dixon, *Chessie: The Railroad Kitten* (Forest, VA: TLC, 1980).

22. 1890 C&O Annual Report, 1.

23. 1890 C&O Annual Report, 12.

24. "The Gang Located," *Wheeling [WV] Daily Intelligencer*, November 11, 1890, 1.

25. H. H. Westinghouse, "Recent Improvements in Air Brakes," *Locomotive Engineers Monthly Journal* 34, no. 12 (December 1890): 948; Thomas Cooley, *The American Railway* (New York: Scribners, 1889), 195.

26. Carroll D. Wright, *Eighteenth Annual Report of the Commissioner of Labor* (Washington, DC: GPO, 1903), (hereafter *Wright Eighteenth Report*), 15. Data cited is of a "normal" family.

27. US Congress, Senate Committee on Finance, *Wholesale Prices, Wages and Transportation* (Washington, DC: GPO, 1893), 20.

28. Carroll Wright, *Sixth Annual Report of the Bureau of Statistics of Labor* (Boston: Wright & Potter, 1875), 414 (hereafter *Wright Sixth Annual Report*); 1903 food expenses from *Wright Eighteenth Report*, 75; the figure of $312.92 is for 25,440 families. Wright also gives a figure of $326.90 for a selected 2,567 families.

29. *Wright Sixth Report*: food (subsistence) p. 414; rent p. 385; fuel p. 411; sundries p. 434; clothes p. 429. The US Bureau of Labor Statistics report of the time contains a table purporting to be a summary of Wright's data, but the amounts do not match the 1875 report. It reports: food $427; rent $117; clothing $106; fuel and sundries $44 each. The differences in amounts and percentages are minor, but the original data is used. See *Wright Eighteenth Report*, 648.

30. Harvey Levenstein, *Revolution at the Table* (Berkeley: University of California Press, 2003), 4; Richard Pillsbury, *No Foreign Food* (Boulder, CO: Westview, 1998); Sylvia Whitman, *What's Cooking?: The History of American Food* (New York: Twenty-First Century, 2001).

31. Arthur Ignatius Judge, *A History of the Canning Industry* (Baltimore, MD: Canning Trade, 1914), 53.

32. Levenstein, *Revolution at the Table*, 22.

33. *Wright Eighteenth Report*, 104. Wright's table is broken down by region but the percentages are for the entire country. As Wright notes, consumption varied by region. For example, beef consumption was higher in the West.

34. US Bureau of Labor Statistics (hereafter USBC), *Historical Statistics of the United States*, "Chapter E: Prices and Price Indexes," table E123–134, 208.

35. US Industrial Commission, *Report on Trusts and Industrial Combinations* (Washington, DC: GPO, 1901), 781.

36. *Wright Eighteenth Report*, 690–98.

37. John Sherman, *John Sherman's Recollections of Forty Years in the House, Senate, and Cabinet*, vol. 2 (Chicago: Werner, 1895), 1082.

38. "Conditions in Europe and America," *Locomotive Fireman's Magazine* 16, no. 6 (June 1899): 617.

39. Robert Higgs, "Railroad Rates and the Populist Uprising," *Agricultural History* 44, no. 3 (July 1970): 296; James Stewart, "The Economics of American Farm Unrest, 1865–1900," ed. Robert Whaples, EH.NetEncyclopedia, accessed February 13, 2022, http://eh.net/encyclopedia/the-economics-of-american-farm-unrest-1865–1900/.

40. The correlation between wheat flour price and overall wheat production is -.771, yielding an R square of -.594.

41. US Department of Agriculture (hereafter USDA), *Wheat Acreage and Production by States, 1866–1943, Statistical Bulletin 158* (Washington, DC: GPO, 1955).

42. Alan Olmstead and Paul Rhode, *Creating Abundance: Biological Innovation and American Agricultural Development* (New York: Cambridge University Press, 2008); Willard Cochrane, *The Development of American Agriculture: A Historical Analysis* (Minneapolis: University of Minnesota Press, 1993); Vernon Ruttan and Yujiro Hayami, *Agricultural Development: An International Perspective* (Baltimore: Johns Hopkins University Press, 1985); William Parker and Judith Klein, "Productivity and Growth in Grain Production in the United States, 1840–60, 1900–10," in *Output, Employment, and Productivity in the United States after 1800*, ed. Dorothy S. Brady (New York: National Bureau of Economic Research, 1966), 523–82; Hadly Quaintance, *The Influence of Farm Machinery on Production and Labor*, PhD diss., University of Wisconsin, 1904.

43. Susan Granger and Scott Kelley, *Historic Context Study of Minnesota Farms, 1820–1960*, vol. 1 (St. Paul: Minnesota Department of Transportation, 2005), 3–91.

44. For the impact of the Deere plow see Neil Dahlstrom and Jeremy Dahlstrom,

The John Deere Story: A Biography of Plowmakers John & Charles Deere (DeKalb: Northern Illinois University Press, 2005).

45. Kansas State Board of Agriculture, *Quarterly Report for the Quarter Ending March 31, 1891* (Topeka: Kansas Publishing House, 1891), 118.

46. US Senate, *Agricultural Depression: Causes and Remedies, Report of Mr. Peffer, Report 787* (Washington, DC: GPO, 1894), 31.

47. Sarah Griffith, "A Tractor Fit for Mad Max," accessed December 4, 2021, http://www.dailymail.co.uk/sciencetech/article-3008162/A-tractor-fit-Mad-Max-Rugged-machine-carves-150-acres-land-day-plough-round-clock.html.

48. US Senate, *Agricultural Depression*, 27.

49. North Dakota State University Archives, "Bonanza Farms," accessed October 9, 2020, https://library.ndsu.edu/fargo-history/?q=content/bonanza-farms.

50. Fred Shannon, *The Farmer's Last Frontier: Agriculture, 1860–1897* (New York: Holt, Rinehart & Winston, 1945), 160.

51. Farm data are from the state reports for the 1920 Census, *Fourteenth Census of the United States, State Compendium*. The respective cites are in volumes as follows: *California*, 59; *Iowa*, 69; *Kansas*, 69; *Minnesota*, 71; *Nebraska*, 63; *Ohio*, 91; *Illinois*, 89; *Indiana*, 71; *Michigan*, 73; *Missouri*, 69.

52. USBC, *Historical Statistics*, "Chapter K: Agriculture," table K502–516, 510–12. Regarding the Wheat Ten, see USDA, "Wheat Acreage and Production by States, 1866–1943," *Statistical Bulletin 158* (Washington, DC: GPO, 1955); Robert McGuire, *An Empirical Investigation of Farmers Behavior Under Uncertainty* (New York: Routledge, 2019).

53. Kansas and Nebraska, "Wheat Acreage and Production," 11.

54. Kansas State Agricultural College Experiment Station, *Report for 1894* (Manhattan: Kansas State Agricultural College, 1895), vii.

55. New Jersey Agricultural Experiment Station, *Seventeenth Annual Report* (Trenton, NJ: J. L. Murphy, 1897), 416.

56. Totals, "Wheat Acreage and Production," 2–26.

57. US Senate, *Report of the Public Lands Commission, 1905, Senate Document 189* (Washington, DC: GPO, 1905); Bureau of Land Management statistics, Center for Great Plains Studies, University of Nebraska–Lincoln, accessed August 4, 2020, http://homestead.unl.edu/projects/homesteading-the-plains/data.html.

58. Granger and Kelley, *Historic Context Study*, 318.

59. Olmstead and Rhode, *Creating Abundance*.

60. Olmstead and Rhode, 36.

61. James Malin, *Winter Wheat in the Golden Belt of Kansas: A Study in Adaption to Subhumid Geographical Environment* (Lawrence: University of Kansas Press, 1944), 170.

62. Accounts of the introduction of hard winter wheat usually place the date as around 1874. The consensus of when the variety had spread through the Wheat Belt is usually the mid-1880s.

63. Malin, *Winter Wheat*, 170.

64. For "planting" see "Stock and Farm," *Western Kansas World* [WaKeeny, KS], October 18, 1890, 3. For "suggestions" see: "Farms and Farmers," *Western News* [Stevensville, MT], August 8, 1900, 3; "Farms and Farmers," *Cottonwood [ID] Report*, August 10, 1900, 3; "Farms and Farmers," *Corvallis [OR] Gazette*, July 24, 1900, 1; and "Farms and Farmers," *Manchester [IA] Democrat*, July 18, 1900, 6. For seed advice, see "Changing Seed Wheat," *The Advocate* [Topeka, KS], July 29, 1896, 7. For the convention, see "For Better Farming," *Bismarck [ND] Weekly Tribune*, May 12, 1899, 8. For fertilizer: see "Nitrate of Soda on Wheat, *Ohio Democrat* [Logan, OH], July 25, 1891, 7; "Nitrate of Soda on Wheat," *Barton County Democrat* [Great Bend, KS], July 16, 1891, 6; and "Nitrate of Soda on Wheat," *The Republican* [Oakland, MD], July 24, 1891, 7.

65. "Meeting of the County Council P. of H. Olmstead County," *Grange Advance* [Red Wing, MN], October 29, 1873, 6; "Clawson Wheat," *Lake County Star* [Chase, MI], September 20, 1877, 2.

66. Alan Olmstead and Paul Rhode, "Biological Innovation in American Wheat Production," in *Industrializing Organisms: Introducing Evolutionary History*, ed. Susan Schrepfer and Philip Scranton (New York: Routledge, 2004), 76.

67. Mark Twain, *A Connecticut Yankee in King Arthur's Court* (New York: Signet, 1965), 220.

68. *Wright Sixth Annual Report*, 194.

69. USBC, *Historical Statistics*, "Chapter G: Consumer Income and Expenditures," 309.

70. Andrew R. Heinze, *Adapting to Abundance* (New York: Columbia University Press, 1990), 22–25.

71. "Silk and Other Gloves," *New York Times*, June 15, 1890, 13.

72. Vivian Perles, *Charles Ives Remembered: An Oral History* (New Haven, CT: Yale University Press, 1974), 56.

73. *Wright Eighteenth Report*, 509, table IV-R, "Summary of Expenditures for Various Items Other than Food, By State."

74. Samuel Gompers, *The Samuel Gompers Papers: The Making of a Union Leader, 1850–86*, vol. 1 (Champaign: University of Illinois Press, 1986), 330.

75. "High Dues Are Necessary to Success," *American Federationist* 3, no. 7 (September 1896).

76. Edward Bemis, "Benefit Features of American Trade Unions," Bulletin of the Department of Labor, No. 22, May 1899 (Washington, DC: GPO, 1899), 371.

77. The 1903 amounts come from page 509 of Wright's report. The 1970 numbers are from USBC, *Historical Statistics*, "Chapter G: Consumer Income and Expenses," table G416–469, 316.

78. USBC, *Historical Statistics*, "Chapter R: Communications," tables R192–217 and R244–257, 808, 810.

79. Carroll D. Wright for Massachusetts Dept. of Labor and Industries, Division of Statistics, *Comparative Wages, Prices, and Cost of Living: From the Sixteenth Annual Report* (Boston: Wright and Potter, 1889), 252. This volume is a reprint from the earlier report but it is cited here because the data are centralized.

80. Carroll D. Wright, *Seventh Annual Report of the Bureau of Statistics of Labor, Cost of Production: The Textiles & Glass, Vol. 2, Cost of Living* (Washington, DC: GPO, 1891), 1929, 1947. The textile and glass data recapitulate the coal, iron, and steel data from the previous annual report.

81. "The Electric Headlight," *Railroad Gazette* 22 (January 17, 1890): 39.

82. Stephen Crane, "Nebraska's Bitter Fight for Life," in *Stephen Crane: Prose and Poetry* (New York: Library of America, 1984), 688–700.

CONCLUSION

A Second Emancipation

James Abrams, Mike Semko, Tom Supey, William Ray, and Joe Janowski, "Anthracite Mining Unionism and the UMW: An Oral History," *Pennsylvania History* 58, no. 4 (October 1991): 330–37.

1. Samuel Gompers, *Seventy Years of Life and Labor*, vol. 2 (New York: A. M. Kelley, 1967), 126–27.

2. Carlos C. Closson, "The Unemployed in American Cities," *Quarterly Journal of Economics* 8, no. 2 (January 1894): 168–217.

3. John Middlemist Herrick and Paul H. Stuart, *Encyclopedia of Social Welfare History in North America* (Thousand Oaks, CA: Sage, 2005), 276.

4. Lawrence Goodwyn, *Democratic Promise: The Populist Moment in America* (New York: Oxford University Press, 1978), 175.

5. George Herron, "Nebraska Commencement Address, 1894," George Herron Papers, Grinnell College Archives.

6. William Jennings Bryan, *Life and Speeches of William Jennings Bryan* (Baltimore, MD: Woodward, 1900), 251.

7. Mary Furner, "The Republican Tradition and the New Liberalism: Social Investigation, State Building, and Social Learning in the Gilded Age," in *The State and Social Investigation in Britain and the United States*, ed. Michael Lacey and Mary Furner (New York: Cambridge University Press, 1993), 172.

8. Craig Phelan, *Divided Loyalties: The Public and Private Life of Labor Leader John Mitchell* (Albany: State University of New York Press, 1994), 4.

9. Phelan, 9.

10. Henry Demarest Lloyd, *A Strike of Millionaires Against Miners, or the Story of Spring Valley* (Chicago: Belford-Clarke, 1890), 67.

11. Walter Weyl, "John Mitchell, The Man the Miners Trust," *Outlook* 82, no. 12 (March 24, 1906): 657.

12. Robert Reynolds, "The Coal Kings Come to Judgment: When the Anthracite Miners Downed Tools in 1902, Economic Feudalism Went on Trial," *American Heritage* 11, no. 3 (April 1960), https://www.americanheritage.com/coal-kings-come-judgment.

13. John Mitchell, "The Miner's Life," *Official Journal of the Amalgamated Meat Cutters and Butcher Workmen of North America* 2, no. 43 (April 1903): 6.

14. Reynolds, "Coal Kings."

15. Reynolds, "Coal Kings."

16. Andrew Roy, *A History of the Coal Miners of the United States* (Columbus, OH: Traubman, 1907), 409.

17. This statement has long been attributed to Mitchell but cannot be found in any of his writings.

18. Joseph Gowaskie, "John Mitchell and the Anthracite Coal Strike of 1902: A Century Later," *The Great Strike: Perspectives on the 1902 Anthracite Coal Strike* (Easton, PA: Canal History and Technology Press, 2002), 128.

19. George Korson, "Me Johnny Mitchell Man," *Songs and Ballads of the Anthracite Miners*, Library of Congress, no. AFS L16, 1976.

20. "Mrs. Martha McCrone," *Record-Union* [Sacramento, CA], October 11, 1897, 6, 7.

21. "Mrs. McCrone the Leader," *Evening Times* [Washington, DC], September 20, 1897, 2.

22. "Mrs. McCrone the Leader," September 20, 1897.

23. "Raids of Amazons," *Herald* [Los Angeles, CA], September 18, 1897, 1.

24. Joseph McKearns, "The 'Faces' of John Mitchell," *The Great Strike*, 29–43.

25. Phelan, *Divided Loyalties*, 115.

26. Christopher J. Cyphers, *The National Civic Federation and the Making of a New Liberalism, 1900–1915* (Westport, CT: Praeger, 2002), 20; also see James Weinstein, *The Corporate Ideal in the Liberal State, 1900–1918* (Boston: Beacon, 1968).

27. "Belmont Made Head of Civic Federation," *New York Times*, December 16, 1904, 1.

28. David Montgomery, *Workers' Control in America: Studies in the History of Work, Technology, and Labor Struggles* (New York: Cambridge University Press, 1979), 66.

29. Philip Foner, *History of the Labor Movement in the United States: 1900–1909* (New York: International, 1964), 71.

30. See Ralph Montgomery Easley, *The National Civic Federation Review*; for "The Assault by Socialism," November 15, 1904, 46; for "Socialism and Revolution," June 1905, 8; for "Socialists Seek to Inflame the Mind of American Youth," June 1905, 9.

31. Marcus Alonzo Hanna, *Mark Hanna: His Book* (Boston: Chappelle, 1904), 30, 32, 34–35.

32. Hanna, 47.

33. Herbert Croly, *Marcus Alonzo Hanna: His Life and Work* (New York: Macmillan, 1912), 317, 315.

34. Croly, 372.

35. Francis Walker, "The Development of the Anthracite Combination," *Annals of the American Academy of Political and Social Science* 111 (January 1924): 234–48.

36. George Baer, "President Baer to the Reading Railway Employees," *Railway Age*, June 18, 1901, 701.

37. "D., L. & W. President Predicts Prosperity," *New York Times*, January 8, 1905, 26.

38. Congressional Record (hereafter CR), January 15, 1903, 871.

39. Eliot Jones, *The Anthracite Coal Combination in the United States* (Cambridge, MA: Harvard University Press, 1914), 70.

40. Anthracite Coal Strike Commission, *Report to the President on the Anthracite Coal Strike of May–October 1902* (Washington, DC: Government Printing Office, 1902) (hereafter Anthracite Coal Strike Commission Report), 218, 220–21.

41. *Indianapolis [IN] Journal*, July 14, 1902, 1.

42. John Mitchell, *Organized Labor: Its Problems, Purposes, and Ideals* (Philadelphia: Dunlap, 1903), 371.

43. Perry K. Blatz, *Democratic Miners: Work and Labor Relations in the Anthracite Coal Industry, 1875–1925* (Albany, NY: State University Of New York Press, 1994), 123.

44. Anthracite Coal Strike Commission Report, 36; "East Is Waiting," *Columbus [NE] Journal*, June 25, 1902, 1.

45. "Either Peace or War with Miners," *Albuquerque [NM] Daily Citizen*, March 21, 1902, 1.

46. Garth Hall for City of Shamokin, "Shamokin and Coal Township: A Brief History," accessed June 21, 2021, http://www.shamokincity.org/history.html.

47. Anthracite Coal Strike Commission Report, 32.

48. Phelan, *Divided Loyalties*, 157.

49. Phelan, 157.

50. Mitchell, *Organized Labor*, 371.

51. Anthracite Coal Strike Commission Report, 35.

52. "It Looks Threatening," *New-York Tribune*, May 15, 1902, 1.

53. Blatz, *Democratic Miners*, 121.

54. Theodore Roosevelt, "At Sioux Falls, South Dakota, April 3, 1903," *Addresses and Presidential Messages of Theodore Roosevelt, 1902–1904* (New York: Putnam, 1904), 152.

55. Carroll D. Wright, "Report to the President on Anthracite Coal Strike," *Bulletin of the Department of Labor, No. 43, November 1902* (Washington, DC: GPO, 1902), 1150.

56. Wright, 165.

57. "Soft Coal Used in New York Freely," *New York Times*, June 4, 1902, 3.

58. "Good Sea Bathing at Cape May," *New York Times*, July 20, 1902, 25.

59. "President Baer," *Official Journal of the Amalgamated Meat Cutters and Butcher Workmen of North America* 2, no. 1 (February 1903): 13–15.

60. United Mineworkers of America, *Minutes of a Special Convention to Consider the Anthracite Strike* (Indianapolis, IN: Hollenbeck, 1902), 3–37.

61. "Standards of Honor and Wisdom," *Public Policy* 7, no. 6 (August 9, 1902): 98.

62. United Mineworkers, 48–51.

63. United Mineworkers, 51.

64. Mary Harris Jones, *Autobiography of Mother Jones* (Chicago: Kerr, 1925), 50.

65. "Cold Atmosphere May Greet Lawmakers," *Evening Times* [Washington, DC], August 14, 1902, 1.

66. "Schools May Close," *Minneapolis [MN] Journal*, September 20, 1902, 2.

67. "Farm, Orchard, and Garden," *Norfolk [NE] Weekly News-Journal*, October 3, 1902, 5.

68. "Operators to Starve Out Miners, *Evening World* [New York, NY], August 22, 1902, night ed., 1.

69. "Strikers," *Akron [OH] Daily Democrat*, August 25, 1902, 1. The Akron article was not about the Shenandoah incident but about another one reputed to have taken place near Cranberry; see also "Non-Union Miners Beaten with Clubs," *Evening Times* [Washington, DC], August 25, 1902, 1.

70. "Coal Miners Control Situation," *The Independent* [Honolulu, HI], August 27, 1902, 1.

71. Croly, *Hanna,* 379.

72. "A Cent a Pound for Coal Now," *Evening World* [New York, NY], September 25, 1902, night ed., 1.

73. Anthracite Coal Strike Commission Report; Stephen Harlan Norwood, *Strikebreaking & Intimidation: Mercenaries and Masculinity in Twentieth Century America* (Chapel Hill: University of North Carolina Press, 2002).

74. Croly, *Hanna,* 397, 398.

75. Walter Wellman, "The Inside History of the Great Coal Strike," *Colliers* 30, no. 3 (October 18, 1902); "Official Statement of the Conference," *New York Times*, October 4, 1902 1; Edmund Morris, *Theodore Rex* (New York: Random House, 2010). Morris writes that the president was already in the room; Robert Reynolds says he was wheeled in; the *New York Times* coverage says the delegates were "presented" to the president, suggesting that he was already in the room. Nathan Miller has him in a gray dressing gown (see his *Theodore Roosevelt* [New York: Harper Collins, 1994], 374). Morris says he was wearing a blue-striped robe.

76. The usually meticulous Edmund Morris missed this symbolism. The normal procedure would have been to replace the flowers in the bowl with fresh ones of the same variety. Using roses was not a spur-of-the-moment decision (they probably came from the Rose Conservatory, which in 1902 Edith Roosevelt was in the process of replacing with the famous Rose Garden). Roosevelt choreographed this meeting down to the smallest detail so it's safe to assume he *meant* for everyone to notice the change of flowers.

77. Mitchell, *Organized Labor,* 388.

78. Theodore Roosevelt, *An Autobiography* (New York: Scribners, 1913), 466.

79. Weyl, "John Mitchell," 659.

80. Reynolds, "The Coal Kings."

81. "The President and the Coal Barons," *Public Policy* 8, no. 17 (October 25, 1902): 269.

82. Croly, *Hanna,* 398.

83. Croly, *Hanna,* 398, 399.

84. Anthracite Coal Strike Commission Report, 11.

85. Mitchell, *Organized Labor*, 390.

86. Croly, *Hanna*, 399 (emphasis in original).

87. Mitchell, *Organized Labor*, 389.

88. Jean Strouse, *Morgan: American Financier* (New York: HarperCollins, 2000), 439.

89. Morris, *Theodore Rex*, 168.

90. Roosevelt, *Autobiography*, 468.

91. *Monthly Weather Review* 30, no. 10 (October 1902): 492.

92. Judge Gray objected to the ICA's pooling provisions: "It would hardly be contended that if it were the only provision of the bill, the power to regulate commerce between the States and foreign nations included the power to interfere with the liberty of contract of those who happened to be engaged in the business of transportation" (CR, January 14, 1887, 661).

93. Eliot Jones, *The Anthracite Coal Combination in the United States* (Cambridge, MA: Harvard University Press, 1914).

94. Jones, 82.

95. John A. Farrell, *Clarence Darrow: Attorney for the Damned* (New York: Random House, 2011), 105.

96. George Baer, *Addresses and Writings of George F. Baer* (Self-published, 1916), 320.

97. Baer, 334.

98. Quotes from Darrow's summation are from Arthur Weinberg, ed., *Attorney for the Damned: Clarence Darrow in the Courtroom* (Chicago: University of Chicago Press, 1989), 327–410.

99. Walter Wellman, "The Settlement of the Coal Strike," *American Monthly Review of Reviews* 26, no. 5 (November 1902): 552.

100. Anthracite Coal Strike Commission Report, 36, 62–63.

101. Anthracite Coal Strike Commission Report, 87.

102. Mitchell, *Organized Labor*, xiv.

103. Roosevelt, *Autobiography*, 479.

104. 193 U.S. 197 (1904), *Northern Securities Company V. United States*, no. 277, 331.

105. Roosevelt, *Autobiography*, 429.

106. Roosevelt, 476.

107. Joseph McKearns maintains that the violence was worse than Mitchell suggested, but he relies on one pro-management newspaper for this view ("'Faces' of John Mitchell," 29–42). Richard Healy makes a similar point in "Disturbance of the Peace: The Operators' View of the 1902 Strike," in *The Great Strike*, 95–123.

108. "John Mitchell," *Plumbers, Gas and Steam Fitters Journal* 34, no. 10 (October 1919): 6.

109. Rebecca Edwards, "Mary Lease and the Sources of Populist Protest," in *The Human Tradition in America: 1865 to the Present*, ed. Charles William Calhoun (Wilmington, DE: Scholarly Resources, 2003), 47–63.

INDEX

Note: Information in figures and tables is indicated by *f* and *t*, respectively.

About the Author

Ralph Brauer brings a unique combination of experiences in teaching, scholarship, research, higher education administration, politics, and grassroots activism to the task of writing about the history of social change. He is a retired professor who served as an administrator at the University of Minnesota and taught at Bowling Green State University in Ohio. Brauer's academic career is complemented by wide-ranging community organizing experience. Brauer is the author of *The Strange Death of Liberal America* (Praeger, 2006); his writing has also appeared in *The Nation* and *New York Times Magazine*. He holds a PhD in American studies from the University of Minnesota.